Towards Human Development

Towards Human Development

New Approaches to Macroeconomics and Inequality

Edited by
Giovanni Andrea Cornia and Frances Stewart

OXFORD
UNIVERSITY PRESS

OXFORD

UNIVERSITY PRESS

Great Clarendon Street, Oxford, OX2 6DP,
United Kingdom

Oxford University Press is a department of the University of Oxford.
It furthers the University's objective of excellence in research, scholarship,
and education by publishing worldwide. Oxford is a registered trade mark of
Oxford University Press in the UK and in certain other countries

First Edition published in 2014

Impression: 1

Published in the United States of America by Oxford University Press
198 Madison Avenue, New York, NY 10016, United States of America

British Library Cataloguing in Publication Data
Data available

Library of Congress Control Number: 2013954858

ISBN 978–0–19–870608–3

Printed and bound in Great Britain by
CPI Group (UK) Ltd, Croydon, CR0 4YY

Preface

This volume discusses a central issue in development, that is the impact of the concept of 'human development' which was initiated with the 1990 Human Development Report and the subsequent debate about objectives, measurement, and policies. This debate has helped to refine the conceptualization and measures of human development and to identify a set of policies needed for realizing this objective. This volume discusses how far development concepts and objectives have shifted as a consequence, and how this has affected global perspectives on development strategies. It also explores whether the observed shift in development goals towards multidimensional, anti-poverty and egalitarian perspectives has been accompanied by concomitant progress on the ground.

Overall economic policy, beyond social and aid policies, is a critical element that can support or inhibit progress in these dimensions. The volume discusses whether the human development debate has led to the re-framing of overall economic policy approaches in ways that would facilitate the achievement of the human development goals, including through a more egalitarian distribution of income and opportunities. Such a focus has become particularly relevant in view of the string of global financial and macroeconomic crises that have affected economic growth and human development directly and indirectly, in both developed and developing countries, from the early 2000s—in particular since 2007–8. Such crises have visibly retarded the achievement of the millennium development goals in several countries. Consequently, the volume argues that the set of policies required to promote human development needs to be greatly broadened beyond the present narrow set (concerning public social expenditure and foreign aid)—which are often identified as the relevant policies for implementing human development strategies—so as to include sustainable policies in the field of pro-poor macroeconomics, and labour-market and financial regulation. In this regard, an innovative aspect of the book is that it tries to relate the two debates, that on human development and that on macroeconomic management, which are normally treated separately in the literature.

The volume argues that efforts of many governments and donors towards human development have had mixed results. There has been limited progress in improving outcomes in the field of education, definite progress in extending social protection, and no progress in terms of employment. There have been some advances in framing a new structuralist macroeconomic approach compatible with human development, involving a more egalitarian and employment-intensive pattern of development. Among developing countries, some improvements were also recorded, relative to the past, in the design of countercyclical fiscal policies during the crisis of 2008, though this policy stance was reversed in many places in 2009–11. Finally, the volume underlines that the quasi-universal rise in domestic income inequality of the 1980s and 1990s was reversed in most of Latin America and parts of South East Asia in the 2000s, partly due to the implementation of a broader set of policies emanating—inter alia—from the human development debate. However, the volume also emphasizes that one of the key problems of our time—the regulation of global finance—which simultaneously affects human development, inequality, and macroeconomic stability—still awaits a solution, and proposes approaches to countercyclical regulation to tackle this problem.

This book includes papers written for a conference which was held at the Institute of Development Studies (IDS) of the University of Sussex on 17–18 November 2011 in honour of Sir Richard Jolly. The festschrift was on the topic *From Structural Adjustment to Human Development: Impact on Poverty and Inequality*, and papers were written on this broad remit. Although each contribution drew on the author's prior experience, all the papers included here were written *ex novo*. Each received detailed comments from the editors of the volume and scholars attending the conference. Overall, the volume offers a message of moderate hope: it shows there was progress in elaborating increasingly more relevant concepts of human development, policies needed to achieve it, and some advances in policy implementation. This suggests that the debates on adjustment with a human face, human development, poverty reduction, the new structuralist macroeconomics, and other progressive approaches, to all of which Richard Jolly made an important contribution, have not been in vain. But it also underlines that these initial gains have been accompanied by the emergence of new problems such as those linked to the informalization of labour markets and the dominance of unregulated and highly volatile global financial markets. Without progress on these fronts, the recent gains in pro-human development policies risk being squandered.

We hope this book will be read by and useful for researchers, graduate students, academics, and the growing number of policymakers who are trying to design and implement a broader policy approach to support human development. The book could also be used as a reader in courses dealing with the nexus between social targets and overall development approaches in emerging and low-income countries.

Giovanni Andrea Cornia and Frances Stewart

Acknowledgements

This volume would not have seen the light of the day without the collective effort of a large number of people working together in many ways. To start with, we would like to thank Lawrence Haddad, Andy Sumner, Hannah Corbett, and all the staff of the Institute of Development Studies (IDS) at the University of Sussex for agreeing to hold the conference in honour of Sir Richard Jolly on 'From Structural Adjustment to Human Development: Impact on Poverty and Inequality' (17–18 November 2011) on the Institute's premises; for developing the conference website <http://www.ids.ac.uk/events/from-structural-adjustment-to-human-development-impact-on-poverty-and-inequality>, and for taking care of the organizational aspects of the conference very efficiently. Our sincere thanks go to the many friends and colleagues of Sir Richard Jolly who attended the conference in his honour. Their written contributions, constructive comments, and frank criticisms helped sharpen the initial presentations as well as the overall articulation of the volume. We also thank the contributors to this volume for their precious time, original analyses, and patience shown in revising their initial drafts on the basis of comments made at the conference, as well as from the editors and two anonymous referees. The structure and content of the volume has benefited substantially from this peer-review process.

We would also like to acknowledge the financial support provided by the two United Nations agencies, that is UNICEF and the Human Development Report Office of UNDP, where Sir Richard Jolly spent several years promoting more efficient and humane economic and social policies and approaches. We would like to thank in particular Richard Morgan and Isabel Ortiz of UNICEF.

Last, but not least, we would also like to express our deeply heartfelt gratitude to Liisa Roponen for her expertise and patience in editing and formatting the volume chapters.

Giovanni Andrea Cornia and Frances Stewart

Contents

Contents

List of Figures

List of Tables

List of Tables

List of Abbreviations

ADB	Asian Development Bank
AIG	American International Group
AT	appropriate technology
AWHF	adjustment with a human face
BCBS	Basle Committee for Bank Supervision
BIS	Bank for International Settlements
BRIC	Brazil, Russia, India, and China
CCTs	conditional cash transfers
CEE	Central and Eastern Europe
CIS	Commonwealth of Independent States
CO	conscientious objector
CPRC	Chronic Poverty Research Centre
CRW	crisis response window
DAC	Development Assistance Committee (of the Organization for Economic Cooperation and Development)
DDO	deferred drawdown option (of the World Bank)
DFID	Department for International Development (UK)
ECLAC	Economic Commission for Latin America and the Caribbean
EDI	education development index
EE-FSU	Eastern Europe and the former Soviet Union
EPAs	economic partnership agreements
EPZ	export processing zone
EU	European Union
FDI	foreign direct investments
FSAP	financial sector assessment programme
FSF	Financial Stability Forum
GATT	General Agreement on Tariffs and Trade
GNI	gross national income

GOBI	(health interventions based on) growth monitoring, oral re-hydration, breast-feeding, and immunizations
GOBI-FF	(health interventions based on) growth monitoring, oral re-hydration, breast-feeding, and immunizations as well as food supplements and family planning
HD	human development
HDI	human development index
HDR	*Human Development Report*
HNWIs	high net worth individuals
ICT	information and communications technology
IDLA	Income Distribution in Latin America (database)
ILO	International Labour Organization
IRB	internal-ratings-based approach
LAC	Latin America and the Caribbean
LDCs	least developed countries
LICs	low-income countries
LSMS	living standards measurement survey
MDGs	millennium development goals
MENA	Middle East and North Africa
MICs	middle-income countries
MPI	multidimensional poverty index
NAIRU	non-accelerating inflation rate of unemployment
n.e.c.	not elsewhere classified
NER	net enrolment ratio
NHDR	*National Human Development Reports*
NIEO	new international economic order
NSF	net stable funding
OPHI	Oxford Poverty and Human Development Initiative
OTC	over-the-counter (derivatives)
PAMSCAD	Programme of Action to Mitigate the Social Consequences of Adjustment
PPPs	public—private partnerships
PTAs	preferential trade agreements
REER	real effective exchange rate
RER	real exchange rate
SCRER	stable and competitive real exchange rate
SEWA	Self-Employed Women's Association (in India)

SIVs	special investment vehicles
SMEs	small and medium-sized enterprises
SP	social protection
SPAP	social protection assessment programme
SSA	Sub-Saharan Africa
SSNs	social safety nets
TNCs	transnational corporations
UCTs	unconditional cash transfers
UNCTAD	United Nations Conference on Trade and Development
UNDP	United Nations Development Programme
UNESCO	United Nations Educational, Scientific, and Cultural Organization
UNICEF	United Nations Children's Fund
UPE	universal primary education
WC	Washington Consensus
WDI	world development indicators
WEO	World Economic Outlook (database)

Notes on Contributors

Christopher Colclough is Emeritus Professor of Education and Development at Cambridge University and Fellow of Corpus Christi College, Cambridge, where he has directed a group of seven research institutions from five countries in a five-year 'Research Consortium on Educational Outcomes and Poverty' (RECOUP). He was the founding Director (2002–5) at UNESCO of the Global Monitoring Report on Education for All. His earlier career was based at the Institute of Development Studies, Sussex, where, as a professorial fellow in economics, he worked mainly on the linkages between primary education and economic development, on education financing, on development theory, and on economic adjustment in Africa.

Since 2000 **Giovanni Andrea Cornia** has taught economics at the University of Florence. Prior to that he was the director of UNU-WIDER and chief economist of UNICEF. He also held research positions in other UN agencies and the private sector. Since 2010 he serves on the UN Committee for Development Policies. His main areas of interest are macroeconomics, inequality, poverty, political economy, child wellbeing, and human development. His latest edited book, *Falling Inequality in Latin America: Policy Changes and Lessons*, was published by OUP in January 2014.

Séverine Deneulin is a senior lecturer in International Development at the University of Bath, UK. She teaches and researches on ethics and development policy. She is the Secretary of the Human Development and Capability Association. Her books include *An Introduction to the Capability Approach and Human Development* (Earthscan, 2009), *Religion in Development* (Zed, 2009), and *Wellbeing, Justice and Development Ethics* (Routledge, 2014). She holds an MSc in Economics from the University of Louvain (Belgium) and a DPhil in Development Studies from the University of Oxford. She was a research assistant in the UN Intellectual History Project in 2001.

Stephany Griffith-Jones is an economist specializing in international finance and development. She is Financial Markets Director at Initiative for Policy Dialogue, Columbia University, and Associate Fellow at the Overseas Development Institute. Previously she was Professorial Fellow at the Institute of Development Studies and has worked at the Commonwealth Secretariat of the United Nations and the Central Bank of Chile. She has been senior consultant to governments in Eastern Europe and Latin America and international agencies. She has published over twenty books and many scholarly articles. Her recent book, edited with José Antonio Ocampo and Joseph Stiglitz, *Time for the Visible Hand*, was published by OUP.

Gerry Helleiner is Professor Emeritus, Department of Economics, and Distinguished Research Fellow, Munk School of Global Affairs, University of Toronto. He has held posts at Yale University, the University of Ibadan, the University of Dar es Salaam, the Institute of Development Studies, Sussex, and the World Institute for Development Economics Research, and served on the UN Committee for Development Planning and numerous development-related boards. He has written and consulted widely on trade, finance, and development policies. From 1991–9, he served as research director of the Group of 24 (the developing countries' caucus at the IMF and World Bank).

Ravi Kanbur is T. H. Lee Professor of World Affairs at Cornell University. He was educated at Cambridge and at Oxford and has taught at the Universities of Oxford, Cambridge, Essex, Warwick, Princeton, and Columbia. He has served on the senior staff of the World Bank, as Chief Economist of the African Region, and as Director of the World Bank's World Development Report. The honours he has received include the Quality of Research Discovery Award of the American Agricultural Economics Association and an Honorary Professorship at the University of Warwick. He is president-elect of the Society for the Study of Economic Inequality.

Raphael Kaplinsky is Professor of International Development at the Open University and previously worked for many years with Richard Jolly at the Institute of Development Studies. He has researched and written on the related themes of technology, industrialization, innovation, commodities, and the impact of China on Africa. His current research focus is on the contribution of inclusive innovation to inclusive growth. He has worked on policy issues in many contexts and particularly in South Africa (his country of origin).

Bruno Martorano is a development economist working at the UNICEF Office of Research in Florence. He has also consulted for UNU-WIDER and UNCTAD. He holds a PhD in development economics from the University of Florence where he lectured on the political economy of development. His main areas of interest are in the fields of economic development, poverty, inequality, social policy, and fiscal policy and child wellbeing.

José Antonio Ocampo is Professor and Co-President of the Initiative for Policy Dialogue at Columbia University. He was UN Under-Secretary-General for Economic and Social Affairs, Executive Secretary of the UN Economic Commission for Latin America and the Caribbean, and Minister of Finance of Colombia. He has received numerous academic distinctions, including the 2008 Leontief Prize for Advancing the Frontiers of Economic Thought. He has published extensively on macroeconomic theory, international financial issues, and international trade. His most recent book with Luis Bértola, *The Economic Development of Latin America since Independence*, was published in 2012 and won the Jaume Vicens Vives award of the Spanish Association of Economic History for the best book on Spanish or Latin American economic history.

Frances Stewart is Emeritus Professor of Development Economics at the University of Oxford. She has an honorary doctorate from the University of Sussex. She received the Mahbub ul Haq award from the United Nations, and the Leontief Prize for Advancing the Frontiers of Economic Thought from the Global Development and Environment

Institute at Tufts University. Books include *Technology and Underdevelopment, Planning to Meet Basic Needs*, and (as co-author) *Adjustment with a Human Face, War and Underdevelopment*, and *Horizontal Inequalities and Conflict: Understanding Group Violence in Multiethnic Societies*.

John Toye was Director of the Institute of Development Studies at the University of Sussex from 1987 to 1997 and is currently Chair of the Advisory Council of the Oxford University Department of International Development and a professorial research associate at the School of Oriental and African Studies, London. He co-wrote with Richard Toye a volume of the UN Intellectual History entitled *The UN and Global Political Economy* (Indiana University Press, 2004)

Rolph Van der Hoeven holds a PhD from the Free University Amsterdam. He is Professor of Employment and Development Economics at the International Institute of Social Studies, Erasmus University, The Hague and a member of the Dutch government's Committee on Development Cooperation. He also serves on the board of several international institutions and journals. Earlier activities include Director of Policy Coherence and Manager of the Technical Secretariat of the World Commission on the Social Dimension of Globalization at ILO, Geneva, Chief Economist, UNICEF, New York, and policy analyst for the ILO in Ethiopia and Zambia.

Robert H. Wade is Professor of Political Economy at the London School of Economics and Political Science. He was a Fellow of the Institute of Development Studies from 1972 to 1995 (but spent much of that time on leave at the World Bank, Office of Technology Assessment of the US Congress, Princeton, and MIT). He won the Leontief Prize for Expanding the Frontiers of Economic Understanding in 2008, and his *Governing the Market* won the Best Book on Political Economy award from the American Political Science Association.

Editors' Introduction

1

Human Development, Inequality, and Macroeconomics

An Overview of Progress and Unresolved Problems*

Giovanni Andrea Cornia and Frances Stewart

1.1 Introduction and Structure of the Volume

Over the past half century, the years in which Richard Jolly has been working as a development economist and practitioner, he led or contributed to some major changes in development thinking. This collection of essays illuminates and evaluates some consequences of these changes in approach. Two broad categories of change can be distinguished: first, from an exclusive focus on aggregate income growth, to one in which the distribution of income, and the consequences for poverty and inequality, came to be regarded as of vital importance; and second, to a recognition that development objectives are multidimensional, covering a range of capabilities or freedoms, and incomes are a means rather than the overriding objective. This evolution in part reflected learning from the consequences of previous approaches, and in part changing political economy, political ideologies, and power.

As a background to the discussions in this book, it is helpful briefly to review these changes, drawing on Chris Colclough's chapter, which categorizes significant stages in this evolution, in most of which Richard played an important part (as shown by John Toye's biography in Chapter 2, which gives a more detailed account of Richard's contribution).

While promoting economic growth was the dominant perspective in the 1950s and 1960s (Mahalanobis 1953; Nurkse 1953; Lewis 1954; Lewis 1955;

* We are grateful to Gerry Helleiner, Richard Jolly, and two anonymous referees for very helpful comments on a previous draft.

Rostow 1960), and did indeed lead to higher growth, the failure of this strategy to reduce poverty and inequality, or to create enough jobs, led to a search for alternatives. Dudley Seers pointed to the need to 'dethrone' GNP and led ILO employment missions to Colombia and Sri Lanka that focused on employment rather than income growth (Seers 1969; ILO 1970; ILO 1971; Seers 1972). Richard was an active member of both these missions. Then, in 1972, Richard himself (together with Hans Singer) led an ILO mission to Kenya, which this time focused on the activities of the poor in the informal sector rather than modern-sector employment, recognizing that the latter could at best provide employment for only a fraction of the working population and that the majority of the poor were not unemployed but working in low-productivity activities in the informal sector. The Kenya Mission called for a set of policies that would ensure 'Employment, Incomes and Equality' (the title of the Report) and recommended a strategy of 'redistribution from growth', by which an increasing share of the fruits of economic growth would be devoted to investment in the assets of the poor and improving their opportunities in the rural and informal sectors (ILO 1972). This was taken up by the World Bank, collaborating with the IDS of the University of Sussex, with Richard a prominent participant, generalizing the approach and modifying it slightly to one of 'redistribution with growth' (Chenery et al. 1979).

These changes in strategy remained predominantly concerned with incomes as a measure of wellbeing. However, the ILO's basic-needs approach directed attention away from income alone to the goods and services people needed to live reasonably satisfactory lives, i.e. to nutrition, education, health services, housing, and so on (ILO 1976; Streeten et al. 1981; Stewart 1985). Income was recognized as a means (among others) to achieve satisfactory levels of basic-needs fulfilment, rather than an end in itself. *Adjustment with a Human Face* (AWHF), which was initiated by Richard at UNICEF, incorporated a focus on both incomes and basic needs, pointing to the adverse impact on incomes of the poor, on essential goods and services, and on human outcomes that resulted from the deflationary adjustment policies adopted in the 1980s under the auspices of the IMF and the World Bank (Cornia et al. 1987). The move away from an exclusive focus on incomes was given major impetus by Sen's capabilities approach, which defined the objective of development as advancing people's ability to be and do valuable things; here basic goods and services as well as income are regarded not as ends but rather as means to enhance such capabilities (Sen 1985; Sen 1999). The initiation of the *Human Development Report* by Mahbub ul Haq in 1990 represented a fusion of Sen's capabilities approach and the rather more pragmatic basic-needs strategy. There followed a series of reports focusing on different aspects of this broad agenda. Richard himself took over from Mahbub ul Haq and was principal coordinator of the *Human Development Reports* from 1996 to 2000 (see Chapter 2).

For the most part, these changes could be regarded as largely a side-show, since the main thrust of development policies was determined by the international financial institutions (IFIs), who adopted a highly ortho-dox, income-oriented and laissez-faire approach, particularly from the early 1980s. However, the adverse consequences of these 'Washington Consensus' (WC) policies on poverty and inequality, as well as the influence of critics, including AWHF and successive *Human Development Reports*, led to an impor-tant change in global perspectives on development, which was embodied in the Millennium Declaration and the global agreement on the millennium development goals (MDGs) of 2000. These goals were supported by govern-ments from across the world and entrenched a broader, human-oriented, multidimensional approach to development.

Richard Jolly thus made major contributions to the shift in focus, from growth to employment, to redistribution with growth, and then to human development; and he also contributed to the questioning of orthodox mac-roeconomic policies as the means to achieve human development and pov-erty reduction. He has continued to contribute in this area, leading the critique of the austerity programmes following the 2008 financial crisis (Jolly et al. 2012). He was involved as a leader of cooperative ventures in this area, both as a practitioner (in the United Nations and elsewhere) and as an advocate.

Since the new millennium there has been definite progress in shifting the goals of development towards egalitarian, anti-poverty, and multidimen-sional perspectives, but how much has actually been achieved? Part Two of this book provides some answers to this question with respect to aid to educa-tion (Colclough), employment (van der Hoeven), social protection (Kanbur), and equality (Wade, Stewart). In brief, on the ground there has been some limited progress in education policy, and definite progress in social protec-tion. But there has been no progress in terms of employment—indeed, there has possibly been regress here. Moreover, the world has generally become more unequal. Even though Séverine Deneulin argues that one can 'read' capabilities and human-development approaches in many different ways— which implies that no single evaluation is universally acceptable—however one reads it, there does seem to be much less progress in reality than in the language of development.

Part Three of this book considers the same issue with respect to macroeco-nomic policies. Cornia analyses some recent changes in macro-fundamentals leading to reduced inequality in a number of developing countries, par-ticularly in Latin America, but also elsewhere, and discusses an alternative strategy ('new structuralist macroeconomics') that would promote a more egalitarian and employment-intensive pattern of development. Helleiner analyses trade, exchange rates, and global poverty. Martorano, Cornia, and Stewart explore whether the human-development paradigm has affected adjustment policies, contrasting fiscal policy in the early 1980s and in the late 2000s, and find some progress. Kaplinsky explores how innovation can contribute to a strategy of redistribution through growth. Finally, Griffith-Jones and Ocampo deal with one of the key unresolved problems of our times, which simultaneously affects human development, inequality, and macroeconomic stability: the regulation of global finance.

1.2 Progress in Human Development?

The idea of human development as representing progress provides the foundation stone for the theory and evidence presented in this book, underlying all our analysis. Hence we need briefly to consider what we mean by human development. As the first *Human Development Report* stated: 'Human development is a process of enlarging people's choices. The most critical ones are to lead a long and healthy life, to be educated and to enjoy a decent standard of living. Additional choices include political freedom, guaranteed human rights and self-respect' (UNDP 1990: 10). Progress in human development consists in the enlargement of people's potential to live productive, creative, and autonomous lives. It thus extends well beyond per-capita income to focus on the many conditions that make this possible, including health, education, work, political freedoms and social cohesion. The human-development approach represents a fusion of the basic-needs approach that preceded it and Amartya Sen's capability approach, the first putting particular emphasis on meeting the most fundamental needs of poor people, and the second on extending the choices people have to lead lives that they value.[1] Both turn away from income as the objective and see it as means to improve human conditions. In this volume, Séverine Deneulin develops a more sophisticated account of the different ways that the capability approach can be interpreted.

Hereafter, we briefly review the main findings of the chapters in relation to this basic question: have policy and outcomes moved in a pro-human-development way, and if not why?

We start by discussing the conceptual framework of capabilities and human development, drawing on Chapter 3 by Séverine Deneulin. The capability

---

[1] Indeed, the people involved in writing the first *Human Development Report* (working for Mahbub ul Haq) included (among others) those previously associated with basic needs (Gustav Ranis, Frances Stewart, Paul Streeten, and Mahbub ul Haq himself) and Amartya Sen and Meghnad Desai.

approach that underlies human development is very open; it defines the space in which progress should be assessèd, but leaves the choice of which capabilities and functionings to choose, and priorities among them, to societies, communities, and individuals. Nor does it dictate a particular way of achieving any chosen direction. As Deneulin argues, the approach has been interpreted in different ways by various authors. She herself describes it as a 'normative language' in which wellbeing, capability, functioning, and agency are critical components, displacing utility as the basis for assessing social arrangements. Others have interpreted it as a partial theory of justice and as such given it more specific content (Nussbaum 2000). Although the approach has been criticized as lacking a political perspective—pointing to a desired, though ill-defined, direction of change, but not to the major obstacles to progress or how to overcome them (Feldman 2010; Stewart 2010)—this does not need to be the case; political analysis can be added to the approach, albeit with some constraints, given its fundamentally individualistic and freedom-oriented basis. Given this openness, following Ricoeur (1981), Deneulin argues that the interpretation of the capability approach will necessarily differ according to the context and the perspectives of the interpreter. Does this mean that anything goes? We believe not. Two aspects are fundamental: one is that progress is multidimensional and is inevitably misinterpreted if measured by a single aggregate, such as GNP or even HDI; the other is that the *process* is important as well as outcomes, which is another reason for not assessing progress with a single number.

The *Human Development Reports* have provided a pragmatic interpretation of the approach, revealed by the topics they have chosen to analyse and the types of policy they have chosen to explore. These provide the framework of interpretation that Mahbub ul Haq, Richard Jolly, and others initiated, and that we adopt in this volume. According to the interpretation of human development (HD) revealed by these reports, HD involves a focus on progress in critical aspects and determinants of human lives, particularly among those who are most deprived. These include health, education, incomes of the poor, employment, and inequality, as well as on environmental sustainability and political freedoms, among others. This multidimensional perspective—with a consistently prime emphasis on the conditions of poor people—represents a major change from a growth-oriented approach, in which one number (income growth) is used to measure progress, ignoring the dimensions just listed except instrumentally. The chapters in this book all interpret human development in these terms.

In Chapter 4, Chris Colclough attempts to trace the impact on policy of the widespread acceptance of human development following the publication of the *Human Development Reports*, starting in 1990, and in particular the agreement on the multidimensional MDGs in 2000, by exploring the impact of aid for education. He notes that the overall volume of aid has increased since 2000, as has the proportion allocated to the social sectors (including education). By comparing the determinants (or correlates) of aid and education in 1998/9 and 2008/9 he is able to capture changes that can arguably be attributed to the change in objectives. He finds no significant correlates in 1998/9, but in 2008/9 the number of children out of school and the enrolment ratio are significantly related to both DFIDs (the UK aid agency) and total aid to education, indicating that the MDG of universal primary education seems to have influenced aid. Per-capita income is also negatively associated with both DFID and aggregate aid, indicating a shift to a poverty focus. However, when a broader range of variables is included in the model, country population size and Commonwealth membership, as well as country income per capita, explain most of the variance. He concludes that 'HD criteria appear to have somewhat increased influence on the allocation of both DFID and global aid to education over the past decade, but they remained of minor significance in comparison with more macro variables'.

A positive spillover of the human development debate is the widely accepted idea that universal social protection is needed to protect the poor against adverse developments and to fight poverty, as argued by Ravi Kanbur in Chapter 5, and this is undoubtedly a change from the pre-1990 era (see also Barrientos et al. 2010). Social protection 'focuses on reducing risk and vulnerabilities' (Shepherd et al. 2004: 8), and includes a range of public, private, and NGO interventions. Kanbur 'presents a broad overview of the main areas of consensus and challenges in the analytical and policy discourse on social protection'. He starts with a framework in which 'improving the wellbeing of the poorest...depends on (i) increasing their assets and opportunities in the medium term, (ii) improving insurance mechanisms, and (iii) addressing the actual outcome of shocks when they hit'. Kanbur emphasizes that an intervention on one of these can have effects (positive or negative) on the others. Protection of the poor against shocks can play a vital role in improving human development, as negative shocks (brought on, for example, by drought, ill health, or unemployment) often have a devastating and long-term adverse effect on poor households. Although there are many informal mechanisms that poor households access as forms of insurance, these are almost invariably inadequate, and state and civil-society action is needed to supplement them. Prominent among state schemes are cash transfers—conditional ones that often exclude the poorest, and unconditional transfers that tend to be more redistributive and inclusive. Among civil-society mechanisms, Kanbur points to the example of SEWA (the Self-Employed Women's Association), which provides insurance for poor self-employed women in India. Kanbur discusses four challenges faced by social protection schemes. The first is whether the schemes only provide insurance or include a redistributive element. While in practice all schemes contain elements of both insurance and redistribution, interventions can differ greatly in the extent of each of these elements. For example, the Mexican *Progresa/Oportunidades* scheme is intended primarily to be redistributive, providing cash transfers for those below a poverty line; but in practice, subject to a major shock, it also acts as a form of insurance, as families who were previously above the poverty line fall below it and are then entitled to receive transfers. In poor countries, both elements are undoubtedly needed. Social protection schemes tend to be concentrated in middle-income developing countries on grounds of affordability as well as institutional capacity. Yet, as Kanbur points out, they are needed even more in low-income countries. A second challenge, then, is to extend social protection comprehensively to low-income countries. A third issue concerns selection of the agents involved. These may include the public sector, the private sector, NGOs, and communities responsible for informal mechanisms. State support is often needed because the private sector typically excludes those most in need, as they cannot finance adequate private insurance and yet may be most vulnerable to shocks. Moreover, NGO-supported or informal mechanisms tend to be inadequate. The challenge for the state is to supplement the activities of other agents, rather than replace them. He cites the successful example of SEWA, which is an NGO but receives some state and donor support. A fourth challenge is whether to adopt conditional or unconditional transfer schemes. Conditional transfers seem to have been effective in changing behaviour (e.g. towards increasing education of children of recipients). But, as Kanbur points out, they may be more regressive than unconditional transfers, while the latter may also generate behavioural changes. He argues for more research in this area.

In any society, there exists a complex mixture of relevant mechanisms that contribute to social protection, and a starting point for evaluating the situation and suggesting reforms is to compile a full inventory, and then to recognize and allow for the fact that new formal schemes may partially or fully displace existing informal ones.

In contrast to the growing acceptance of the need to fight poverty—including through social protection—there has been no parallel consensus shift about the need to reduce income inequality. In Chapter 6, Robert Wade reports that inequality has increased in most regions of the world since the 1980s, though improvements have been recorded recently in a number of developing countries (see Table 9.4). Large increases in inequality were recorded, for example, in the USA, where the share of the top 1 per cent rose from 8.5 per cent to 23.5 per cent of GNP between 1978 and 2007, partly due to a concentration of corporate power. Wade argues that there is no strong political force challenging this rise. In developed countries, changes in the tax system have been mainly in an unequalizing direction, while for developing countries poverty reduction rather than reduced inequality is widely accepted as the most important objective, as indicated by the MDGs, which notably omit reference to inequality. He contends that the neoliberal philosophy, which opposes government interventions for ideological as well as 'efficiency' reasons, is largely responsible. He argues against the so-called efficiency costs of equality put forward by some economists, pointing to the fact that the more equal Nordic economies performed just as well as the more unequal UK and US economies. Moreover (Lansley 2011) shows that high inequality can raise the risk of financial fragility, which also threatens growth.

The surprising fact is that democratic electorates have mainly accepted this inegalitarian philosophy. Wade suggests this is due to a combination of 'ideas' and 'interests'. The ideas stem largely from mainstream economists who argue that the market produces an optimal and 'fair' distribution, and that any intervention would have high efficiency costs by reducing incentives. Their views are well publicized by right-wing think tanks. The 'interests' arise because, while income distribution has become more unequal and the share of the rich has soared, this has been at the expense of the bottom 40 per cent, while the middle 50 per cent have not seen a squeeze of their incomes. This middle, who could swing politics in a redistributive direction, fear that any redistribution would be mainly from them to the poorest 40 per cent, and they would therefore stand to lose, or at best would find their position unaffected. Moreover, this middle group feels no solidarity with the poorer deciles. For these reasons, as well as the power of corporations through political financing, even centre-left political parties have supported strategies of poverty reduction rather than egalitarianism.

Frances Stewart's Chapter 7 is also concerned with why countries do not adopt more egalitarian policies, with a particular emphasis on horizontal (or group) inequality. While Wade focuses mainly on developed countries, Stewart uses evidence from four African countries. She starts by reviewing the implications of some major philosophical approaches to justice in relation to both vertical and horizontal inequality, as well as—like Wade—the arguments of economists. While both philosophers and economists provide some justification for vertical inequality (for efficiency reasons, as Wade indicates), in neither case can one find much justification for horizontal inequality, or inequality between major groups, divided by race, gender, or ethnicity. Although some incentives may be needed to motivate individuals, there seems no good reason why this should lead to inequalities across groups, since one can expect a similar range of talents and motives within every major group. Consequently, from the perspectives of both justice and of efficiency, the case for horizontal equality appears to be stronger than for vertical inequality. Yet, ironically, social psychology suggests that people's view of the 'scope of justice'—or the universe of people among whom it is broadly accepted that justice and a fair distribution should apply—is likely to apply more within groups than across them. Consequently, one might expect more support for policies to reduce vertical than to reduce horizontal inequality.

The second part of Stewart's chapter uses data from perceptions surveys in Ghana, Kenya, Nigeria, and Uganda to explore how far there is indeed objection to cross-group transfers. This shows strong support for redistribution across groups in Ghana and Uganda, but much less support in Kenya and Nigeria. Using logit analysis, the chapter explores some possible determinants of support for redistribution. It finds that while significant relationships vary across countries, a person's perception of being *politically excluded* is associated with approval for redistribution in all four countries. It finds no evidence to support the view that a person's expressed identity, ethnic or national, determines their support for redistribution, thus challenging the 'scope of justice' hypothesis. Stewart concludes that the country differences observed are likely to stem from the different histories of the four countries. The findings suggest, however, that it is possible to find support for redistribution in multi-ethnic societies, and the different histories of the countries may suggest ways in which such support can be further promoted.

A rather negative assessment of progress towards human development is told in Chapter 8 by Rolph van der Hoeven with respect to employment. Employment was at the forefront in the 1970s, given prime emphasis by Seers and others. However, the era of stabilization and adjustment in the 1980s and then the increasing focus on poverty in the 1990s and 2000s gave it rather low priority. While the ILO has led the call for 'decent work' and it has always been recognized as an important feature of human development, it was not at first part of the MDGs and was only added to them in 2005. Employment has once more come to prominence, however, with the widespread attribution of the Arab Spring rebellions to unemployment among youth, as well as the rising unemployment in advanced economies due to the recession. Trends in employment have not been encouraging, as van der Hoeven reports. There has been a decline in the employment-to-population rate in most regions and a high rate of informal work (at 70 per cent of the total in low-income countries, 64 per cent in middle-income, and as much as 46 per cent in high-income countries), partly due to the rising share of services in total employment. The wage share has been declining in two-thirds of developing countries, with some Latin American countries being the major exception. There has also been a rise in inequality among wage earners. As van der Hoeven notes, these trends may be associated with the growing internationalization of the production process. Taken as a whole, the employment situation does not seem to have improved in the last few decades. The switch in aid towards the social sectors—contributing to some aspects of advance in human development—has been at the expense of economic infrastructure and possibly of job creation. Van de Hoeven concludes with some recommendations for policy change to support employment creation. He emphasizes the need to consider the quality as well as the quantity of employment in designing policy. Relevant policies include macro policies designed to increase capacity utilization, management of real exchange rates to promote labour-intensive activities, support for minimum wages to achieve reasonable living standards without raising minimum wages so high that they inhibit employment, and, in the longer term, policies to support structural change. Aid donors need to include considerations of employment (both quantity and quality), particularly as aid in the past has sometimes had a negative effect on employment. Ways in which aid can contribute to the employment objective include supporting infrastructure, education, vocational training, and small enterprises.

Van der Hoeven concludes that 'if the growing concern for employment and inequality is taken seriously, a refocus of development efforts is necessary, combining a greater share of development aid for employment and productivity-enhancing activities with a change in national and international economic and financial policies, so as to make employment creation (as well as poverty reduction) an overarching goal'.

The major conclusions of Part Two are that there has been some progress towards human-development-oriented goals, not only a change of rhetoric. In particular, in contrast to the income focus and exclusive market-orientation of the 1980s, the MDG process represents a considerable advance towards multidimensionality, explicit and time-limited social objectives, and the recording and monitoring of progress in achieving the specific objectives. Previous development targets, such as those of the United Nations Development Decades of the 1960s and 1970s, were by no means as focused or comprehensive in their targets and monitoring of progress. There has been a radical shift in attention of the international community towards social policy, in contrast to its virtually complete neglect in earlier decades. However, as the chapters in this book show—as well as many other investigations (ODI 2010; Hailu and Tsukada 2011)—actual progress on the ground has been mixed. The chapters here record some advance in education and social protection, but a worsening in employment and inequality. One reason for these limited achievements is that the MDG approach has tended to neglect economic policy as an important element in determining human outcomes. Achievements on the MDGs depend not only on expenditures on and policies towards the social sectors, but also on the growth of incomes of the poor, which depends on aggregate growth and its distribution.

These last concerns are explored in the next section, which focuses on the national and international macroeconomy and investigates whether the changes that have occurred in this area have led to progress in the direction of advancing human development and reducing inequality.

1.3 New Approaches to Macroeconomics and Innovation, Human Development, and Income Inequality

Part Three of the volume comprises Chapters 9 to 13, which deal with the relation between macroeconomic, trade, and regulatory policies on the one side and human development and inequality on the other. A main question in this section is whether the human-development debate (including its call for greater democracy and popular participation) has inspired or inhibited the adoption of more pro-growth and equitable macroeconomic, trade, and innovation policies with a more favourable impact on human development than the traditional Washington Consensus policies and World Trade Organization (WTO) arrangements. The final chapter of Part Three discusses possible ways of dealing with the main unresolved macroeconomic problem that has had negative effects on human development during the last 20 years, and especially since 2007: the regulation of domestic and global finance so as to minimize the occurrence and impact of devastating financial, banking, and currency crises.

To start with, in Chapter 9, Giovanni Andrea Cornia compares and assesses the income-inequality impact of the macroeconomic policies adopted under the 'real-life' Washington Consensus with that of the new structuralist macroeconomics that has evolved during the last decade in several countries of Latin America and in some countries of Sub-Saharan Africa and South East Asia—though much less in the OECD and the former Communist economies in transition. He argues that while income disparity rose in the majority of the many countries that followed 'real-life' Washington Consensus policies during the last thirty years, inequality fell during the 2000s in most countries that adopted packages inspired by the new structuralist macroeconomics. The earlier 'real life' WC-motivated adjustment policies focused essentially on balance of payments and budget equilibrium and rejected any evaluation in relation to a broad concept of economic efficiency (including the growth of output, investments, and employment), let alone human development, a concept which had limited currency at that time. In contrast, the new approach adopts development-oriented, and yet rigorous, macroeconomic (and other) policies, which have helped achieve more favourable distributional outcomes.

Thus, in line with the points made in Part Two by Deneulin, Colclough, and Kanbur, Chapter 9 argues that since the late 1990s the emphasis in a number of developing countries has shifted towards a broadening of policy objectives (including human development, social protection, and employment) and towards the reliance on a broader set of instruments. Even the IMF seems to have reconsidered its exclusive focus on inflation, budget deficits, and foreign debt and recently to have questioned the wisdom of the austerity measures recommended in the OECD countries.[2] In fact, the new structuralist macroeconomics aims at several objectives simultaneously, including some of the traditional ones—low inflation, budget deficits, and output gaps— but also at sustaining long-term growth of output and employment in the traded sector and reducing inequality, as well as at preventing external and internal crises. These multiple objectives are to be achieved by a substantially broader array of macroeconomic and financial policies that includes mobilizing domestic savings and lowering foreign indebtedness, controlling capital inflows including in non-crisis periods, a stable and competitive exchange rate shifting resources towards the relatively labour-intensive traded sector, achieving long-term equilibrium in the current account balance, and sectoral policies that aim at diversifying export composition and destination. It also comprises a countercyclical fiscal policy avoiding the deflationary bias of the orthodox approach and assigning a greater role to discretionary stabilizers through the expansion of equalizing social assistance programmes that have developed during the last two decades (but were not considered as a component of macro policy), a proactive tax policy emphasizing a rise of the revenue/GDP ratio through greater reliance on progressive tax instruments, a countercyclical monetary policy broadly driven by flexible inflation targeting, a monetary policy providing liquidity in crisis years, capital controls to preserve monetary autonomy, and the countercyclical regulation of finance to prevent asset-price bubbles and excessive risk-taking. Finally, the chapter argues that an essential tool of the new approach is stricter banking regulation and supervision as already applied, for instance, in a number of Latin American countries. Chapter 9 also discusses the pathways through which such policies affect inequality and provides initial econometric evidence supporting the conclusions about the beneficial impact of this new macroeconomic approach on income inequality.

In Chapter 10 Gerry Helleiner elaborates in greater detail the effects of changes in trade, exchange rate, and capital account policies discussed in the previous chapter. He focuses on the importance of the recent shifts in exchange rate regimes and capital controls for poverty alleviation and, by implication, inequality. He argues that while trade and exchange rate policies can have a significant impact upon global poverty, there is continuing

---

[2] See <http://www.washingtonpost.com/blogs/wonkblog/wp/2013/01/03/an-amazing-mea-cu lpa-from-the-imfs-chief-economist-on-austerity/>.

controversy as to exactly how. The results of preferential trade arrangements (such as the duty-free, quota-free market access) are not politically promising, while 'aid for trade' measures for the poorest countries have proved rather ineffective, although they enjoy considerable political support. Improvements in developing countries' own trade and exchange rate policies are potentially a more effective means of reducing poverty. Success of the latter, however, depends on a sophisticated understanding of such policies' potential role in stimulating growth and addressing poverty and often requires the development of specific training programmes. Yet professional assessments indicate considerable uncertainty as to the probable impact of trade and trade policy upon growth (and therefore poverty and inequality) in developing countries. Appropriate trade policy will depend upon the particular circumstances of time and place, and upon trade composition. Efforts to better understand and improve the developmental and poverty-reducing impact of trade and trade policies in individual developing countries are thus required. Helleiner argues, however, that, be that as it may, the real exchange rate is a major determinant of the structures of production and demand, especially in the short to medium term, and that the impact on trade of recent shifts of many countries to a competitive real exchange rate easily swamped that of more slowly changing tariffs and trade barriers on imports, taxes, and other barriers or subsidies. Indeed, short- to medium-term movements in the real exchange rate in most cases greatly exceed the height of tariffs and trade barriers, which often remain unchanged for long periods. This implies that sensible overall development- and poverty-oriented incentive policies must involve central banks and treasuries no less than trade ministries. Yet, with financial globalization, volatile capital flows have rendered it more difficult for poor countries to maintain a development-sensitive real exchange rate. Capital controls and an accumulation of reserves are therefore in order to support the real exchange rate target.

A great many governmental policies other than those towards trade and the exchange rate may also significantly influence production and trade incentives, including directed and/or subsidized credit, favourable government procurement policies, conditions concerning local content and hiring requirements, and the provision of infrastructure and skills. Thus, an exclusive focus upon trade policy, even broadened to incorporate exchange rate policy, would clearly miss much of what determines export- and import-competing production, trade, and development. Ultimately, in Helleiner's view, there is no escape from the need for each poor country to build the capacity to develop its own uniquely appropriate trade and exchange rate and other policies. This is a matter not only of individual skills but also of strong and relevant institutions and processes, including political ones.

In Chapter 11, Martorano, Cornia, and Stewart discuss the consequences of another important aspect of the macroeconomic policy changes that have taken place in several countries during the last decade, in particular the greater emphasis placed by governments on countercyclical fiscal policy and the protection of social investments during adjustment. It does so by juxtaposing the fiscal policies—and in particular the changes in social expenditures—adopted during the debt crisis of 1982–5 and the financial crisis of 2008–11. The authors show that, in contrast to the early 1980s, in 2008 governments' responses to the crisis were generally characterized by the adoption of Keynesian stimulus packages in which an increase in social spending represented one of the main components. As a result, in 2008 public expenditure on health increased on average in every region and in four-fifths of the OECD and Latin American countries and in about half of Sub-Saharan African and Asian economies (see Table 11.5). Similar results were observed in the field of education, except for MENA.

The authors then argue that in 2009–10 fear of debt default and continuous pressures coming from the financial markets pushed many policymakers to introduce austerity packages and cut public social expenditure, as had occurred in the early 1980s, offsetting in this way part of the prior countercyclical policy decisions. This approach was particularly pronounced in the European Union, where the austerity measures were very deep and their impact particularly marked, as noted by Richard Jolly and co-authors in *Be Outraged* (Jolly et al. 2012). Yet, in the developing countries the size of the social cuts adopted during the fiscal consolidation of 2009–10 (with the exception of Africa, where social expenditure continued to expand) was not large enough to offset the previous increase. Of course, the sovereign debt crisis and related fiscal adjustments in Europe and the developing economies closely connected with Europe are not yet over, and continued cutbacks in the future may mean a net worsening in expenditure during this economic crisis when the subsequent years are included. In addition, the authors find that, comparing government responses in the two crises, unlike the crisis of 1982–5, when social expenditure was cut more than proportionately to total government expenditure, in the crisis of the 2000s, even during the recent fiscal contraction, countries protected health and education relatively more than other lines of public expenditure. Indeed, even during the fiscal consolidation of 2009–11, the share of public expenditure on social protection, health, and education continued to increase or remained stable in most regions, while that of economic affairs was cut most frequently.

Econometric evidence included in Chapter 11 suggests that the factors explaining the difference in policy approaches between the early 1980s and 2008–9 include greater country autonomy compared with the past (which permitted the introduction of countercyclical Keynesian policies proportional to the size of the economic shock experienced), the spread of democracy (independently of the political orientation of the new regimes), and the greater attention paid to human development and the MDGs by policymakers during fiscal adjustments. In particular, a worsening of economic conditions led to a countercyclical expansion of social protection spending. The evidence also shows that countries undertaking an IMF programme were less likely to adopt expansionary fiscal policies during the crisis. In fact, although the IMF favoured an expansionary adjustment in several countries in 2008, and in 2009–10 imposed less stringent conditions with respect to the past, its late 2000s stance did not differ much from that of the previous crisis.

A better distribution of income can also be generated by the endogenous forces operating in the market. In this regard, Chapter 12 by Raphael Kaplinsky investigates how innovation can contribute to a strategy of redistribution through growth. He notes that, despite an accelerating pace of growth over the past two decades, most low- and middle-income economies (apart from China and a few other countries) have seen an increase in the number of people living below $1.25 per day. This trend is due to the structurally unequalizing character of the dominant global growth pattern, and in particular to three factors. The first is deepening globalization, which allows high-income earners relying on various types of scarce resource (natural resources, skills, entrepreneurship, and patents) to receive large rents from an expanding global market while exposing those with low human capital and resources to the intensified competition triggered by the entry of China and other low-wage producers into the global economy. Inequality has also risen because of the financialization of the global economy, which has led to a change in the terms of trade between financial services and the other sectors of the economy. The third component of this exclusionary growth is the dominant pattern of innovation. The northern locus of much of global innovation in the twentieth century meant that the bulk of it was inappropriate for meeting the needs of the poor. Such innovation is highly capital-, skill-, and scale-intensive, depends on high-quality infrastructure, and focuses on producing goods that meet the needs of the rich.

However, a series of disruptive factors are nudging the pattern of innovation in new and potentially pro-poor directions, such that the search for appropriate technologies will increasingly be driven by the market rather than (as in the past) by non-profit organizations. Kaplinsky underscores how this has resonance with the 'redistribution from/with/through growth' debate in which Richard Jolly was a prime mover in the 1970s. It also has implications for policies that might speed up the diffusion of new efficient, appropriate technologies, hence contributing to the adoption of pro-poor growth strategies in low- and middle-income economies.

The potential for global redistribution with growth through the market depends closely on the fact that, unlike in the past, the market (at times helped by adequate public policies) is generating endogenous processes of innovation in the fields of readily divisible information and communication technologies (starting with mobile phones), new forms of energy production, renewables such as solar and wind power, and biomass, which, as in the case of mobile telephony, enhance both consumer welfare and producer incomes, providing the potential for low-cost and widely distributed energy supplies. Two further sets of emerging pro-poor technologies are nanotechnology and biotechnology, which have important potential applications in meeting the needs of poor people and can be applied on a small scale. Examples are new diagnostic kits and water purification systems.

Other endogenous trends that will facilitate the application of these new pro-poor technologies are the global diffusion of innovative capabilities made possible by the spread of education in developing economies, the rapid expansion of a low- and middle-class consumer market (the 'bottom of the pyramid') in emerging economies less affected by the current crisis, and the rapid diffusion of 'disruptive entrepreneurs' concentrating on the efficient production of low-cost wage-goods in developing countries.

Finally, in Chapter 13, Stephany Griffith-Jones and José Antonio Ocampo discuss the countercyclical regulation of financial activities, which during the last decades has often caused devastating worsening of economic and social conditions in a large number of countries due to excessively liberalized and volatile national as well as global finance, too great risk-taking by unregulated or under-regulated national and international financial institutions, and the spread of unregistered transactions, which have tended to circumvent improvements in regulatory policy.

The procyclical nature of finance, which is one of its key market failures, calls for countercyclical prudential regulation to be put in place in the context of a broader countercyclical macroeconomic policy framework. Yet, prior to the current crisis, support for countercyclical regulation was mainly restricted to a few academics and some international organizations, such ECLAC and the BIS. However, Griffith-Jones and Ocampo argue that in recent times support for countercyclical regulation seems to be shared by more scholars, and is increasingly prevalent among policymakers. Such consensus indicates that it is not enough just to reduce the procyclicality of existing approaches, but that it is also necessary to design new, proactive countercyclical regulations—to offset the impact of unavoidable procyclicality elsewhere in the financial system.

The authors argue that most of the aims of macro-prudential regulation are widely shared, including the following: limiting the extent to which capital regulation and accounting frameworks permit the accumulation of risky loans during booms, thus exacerbating credit cycles; forcing banks to build large capital cushions in good times; raising capital requirements for bank and non-bank financial firms that pose a threat to financial stability; and improving the ability of banks to withstand specific and system-wide liquidity shocks. There are, however, a number of outstanding issues on which the discussion is still open, including in the field of rule-based versus discretionary interventions, the regulation of liquidity, accounting rules that would require provisions for latent loan losses to be built up during periods of credit growth, and complementary regulations about currency mismatches, limiting and/or adjusting cyclically loan-to-value ratios in the real estate sector, and setting minimum down-payments by borrowers for mortgages. The authors emphasize that the main problem with using such a large array of instruments may be their considerable complexity, which partly reflects the complexity of problems posed by the financial system. An alternative, more direct approach would be for regulators to limit the growth of bank credit.

In conclusion, and as with the discussion in Part Two, Part Three of the volume suggests that some progress has been recorded in several developing countries that in recent years have adopted macroeconomic and trade policies inspired by and leading to more country autonomy, with greater attention to their social and inequality impact. There is a suggestion that, in addition to the policies introduced to combat the downside risks of global economic integration, the recent spread of democracy and the long-standing debate on 'adjustment with a human face', human development, the need for Keynesian policies, and attempts at structural change have been major drivers of these policy changes that have occurred among low- and middle-income countries, even while the OECD countries and most European economies in transition seem to be mired in traditional austerity and liberal policies. Some improvements in the resources, lending volumes and conditionality of the IMF have also possibly helped, though the Fund largely returned to orthodox policies with the intensification of the crisis in 2009–11. Improvements in terms of trade for many of the commodity-producing countries and the increased size of markets of Asian countries (which had adopted unorthodox development policies) also played a role in these policy improvements by lessening the balance-of-payments constraint in many developing countries. Finally, the drive for a more equitable pattern of development may be achieved endogenously by the market, as emphasized by Kaplinsky, who suggests that, unlike in the past when technological innovation mainly had an exclusionary character, inequality and poverty may be alleviated thanks to processes of innovation in the field of easily divisible technologies, the spread of education, and the efficient production of low-cost wage-goods for the masses.

But it is certainly too soon to claim victory with regard to human-development-oriented macro policies and technology, as it is not clear whether such policy shifts are permanent or temporary. As noted, several of the MDG targets (particularly in the field of nutrition and maternal mortality) have been only partially achieved, while progress has been uneven across countries and regions, partly due to the failure of northern countries to reach the ODA targets that they had agreed on the occasion of the 2000 Millennium Development Assembly (UNDP 2012). Optimism about the recent virtuous evolution of public policy in several developing countries must also be tempered by the apparently persistent inability to find a global solution to the recurrent financial crises that have been increasingly hitting the world economy and, given the greatly augmented economic integration among countries, many developing countries as well. The impact of such crises often offsets progress realized by means of social and aid policies. In this regard, the chapter by Griffith-Jones and Ocampo outlines a series of countercyclical regulatory measures towards the financial system on which a consensus seems to be forming. Yet, so far, real-life political agreements in this field have been very few in both the USA and Europe, though some progress was realized during the last decade in a few regions (such as East Asia and Latin America) that previously had suffered from distressing financial crises. Such countries seem to have learned from their past mistakes. If this is a general rule, Europe and the USA will also, in due time, solve the financial regulation challenge, though it may well be that the resistance of financial interest groups will hamper any serious advance in these countries—and by implication in the low- and middle-income countries also—leading to prolonged stagnation and slow progress on human development.

Two major issues arise from the main conclusions of this book. The first concerns why policy and practice have only partially kept up with the rhetoric. Here, as suggested earlier, we must turn to political economy and political power to find some answers. The second issue is whether the human-development paradigm is itself sufficient. Some clear defects are apparent. First, it is a very loose portmanteau, lacking precision and subject to numerous interpretations, which lends itself to failures of implementation. Potential conflicts between the various elements that it covers—e.g. between political and economic freedoms, or between reducing inequality and poverty and supporting free markets—are generally not elucidated, nor is there guidance as to priorities and trade-offs. Secondly, despite its broad embrace, it neither offers guidance on the macroeconomic and development approaches best suited to achieve human development nor does it do justice to environmental issues, which clearly need to be at the forefront of global concerns. This is indicated by debates over the post-2015 agenda, with environmentalists aiming to make sustainability central, while those who support the human-development approach tend to put prime emphasis on enlarging the goals to give priority to those socioeconomic areas where the 2000 MDGs appear to have failed, such as in reducing inequality and promoting employment. Attempts to synthesize the two tend to produce fudges rather than solutions, again failing to recognize real trade-offs and dilemmas.

References

Barrientos, A. and D. Hulme (2010). *Social Protection for the Poor and Poorest: Concepts, Policies and Politics*. Basingstoke and New York: Palgrave Macmillan in association with the Brooks World Poverty Institute at the University of Manchester and the Chronic Poverty Research Centre.

Chenery, H., M. S. Ahluwalia, C. L. G. Bell, J. H. Duloy, and R. Jolly (1979). *Redistribution with Growth: Policies to Improve Income Distribution in Developing Countries in the Context of Economic Growth*. London: Oxford University Press.

Cornia, G. A., R. Jolly, and F. Stewart (1987). *Adjustment with a Human Face*. Oxford: Oxford University Press.

Feldman, S. (2010). 'Social Development, Capabilities, and the Contradictions of (Capitalist) Development'. In S. L. Esquith and F. Gifford (eds), *Capabilities, Power and Institutions*. Philadelphia: Pennsylvania University Press, 121–42.

Hailu, D. and R. Tsukada (2011). *Achieving the Millennium Development Goals: A Measure of Progress*. Working paper. Brasilia: International Policy Centre for Inclusive Growth.

ILO (1970). *Towards Full Employment*. Geneva: ILO.

ILO (1971). *Matching Employment Opportunities and Expectations. A Programme of Action for Ceylon*. Geneva: ILO.

ILO (1972). *Employment, Incomes and Equality*. Geneva: ILO.

ILO (1976). *Employment, Growth and Basic Needs: A One-World Problem*. Geneva: ILO.

Jolly, R., G. A. Cornia, D. Elson, C. Fortin, S. Griffith-Jones, G. Helleiner, R. van der Hoeven, R. Kaplinsky, R. Morgan, I. Ortiz, R. Pearson, and F. Stewart (2012). *Be Outraged*. Oxford: OXFAM.

Lansley, S. (2011). *The Cost of Inequality: Three Decades of the Super-Rich and the Economy*. London: Gibson Square.

Lewis, A. (1954). 'Economic Development with Unlimited Supplies of Labour'. *Manchester School of Economic and Social Studies*, 22: 139–91.

Lewis, A. (1955). *The Theory of Economic Growth*. London: Allen and Unwin.

Mahalanobis, P. C. (1953). 'Some Observations on the Process of Growth in National Income'. *Sankya*, 12(4): 307–12.

Nurkse, R. (1953). *Problems of Capital Formation in Underdeveloped Countries*. Oxford: Blackwell.

Nussbaum, M. (2000). *Women and Human Development: A Study in Human Capabilities*. Cambridge: Cambridge University Press.

ODI (2010). '*Millennium Development Goals: Report Card. Measuring Progress Across Goals*'. London: Overseas Development Institute.

Rostow, W. W. (1960). *The Stages of Economic Growth: A Non-Communist Manifesto*. Cambridge: Cambridge University Press.

Seers, D. (1969). 'The Meaning of Development'. *International Development Review*, 11(4): 3–4.

Seers, D. (1972). 'What Are We Trying to Measure?'. *Journal of Development Studies*, 8(3): 21–36.

Sen, A. K. (1985). *Commodities and Capabilities*. Amsterdam: North-Holland.

Sen, A. K. (1999). *Development as Freedom (DAF)*. Oxford: Oxford University Press.

Shepherd, A., R. Marcus, and A. Barrientos (2004). *'Policy Paper on Social Protection'*. London: Overseas Development Institute.

Stewart, F. (1985). *Planning to Meet Basic Needs*. London: Macmillan.

Stewart, F. (2010). 'Power and Progress: The Swing of the Pendulum'. *Journal of Human Development and Capabilities*, 11(3): 371–95.

Streeten, P. P., S. J. Burki, M. Ul-Haq, N. Hicks, and F. Stewart (1981). *First Things First, Meeting Basic Human Needs in Developing Countries*. New York: Oxford University Press.

UNDP (1990). *Human Development Report*. Oxford: Oxford University Press.

UNDP (2012). *The Millennium Development Goals 2012 Report*. New York: UNDP. Available at: <http://www.undp.org/content/dam/undp/library/MDG/english/The_MDG_Report_2012.pdf> (accessed 29 January 2013).

Part I

Sir Richard Jolly's Contribution to the Analysis of Economic Development

2

The Achievements of an Optimistic Economist*

John Toye[1]

I first met Richard Jolly at the end of January 1968 when, as part of my training as a civil servant, I was sent on a week's course at the newly established Institute of Development Studies at the University of Sussex. After a scary drive through the snow down the A23, it was a wonderful relief to be welcomed to the Institute by this genial man, who seemed genuinely glad to see us. We obviously did not impress him and his colleagues as much as he and they impressed us. In the next *IDS Annual Report*, some anonymous person wrote that it was 'worrying that they [i.e. my group of trainee civil servants] did not seem to be particularly interested in overseas development' (IDS 1968). That was far from true in my case. The encounter with Richard and his IDS colleagues changed my professional trajectory and began my lifetime engagement with development studies. So it is a special pleasure now to recount Richard's own life and career.

2.1 Youth, Cambridge, and Kenya

Richard Jolly, born in the summer of 1934, was the only son of Arthur Jolly and his wife Flora Doris (née Leaver) in Hove, Sussex. They also had two daughters, and his sisters were very important to Richard. His father, an accountant, had settled in Hove just before the First World War and started a successful accountancy partnership. Both parents were religious, though

* I am grateful to Frances Stewart and Giovanni Andrea Cornia for their very useful comments on an earlier draft.

[1] This chapter is based on three interviews with Richard Jolly conducted during 2011.

in different degrees. Arthur was treasurer of the local English Presbyterian Church for many years, a man of strong practical faith and conviction. His forte was voluntary youth and community work. The Borough of Hove recognized his lifetime of public-spirited activity by making him an Honorary Citizen. Flora was a keen supporter of Frank Buchman's Oxford Group (renamed the Movement for Moral Rearmament in 1938), which emphasized the need for personal change, and which focused its recruitment on the wealthy and famous (Overy 2009: 69–70).

Richard enjoyed only six years of childhood with his sisters in the large family house in Wilbury Gardens. In September 1940 the fear of an imminent German invasion led his parents to dispatch him and his sisters to foster homes in Canada, where he stayed until early 1945. On return, he was enrolled at Brighton College, not then in one of its most academically impressive phases, where after reaching school certificate level he specialized in mathematics and physics. Receiving excellent tuition in small classes, he passed his examinations at Advanced and Scholarship level. He missed the Cambridge scholarship examinations because of illness (encephalitis), but gained admission to Magdalene College, where a distant cousin, A. S. Ramsey, had been a fellow in mathematics.[2] Richard found the college to be friendly and comfortable and spent his first year there doing Part I of the Mathematical Tripos, or undergraduate degree course, under the supervision of Dennis Babbage.

Although feeling rather isolated in his maths studies, he found sociability in the Cambridge Inter-collegiate Christian Union (CICU), a student club whose mission is to bring the good news of the Gospel to fellow Cambridge students. It was a CICU friend who suggested to Richard that he should consider switching from maths to economics, pointing out to him Marshall's opening pronouncement (1890: 1) that 'the two great forming agencies of the world's history have been the religious and the economic'. Before deciding to switch, Richard spent the summer of 1954 reading *Economic Analysis* by Kenneth Boulding, an economist who was also a lifelong Quaker.

Michael Farrell supervised Richard's work for Part II of the Economics Tripos. Farrell was an economic theorist and econometrician whose main research focus was the efficiency of the firm. His work was neoclassical in its approach and therefore uncongenial to the self-identified disciples of Keynes who at that time dominated the Economics Faculty.[3] Richard was little aware of these professional differences and, under Farrell's tuition, became for a

---

[2] A. S. Ramsey was the father of Frank P. Ramsey, the brilliant Cambridge economist who died at the age of 27, and of Michael Ramsey, who in 1961 became Archbishop of Canterbury.

[3] See Christopher Bliss's entry for Michael Farrell in the *Oxford Dictionary of National Biography*. Farrell advised Richard not to read Joan Robinson's *The Accumulation of Capital* (1956), but did allow him to read her *Economics of Imperfect Competition* (1934).

while as true a believer in neoclassical economics as he was in evangelical Christianity. He graduated with first class honours in 1956.

At that time, conscription was still in place in the UK, so Richard still faced the prospect of two years of National Service in the armed forces. He spent the Christmas of 1955 reading the arguments for and against pacifism, finally opting for entry as a medical noncombatant—i.e. someone who supplied medical services to army personnel but did not fight. He wrote to the War Office enquiring how many medical noncombatants were currently enlisted in the British army and received the surprising reply that there were none. So he changed his mind and applied for registration as a conscientious objector (CO). At the tribunal hearing in Fulham in 1956, he heard several previous applications for CO status dismissed on the grounds that the applicants had not offered to enlist as medical noncombatants. After his own application had been approved, Richard challenged the panel judges about the grounds for their refusal of the preceding applications, flourishing the letter from the War Office stating that there were no medical noncombatants in the army. This information produced consternation in court, since the judges seemed to know nothing of this. Richard's eyes were opened to the fallibility of officialdom. It was something of a political awakening for him.

Separately from his application for CO status, Richard had been exploring the possibility of going to Kenya to work for the colonial Ministry of Community Development and Rehabilitation. The CO tribunal approved this occupation as an appropriate alternative to military conscription. He was fortunate in being sent to the community development wing, where he first learned Kiswahili, and not being assigned to the rehabilitation wing of the ministry, which was dealing with the re-integration of former Mau Mau guerrillas. He was then posted as community development officer to Baringo district in Rift Valley province, one of Kenya's more underdeveloped districts, especially in the matter of school provision. One of the community development assistants, Grace Mahbub, pointed out that almost all of the colonial services were targeted at men, while women did most of the actual work. Richard concentrated his efforts on working with women, for which he earned the local sobriquet, Bwana ya Wanawake ('man of the women')— one that may have been misinterpreted in the late 1950s but can now be worn with pride.

His two years in Baringo district were formative for three main reasons. First, they were the time when he lost his Christian beliefs. At the start, he found friends in the African Inland Mission; by the end, he came to see them as operating inside their own cultural bubble and unable, because of their own religious doctrines, to connect properly with the people whom they had come to Kenya to serve. Second, Baringo was his first face-to-face exposure with problems of development, which previously he had only read about in Arthur Lewis's *The Theory of Economic Growth* (1955). Third, the disparity between the economics that he had learned and lives of the people of Baringo was sufficient to make him eager to go on to further study in the hope of bringing academic and practical knowledge a little closer to each other. At the same time, his loss of Christian faith also made him suspicious of other kinds of fundamentalism, such as the various closed belief systems to be found lurking in economics and social science.

2.2 Yale and After

Michael Farrell had originally advised Richard to apply for postgraduate entry to the University of Chicago, where Farrell had worked in the Cowles Commission in 1951–3.[4] Because of Baringo's rudimentary postal service— the mail was still brought by runner—the Chicago application forms arrived after the submission deadline, and meanwhile Richard had applied to and been accepted by Yale University. Before leaving for Yale, Richard worked as Farrell's temporary research assistant on an investigation into the determinants of labour productivity in coal mining. They used a large dataset (818 mines) and seventy-seven independent variables for econometric testing, running regressions on the early computer EDSAC 2, but succeeding in explaining about half of the productivity differences. Richard at the time took this to be a poor result, which threw doubt on the usefulness of econometric methods—a view that he now considers to have been a serious professional misjudgment, a sign of youthful inexperience.

In his first year at Yale, Richard completed his MA successfully, but felt disappointed with the courses on economic development that were on offer. He applied for doctoral studies at Nuffield College, Oxford, but was too late and Norman Chester, then Warden, turned him down. The situation at Yale then changed for the better for two reasons. First, during his second year he was found an attractive sinecure, which paid his fees and required him only to organize occasional visits to the university by high profile personalities. One of these was the *New York Times* journalist Herbert Matthews, who had interviewed Fidel Castro in the Sierra Maestra in 1957.[5]

---

[4] At this time, researchers at the Commission were developing simultaneous equation models of the economy, and a variety of methods for the statistical estimation of such models. The Cowles Commission moved from Chicago to Yale University in 1955, with the new name of the Cowles Foundation.

[5] The significance of the interview was that it established that Castro was alive and well in Cuba after the Batista government had declared him dead, publicity that was instrumental to the success of the Cuban revolution.

The second and more important reason why the Yale experience improved was the arrival in 1961 of Dudley Seers, someone who was to play a major role in shaping the first half of Richard's career. Dudley came to Yale fresh from four years working at the UN Economic Commission for Latin America, alongside Raul Prebisch and Osvaldo Sunkel. Dudley brought to Yale his discovery of ECLA's 'structuralism'. This was not so much a theory as an approach to the analysis of development. Rather than relying on imported models derived from the developed countries' experiences, which could be exceptional, the structuralist approach analysed the key structural features of the country and sought to understand their implications for its development prospects.[6]

Dudley, by training a statistician, was dismissive of GDP growth as an indicator of development. He preferred to focus on the reduction of unemployment, inequality, and poverty (Seers 1969). He also brought a breath of realism to economic statistics. To measure development he told the class of startled Yale graduates, 'I prefer the shoe index'. His proposed index would use data on how many people were barefoot, how many had on their feet soles cut from car tyres, how many wore Bata imports, how many were leather-shod, and how many flaunted fancy footwear. The interesting point, Dudley explained, was the number and variety of shoes possessed by the top few per cent of the population—not only brown and black ones, but specialist shoes such as riding boots, tennis plimsolls, and dancing pumps. This was long before Imelda Marcos's hoard of nearly three thousand pairs of designer-label shoes was revealed.[7] It was a typical Dudley provocation, but it rang a bell with Richard.

Richard had already visited Cuba twice when Dudley asked him in his third year to join a research project that he was leading on the economic and social aspects of the Cuban revolution. He had negotiated access for this project through his former ECLA colleague, Regino Boti, then a Cuban economics minister. Dudley thought that the Castro revolution was 'one of the most important political developments in [the twentieth] century' (Seers 1964: xi). He wanted to know whether the ECLA goals of faster economic growth and social reform could indeed be achieved by means of the power of revolutionary nationalism. He assembled a small team, including Richard, Andres Bianchi of Chile, also doing graduate studies at Yale, and Max Nolff. Together they researched in Cuba in August and September 1962.

---

[6] Seers elaborated this view in his much re-published article 'The Limitations of the Special Case' (1963).

[7] Her extravagance was revealed after she fled the Philippines with President Ferdinand Marcos in 1986. In 2001, the former First Lady opened a shoe museum in the Mankina district of Manila, in which most of the exhibits were her own shoes.

Richard set to work on the Cuban education sector. What he produced was less of a chapter than a small monograph, running to over one hundred pages of the subsequent edited book. The economic aspects of education were in the foreground, because of their relevance for other poor Latin American countries. There were good descriptions of the initial conditions of Cuban education infrastructure and the new regime's changes to primary school enrolment, secondary teaching, and university-level education, plus the massive adult literacy campaign. Yet the statistics that could be assembled were not sufficiently detailed or comprehensive to enable the net benefits of the additional investment in education to be estimated. In any case, both Richard and Dudley were clear that investment in education might not be sufficient to relax the constraints holding back Cuban agriculture and industry.

In a separate appendix, Richard expressed his distaste for the Marxist-Leninist political ideas that were being propagated through the education system. At the same time, he acknowledged that there was 'more than a touch of relevance in the message: much of what is emphasized about economic imperialism, land reform and the privileges of the rich, for example, already finds a ready market in Latin America' (Seers 1964: 347). Perhaps it was this comment that prompted a hundred critical reviews in the newspapers of the southern states of the USA—although the book went on to sell 5,000 copies.

During his time at Yale, Richard met many people, as well as Dudley, who were to be part of his professional future. They included Gerry Helleiner, Hollis Chenery, Brian van Arkadie, Reginald Herbold Green, and Michael Intriligator. The most important of all for his personal future was Alison Bishop, who was studying the behaviour of the lemurs of Madagascar for her doctorate.[8] Richard later managed to extend his African field research to include Madagascar, but on his way there stopped off in Addis Ababa for a two-month assignment for the Economic Commission for Africa.[9] His letters warning Alison of this delay failed to reach her, in circumstances reminiscent of a Hardy novel, and it was only by the sheerest good fortune that she was able to meet his plane when he finally arrived.[10] In 1963 Richard and Alison

---

[8] Lemurs tended to be more fancied by the wealthy as exotic pets than studied in their natural habitat. Virginia Courtauld, for example, built in a cage for her pet lemur, Mah Jong, when refurbishing Eltham Palace in the late1930s.

[9] Hans Singer was working for the Economic Commission for Africa, and Dudley Seers also worked on this assignment. In his *Short History of IDS*, Richard mentions conversations with Hans and Dudley about the Bridges Report and the shape that a future national institution for development studies (i.e. what was to be IDS, Sussex) might take.

[10] Alison tells the story in Chapter 7 of *Lords and Lemurs* (Jolly 2004), entitled 'A Very Cheap Wife'. Richard had given Alison's father a cow and a calf to provide milk for his morning coffee, which was a very small payment by the going standards of the Antandroy of Southern Madagascar at the time.

were married in the Royal Pavilion in Brighton, and they subsequently had two daughters and two sons. The marriage proved to be a strong foundation on which both of their careers could flourish. Alison had already found her lifetime scientific interest and built an international reputation through her research and writing—her textbook *The Evolution of Primate Behaviour* had sold over 50,000 copies by the 1990s. However, she sought only visiting appointments at universities and so was able to accompany Richard when his career took him to different places at different times.

While at Makerere University in 1964, Richard responded to an advertisement by the Department of Applied Economics (DAE) in Cambridge for a researcher working on developing economies for a project funded by the UK Department of Technical Cooperation. He told the DAE that he intended to research on education in Northern Rhodesia, soon to be Zambia, and was appointed. In his long and distinguished career, this was the only occasion on which he ever applied for a job. A few months later, when Dudley Seers was leading a mission to Northern Rhodesia, he asked Richard to cover the education sector, which he did, focusing on the education needs in what was a copper-rich country and, for the first five years after independence, the fastest-growing country in Africa.[11] Richard then returned to Makerere for the rest of the academic year, but later went back to Zambia to work at the ministry of national planning on manpower planning. They were able to get a good picture of the whole of the supply side of the labour market. However, estimating the demand side was a more doubtful business. Richard was sceptical of the Harbison and Myers (1964) rules of thumb for inferring labour requirements from economic growth rates. In any case, the key issue for the Zambians was not future demand but the speed of the Zambianization of the labour force.

2.3 The Institute of Development Studies at Sussex University

Dudley Seers was appointed as director general of the newly created Ministry of Overseas Development in 1964, and supported the minister, Barbara Castle, and the permanent secretary, Sir Andrew Cohen, in bringing to birth the Institute of Development Studies at the University of Sussex in 1966. This was the incarnation of the idea of a national institution for development studies that Dudley, Hans Singer, and Richard had discussed in Addis Ababa in 1963. By October 1967, Dudley had become the director of the IDS and

---

[11] The report of the UN/FAO mission *The Economic Development of Zambia* (1964) used a modified (i.e. non-square) input-output table devised by Dudley and Michael Ward.

Richard, then at the Department of Applied Economics in Cambridge, had been invited to become a fellow.

The end of the 1960s was a time when confidence in the ability of conventional development planning to engender economic development was fast eroding. The report of the Pearson Commission on International Development, *Partners in Development* (1969), was an official and high-profile attempt at reappraisal and renewal of the development project. Barbara Ward, then Professor of International Economic Development at Columbia University and well known for her best-selling publications, came to the IDS in late 1969 to ask Dudley Seers to recommend people of the younger generation to animate a conference on the Pearson Report, and Dudley suggested Richard among others. Richard's paper to the conference was critical of Pearson on the grounds that, even if the measures advocated by the report were implemented, the 'widening gap' between rich and poor nations of which the report complained would continue to widen. With Reginald Green, Gerry Helleiner, Michael Bruno, and a few others, Richard drafted a statement (the Williamsburg Declaration) calling for much bolder approaches to development—and, somewhat to their surprise, most of the conference participants agreed to sign it.

In 1969 the ILO inaugurated its World Employment Programme, which began with a series of country missions to examine employment problems and make recommendations. Dudley Seers led the first two, to Colombia (1970) and Sri Lanka (1971), and Richard, who had been on the first two, was co-leader with Hans Singer of the third to Kenya (1972). One novel aspect of the Kenya Report was its emphasis on the positive contribution that the informal sector could make to the generation of employment and income—the first mention of the informal sector in an international report. This raised the critical question for economic development of whether informal enterprises could ever expand beyond a certain size and formalize themselves. Another pioneering feature was Hans Singer's concept of 'growth with redistribution', which resulted in a subsequent IDS–World Bank collaborative volume, *Redistribution with Growth* (1974). In this case, the query was a political one: why should a dominant elite agree to make the sacrifices that redistribution would entail for them?

By 1972, Dudley Seers wanted to lay down the role of IDS director, but Richard persuaded him that they should make a joint application for the post, for what today would be known as a job share, over the next five years. The appointing committee was not keen on this proposal, probably sensed that Dudley was not too keen on it either, and offered the job instead to Sidney Dell, who at that time headed the UNCTAD office in New York.[12]

---

[12] For more on Sidney Dell, see Toye and Toye (2004: 57 *et passim*).

However, Dell decided that he did not really want to leave New York and declined the offer, and Richard was then appointed as sole director.

As director, Richard felt called upon to focus more directly on major world events, such as the oil-price crisis and the UN resolution on a 'new international economic order' (NIEO). He valued his membership of the international development network that Barbara Ward had gathered around herself while chair of the North–South Round Table, which included Mahbub ul Haq, Gerry Helleiner, Enrique Iglesias, and Sartaj Aziz. Barbara Ward moved to Lodsworth, Sussex, in 1973 and became a governor of the IDS, despite suffering from cancer. Her guiding principle was the moral unity of humankind (Ul Haq 1995: 200–4). At a round table meeting to discuss the Brandt Report held at IDS in 1980, the last that Barbara Ward attended before her death, she voiced her credo: 'our visionary perspective is the true realism'.

For Richard, however, leadership was not only about envisioning a more just world, important as vision is to him. He wanted to find the political purchase that would realize actions for justice. In a paper titled 'The Judo Trick' (1974), he asked that question in the context of education reform. He suggested, following Tony Somerset, that the reform of the examination system was the fulcrum on which reform of the entire system would turn, because it could mobilize a reforming coalition of teachers, parents, and pupils. What then was the judo trick that would produce an NIEO? Many people hoped that an alliance between OPEC, the Organization of Petroleum Exporting Countries, and the oil-importing developing countries—informally called the 'NOPEC'—would be the key move that would re-shape world income distribution. That hope left out of account the matter of where the OPEC countries wanted to invest their surpluses and whether they would be willing to act against the interests of their bankers in the developed world. They were not.[13]

This search for convergent interests implied a challenge to both neo-Marxists, who think that policy initiatives are futile, given the laws of motion of capitalist society, and neoliberals, who think they are unnecessary or counterproductive, since the unfettered market will induce desirable adjustments. To challenge both at once recalls Dudley Seers' rejection of 'Marxism and other neoclassical doctrines'.[14] Yet Dudley was also critical of muddling mutuality and morality, a criticism that might apply to a tactic of locating convergent interests for benevolent action.[15] The tactic was

---

[13] The search for mutual interests between North and South motivated Robert Cassen, Richard Jolly, John Sewell, and Robert Wood to write *Rich Country Interests and Third World Development* (1982). However, as noted ruefully in the preface, 'bold and simple truths tend to vanish into thickets of multidimensional reconsideration' and, moreover, by this time the North–South dialogue had already been extinguished.

[14] The reference is to Seers (1979).

[15] His criticism of the Brandt Report for doing this is in Seers (1980).

much more in line with the thinking of Hans Singer, who was always seeking opportunities in the current turn of events for good outcomes to be set in motion.

Quite apart from the snuffing out of the North–South dialogue, the Conservative government of Mrs Thatcher meant trouble for the IDS. Richard had to mount defence and damage-limitation exercises. One threat was the placing of the IDS on a list of QUANGOs (or 'quasi-autonomous non-governmental organizations') to be closed down. Richard has told elsewhere the story of how he campaigned successfully against that listing—even by putting the IDS case to the Queen![16] Equally worrying was the ODA demand to taper off the full funding of the Institute that it had enjoyed since 1966. Richard got agreement that the taper should extend over five rather than three years. The ingenious way of closing the resulting financial gap that Richard negotiated with the fellowship was a system of work points. Inspired by Gordon White's account of the practice on Chinese collective farms, but also combined with capitalist incentives, work points, to put it simply, linked specific tasks undertaken by fellows with an overall income target for the Institute. Although the precise functioning of the system was endlessly contentious, its introduction produced a Stakhanovite response from the fellowship, and this allowed the IDS to build reserves against the rainy day that eventually came when government funding was slashed even further.

2.4 UNICEF Policies and Programmes

When the IDS was under threat, one of those whom Richard mobilized to write a protest letter was Jim Grant, then head of the Overseas Development Council in Washington DC. In 1980 Grant became executive director of UNICEF in New York, and following on from their interaction over IDS Grant invited Richard to join UNICEF as deputy executive director (programmes). At this point Richard still knew rather little about the UN or UNICEF, but after nine years as IDS director and the alarms of 1979/80, he was willing to try pastures new. Initially, he settled for a three-year contract, opting to keep on the home he and Alison had made in Lewes. He soon discovered the strengths of UNICEF, whose reputation as one of the most effective and respected parts of the UN was enhanced by the leadership of Jim Grant.

Giovanni Andrea Cornia was UNICEF's chief economist, and reports were coming in from some of the field offices of increases in child malnutrition.

---

[16] Jolly (2008).

In 1982, it was decided to research the impact of the world recession on children, and when Dudley Seers declined to head the team, Richard took on an internal leadership role. Cornia designed a matrix for twelve country case studies to reflect country differences in per-capita income, openness to trade, infant mortality rate, and political ideology. The aim was to capture a representative picture. A synthesis of the case-study results, often based on fragmentary but timely field information provided by UNICEF offices in developing countries, and published in March 1984, argued that the effects of recession in developed countries were being felt with augmented force in developing countries, especially by the rural poor and their children.[17]

This pointed to the need for countervailing policies. Discussion then started between UNICEF and the IFIs about how these concerns bore on IMF stabilization policies and World Bank structural adjustment programmes. In 1984, UNICEF got involved in an inter-agency team to plan Ghana's Programme of Action to Mitigate the Social Consequences of Adjustment (PAMSCAD), which eventually started in 1988. Richard believed that 'the Ghana case provides probably the most useful operational example of the international agencies working with a country to develop a programme of human recovery linked to adjustment' (Jolly 1988: 169). Yet PAMSCAD was a big flop, which in part could be attributed to the flawed policymaking processes of the Ghanaian government and in part to the reluctance of the World Bank to get involved in the provision of social safety nets.

Because of its previous history of economic misrule, Ghana's structural adjustment programmes under IMF–World Bank auspices were being conspicuously successful. Even without PAMSCAD, incomes not least of farmers were growing, public expenditure was expanding, and so was the spending on the social sectors. Social services improved as trained teachers replaced the untrained and health clinics were re-stocked with drugs.[18] The doubling of the incidence of child malnutrition that had triggered UNICEF's initial concern belonged to the period 1980–3, that is, the period before the first economic recovery programme had begun.

Nevertheless, the adjustment policies of the IFIs were now under the spotlight, displacing recession in the developed world. In July 1985, Richard gave the second Barbara Ward Memorial Lecture to SID in Rome on the topic 'Adjustment with a Human Face'. The title echoed the subtitle of Fritz Schumacher's popular little book *Small Is Beautiful: Economics as if People Mattered*. The human face became part of the populist rhetoric of development, which had a wide appeal.[19]

---

[17] This was in a special issue of *World Development* (12.3) edited by Richard and Andrea Cornia.
[18] I have described Ghana's structural adjustment experience in the 1980s in Volume 2 of Mosley, Harrigan, and Toye (1991: 150–200).
[19] Not everyone was charmed. A disgruntled colleague sent me the following lines: 'I wish I loved the Human Race / I wish I loved its silly face / And when I'm introduced to one / I wish I thought *What Jolly Fun!*' This turns out to be an extract from 'Wishes of an Elderly Man' by Walter Raleigh (1861–1922), according to the *Oxford Dictionary of Humorous Quotations*.

Adjustment with a Human Face was also the title of the book by Giovanni Andrea Cornia, Richard, and Frances Stewart published by Oxford University Press in 1987. In these volumes it was acknowledged that adjustment policies were not the primary cause of the social setbacks suffered by vulnerable groups, yet adjustment policies were said to be 'not doing enough' to prevent further such setbacks.

Conceptual clarity about the nature of those social consequences of adjustment programmes that needed to be mitigated remained elusive. *Adjustment with a Human Face* adopted the position that it was impossible to distinguish the negative social consequences of prior bad economic policies from the negative social consequences of subsequent corrective economic policies.[20] The book was, in effect, a general plea for less contractionary adjustment policies as well as for more international action to combat poverty and malnutrition. And a very successful plea it was. UNICEF's unrelenting advocacy undoubtedly contributed to the World Bank's return to issues of poverty reduction in 1990. It was also effective in inter-agency politics, bringing UNICEF to the front of the public stage in a way seen neither before nor since. This new prominence was greatly appreciated by UNICEF's staff members and high staff morale eased management problems within the organization.

UNICEF's own programme strategy was born at a meeting held at UNICEF headquarters in September/October 1982 on the subject of nutrition. With the aim of improving child survival rates across the world, UNICEF devised a quartet of simple and cheap health interventions that it would promote in over a hundred countries. These were growth monitoring, oral re-hydration, breast-feeding, and immunizations—known for short as 'GOBI'. These elements were all low-cost and possible to implement on scale. To these were added two further elements called 'FF', these being food supplementation and birth spacing and family planning. GOBI-FF was later extended to GOBI-FFF, when female education was added to the list of desirable actions. GOBI-FFF was a strategy of selective primary healthcare that followed on from the joint WHO–UNICEF primary healthcare strategy adopted at Alma-Ata in 1978. As such, it ran into some concerns that it could detract from local efforts to evolve a more rounded locally determined primary healthcare strategy. These anxieties do not seem to have been borne out by subsequent evaluations.[21]

UNICEF was in a good position to advance its child survival strategy because, since the 1960s, it had been gradually shifting staff from its headquarters to its network of country offices. The task of each country office was to make an analysis of children's needs in the country concerned, to

---

[20] Richard defended the UNICEF position in an essay 'Adjustment with a Human Face: A Broader Approach to Adjustment Policy' (Jolly 1987).
[21] See, for example, McPake et al. (1993).

specify the relevant action to be taken by the government, by NGOs, and by aid donors, and to recommend how UNICEF could act as a catalyst for the specified actions. Each office had GOBI goals, approved by the country representative. Richard insisted on a more systematic approach, codified in a manual, and pressed offices to supply headquarters with basic statistics on child nutrition. He advocated collection by multi-indicator cluster surveys, for which the enumerators were local medical students—thereby making future doctors more conscious of child nutrition. The figures indicated significant declines in the number of children dying from diarrhoea, infectious diseases, and other common killers.

The event that really raised the profile of this effort was the 1990 World Summit for Children, the first of a number of UN summits that were to follow. At first there were doubts as to whether the UN had the power to call a summit meeting, so Canada, Sweden, Egypt, Pakistan, Mali, and Morocco convened it and the UN provided the venue. Seventy-one heads of state attended and 87 other countries sent lower-level representatives. The summit set new goals for reduction in child mortality, and for access to education and healthcare, with special attention to girl children. Major progress was made towards country ratification of the Convention on the Rights of the Child. The event started a trend for world summits on other socioeconomic issues, and its goal-setting foreshadowed the millennium development goals.[22]

Other UN agencies looked enviously at UNICEF's claims of goal achievement, its flair for high-level publicity, and the influx of donor funds that these brought. All the same, Richard was able to play a coordinating role between UNICEF, UNDP, UNFPA, WHO, and WFP—and at times other UN agencies. In the cause of UN reform, this coordination involved the clarification of agency mandates and the cutting out of overlaps and, in Richard's view, the building of value added by focusing on the achievement of common goals.

When Jim Grant came to the end of his time as executive director of UNICEF, Richard had only the support of the UK government in his bid to be the successor. Carol Bellamy, who was chosen as the new head of the agency, gave Richard no encouragement to stay. So, sponsored by John P. Lewis, he became a visiting fellow at the Woodrow Wilson School of Advanced Studies in Princeton University, where Alison was teaching. His aim was to write a book about UNICEF.

---

[22] See Emmerij et al. (2001: 112–13).

2.5 The Human Development Report

Meanwhile, in another part of the UN forest, Gus Speth, administrator of the UNDP, was stirring, because he believed that the UNDP board had some unease with Mahbub ul Haq's leadership of the office of the *Human Development Report* (HDR). Mahbub decided to return to his roots and establish a new South Asian HDR Office in order to bring out a South Asian regional version of the HDR. He then asked Richard if he would like to take over the vacant post in New York.

For Richard, to do so would be to make a significant but welcome change of gear. He had been away from the world of development thinking for a long spell, so to return to reading, learning, and writing full time would be a challenge. He was also doubtful about the human development index, which Mahbub had insisted should be part of the HDR, but which Richard regarded as an arbitrary construction. Amartya Sen had also advised against the inclusion of the index when the HDR was first being launched, but he had taken a more pragmatic view later, agreeing that the index served as a useful weapon to combat the centrality of GDP as an indicator of development. 'We need a measure of the same level of vulgarity as GNP—just one number, but a measure that is not as blind to social aspects of human lives as GNP is,' Mahbub is said to have remarked to Sen by way of explanation.[23] Richard decided to make the move to UNDP and to retain the index in the HDR, a decision that he saw as essentially political.

Richard oversaw the publication of five HDRs between 1996 and 2000, selecting a series of important themes. These ranged from growth, through poverty and consumption, to globalization and human rights. He worked with Sudiko Fukuda-Parr and had assistance on the conceptual and statistical side from Amartya Sen and Sudhir Anand. They devised a new logarithmic function to provide a measure of 'adjusted income' for the report on growth. For the poverty issue they worked on a measure of interlocking deprivations: illiteracy, low life expectation, lack of access to water, and malnutrition. For the consumption issue, they tried to find a way to include—in the spirit of Keynes's *Economic Possibilities for Our Grandchildren* [24] —the finer things in life in a measure of consumption, but failed. Richard regarded the 2000 report as the most important of his series. For this one, Sen wrote about how human-rights discourse can add value to the concept of human development, and vice versa.

[23] Sen (1999).
[24] 'We shall honour those who can teach us how to pluck the hour and the day virtuously and well, the delightful people who are capable of taking direct enjoyment in things, the lilies of the field who toil not, neither do they spin.... There will be no harm in making mild preparations for our destiny, in encouraging, and experimenting in the arts of life...' (Keynes 1972: 330–1).

Richard maintained good relations with the governments represented on the UNDP board, but when Mark Malloch-Brown came in as the new administrator of UNDP, he offered his resignation. He was now 65, and he was aware that there were too many UK nationals in the upper reaches of the UNDP. Unlike Carol Bellamy, Malloch-Brown urged Richard to stay on, which he did for another year, before returning to IDS as an honorary fellow.

2.6 The UN Intellectual History Project

Richard had by now long been a champion of the UN. This was the other face of his critical stance towards the international financial institutions. Giving the John W. Holmes memorial lecture to the Academic Council of the UN system in 1996, he made this assessment:

> The UN has, over the whole of its fifty years, often demonstrated both awareness of…global issues [of debt, trade, technology, and aid] and intellectual creativity in analysing them and suggesting solutions. In this respect, the UN record is more successful than is often acknowledged.

That judgment was the basis of his interest in promoting the production of a history of UN ideas, particularly ideas in the area of social and economic development. Sidney Dell, another dedicated servant of the UN ethos, had projected such a history some years before. Dell had wanted a twenty-volume history, and started to raise money for it in the 1980s. Only the Japanese government offered any money for Dell's plan, of which one volume was completed before Dell's death in 1991. After leaving UNICEF, Richard began to look for finance for a UN history, but without initially seeing himself as one of the leaders of such a project. Tom Weiss also took a leading role, and Louis Emmerij was identified as the third member of the managing triumvirate at an EADI meeting in 1999.

The financial breakthrough came with support for the project from Lincoln Chen, the deputy head of the Rockefeller Foundation, who advised Gordon Conway, the president to offer US$300,000. This grant encouraged other donors to come in with additional financial support. The original plan was for fourteen volumes, produced over a span of six years. Unsurprisingly for such a project, the time span extended to ten years (1999–2009), and sixteen volumes in all appeared, plus a seventy-page booklet on *The Power of UN Ideas* for the UN's sixtieth anniversary in 2005. Richard himself was co-author of five of the series.

As with any series, it had some unevenness in approach and quality. Three of the volumes won prizes. The best-selling volume was *UN Ideas that Changed the World*, followed by *Ahead of the Curve?* Both of these were multi-author overview volumes to which Richard contributed. The sales figures were quite moderate relative to those achieved by other publications with which Richard had been involved, such as the ILO Report on Kenya, *Adjustment with a Human Face*, and the *Human Development Report*. Nevertheless, the UN Intellectual History Project, including the seventy-nine interviews with UN staff for the Oral History Archive at the City University of New York, was a monumental project that succeeded in shining a spotlight on the intellectual and practical contributions of the world body.

2.7 The Achievements of an Optimistic Economist

Richard's long and distinguished career in development has been recognized by the award of a knighthood, in 2001, for services to the United Nations and to international development. In addition, the University of East Anglia, the University of Sussex, and the former Institute of Social Studies in The Hague have awarded him honorary degrees. His outstanding mature achievements in leading a major UN agency, further developing the human-development concept, and realizing Sidney Dell's ambition of a history of UN ideas and actions speak for themselves.

If one delved into the causes of his success, the first to come to mind would be his temperament. Alison commented on it, recalling their first stay together in Madagascar: 'I was learning fast that it was possible to become totally involved with Malagasy people if you hung out with a cheerful economist with curly red hair and a passion for local life' (Jolly 2004: 172). I certainly have never seen Richard out of countenance, or anything other than good tempered and serene. This optimistic exponent of the dismal science constantly warns against development pessimism and stresses the forward strides in wellbeing that history has already recorded. Acknowledging past success, however, always prefaces powerful words of encouragement to envisage the next steps needed to make new strides in the future. 'Why Falter Now?' is the characteristic title of one of his lectures.[25] This is the very opposite of Ogden Nash's invitation to complacency: 'Progress is fine, but it has gone on too long.' Rather it is the kind of bracing persuasion that is used by a man who once led an elephant over the Alps.[26]

Optimism must be sustained, and the best way to sustain it is through a supportive home life. Richard has been blessed in that respect, and enabled to take on assignments that could have wrecked less resilient lives. The

[25] Third Bradford Development Lecture, 22 October 1993.
[26] Richard's first publication in *Alpine Journal* (1962) was 'Hannibal's Route across the Alps: Results of an Empirical Test'.

ability to make and keep long-term relationships outside as well as inside the home must also have been crucial to his success. His professional network has been highly durable, as well as ever expanding.

Jo Beall has highlighted 'Richard Jolly's unique combination of intense optimism and measured pragmatism'.[27] Her emphasis on pragmatism is well merited. Richard is always looking for the opportunity for another 'judo trick', that quick move that makes a big impact because the forces of nature are on one's side. At present, he is looking to the concept of human security in the broadest sense to integrate the many concerns that comprise the notion of human advancement. It does indeed integrate those issues to which he has devoted himself for more than 50 years—education, employment, disarmament, health, poverty reduction, and greater equality—issues that he has helped to make into goals for the whole world.

References

Boulding, K. (1941). *Economic Analysis*. New York: Harper and Brothers.

Cassen, R., R. Jolly, J. Sewell, and R. Wood (eds) (1982). *Rich Country Interests and Third World Development*. London: Croom Helm.

Emmerij, L., R. Jolly, and T. Weiss (2001). *Ahead of the Curve? UN Ideas and Global Challenges*. Bloomington, IN: Indiana University Press.

Harbison, F. and C. A. Myers (1964). *Education, Manpower and Economic Growth: Strategies of Human Resources Development*. New York: McGraw-Hill.

IDS (1968). 'January Course for Home Civil Servants'. *IDS Annual Report 1967/8*. Brighton: IDS.

Jolly, A. (2004). *Lords and Lemurs*. Boston: Houghton Mifflin.

Jolly, R. (1962). 'Hannibal's Route across the Alps: Results of an Empirical Test'. *Alpine Journal*, 67: 243–9.

Jolly, R. (1987). 'Adjustment with a Human Face: A Broader Approach to Adjustment Policy'. In E. Clay and J. Shaw (eds), *Poverty, Development and Food: Essays in Honour of H. W. Singer on his 75th Birthday*. London: Macmillan, 61–77.

Jolly, R. (1988). 'Poverty and Adjustment in the 1990s'. In J. P. Lewis (ed.), *Strengthening the Poor: What Have We Learned?* New Brunswick: Transaction Books for the Overseas Development Council, 163–75.

Jolly, R. (1993). 'Why Falter Now? The Case for Development Commitment'. Third Bradford Development Lecture, 22 October. Bradford: University of Bradford.

Jolly, R. (2008). *'A Short History of the IDS: A Personal Reflection'*. IDS Occasional Paper 388. Brighton: IDS.

Jolly, R. and G. A. Cornia (1984). *The Impact of World Recession on Children*. Oxford: Pergamon Press.

---

[27] In Simon (2006: 133).

Keynes, J. M. (1972). *The Collected Writings of John Maynard Keynes*, Vol. XI. London: Macmillan and Cambridge University Press.

Lewis, A. (1955). *The Theory of Economic Growth*. London: Allen and Unwin.

McPake, B., F. Ajnong, B. Forsberg, W. Liambilla, and J. Olenga (1993). 'The Kenyan Model of the Bamako Initiative'. *International Journal of Health Planning and Management*, 8(2): 123–8.

Marshall, A. (1890). *Principles of Economics*. London: Macmillan.

Mosley, P., J. Harrigan, and J. Toye (1991). *Aid and Power: The World Bank and Policy-based Lending*. London: Routledge.

Overy, R. (2009). *The Morbid Age: Britain between the Wars*. London: Allen Lane.

Robinson, J. (1934). *Economics of Imperfect Competition*. London: Macmillan.

Robinson, J. (1956). *The Accumulation of Capital*. London: Macmillan.

Seers, D. (1963). 'The Limitations of the Special Case'. *Bulletin of the Oxford University Institute of Economic and Statistics*, 25(2): 77–98.

Seers, D. (ed.) (1964). *Cuba: The Economic and Social Revolution*. Chapel Hill, NC: University of North Carolina Press.

Seers, D. (1969). 'The Meaning of Development'. *International Development Review*, 13(4): 2–6.

Seers, D. (1979). 'The Congruence of Marxism and Other Neoclassical Doctrines'. In K. Hill (ed.), *Towards a New Strategy for Development*. New York: Pergamon Press, 1–17. (Reprinted in R. Jolly (ed.) (2012), *Milestones and Turning Points in Development Thinking*. London: Palgrave, Macmillan, 43–56.)

Seers, D. (1980). 'Muddling Mutuality and Morality: A Review of the Brandt Report'. *Third World Quarterly*, 2(4): 681–93.

Sen, A. (1999). 'Assessing Human Development'. In R. Jolly (ed.) *Human Development Report 1999*. New York: UNDP, 23.

Simon, D. (ed.) (2006). *Fifty Key Thinkers on Development*. Abingdon: Routledge.

Toye, J. and R. Toye (2004). *The UN and Global Political Economy*. Bloomington, IN: Indiana University Press.

ul Haq, M. (1995). *Reflections on Human Development*. New York: Oxford University Press.

Part II

Human Development and Inequality: Progress in Concepts and Policies?

3

Constructing New Policy Narratives
The Capability Approach as Normative Language*

Séverine Deneulin

After years of negotiations and persuasion, in 1990 Mahbub ul Haq launched a new office at the United Nations Development Programme. Its mandate was to produce an annual report that would monitor how well countries were doing, using different criteria from those of the World Bank's *World Development Reports*. For more than twenty years, the *Human Development Reports* have been reporting on how successful countries are in terms of 'human development'. The reports have now become a basic reference for those looking for information on how well governments have succeeded in enabling people to live well in some selected dimensions, such as health, knowledge, political freedom, political empowerment, and employment.[1]

By collecting data about the quality of people's lives and computing a composite index, the human development index, to replace gross domestic product as the indicator of success, the *Human Development Reports* have sought to bring about a paradigmatic shift and to develop an alternative to the neoclassical economic paradigm, which had underpinned many policies worldwide since the early 1980s. Human development growth, approximated by better health and education outcomes and improved standards of living, should be the ultimate measure of development or progress, not economic growth. Replacing the neoliberal paradigm with the human development paradigm has been a running theme and main driver of Richard Jolly's professional career. It has best been summarized in a short article he wrote soon after retiring from UNICEF.

* I thank Frances Stewart and four anonymous referees for their comments on an earlier draft.
[1] See <http://hdr.undp.org/en>.

Human development puts 'people first' (Jolly 2009). The economy is important but is only a means to an end. Economic growth can sometimes lead to greater inequity and fewer opportunities for people to live well. Investments in education and health matter, not only because they make the workforce more productive but because a healthy life and the pursuit of knowledge are part of what it means to live well as human beings. People's experience of poverty is multidimensional and not simply a matter of income. Poverty is also lack of voice, lack of access to knowledge, lack of access to healthcare, and lack of dignified employment opportunities, among other things. In sum, what human development is, is very simple: it is a paradigm according to which concern for people, and the quality of their lives, should come first in every decision at all levels, whether individual, organizational, or governmental.

Human development draws heavily on the conceptual works of economist Amartya Sen, and his 'capability approach'.[2] This chapter interprets the capability approach as a new normative language for policy. It argues that it is characterized by some fundamental words—wellbeing, functionings, capabilities, agency, freedom—but speakers/social actors are left free to combine these words in multiple ways, interpret them according to different policy settings, and construct context-dependent policy narratives. The chapter highlights two areas of interpretative differences: the purpose of the normative language and its conception of the person. It illustrates how the capability approach language is interpreted differently according to various policy settings and used to construct different normative policy narratives. The chapter argues that this plurality of interpretations is one of the capability approach's greatest strengths, and the main reason why it is to date the most comprehensive and compelling normative language with which to frame social action for improving people's lives. This openness to interpretative differences may, however, sometimes be a liability.

3.1 The Capability Approach as Normative Language

The concept of 'capability' first appeared in the late 1970s, in Sen's Tanner Lectures 'Equality of What' (Sen 1980), as an alternative formulation of equality to utility and primary goods. Sen vowed then 'not to desist from doing some propaganda on its behalf' (1980: 197). Many voices have joined in this advocacy in the three decades after the concept was first introduced,

---

[2] There were other influences such as the North–South round tables and the 'basic-needs approach' adopted in the late 1970s by the International Labour Organization and later on by the World Bank. See Stewart (2006).

and some of these voices are now collectively organized in the Human Development and Capability Association, launched in 2004.[3]

The concept of 'capability' appears rather obscure to the uninitiated audience. As Sen acknowledges, '[c]apability is not an awfully attractive word', a 'nicer word could have been chosen' (Sen 1993: 30). As a more attractive word, the *Human Development Reports* have translated 'capability' as 'choice'. This has created some misunderstanding, for human development is not about expanding consumer choices, such as a greater choice of brands or between different healthcare providers, but about expanding the opportunities people have to function. Sometimes an increase in 'choices' in the latter sense, such as the choice between a public and private health system, may lead to a decrease in people's opportunities to function—the introduction of a dual health system, for example, may lead to a disinvestment in the public health system and exclude some people from accessing healthcare.

This section presents the concept of 'capability', and the approach based on it, as a normative language. It is a language because it possesses some basic words and a grammar structure that define it. It is a *normative* language because words are used to construct moral narratives and moral judgments. The capability approach is concerned with providing a normative approach to framing decisions, especially at the policy level. Should the British government cut university education expenditures and cease to subsidize students? Should the Peruvian government give a special tax allowance for agrobusiness exporters? Should the Ethiopian government invest large financial resources in building a dam on the Nile to generate more electricity for Addis Ababa?

The capability approach can also provide a frame for moral judgments at the individual level. Should one work part-time in order to devote more time to other activities? Should a household own one or two cars, or none at all? When Gary Becker won the Nobel Prize in Economics in 1992, in his Nobel lecture he reported that he had had the insight of applying utilitarian economic theory to crime when he arrived late for an oral examination and had to decide whether to park in a paying car park or to park illegally and get a ticket.[4] He calculated the risk of getting fined, the cost of the fine, and the cost of the parking, and decided to park illegally, given the low likelihood of getting fined. Using the capability approach would have led to a rather different process of deliberation and judgment.

The words of the capability normative language are few. They have been laid out most comprehensively in Sen's Dewey Lectures, entitled 'Wellbeing, Freedom and Agency', given in 1984 at Columbia University and published in 1985 in the *Journal of Philosophy*. The opening sentence says it all: 'The

---

[3] See Human Development and Capability Association at <http://www.hd-ca.org>.
[4] See <http://www.nobelprize.org/nobel_prizes/economics/laureates/1992/becker-lecture.pdf>.

main aim of the lectures is to explore a moral approach that sees persons from two different perspectives: *wellbeing* and *agency'* (Sen 1985: 169). Sen does not yet talk of a 'capability approach', but he talks of an approach to morality, the domain of what should be done, which conceives of persons as functioning bodies and minds and as agents. Any moral judgment, whether at the individual or policy level, is to be based on these two perspectives: wellbeing and agency. The opening paragraph of the Dewey Lectures concludes by saying that 'each aspect [wellbeing and agency] also yields a corresponding notion of freedom' (Sen 1985: 169). In later writings, Sen talks of the 'opportunity' and 'process' aspect of freedom (Sen 2002). Thus, it is a moral approach based on freedom, but a freedom inescapably connected to the twin concepts of wellbeing and agency, and not a freedom to express whatever desire one may have.

Sen contrasts having wellbeing with being well-off. The latter is concerned with opulence, with how much a person has, the former with how a person functions, what he/she succeeds in being or doing:

> The primary feature of wellbeing can be seen in terms of how a person can 'function'. I shall refer to various doings and beings that come into this assessment as *functionings*. These could be activities (like eating or reading or seeing), or states of existence or being, e.g., being well nourished, being free from malaria, not being ashamed by the poverty of one's clothing or shoes. (Sen 1985: 197–8)

The moral approach that Sen presents is one in which the central moral question is 'What kind of a life is he/she [a person] leading? What does she succeed in doing and in being?' (Sen 1985: 195). A social arrangement is good if it enables a person to succeed in doing and being things in areas they consider worthwhile. Sen does not give any indication as to what these activities or states of existence may be beyond the ones given above.[5] The 'functioning approach is intrinsically information-pluralist' (Sen 1985: 200). A person functions in many aspects and there are many activities she can do and many states he/she can be.

To this functioning moral approach, Sen adds another layer and extends it to a person's capability to function:

> The information pluralism of the functioning approach to wellbeing has to be further extended if we shift attention from the person's actual functionings to his or her *capability* to function. A person's *capability set* can be defined as the

---

[5] In his Tanner Lecture, Sen speaks about 'basic capabilities', which he associates with 'a person's being able to do certain things', such as 'ability to move about' and 'ability to meet one's nutritional requirements, the wherewithal to be clothed and sheltered, the power to participate in the social life of the community' (Sen 1980: 218).

set of functioning vectors [a functioning vector being the set of functionings a person actually achieves] within his or her reach (Sen 1985: 200–1)

Sen shifts his moral approach from a functioning to a capability approach so that one can include another type of information in moral evaluation: positive freedom or 'the freedom "to do this" or "to be that" that a person has' (Sen 1985: 201). When one compares two states of affairs and judges whether one is better than the other, the capability approach allows for 'comparison of actual opportunities that different persons have' (Sen 1985: 201), and not simply for comparison of actual activities or states of existence. Two students may fail their exam and share the same state, a failed degree, but if one student had to work full time and look after siblings and did not find time to study, and the other spent her days partying with her parents' money and did not find time to study, the opportunity sets of these two students were very different.

In addition to wellbeing, functionings, and capabilities, the normative language contains another central word: agency. Agency and wellbeing are connected but do not always go in the same direction. Agency is the 'pursuit of whatever goals or values he or she regards as important' (Sen 1985: 203). A peasant in the Amazon who resists illegal logging and campaigns to protect the forest may risk his or her own life. Despite the obvious loss of wellbeing, that person exercises agency. In Sen's moral approach, information about agency, and not only wellbeing, has to be included in moral judgments. Sen justifies the inclusion of agency in the informational basis of moral judgment on the grounds of recognition of responsibility. Persons are not only functioning, doing, or being certain things, but they are also responsible: 'The importance of the agency aspect, in general, relates to the view of persons as responsible agents' (Sen 1985: 204).

The language does not say that one type of information—functioning, capability, agency—is more important than another. Their importance varies according to context:

> The wellbeing aspect may be particularly important in some specific contexts, e.g., in making public provisions for social security, or in planning for the fulfilment of basic needs. In judging what a person may expect from social arrangements, the demands of wellbeing may loom rather large. On the other hand, in many issues of personal morality, the agency aspect, and one's responsibility to others may be central. The wellbeing aspect and the agency aspect both demand attention, but they do so in different ways, and with varying relevance to different problems.

Sen presents his moral approach as an alternative to the moral approach widespread in the discipline of economics. Instead of using utility as information for moral judgment, one should use wellbeing, understood as the ability to function, and agency. To take Gary Becker's decision of paying for parking or parking illegally, acting with respect for the law (agency) and therefore paying the car park, even if one would have preferred to spend the money in other ways, is as relevant a consideration in coming to a decision as the likelihood of being fined. Or consider a household decision to buy a car. Becker's approach would be to maximize the household's utility by weighing up the benefits and costs of having a car for the household, such as the costs of public transport, as against those of having a car. Sen's approach would be to include information about wellbeing and agency. If there is a disabled person in the household, then considerations for that person's wellbeing and mobility may override cost considerations. Or if the household has a strong environmental commitment, its members might continue to use public transport despite wellbeing losses (lower mobility and maybe higher monetary costs). Agency is in this last case the most important information taken into account in the decision.

The moral approach presented in Sen's Dewey Lectures, i.e. the capability approach, can also be used to articulate policy narratives. The capability approach is essentially about a space for evaluating social arrangements, and holds that the relevant information to use in evaluation is capabilities, functionings, and agency. For example, is the UK government decision to increase university fees good? If it leads to young people having fewer opportunities to access university education, this social arrangement may not be good. But the public resources saved on university education could be redirected to support housing for people on low incomes or to address child poverty. In such cases, the social arrangement may be good because it gives people more opportunities for affordable housing. There may be trade-offs. Is the construction of the Gibe dam in Ethiopia a good social arrangement? If the construction of the dam leads to people being forced to leave their land, to public resources being diverted from key social services and people having more limited access to healthcare, and to environmental degradation and loss of livelihood for many farmers, these are relevant considerations to use in the evaluation of the social arrangement in addition to information about economic resources generated by the dam.

The capability approach is thus a normative language which enables us to articulate a social reality from the perspective of wellbeing and agency. How its key words are combined, which words are more important, depends on the situation. In relation to equality, the capability approach advocates that equality be assessed in the functioning and capability space rather than that of incomes or utility. In some contexts, one will use information about functionings, in other contexts, one will be able to use information about capabilities, the real opportunities or freedoms people have to do or be certain things. In other contexts, one will use information both about wellbeing and agency, or the opportunity to pursue goals beyond one's wellbeing.

There are thus many levels and perspectives from which the capability approach can be used, and many ways in which its key words can be combined to construct various narratives to evaluate a given social reality. This is why the capability approach has been so versatile. It is used in the fields of education, health, and disability, among many others. It is used to analyse social arrangements for women, indigenous peoples, and other marginalized groups. Each context will yield different uses of the approach.

To sum up, the capability approach is a normative language based on freedom: the freedom a person has to pursue his/her wellbeing and the freedom he/she has to pursue other goals beyond his/her wellbeing. Wellbeing is conceived in terms of functionings, or beings and doings. Wellbeing can also include freedom: a person's wellbeing depends not only on what he/she does or is, but on *how* he/she has achieved that functioning. Eating a ready meal from a set menu or eating a meal cooked from scratch by one's chosen ingredients may lead to a similar functioning, being nourished, but one may derive greater wellbeing from the latter than the former because of the process involved in reaching that functioning. Whether wellbeing is a matter of functioning or a matter of agency foremost, the capability approach is open to both characterizations. In Sen's words (1992: 150):

> If the wellbeing that a person gets from what she *does* is dependent on *how* she came to do it (in particular, whether she chose that functioning herself), then her wellbeing depends not just on x, but on the choice of x from the set S. [...] The crucial question here, in the context of wellbeing, is whether freedom to choose is valued only instrumentally, or is also important in itself. The capability approach is broad enough to permit both the rival—but interrelated—characterizations of wellbeing, and can be used in either way. (Sen 1992: 150)

Freedom is an ambiguous concept, and the capability approach, as a moral approach that sees persons from the perspective of freedom, is therefore also ambiguous:

> Insofar as there are genuine ambiguities in the concept of freedom, that should be reflected in corresponding ambiguities in the characterization of capability. This relates to a methodological point [...] that if an underlying idea has an essential ambiguity, a precise formulation of that idea must try to *capture* that ambiguity rather than hide or eliminate it. (Sen 1993: 33)

The capability approach is deliberately incomplete and does not provide 'a comprehensive theory of valuation' (Sen 1993: 48). It can be used with many other theories. It is a general approach 'with various bits to be filled in' (Sen 1993: 48). Sen provides the words of a new normative language, but its ambiguity gives rise to a plurality of interpretations. The next section discusses different, sometimes conflicting, interpretations of the capability approach. It highlights that this need not be a problem as the plurality of interpretations is a mirror of the deliberate incompleteness and openness of the capability approach.

3.2 Plurality of Interpretations

The basic structure of the normative language of the capability approach has been written in many texts. This study has focused on four (Sen 1980, 1985, 1992, 1993). Like any text, these texts were written by a specific author, situated in a specific reality, with a specific intention and audience. Sen wrote primarily for neoclassical economists with the intention to demonstrate some problems with neoclassical economics (the use of utility as an approximation of human wellbeing and the assumption of rational choice), and for liberal egalitarian philosophers with the intention to demonstrate some problems with Rawls's theory of justice (the use of primary goods as the informational basis of justice).

As a 'discourse fixed by writing' (Ricoeur 1981: 144), a text is there to be read but to read it is 'to fulfil the text in present speech' (Ricoeur 1981: 144), 'to conjoin a new discourse to the discourse of the text' (Ricoeur 1981: 158). To read a text is always to relate its basic structure to the specific reality of the reader. Reading Sen's texts is about translating their basic structure in the world of the reader. A feminist economist working in the reality of rural India does not read the texts of the capability approach in the same way as a liberal philosopher does in the reality of academia in New England, and they will not communicate the insights of the capability approach in the same way, for their reality, audience, and intentions are different.

Like any text, the texts that fix the basic structure of the capability approach are open to interpretation, in the sense that the meaning of the original texts is always to be reconstructed by the reader according to his/her own reality. The work of interpretation is particularly needed as Sen has left the basic structure of the capability approach purposively ambiguous. This section highlights two main areas of multiple interpretations: the purpose of the normative language and the conception of the person that underpins it.

3.2.1 Purpose of the Capability Approach

In a review article, Alkire (2005: 122) interprets the capability approach as a 'proposition' that 'social arrangements should be evaluated according to the extent of freedom people have to promote or achieve functionings they value'. It provides an alternative informational basis for moral judgments to that of utility but falls short of being prescriptive about what type of information to include. It only advocates that the evaluation of social arrangements be in the capability space, which can include a whole range of functionings and capabilities. The relevant information for evaluating, say, the wellbeing of female pensioners in rural Wales will be different from the one used to evaluate the wellbeing of migrant construction workers in Dubai.

As an evaluation space for assessing whether social arrangements are good or bad, the capability approach can be used to evaluate very diverse realities. For example, it can help articulate the reality of introducing information and communications technology (ICT) in a remote African village. Instead of analysing the economic impact of ICT, the capability approach constructs a story about whether ICT has generated more opportunities for the villagers to be or do what they have reason to value. Or it can help evaluate a certain type of school pedagogy. Instead of articulating a new pedagogy in terms of its impact on young people's performance at tests, the normative language of the capability approach articulates this specific social arrangement in terms of young people's wellbeing and agency.

In another review article, Robeyns (2005: 96) talks of the capability approach as being 'primarily and mainly a framework for thought', a 'broad normative framework for the evaluation and assessment of individual wellbeing and social arrangements' (Robeyns 2005: 94). She argues that poverty, inequality, and social exclusion are not social phenomena that the capability approach seeks to explain. It aims only at conceptualizing them in the light of individual freedom, and would need to be accompanied by explanatory theories. For example, it provides a structure for analysing the situation of some farming community whose livelihoods are affected by climate change. Instead of telling a story about income losses caused by failed crops, the capability approach tells the story of people no longer having opportunities to do or be what they value, such as opportunities to hold events that brought the community together and strengthened solidarity links between the members, or opportunities for women to cultivate land. But on this interpretation, the capability approach does not explain why that farming community is losing opportunities to be or do what they value.

But the capability approach is subject to another interpretation. According to this, it is not only a normative language relevant to the evaluation of social arrangements, but also a language that is relevant to political action and social transformation. In other words, the capability approach is not only a framework for the evaluation of social arrangements or a framework for the analysis of social phenomena, but it can also be interpreted as a partial theory of justice.[6]

---

[6] Alkire (2008) refers to the 'narrow' interpretation of the capability approach when used for evaluation, and 'broad' or 'prospective' interpretation when it is used for informing social action.

In his *Idea of Justice*, Sen (2009) argues against the need for a theory of justice, such as that of Rawls. Asking the question of what a just social arrangement is, he contends, is not a good starting point for thinking about justice. He argues that a comparative framework that enables one to decide between alternative social arrangements, whether one is better or worse than another, is a better starting point for making societies more or less just. He argues that the capability approach should be used as a comparative framework. One situation is more just than another if more people have more opportunities to reach valuable states of being or doings than another. A society where women have more opportunities for meaningful employment is more just than one in which women are denied the opportunity to work outside the home. But it is not the task of the capability approach, Sen would argue, to offer an idea of what a just social arrangement would be or to prescribe principles or programmes of action to bring about just social arrangements.

Martha Nussbaum's writings figure most prominently in the alternative interpretation of the capability approach—as a normative language to articulate political action and as partial theory of justice.[7] She proposes a list of ten central human capabilities and argues that these need to be inscribed in constitutions as fundamental human rights (Nussbaum 2000, 2011). Nussbaum has 'filled in the various bits' (Sen 1993: 48) of the capability approach with a combination of Aristotelian social democracy and Rawlsian political liberalism (Nussbaum 1992, 2006).

Another way of using the normative language of the capability approach to frame political action for new social arrangements is to link it to social movement theory. One critique of Sen's writings on poverty and injustice is their silence regarding the unjust and alienating nature of the capitalist economic system (Dean 2009; Bagchi 2000; Feldman 2010). This has led some authors to reject the capability approach as a credible alternative to utilitarianism and neoliberalism, and even to perceive it as an ally of global capitalist expansion. These are, however, unjustified critiques. The purpose of Sen's writings was not to offer an alternative to capitalism but to offer a normative approach to analyse social arrangements from the perspective of wellbeing and agency. But this does not mean that one cannot interpret the basic structure of the capability approach in order to inform social action and political transformation. Every reader of the text will read the text and transfer it into his or her reality, and communicate it in a certain way given his or her intention and audience.

---

[7] Nussbaum's latest book, *Creating Capabilities: The Human Development Project*, has been published in French as *Capacités: Comment créer les conditions d'un monde plus juste?* (Capabilities: How to Create the Conditions of a More Just World).

The normative language of the capability approach could help social move-ments analyse the reality of an unjust situation, and each movement can 'fill in the bits', to paraphrase Sen. To advocate employment opportunities for women, some organizations may use feminist Marxist theories of patriarchal alienation; others may use liberal legal theories of individual rights. Both are valid uses of the language to frame political action to promote opportuni-ties for valuable functionings, as long as the theories 'used to fill in the bits' are compatible with a perspective of the person in terms of wellbeing and agency.

To the critique that the capability approach does not challenge the global capitalist mode of relations and only offers a way of assessing its symptoms rather than proposing a new configuration of power and social relations (Feldman 2010), one can answer that this was not the original purpose of the author of its basic texts but there is no reason why one cannot adopt the basic structure of the capability approach, and fill it in with other theories, to offer a new model of economic relations that respects people's agency and promotes people's wellbeing better than the capitalist mode of production.

3.2.2 Conception of the Person

A second area of plurality of interpretations relates to how the capability approach conceives the person. It is a moral approach that holds a concep-tion of the person as free. This freedom has two perspectives: wellbeing and agency. A person is free when he/she has the opportunity to function [as a human being] and to pursue goals he/she values.

The central place of human freedom in the capability approach has made some interpret it as a form of liberalism, philosophically speaking (Robeyns 2009). In Sen's basic structure, the capability approach does not presuppose a comprehensive doctrine of the good and, consistent with the basic tenets of liberalism, leaves people free to decide what conception of the human good they want to pursue. In an argument with John Rawls about his con-cern that capabilities are in essence judgments about what is worthwhile and implicitly rely on a judgment about the nature of a good human life, Sen (1990: 118) responds, 'Capability reflects a person's *freedom* to choose between alternative lives (functioning combinations), and its value need not be derived from one particular "comprehensive doctrine" demanding one specific way of living.' This is why Sen does not define the valuable capabilities that should enter the evaluation space, and talks of the 'capabilities people have reason to value'. It is up to processes of public reasoning within each society or context to define the 'valuable' capabilities that should enter the evaluation space of social arrangements. This is to respect people's freedom to define their own priorities and what capabilities are valuable in their own realities.

But this non-teleological view of human wellbeing need not be the only interpretation of the capability approach. When Sen wrote the basic texts of the normative language, his audience was that of political philosophy in which most academic arguments evolved around Rawls's theory of justice. The basic structure of the capability approach can be interpreted differently when taken to another audience. Martha Nussbaum takes the capability approach in another direction by linking valuable capabilities to a particular conception of the human good, thus adopting a teleological conception of the person. What constitutes human wellbeing, to live well as a human being, is not, according to her, whatever people freely decide. In that context she proposes a 'thick vague theory of the good' with her list of central human capabilities (Nussbaum 1992, 1993). Sen (1993) has no objection to this interpretation, as long as it is not the only one.

Whether human life has an end, the perfection of the human good, or not, is not the only area of plurality of interpretations regarding the underlying conception of the person of the capability approach. Whether human life is individual or structural has been another area of disagreement.

The basic structure of the capability approach, as Sen presents it, is 'ethically individualist' because it affirms that states of affairs should be evaluated only according to their goodness or badness for individuals (Robeyns 2005, 2008). Economic structures, social norms, informal and formal institutions are assessed according to their impact on individual lives. For example, the structure of the caste system, or the quality of family relations, does not enter into wellbeing evaluation, only their effects on individuals via, among others, lack of employment opportunities, higher morbidity, lack of bodily integrity for women, higher malnutrition, or lower educational opportunities among the lower caste. The caste system or family relations as such are not part of the assessment of social arrangements.

One reason for this commitment to ethical individualism is that a focus on groups or institutions may hide forms of oppressions and inequalities within the group (Alkire 2008). Focusing on the family, for example, as a collective unit may hide the fact that, while enabling the flourishing of some members, usually males, it may be oppressive to other members, usually females. How a 'good' family is defined is often the product of power relations with women having no voice: men may define a 'good' family as one in which women stay at home and are subject to their husbands (Robeyns 2008). Therefore, it is individuals, and the opportunities they have to function, not groups, who are the object of justice:

> There is indeed no particular analytical reason why group capabilities must be excluded a priori from the discourse on justice and injustice. The case for not going that way lies in the nature of the reasoning that would be involved. [...] Ultimately, it is individual evaluation on which we would have to draw, while

recognizing the profound interdependence of the valuation of individuals who interact with each other. [. ..] In valuing a person's ability to take part in the life of society, there is an implicit valuation of the life of the society itself, and that is an important enough aspect of the capability perspective. (Sen 2009: 246)

Thus, on this interpretation of wellbeing and agency, it is sufficient to recognize individual interdependence and interaction, but the structures that emerge from that interdependence are not part of the moral evaluation.

There is, however, another interpretation of the conception of the person in a moral approach, which adopts the perspective of freedom. Because persons interact and are in relation with each other, they create something that is beyond them and that therefore should be part of any normative language that aims at articulating the goodness or badness of social arrangements. Because relations are constitutive of human life, these relations acquire an existence beyond the control of any individual life (Deneulin 2008). This does not mean that they are immune to change, but no individual as such has control over it; only multiple individual actions or collective actions do.

The economic system that provides the basis for the exchange of goods may be the result of individual interactions, but it also constitutes a structure that profoundly shapes the opportunities people have to live well, and should therefore be part of the evaluation of justice (Deneulin 2011). A society structured by an unregulated economic system based on giving priority to the maximization of short-term profits over human wellbeing may create fewer opportunities for valuable functionings than one structured by an economic system based on the subjugation of profits to concern for the wellbeing of the workers. A society structured by a political system based on racial superiority of a few creates fewer opportunities for valuable functionings than a society based on a political system that sees everyone as having equal political, social, and economic opportunities. Collecting information about individuals' wellbeing only, including their ability to participate in society and collective action, omits a very important aspect of human life, namely that human life is embedded into a complex web of structural relations that do not belong to any individual as such. The quality of these structural relations matters in judging the goodness or badness of social arrangements. Analysing the nature of social institutions, from the caste system to the global financial architecture, should be a major concern for human-development policy (Stewart 2012).

3.3 The Construction of Policy Narratives

Each interpretation gives rise to the construction of different policy narratives. The normative language of the capability approach was introduced in order to provide an alternative to utilitarianism as a foundation for economic decision and policy. This section describes some examples of how the basic structure of the language of the capability approach gives rise to the framing of alternative policy narratives. It has selected two narratives that broadly reflect the plurality of interpretations of the language described in the previous section: the multidimensional poverty index (MPI) and the National Human Development Report of the Dominican Republic.

3.3.1 The Multidimensional Poverty Index (MPI)

For decades, international poverty measures have consisted in counting the number of people living below the poverty line—usually set at the amount of money a family needs to meet some minimal food and shelter requirements. These measures have been based on the language of neoclassical economics and its approximation of wellbeing in terms of preference satisfaction and income and consumption levels. The multidimensional poverty index uses instead the language of the capability approach to measure poverty. It singles out three dimensions of wellbeing and is measured by ten indicators, which have been chosen for international comparison purposes on the basis of existing data availability: health (nutrition, child mortality), education (years of schooling, school attendance), and living standards (cooking fuel, sanitation, water, electricity, floor, and assets).[8] A person is poor if he/she is deprived in at least one dimension. In 2010, the Oxford Poverty and Human Development Initiative (OPHI) estimated that 53.7 per cent of the Indian population was multidimensionally poor. This compares to the 37.2 per cent of the population below the national poverty line according to data from Indian government.[9]

According to whether one uses data on income poverty or multidimensional poverty, different policy narratives unfold. If one uses the neoclassical language, policies will focus on raising people's incomes and pushing people above the income level. For example, the Indian government pursued market liberalization, which led to an unprecedented rate of economic growth, at an average of about 8 per cent in the last ten years (Drèze and Sen 2011). These policies reduced the number of income-poor significantly. According to World Bank estimates, the poverty headcount ratio, calculated at the national poverty line, was 45.3 per cent in 1994. In 2010, only 29.8 per cent of the population was estimated to be poor.[10]

[8] See policy brief 'Multidimensional Poverty Index 2011' at <http://www.ophi.org.uk>.

[9] See 'MPI Country Brief: India' at <http://www.ophi.org.uk/wp-content/uploads/India.pdf?cda6c1>.

[10] See <http://data.worldbank.org/country/india>.

In contrast, if one uses the capability language, policies will focus on redistribution and social policies to ensure that people have opportunities to be or do some valuable things, such as being healthy. In that regard, the assessment of India's economic policies is less of a successful story. Despite the high rate of economic growth, child malnutrition has more or less stagnated. Deaton and Drèze (2009) report that the proportion of underweight children in the 0–3 year age group fell only from 47 per cent in 1998–9 to 46 per cent in 2005–6. The economic policies pursued by the Indian government, and the neglect of investment in agriculture and rural areas, have also led to higher levels of mortality among the farming community, with farmer suicide rising at alarming levels in some Indian states (Nagaraj 2008).

The multidimensional poverty index sits clearly within the interpretation of the normative language as an evaluation framework for social arrangements, and not as a partial theory of justice. The MPI is not designed to understand the causes of poverty and to propose a programme of action to remedy it. It simply evaluates the state of affairs. It also has a conception of the person based on individuality. The MPI looks at how deprived each person is. It 'assesses the nature and intensity of poverty at the individual level' (Alkire and Santos 2010: 1).

However, this interpretation is not necessarily exclusive of other interpretations. The MPI can be seen as the first stage of a partial theory of justice. By offering a vivid description of the nature and intensity of deprivation, it does point to policy failures, such as the failure to provide adequate nutrition and sanitation. Neither does the MPI's strong individual focus rule out the assessment of social arrangements at a more structural level. The OPHI 2011 MPI policy brief describes the life of Adil in West Bengal beyond the three dimensions and ten indicators that constitute the index. His employment opportunities depend on personal and social relations that are often exploitative. The securing of basic functionings, such as being nourished and being sheltered, is immersed in a complex set of patron–client relationships which, on the one hand, give him some functionings but, on the other hand, strip him of his agency. The evaluation space of social arrangements can be broadened to include data on the quality of structural relations, such as the nature and intensity of clientelism, or the nature and intensity of political inequality in democratic institutions. Creating measures of structural relations, in addition to measures of individual functionings, remains a challenge, but one could envisage supplementing quantitative assessments of individual characteristics with qualitative assessments of structural characteristics.

The MPI is an example of how different policy narratives can be constructed on the basis of the normative language of the capability approach and illustrates how the language can be *interpreted*, that is, the reader reads the basic texts of the capability approach within his/her own context and transmits them to a specific audience. In the context of the MPI, the audience is economists and statisticians working for governments and international institutions, who had previously measured poverty in terms of income. Were the audience different (say, social movements who drew their inspiration from Marxist thought), the interpretation of the basic texts would have been different.

3.3.2 The National Human Development Reports

The *Human Development Reports* were one of the first attempts at communicating the normative language of the capability approach to a wider non-academic public. In doing so, they have interpreted the basic language in a certain way, with a given audience and intention in mind: offering an alternative to the annual *World Development Reports* of the World Bank. They have gone beyond the evaluative and individual interpretation of the capability approach and offered a rich analysis of some of the causes for high and low achievements in wellbeing outcomes, and suggested a programme of action for influencing these achievements.[11] Some national human development reports (NHDRs) have also attempted to go beyond the evaluation of wellbeing at the level of individual characteristics to include structural relations. The NHDR from the Dominican Republic of 2008, entitled 'Human Development: A Question of Power', included an analysis of the configuration of power in the country, in addition to collecting data of functionings at the individual level.[12] It concluded that one of the main obstacles to people having opportunities to be or do some valuable things, such as being educated or healthy, was inequality. The range of opportunities available for particular people and groups depends on how much power certain groups have (UNDP 2008: 3). It is symptomatic in that respect that significant public resources have been allocated to building a metro line in a low-population-density area of Santo Domingo and not in a high-density area where it would benefit more people, and that public resources have been diverted from social investment in the poor urban areas where the vast majority of people lacking basic opportunities live (UNDP 2008: 139).

In the context of the Dominican reality, the normative language of the capability approach acquires another meaning. Reading the basic texts of the

---

[11] The capability approach and human development have often been used as synonyms. However, as the study has demonstrated, the interpretations of the capability approach are multiple and 'human development' is one interpretation, one that emphasizes the need to go beyond evaluation to include an analysis of the causes of deprivations, why people lack the freedoms to do or be valuable things, and how to remedy the situation and remove these unfreedoms.

[12] This is available only in Spanish, at <http://www.hdr.undp.org/en/reports/national/latinamerica thecaribbean/dominicanrep/NHDR_2008_DominicanRep.pdf>.

capability approach entails taking them outside their initial contexts (neo-classical economics and liberal political philosophy) to the context of the reader. This is why the authors of the report take development beyond its individual dimension to the collective, and bring a specific perspective on human development: 'Capabilities, that is, the personal capacities and con-ditions to be able to do or be what one values in life are carried by individu-als, but they are socially constituted' (UNDP 2008: 3, translation mine). In other words, individuals are socially constituted, and limiting the evaluation space of wellbeing to individual characteristics leaves out the social constitu-tion of human life. Individuals are who they are through the relationships in which they engage, whether at interpersonal family level or structural national and global level.

In the Dominican context, analysing the social reality from the perspec-tive of individual capabilities would deform the reality, as key individual capabilities such as the opportunity to be educated are collective:

> The possibilities of having an education of quality or having access to an effec-tive justice system depend on institutional circumstances [...]. But, moreover, persons live in society and, therefore, the quality and form of interpersonal relations are part of the equation of the wellbeing of people. (UNDP 2008: 3, translation mine)

Institutions are therefore not only instrumental to people's wellbeing, the quality of relations and structures built on these relations (such as political and economic structures) are constitutive of human wellbeing.

Given that the NHDR is written under the auspices of the UNDP, which depends on the approval of a country's government for its presence, the Dominican NHDR could not give an in-depth rendition of the power rela-tions that structure the Dominican society, but it nonetheless provided a framework for other groups, such as civil-society organizations to do so. The NHDR calls on the Dominican civil society to exercise its agency col-lectively and change the distribution of power in the country so that certain economic groups do not trump the interests of the marginalized. It defines power as a 'relation between people and groups' (UNDP 2008: 4, translation mine). Power becomes problematic when the relation between people and groups becomes one of exploitation and domination.

The Dominican NHDR talks of 'collective capabilities' as 'referring to the capabilities that people have to influence decisions that affect them and to the institutional framework that guarantees access to opportunities, such as achievements that are only possible in a collectivity' (UNDP 2008: 4, trans-lation mine). Indeed, the capability that people have to affect decisions is something that belongs to a structure. An individual, or even a group of peo-ple, has no capability to influence the decisions of an autocratic government that uses violence against dissent. The opportunity they have to influence policy decisions depends on the political structure, which is beyond any individual's reach. It is therefore paramount to extend the wellbeing evaluation space to collective functionings, or what Stewart (2012) calls 'social competencies': what institutions can do or the relationships that structures allow or do not allow. An autocratic violent political structure does not allow for relationships of trust and equality between people. A financial economic structure based on risk and greed does not allow for relationships of respect and mutual concern between economic actors.

3.4 Conclusion

Amartya Sen has constructed a new normative language in the social sciences, a language based on 'freedom', understood as wellbeing and agency. This language is introducing a paradigmatic shift in the social sciences. People, their wellbeing and agency, are to be the centre of concern of all social analysis and social action. But Sen wrote the basic structure of the language in a given context with a given audience. Readers of the text will unavoidably have to interpret the texts, the words and structure of the capability approach, within their own context, audience, and purpose. This chapter has highlighted two major interpretations. The first relates to the purpose of the language: is it a language to be used only for evaluation of social arrangements or is it to be used also for social transformation? The second relates to the conception of the person on which the language rests: does a person have an end beyond his or her own freedom and is a person the ultimate unit of moral concern or does he/she create relationships and structures which are also ultimate units of moral concern?

The chapter has emphasized that these interpretations are not mutually exclusive, for interpretation is always context-dependent. In some contexts, such as economic analysis of poverty, one interpretation will prevail. In others, such as political analysis of social change, another interpretation prevails. However, not all interpretations are equally valid. Interpretations that read the texts of the capability approach as another name for human resources and a justification for investment in health and education for the sake of economic growth do misinterpret the capability approach. Or interpretations of the capability approach that reduce it to a matter of 'expanding choices', especially consumer choices, equally misinterpret the texts.

There will unavoidably be a conflict of interpretations. Sometimes it will be possible to arbitrate between them, such as the difference between interpreting capabilities as 'choices' or 'genuine opportunities for human flourishing', sometimes the disagreement will remain, such as whether individuals should be the ultimate unit of moral concern for wellbeing evaluation and whether human life as an end goal. As Ricoeur (1981: 213) points out in his discussion of hermeneutics:

> If it is true that there is always more than one way of construing a text, it is not true that all interpretations are equal. [...] The text is a limited field of possible constructions. The logic of validation allows us to move between the two limits of dogmatism and scepticism. It is always possible to argue against an interpretation, to confront interpretations, to arbitrate between them and to seek for an agreement, even if this agreement remains beyond our reach.

The chapter has sought to lay bare two main interpretations of the basic texts of the capability approach and describe various policy narratives constructed on the basis of these interpretations. The *Human Development Reports* started the work of constructing narratives on the basis of this new normative language of the capability approach in 1990. The reality of the world of 2013, with global inequality and environmental degradation at their highest levels ever, points to the urgency of constructing new policy narratives. It is in the struggles to change the economic, social, and political structures that have led to such a reality that a plurality of interpretations of the capability approach is essential. And in this regard, the normative language of the capability approach cannot be left on its own but has to be filled in with the many bits that different social and political theories, and indeed ethical theories, offer.

References

Alkire, S. (2005). 'Why the Capability Approach'. *Journal of Human Development*, 6(1): 115–33.

Alkire, S. (2008). 'Using the Capability Approach: Prospective and Evaluative Analyses'. In S. Alkire, M. Qizilbash, and F. Comim (eds), *The Capability Approach: Concepts, Measures and Applications*. Cambridge: Cambridge University Press, 26–49.

Alkire, S. and M. E. Santos (2010). *Multidimensional Poverty Index*. OPHI Research Brief. Oxford: Oxford Poverty and Human Development Initiative. Available at: <http://www.ophi.org.uk/wp-content/uploads/OPHI-MPI-Brief.pdf>.

Bagchi, A. K. (2000). 'Freedom and Development as End of Alienation'. *Economic and Political Weekly*, 35(50): 4409–20.

Dean, H. (2009). 'Critiquing Capabilities: The Distractions of a Beguiling Concept'. *Critical Social Policy*, 29(2): 261–78.

Deaton, A. and J. Drèze (2009). 'Food and Nutrition in India: Facts and Interpretations'. *Economic and Political Weekly*, 44(7): 42–65.

Deneulin, S. (2008). 'Beyond Individual Agency and Freedom: Structures of Living Together in the Capability Approach'. In S. Alkire, M. Qizilbash, and F. Comim (eds), *The Capability Approach: Concepts, Measures and Applications*. Cambridge: Cambridge University Press, 105–24.

Deneulin, S. (2011). 'Development and the Limits of Amartya Sen's *The Idea of Justice*'. *Third World Quarterly*, 32(4): 787–97.

Drèze, J. and A. Sen (2011). *Putting Growth in Its Place*. *Outlook India*, 14 November. Available at: <http://www.outlookindia.com/article.aspx?278843>.

Feldman, S. (2010). 'Social Development, Capabilities, and the Contradictions of (Capitalist) Development'. In S. L. Esquith and F. Gifford (eds), *Capabilities, Power and Institutions*. University Park, PA: Pennsylvania University Press, 121–41.

Jolly, R. (2009). 'Human Development and Neoliberalism: Two Paradigms Compared'. In S. Fukuda-Parr and A. K. Shiva Kumar (eds), *Handbook of Human Development*. Delhi: Oxford University Press, 106–16.

Nagaraj, K. (2008). *Farmers' Suicides in India: Magnitudes, Trends and Spatial Patterns*. Madras Institute of Development Studies Working Paper, March. Available at: <http://www.macroscan.org/anl/mar08/pdf/farmers_suicides.pdf>.

Nussbaum, M. (1992). 'Human Functioning and Social Justice: In Defence of Aristotelian Essentialism'. *Political Theory*, 20: 202–46.

Nussbaum, M. (1993). 'Non-Relative Virtues: An Aristotelian Approach'. In M. Nussbaum and A. Sen (eds), *The Quality of Life*. Oxford: Clarendon Press, 242–69.

Nussbaum, M. (2000). *Women and Human Development*. Cambridge: Cambridge University Press.

Nussbaum, M. (2006). *Frontiers of Justice*. Cambridge, MA: Belknap Press.

Nussbaum, M. (2011). *Creating Capabilities*. Cambridge, MA: Harvard University Press.

Ricoeur, P. (1981). *Hermeneutics and the Human Sciences* (edited and translated by J. B. Thompson). Cambridge: Cambridge University Press.

Robeyns, I. (2005). 'The Capability Approach: A Theoretical Survey'. *Journal of Human Development*, 6(1): 93–114.

Robeyns, I. (2008). 'Sen's Capability Approach and Feminist Concerns'. In S. Alkire, M. Qizilbash, and F. Comim (eds), *The Capability Approach: Concepts, Measures and Applications*. Cambridge: Cambridge University Press, 82–104.

Robeyns, I. (2009). 'Equality and Justice'. In S. Deneulin (ed.), *An Introduction to the Human Development and Capability Approach*. London: Earthscan, 101–20.

Sen, A. (1980). 'Equality of What?' In S. McMurrin (ed.), *Tanner Lectures on Human Values*. Cambridge: Cambridge University Press, 196–220.

Sen, A. (1985). 'Well-Being Agency and Freedom: The Dewey Lectures 1984'. *Journal of Philosophy*, 82(4): 169–221.

Sen, A. (1990). 'Justice: Means versus Freedoms'. *Philosophy and Public Affairs*, 19(2): 111–21.

Sen, A. (1992). *Inequality Re-examined*. Oxford: Clarendon Press.

Sen, A. (1993). 'Capability and Wellbeing'. In M. Nussbaum and A. Sen (eds), *The Quality of Life*. Oxford: Clarendon Press, 30–53.

Sen, A. (2002). *Rationality and Freedom*. Cambridge, MA: Harvard University Press.

Sen, A. (2009). *The Idea of Justice*. London: Allen Lane.

Stewart, F. (2006). 'The Evolution of Economic Ideas: From Import Substitution to Human Development'. In E. V. K. FitzGerald and R. Thorp (eds), *Economic Doctrines in Latin America*. London: Palgrave Macmillan.

Stewart, F. (2012). *Capabilities and Human Development: Beyond the Individual—The Critical Role of Social Institutions and Social Competencies*. Available at: <http://www.undp.org/content/india/en/home/ourwork/humandevelopment/videos/lecture-frances-stewart.html>.

UNDP (2008). *'Human Development: A Question of Power'*. Santo Domingo: UNDP and the Dominican Republic.

4

Human Development as the Dominant Paradigm
What Counts as Success?*

Christopher Colclough

4.1 Introduction

Has human development yet become the dominant paradigm? This chapter argues that it has provided a very influential critique of orthodoxy, but that it has as yet been somewhat less successful as a full-fledged alternative strategy. The chapter argues that it has worked strongly as a filter through which to assess the effects of policy and of available alternatives. It has both been informed by, and has stimulated, new theory. It has had a substantial impact on metrics—the human development index (HDI) is now a strong competitor with GDP rankings as the preferred index for measuring development performance. It has had substantial impact on aid intentions. Here, adoption of the millennium development goals (MDGs) was the major breakthrough—against which the impacts of aid, and of development policy more generally, are frequently assessed and measured. But its impact on development outcomes is much more difficult to map. Important reasons for this—apart from our not knowing the counterfactual—include the impact of lags, politics, and history. The argument is illustrated by examining the allocation of aid to education—the key human-development sector—which, despite rhetoric, good intention, and some limited improvements in terms of resource allocation, has remained primarily determined by factors other than those suggested by objective poverty/human-development needs.

* The author thanks Gerry Helleiner, Ravi Kanbur, Frances Stewart, Andy Sumner, John Toye, and other participants at the Sussex conference for helpful comments, but absolves them from responsibility for any remaining errors and omissions. Katrin Keuzenkamp provided excellent research assistance for parts of the chapter.

4.2 Human Development and Development Economics

Work on the economics of developing countries was characterized from the late 1950s onwards by writers who drew attention to the ways in which the structures of such countries differed from those of the more industrialized world, and who questioned the relevance of standard neoclassical assumptions as a basis for prediction and policy. These 'structuralist' writers gradually built up a formidable critique of orthodoxy, pointing to the ways in which market imperfections and rigidities in developing countries led to a different set of outcomes than those that the market could normally be expected to deliver. Development economics began to adopt a separate identity, with a subset of theoretical approaches to the analysis of trade, industrialization, agricultural development, and labour markets, which was distinctly different from those offered by more orthodox approaches.[1]

Generally, however, the emerging corpus of work in development economics continued to utilize standard economic tools of analysis in this modified theoretical setting. It was the *assumptions* of the standard model that were changed and, in doing so, writers were building on aspects of the new macroeconomics set out by Keynes and upon the work of Joan Robinson, Michael Kalecki, and others who had concerned themselves increasingly with building an economics of imperfect competition in the context of industrialized societies. The major objective of the new development economists became one of understanding and, in turn, learning how to ameliorate, the fallibility of markets in low-income states—usually indicating the different types and extent of public intervention needed, in order to achieve the growth objectives that better-functioning markets might otherwise deliver. A shortage of savings and the presence of low 'absorptive capacity' in newly independent countries required an emphasis upon supplementing capital from abroad via aid and foreign investment, and on strengthening domestic supplies of human capital via the expansion of education and training systems.[2]

During the late 1960s, however, a more profound critique began to emerge. This was concerned not merely to demonstrate the limitations of the orthodox model when applied to the circumstances of (often) mono-export, labour-surplus economies, but rather to question the very *objectives* of theorizing in the neoclassical tradition. In a seminal paper, Dudley Seers questioned whether in circumstances of poverty and deprivation experienced by a majority of those living in developing countries, the appropriate objective and ultimate indicator of development should be to maximize the value of

[1] A useful overview of such writings remains Meier and Seers (1984).
[2] A whole generation of so-called 'two-gap' models, in the Harrod–Domar tradition, demonstrated the aid allocations needed to achieve alternative target rates of economic growth.

produced goods and services—i.e. to be somewhere on society's production possibilities frontier—or to adopt objectives more directly related to poverty alleviation, such as increasing the availability of employment for all adults, and promoting a more equitable distribution of income. Although over the long run, economic growth was a necessary condition for reducing poverty, it was not a sufficient condition in either the short or the longer term (Seers 1969).

The new message of this argument lay not so much in the re-specification of development goals (although they had rarely been so clearly set out in earlier literature), but in the assertion that they would not necessarily be delivered by the mere achievement of economic growth. Seers attacked the conventional view that the benefits of growth would 'trickle down' to reduce poverty in the most cost-effective ways. His argument introduced a sceptical analysis both of the technical relevance of the national income concept (or at least of how it was measured and applied in poor countries) and of the political integrity of many of the ruling regimes in developing countries, in the sense that their own interests were not necessarily allied with those of the poor. Power was increasingly concentrated in the hands of those who benefited from growth, and was used, by implication, often repressively, to preserve those benefits.[3]

In retrospect, these arguments marked a turning point between the dominance of the earlier 'growth paradigm' and the ascendancy—albeit with many stumbles along the way—of a new one, characterized by the aims of removing absolute poverty, increasing productive employment and meeting the basic needs of all the people.[4] By implication the work of planners and statisticians would need to move away from a focus upon growth accounting, towards developing measures and models for monitoring the distribution of income, the reduction of poverty, and, particularly, the changing characteristics of employment in both formal and informal sectors to support the new policy emphasis. This marked an important shift towards an emphasis upon 'human development'.[5]

---

[3] These political-economy points were set out more fully in a 'postscript' to the original paper (Seers 1969), which was appended to one of its several reprintings (Seers 1979).

[4] The theoretical and empirical underpinnings of the new approach were set out in the joint IDS/World Bank volume entitled *Redistribution with Growth* (Chenery et al. 1974).

[5] As indicated above, the development of human resources had not been neglected by planners during the 1960s. Naturally enough, their preoccupation with economic growth had been marked by a strong interest in the productive value of investment in education and training. The problem of increasing the 'absorptive capacity' of developing countries was judged to be central to the enhancement of their growth prospects and, as suggested by Table 4.1, the enhancement of 'human capital' became a central concern of economic planners. It resulted, however, in a preoccupation with the high-level skills that an acceleration of economic growth was perceived to require. It would be some time before a focus upon expanding and improving primary schooling was recognized to be a critical means of providing resources and productive capacity to the poor.

The new focus upon poverty and redistribution became influential amongst international agencies and aid organizations, but it had only marginal impact upon national development policies. As to the former, by the mid-1970s the president of the World Bank had announced that the development record should be judged not by economic growth, but by the extent to which poverty was reduced in the world. Reflecting this ambition, the pattern of World Bank lending shifted somewhat over the decade towards projects that were expected to bring greater benefits for the poor. Sectors were now included that had a direct impact upon their welfare, such as primary healthcare and primary schooling, which had earlier not been thought proper targets for development loans.[6] Equally, the British and Scandinavian aid agencies were prominent amongst the bilateral donors in reorienting their aid policies to adopt an explicit focus upon the poorest peoples, regions, and countries. There were signs during the early 1970s that the emphasis of development policy, at least as advocated by some of the more influential development institutions, had shifted towards a more people-centred approach that placed the problem of poverty alleviation centre-stage (Table 4.1).

The critique presented by Seers and others was thus translated into a powerful set of messages along two dimensions. First, at a theoretical level, the notion that gainful employment growth and poverty alleviation would not necessarily be delivered automatically by growth maximization (and that thus a different policy set may well be required) amounted to a radical assault upon orthodoxy. Second, in terms of praxis and policy, it directly raised the notion that the distribution of the benefits of growth needed to be articulated as one of the fundamental objectives for economic analysis (rather than its being relegated, as in traditional analysis, to the political domain). Some of the more important policy differences between the two approaches were demonstrated by a high-profile set of employment 'mission' reports undertaken under ILO auspices during the 1970s, and by more formal analysis from Chenery et al. (1974). These studies further articulated and operationalized Seers' ideas, and they were extended again by UNICEF during the 1980s in its influential work on 'adjustment with a human face'.[7]

---

[6] Alkire (2010) provides a careful analysis of the extent to which poverty concerns were present in World Bank statements and policies over the 1960–90 period.

[7] Richard Jolly took a major part in all of these developments. He had worked closely with Dudley Seers over a number of years, and followed him as director of the Institute of Development Studies at the University of Sussex in 1972. He worked with Seers on the early ILO employment missions to Colombia and Sri Lanka, and co-led, with Hans Singer, the employment mission to Kenya in 1972. He was a co-author of the joint IDS/World Bank volume *Redistribution with Growth* (Chenery et al. 1974), and subsequently, as deputy executive director of UNICEF, led its initiative on 'adjustment with a human face'. Much of the tenacity with which the international critique of orthodox adjustment policies was pursued was inspired by his leadership.

Table 4.1 Approximate sequencing of development paradigms, 1960–2010

	Dominant paradigms	Constraints identified	Strategy proposed	Competing paradigms
1960–70	Maximization of growth	Absorptive capacity Low savings	Aid Foreign investment Human capital formation	Socialist accumulation
1970–80	Structuralism	Structural rigidities Market imperfections Patterns of ownership Domestic politics	Redistribution with growth Basic needs Employment generation	State socialism Dependency and neo-Marxism
1980–90	Neoliberalism and stabilization	Balance-of-payments disequilibrium Constrained markets State as pariah Rent-seeking	Liberalize markets and prices Reduce role of state	Modified structuralism Adjustment with human face
1990–2000	Washington Consensus	Recession Stagnation Deepening poverty	Liberalize Stabilize Privatize	Human development
2000–10	Human development Poverty alleviation Growth	Resources Political interests Credit crunch	MDGs Context important	Modified Washington Consensus

Note: The above table provides a suggestive sequencing of the ways in which ideas associated with different analytic approaches have been prominent in the international dialogue about development, and have influenced conventional wisdom as to what makes for 'good' development policy over the past half century. Too much emphasis should not be placed on the precise decadal periodicity: it is intended to provide an approximate but useful set of signposts for the ways in which competing intellectual ideas came to prominence at different times. Some of the main academic and policy documents that affected the balance of development advice, in ways summarized by the table, are indicated in the text.

4.3 The Neoliberal Counterattack

By the end of the 1970s, however, this approach nevertheless began to have an air of unreality about it. There had been few signs of policy change at the national level in directions advocated by ILO. Even the World Bank, in its new series of *World Development Reports* launched towards the end of McNamara's tenure as president, continued to be pessimistic about the prospects for serious reductions in the incidence of absolute poverty by the end of the century (World Bank 1979: 19). Equally, the impact of the second oil crisis was beginning to be felt, in ways which shifted the attention of the international community back towards growth concerns. The *World Development Report* of 1980 was the first to indicate that Sub-Saharan Africa faced stagnation during the 1980s, even on moderately optimistic projections for commodity price trends and for growth in other regions (World

Bank 1980: 6). The 'Berg' Report of the following year both confirmed this dismal prognosis, and laid the blame for Africa's demise firmly at the door of policy 'failures' by African states, rather than of external circumstances and events (World Bank 1981).

The new critique of African policy was strongly revisionist in tone. It reasserted the primacy of 'getting the prices right' amongst policy objectives, arguing—as had been typical fifteen years earlier—that growth would thereby be best promoted and poverty would be most effectively reduced. This reflected a new orthodoxy on development theory and policy that was emerging from the Bank under the leadership of a group of 'new liberals' who were increasingly influential with McNamara's successor, Clausen, and who were themselves reflecting wider trends and fashions shaping the economics profession as a whole (Balassa 1982; Krueger 1974; Lal 1983). These economists argued that the slow progress made by developing countries had been mainly caused by excessive economic intervention by their own governments. Its costs had been much greater than its benefits, in part because an important part of bureaucratic endeavour is taken up with securing private benefits for the officials concerned. Moreover, the direct and indirect impact on prices of a wide variety of state interventions had resulted in a sharp difference emerging between market and 'shadow' prices, resulting in inefficient resource allocation. Thus, far from calling for an extension to the state's role—in support of either production or redistributive activity—the new orthodoxy argued for its sharp reduction and replacement by the market whenever and wherever this could be achieved.

This is not the place to explore the pros and cons of the neoliberal case, which became the new policy orthodoxy during the 1980s (Table 4.1).[8] The important point, for present purposes, is that over that decade, the fairly central position of distributional concerns in the paradigms that had been influencing policy advocacy at the international level all but disappeared. Based upon some important theoretical insights, but rather little empirical evidence (Krueger 1974; Bates 1981) states rapidly became viewed as predatory—net consumers of resources, inefficient (not only in the directly productive sectors, but also in those 'public goods' areas where few economists from Adam Smith onwards have believed that private alternatives would be either sensible or viable), self-serving, and, more often than not, corrupt. The neoliberal approach, which advocated reductions in the role of the state and a shift to market pricing, even in the social sectors, did not merely ignore the

---

[8] An earlier paper (Colclough 1991) argues that the neoliberalism that emerged at this time was a version of state-minimalism more extreme than even that of the classical economists, let alone of the later neoclassicals, who were more aware of the implications of widespread market imperfections.

potential importance of state actions in support of human development, but it actually placed the latter in some considerable jeopardy.

4.4 Human Development Fights Back

The blindness towards human development of 'pricist' approaches to adjustment, and to development policy more generally, informed its main critiques. Cornia et al. (1987) focus upon the extent to which such approaches damaged equity, employment, and social-sector development. They argue that the emphasis placed by orthodox adjustment policies upon demand reduction, the elimination of subsidies, including those for staple foods, contraction of public expenditures (which reduced both the number of employees in the public sector and the quantity of public services available), and increases in user charges for social services had each tended to threaten important dimensions of human development.[9] These criticisms stimulated the World Bank to take more account of the human dimension by introducing, towards the end of the 1980s, programmes on the social dimensions of adjustment and they were reflected in a range of new initiatives by the international community that initially appeared to be harbingers of change. For example, a series of UN world conferences and summits—on education (1990), population (1994), gender (1995), and social development (1995)—resulted in declarations signed by almost every government, reaffirming their commitments to reach a wide array of human development goals over the coming decade.

Meanwhile, the UNDP had begun its annual series of *Human Development Reports*, which provided a new synthesis of the case for the overriding importance of human development in national strategies (UNDP 1990). These reports, from the outset, took the view that human development offered a more worthy—albeit more complex—set of objectives than merely the maximization of income. The writings of Amartya Sen (who had been directly involved in the UNDP's *Human Development Reports* since their inception in 1990) provide the clearest intellectual underpinning for these kinds of argument.

Sen took up the critique of neoclassical economics, as applied to development policy, in a manner that extended well beyond the beginnings advanced by Dudley Seers a decade or so earlier (Sen 1980, 1985, 1989, 1999). But his fundamental question is rather similar to that posed by Seers (1972) in 'What

---

[9] A more general set of structuralist critiques can be found in Colclough and Manor (1991), which uses argument and evidence to demonstrate the fallibility of neoliberal policies, even in their own terms.

Are We Trying to Measure?'. Essentially Sen argues (with Aristotle) that maximizing material wealth is a means to a more valued end, rather than the end itself. It is not that the pursuit of economic prosperity is unreasonable, but rather that it is often taken to be the ultimate goal rather than being a useful intermediate step towards a more fundamental set of objectives.

What we should wish to achieve, he argues, is the maximization of the ability to choose valued states of life—of 'beings and doings'. Income is important as a means of facilitating more rather than fewer of these states. But it is by no means the only one and, in any case, there may, even for rich people, be many other constraints (such as poor health, limited education, or constrained political circumstances) that prevent them from improving their range of feasible choices. Accordingly, he proposes a different measure to maximize—capabilities—of which utility is a by-product rather than a central element.

It sometimes appears to be the case in writings about human development (HD), that the neoclassical problem of the impossibility of interpersonal comparisons of utility (and thus the essentially political nature of the advocacy of a particular distribution of income) has been overcome. However, the HD literature does not escape the problems associated with the subjective calculus of neoclassical theory. Sen demonstrates that distribution is of the essence, yet the valuation of capabilities is still ultimately a matter of individual choice. Thus, in a rigorous sense, interpersonal comparisons cannot be avoided in generalizing the capabilities approach.[10] On the other hand, it is somewhat easier to include some things as rights, as being desirable in themselves, and as constituents in any list of human freedoms—basic education and health being prime candidates for such inclusion.

The influence of these ideas—as developed theoretically by Sen, and explored in policy terms in the *Human Development Reports*—increased significantly during the 1990s. However, a 'compact' about wise development policy remained generally dominant amongst international institutions at this time (Table 4.1). This so-called 'Washington Consensus' (Williamson 1989) contained many elements of the neoliberal agenda—including the perceived need for fiscal discipline, financial-sector reform, market-based exchange rates, liberalization of trade, and privatization[11]—which were attached as conditions to many of the cooperation and financing agreements

---

[10] Sen acknowledges that metrics would often need to concentrate on achieved functionings, rather than valuations that include assessment of freedoms to choose alternative ones. How far such a restricted approach to assessing capabilities is used 'would depend much on the practical consideration of what data we can get and what we cannot' (Sen 1989: 46).

[11] Notwithstanding its three touchstones, as characterized by Rodrick (2006)—liberalize, stabilize, privatize (Table 4.1)—the neoliberal nature of the package is actually strongly denied by its architect (Williamson 2004), who acknowledges only privatization amongst his list of ten 'consensus' items as being a neoliberal legacy.

entered into during that decade. The empirical evidence for adjustment failures, and for deepening poverty, led to some modifications of this list, particularly as regards the importance given in the agenda to tackling corruption
and to improving governance more generally, to introducing social 'safety
nets', and to targeting poverty (Rodrick 2006).[12] Nevertheless, the balance of
advice, and conditions, affecting loans and grants to low-income countries
remained strongly orthodox over the 1990s, changing only gradually over
the decade.

4.5 The MDGs—Metrics and Human Development

A step change in the balance of international opinion, however, was signalled at the turn of the century, with the promulgation of the millennium
development goals (MDGs). These specified a particular set of time-bound
objectives for the reduction of poverty to be achieved across all societies,[13]
which were closely related to the objectives of human development. As the
2010 HDR points out, early editions of the report espoused such goal-setting
as a means of concentrating attention on the record of progress in human
development across the world. The UNDP was not, of course, the first agency
to see the importance of such an approach. On the contrary, the UN had
already had much experience of setting (yet often failing to secure) major
human goals since the first UN conventions on human rights half a century
earlier. As indicated earlier in this chapter, a succession of UN conference
declarations—on human rights, on the rights of the child, on gender, on
education, and others—had signed up governments through their delega-
tions to pursue public action in their own countries so as to achieve the
targets and goals. Essentially, the UN became involved in a major political
process of international advocacy, opening the way to applying both legal

---

[12] Anyone who has closely followed the history of World Bank analyses over the period since
the mid-1960s could be forgiven for believing that development economics and the development strategies that derive from it have been increasingly dominated by a concern to address
poverty. Even the sharp endorsement of neoliberalism during the early 1980s was interpreted by
some commentators as a disillusionment with intervention in markets, which had often led to
further impoverishment of populations in the developing world, and the appearance of alternative models of development success, led by the market, which in turn appeared to be remarkably
successful in tackling poverty. As Robert Wade (1990) first showed, we know that that is a faulty
interpretation of what actually happened. Intervention continued in new and subtle ways for
those states that succeeded, and that success could not in any case be replicated in the ways
imagined by those initially convinced by the Asian 'miracle': the Washington Consensus soon
needed to be expanded and redesigned, even for those whose faith in its central tenets remained
undimmed.
[13] Tackling poverty in low-income countries was, however, given much more attention by the
MDGs than was its alleviation in the more industrialized world.

and moral suasion on states to honour the obligations to which they had willingly, and very publicly, signed up.[14]

While the HDR did not, by any means, start this process, it is, however, reasonable to argue that its role in pointing to the complementarity of a range of human development goals via a multidimensional index helped to strengthen the notion, and the presumed validity, of goal-setting through the 1990s and beyond. The human development index (HDI) has had many detractors, and has been criticized on grounds of false aggregation, arbitrariness, incommensurability, and a range of other points.[15] Most such criticisms do not undermine its analytic usefulness, and still less its intuitive appeal (an indicator of development that allows comparison of levels of education, longevity, and average living standards amongst national populations being difficult to dismiss as unimportant).[16] The HDI has also had a range of didactic externalities by, *inter alia*, strengthening the seriousness with which politicians—and journalists—take notice of their own relative national performance on the HDI, instead of paying exclusive attention to GDP per capita.[17]

The MDGs adopted a set of goals, many of which had been identified and agreed at the earlier, more specialist, UN conferences. But articulating them as part of an integrated package that was intended to address the reduction and eventual elimination of poverty, embraced a familiar HDR theme: that poverty was not directly amenable to alleviation via economic growth alone, and needed separate action on specific components of development. It served to emphasize that matters of distribution were paramount, that policies were needed to tackle it head-on if poverty were to be rapidly reduced, and that distributive objectives needed to be disaggregated to the sectoral level so as to be targeted in a coordinated way. As we have seen, this same critique had been advanced by Dudley Seers thirty years earlier and had, in turn, been part of the explicit agenda of the HDR since the report's inception. However, the MDGs operationalized it in a much more concrete way, in circumstances that also secured both its formal endorsement by

---

[14] A more detailed discussion of the ways in which the UN has used conference declarations to reinforce legally binding commitments, often to good effect, is given in Colclough (2005).

[15] A useful review is provided by Raworth and Stewart (2003).

[16] In that context, the riposte contained in the 2010 report to earlier criticisms of the HDI, that 'the objective is not to build an unassailable indicator of wellbeing—it is to redirect attention towards human-centred development and to promote debate about how we advance the progress of societies' (UNDP 2010: 25) seems, at least to this author, a trifle weak.

[17] Experience with a more recent UN index—the Education Development Index (EDI)—has been closely similar. Its annual publication over the years since 2003 (UNESCO 2002–), whilst often causing heated political battles about the basis for the rankings, has sometimes led to the adoption of explicit targets by national politicians in particular countries, who have committed their governments to secure some movement in their placement in the international EDI rankings over time.

most of the world's heads of government and the technical support of most aid agencies and international financial institutions. It appeared, then, (as suggested in Table 4.1) that the human-development paradigm was strongly set to have a dominant impact upon the design of development policy in the new century.

4.6 Has HD Made a Difference?

4.6.1 The MDGs and Aid Behaviour

Given the comprehensive nature of the goals, and the extent to which they were championed by the international community, the least one might expect is that they would have had some tangible impact upon development policy over the past decade and indeed upon the allocation of aid resources in support of such policy change. The tracing of impact on policy change is notoriously difficult, since the counterfactual cannot be known. Some writers have attempted to document the extent to which the HD paradigm, and specifically the HDRs themselves, have influenced policy (ul Haq 2003) but the evidence in most cases is inevitably impressionistic rather than decisive. Those who have examined aid flows from this perspective generally find that the main determinants of aid allocation are factors other than the MDGs (Alesina and Dollar 2000; Wood 2008). The authors of a more recent study, which demonstrates the undoubted increase in aid flows after agreement on the MDGs in comparison with the earlier decade, conclude that aid may, of course, have increased even in their absence, and that there is in any case only weak evidence of country policy change and of improved outcomes (Kenny and Sumner 2011).

Aid, then, has increased in volume. Also, its proportionate allocation to the social sectors appears to have increased relative to the directly productive sectors (Sumner and Tiwari 2011). But the intra-sectoral patterns of allocation may tell a different story. It will be recalled that education is specifically targeted by the MDGs: the objective of Goal 2 is to 'achieve universal primary education', and its associated target is 'to ensure that, by 2015, children everywhere, boys and girls alike, will be able to complete a full course of primary schooling'. It would, then, be useful to know whether the earlier macro findings, which indicate a weak, or uncertain, overall influence of the MDGs on aid behaviour, are also true of aid flows to education, one of the most critical sectors for HD. In that connection, Table 4.2 shows the extent to which, in the late 1990s and again a decade later, the allocation of aid to education by DFID, and by all agencies taken together, was variously influenced by income (GNI) per capita, the number of children out of school, the primary net enrolment ratio (NER), and the survival rate to grade 5 (the

Table 4.2 HD influences on aid to education

	DFID aid 1998/9	DFID aid 2008/9[1]	Total aid 1999/00[2]	Total aid 2007
Log GNI per capita	−0.155 (−0.45)	−1.208** (−3.25)	−0.041 (−0.28)	−0.242 (−1.68)
Log out-of-school children	0.287 (1.70)	0.552*** (4.32)	0.361*** (5.03)	0.476*** (7.02)
Total primary NER	1.589 (1.75)	1.599* (2.34)	0.632 (1.79)	1.444*** (4.12)
Survival rate to grade 5	−0.745 (−0.85)	0.476 (0.61)	−0.210 (−0.59)	0.157 (0.416)
Intercept	4.395** (3.53)	6.745*** (7.26)	0.568 (1.16)	0.026 (0.06)
No. of observations	59	43	78	93
R²	0.099	0.457	0.295	0.422
Adjusted R²	0.032	0.400	0.256	0.395

Notes:
[1]Excludes one case receiving less than £10,000 in aid for education.
[2]Excludes 15 countries receiving aid for education where sufficient data are not available.
Dependent variables: Log of DFID aid to education 1998/9, log of DFID aid to education 2008/9, log of total aid commitments to education 1999/00 (average), log of total aid commitments to education 2007.
t-values in parentheses.
* p < .05. ** p < .01. *** p < .001.
Source: Colclough (2011).

latter being taken as a proxy for education quality).[18] The analysis excludes countries not receiving educational aid in those years. If aid agencies have been serious about promoting the MDG targets, one would expect these variables to have become more prominent in the cross-country distribution of aid to education over the past decade.[19]

In the case of DFID's aid to education, it can be seen that in 1998/9 none of these variables were significant determinants of the amounts of aid provided. Ten years later, on the other hand, per-capita income, the numbers out of school, and the enrolment ratio (though not the survival rate) had each become significant predictors, each with expected signs. Somewhat unexpectedly, the relationship between aid and NER is positive—implying that amongst low-income countries with large numbers of children out of school, those with higher NERs tended to be allocated more aid than those with lower net enrolments. This might suggest that DFID's aid allocation targeted, perhaps on efficiency grounds, those countries that were closer to achieving universal primary education (UPE) rather than others where a large absolute enrolment gap nevertheless remained to be closed. Taken together, these variables explained

[18] Learning outcome measures would provide the most appropriate proxy for the quality of education, but comparable data are not available for many countries. There is, however, a strong link between survival within the primary cycle and educational achievement. It also captures aspects of grade repetition, promotion policy, and early drop-out, which are useful signifiers of quality. For further discussion, see UNESCO (2003: 284–5).
[19] The database used, and a more extended technical discussion of the analysis summarized in Tables 4.2 and 4.3 can be found in Colclough (2011).

about 40 per cent of the variance of DFID's aid to education in 2008/9, compared to only about 3 per cent ten years earlier.

The final two columns of Table 4.2 give a comparable analysis of the determinants of aid to education from all agencies taken together. In this case, for the earlier year (1999/2000) the number of children out of school is a significant predictor of total aid to education, explaining (together with the other non-significant variables) about 26 per cent of the variance in education aid volumes. However, the later (2007) model for total aid explains rather more (about 40 per cent) of the variance, with both out-of-school children and NER (again, with a positive sign) now reaching strong levels of significance. This indicates that, across all agencies, for given enrolment ratios, poorer countries with larger numbers of primary-school-aged out-of-school children tended to receive more aid for education than others.[20] Accordingly, using an MDG lens, the allocation of aid to education appears to have improved over the first decade of the century: education aid, both from DFID and from all sources, became increasingly influenced by these factors and, accordingly, the cross-country allocation of aid to education appears to have become more influenced by HD criteria during this period.[21]

Nevertheless, expanding the analysis to include a wider range of variables shows that this apparent shift in direction was marginal: additional factors, beyond those deriving from the MDG goals, ultimately remained more influential in determining aid allocations to education. Table 4.3 presents a 'best-fit' model of the determinants of the allocation of aid to education for recent years, using stepwise modelling. The list of candidate predictor variables included all those shown in Table 4.2, together with a range of other enrolment ratios, and proxies for education quality, for gender inequality, and for the incidence of corruption. However, it can be seen that for DFID aid, education variables now no longer appear. The most important influences become total population, per-capita income, and Commonwealth

---

[20] In one sense this could be judged to be evidence for a large country effect, in the sense that the high-population countries also happen to be those with most children out of school. However, there is little reason to suppose that more aid would accrue to education (as opposed to other sectors) unless it were believed by agencies and governments to be useful in that sector. That this has been so is suggested by the result that, for given enrolment ratios, those countries with more out-of-school children have been receiving more aid for education than those with less.

[21] It should be noted, however, that the smaller sample of countries used for the 1999 analyses may constrain the direct comparability of the two sets of results in the total (though not the DFID) aid case. To test this, the 2007 regression was re-run using only the seventy-eight countries included in the 1999/2000 analysis. This produced an R-square of 0.421 (adjusted 0.390), almost identical to that obtained with the larger sample, shown in Table 4.2. The levels of significance achieved were the same, with $p < .001$ for log out-of-school children and NER and log GNI per capita and survival rate to grade 5 being insignificant. The coefficients were also of similar magnitude. Thus, we can conclude that the differences between the results for the two dates are not caused by sample selection bias.

Table 4.3 Determinants of aid to education, DFID and global aid

	DFID education aid 2008/9	Total education aid 2007
Step 1		
Log total population	0.504** (2.90)	0.585*** (8.77)
Intercept	4.313*** (5.71)	−0.736** (−2.67)
R²	0.170	0.458
Adjusted R²	0.149	0.452
Step 2		
Log total population	0.600*** (3.95)	0.572*** (8.81)
Log GNI per capita	−1.145*** (−3.91)	−0.235* (−2.52)
Intercept	6.983*** (7.40)	0.012 (0.03)
ΔR²	0.229	0.036
Adjusted ΔR²	0.220	0.031
Step 3		
Log total population	0.604*** (4.44)	
Log GNI per capita	−1.193*** (−4.54)	
Commonwealth membership	0.622** (3.30)	
Intercept	6.818*** (8.05)	
ΔR²	0.131	
Adjusted ΔR²	0.125	
No. of observations	43	93
Final R²	0.530	0.494
Final adjusted R²	0.494	0.483

Notes:
Dependent variable: log of DFID aid to education 2008/9, and of total aid commitments to education 2007.
t-values in parentheses.
* p < .05; ** p < .01; *** p < .001.

Source: Colclough (2011: Tables 5 and 6).

membership, which together explain about 50 per cent of the variance in aid allocations to education. Each of these three variables contributes strongly to the amount of variance explained. It seems, then, that DFID's aid allocation practice in education reflects its more general aid priorities—countries with low incomes, large populations, and with political and historical ties to the UK (proxied by Commonwealth membership) receive more favoured treatment than other countries in the allocations of aid for education.[22] The parallel analysis for global education aid also explains roughly half of the variance in aid allocations in 2007—almost all of which is accounted for by the total population variable. The fit is very similar to that shown for DFID education aid. Here, too, it seems that low-income countries with large populations are given preference in the allocation of global aid to education, and

---

[22] See also McGillivray and Oczkowski (1992) and Thiele et al. (2007).

that these factors have a stronger influence than other, education-related variables.

We can conclude that HD criteria appear to have had a somewhat increased influence on the allocation of both DFID and global aid to education over the past decade, but they remained of minor significance in comparison with more macro variables—including strategic/historical factors, overall population size, and per-capita income—which continued to have the major influence on patterns of allocation.

4.6.2 Paradigm Shifts

There is an issue as to whether HD provides mainly a set of insights and emphases, or whether it represents a paradigm shift in comparison with earlier development theories and their associated policy agendas. Alkire (2010: 48) puts the case thus:

> The human development paradigm purported to *add value* by making two fundamental changes. First, it changed the *unit of analysis* from the economy to the person. This allowed considerations of equity and of poverty to accompany assessments of wellbeing. Second, it changed the *space* in which progress was tallied from income to capabilities or freedoms. In the earlier framework, the healthy economy was one that was growing in terms of income per capita. In the human development framework, a healthy economy is one that is growing in terms of people's freedoms and capabilities. (emphasis in the original)[23]

We earlier suggested that a paradigm shift requires not merely a change in the *assumptions* of the analytics (as was secured by much of the work in the development economics tradition), but also a change in the *objectives* of the analysis (or a change in the ways in which, to use Alkire's vocabulary, progress is *tallied*).

Perhaps recognizing this, some writers in the orthodox tradition have objected to the charge that they espouse economic growth for its own sake. Rather, they point out that it is sought precisely because it is instrumental in achieving these other objectives (see Srinivasan (1994), who cites also Arthur Lewis (1955: 422) on this). They criticize HDRs for their strong emphasis on the range and diversity of national experiences in translating economic growth into human development—thereby placing most of their attention on the deviations from the regression line.[24] In so doing, the critics argue,

---

[23] Although in theory the HD paradigm shifted the unit of analysis towards the individual, as Alkire suggests, in practice the unit of measurement, as expressed in the HDI, remained firmly at the national level.

[24] It is worth noting that criticisms by World Bank staff that the HDR is selective in its use of evidence can be judged with some scepticism in the light of its own research record. A recent high-profile external evaluation of World Bank research found a great deal of work that was undistinguished, some of which was 'technically flawed and in some cases strong policy positions have

HDRs consistently overlook, or downplay, the big and important message that economic growth does alleviate poverty and improve human development indicators—and that 'it is not bad at it' (Ravallion 1997: 637). These critics wish to argue that what is at issue between them and the advocates of HD is not so much the choice of criteria for measuring development success as disagreement about the most effective means by which such success can be secured. The defenders of orthodoxy claim that increases in per-capita income provide a more efficient means of achieving poverty reduction than other approaches.

There is an alternative way, of course, of characterizing these differences. Just as orthodoxy argues that HD ignores the growth–HD route, so HD can argue that orthodoxy ignores the importance of the residuals. There is plenty of evidence from HD writings that economic growth continues to be judged a central plank for policy (and earlier building blocks of the paradigm, such as *Redistribution with Growth*, explicitly argued that growth was necessary, but not sufficient). HD analysts are concerned to place attention on the extent to which, at given bands of per-capita income, and at given rates of economic growth, country ability to translate growth into better HD varies widely. It is obviously of great interest to ask what it is that separates the good from the bad performers—is it initial structural circumstances, is it the constrained options available, or is it the particular policies that have been adopted that make the difference?

There is, moreover, a clear and revealing disagreement about both policy content and time-frames. Even without fundamental divergence over whether poverty should be eliminated, there is variation between the strategies proposed by HD and by orthodoxy to achieve it. A key difference, of course, is that HD analysts argue for a multidimensional criterion for measuring progress, rather than just incomes and income poverty. Nevertheless, the introduction of time-bound targets for HD also involves a different

---

been supported by such (non) evidence'. It found evidence that researchers were 'under pressure from the Bank presidency and elsewhere not to say things that go directly against the broad policy line that the Bank is espousing' and that researchers themselves said it was not unusual to be told that 'we should do an evaluation to prove that X programme works' (Deaton et al. 2007). This evidence is compelling since its authors were senior academics who themselves work within the orthodox economics paradigm. It is broadly supported by separate independent research that indicates the ways in which the neoliberal orthodoxy at the Bank has been instrumentally underpinned by its own research evidence and procedures. Broad (2006) presents evidence to suggest that the Bank's Development Economics Research Department conducts biased hiring and promotion practices, uses uneven and discriminatory peer-review procedures, labels internal critics as 'idiosyncratic' or 'disaffected' so as to stifle internal debate on key policy areas, manipulates data, and selectively promotes and publicizes particular conclusions or lines of work. This mutually reinforcing set of mechanisms establishes a set of incentives that causes research staff to tow the ideological line of current senior managers and produce analyses and publications that strengthen, rather than undermine, the commitment to neoliberalism amongst international institutions.

policy agenda from that prescribed by orthodoxy—not, for example, easily indulging a 'grow now, redistribute later' praxis. This implies a contrast in rates of time preference for poverty alleviation as between advocates of HD and of orthodoxy. Furthermore, if indeed there were no real differences about objectives, the fact that orthodox analytics remain singularly agnostic about questions of distribution seems hardly a promising basis for securing the poverty reductions that are desired (or indeed for knowing anything about whether or not they are being achieved). These are fundamental divergences that cannot be brushed aside as indicating simply contrasts in emphasis. The HD approach embraces, but goes well beyond, growth analytics: it poses from the outset a different, and more complex, set of questions than those usually addressed by more orthodox approaches.

4.7 Conclusion

Much of development economics in the structuralist tradition demonstrates the results of replacing the standard assumptions of the neoclassical model with others that are deemed more realistic in the typical circumstances of developing countries. It has challenged received wisdom about the impacts that certain categories of policy change bring for individual behaviour and for national prosperity, by showing that the underlying assumptions of the orthodox model are inappropriate in the particular structural circumstances of many low-income countries. However, most of the insights it has generated can be accommodated within the orthodox paradigm: in that sense, it has helped to ground economic analysis much more clearly within the particular circumstances and contexts of low-income states.

Quite separately, over the past forty years, a more challenging body of critical thought has developed, which asserts a different notion of 'development' and a different set of objectives for development policy from those espoused by orthodoxy. The call to shift the overriding policy objective from commodity production to human development began in the late 1960s with the contributions of Dudley Seers and a group of political economists at IDS and elsewhere. It was further developed via both theoretical work and policy analyses in collaboration with international institutions, notably the World Bank, the ILO, and UNICEF. Its post-1990 flourishing has been led by UNDP and theoretically informed particularly by the work of Amartya Sen. This HD tradition represents a potential paradigm shift in the Kuhnian sense (Kuhn 1962) that, if fully embraced, would change the regular objectives and conduct of those working in the orthodox economic tradition, and of what properly counts as 'economic science'.

This new tradition has been enormously influential in a number of ways. It has reasserted a whole set of important criteria with which to assess development achievements. This happened most directly with the introduction of the HDI, which rather quickly became competitive with income rankings as a preferred (or at least equal) means of assessing development performance. It was confirmed, and extended, by the adoption of the MDGs—a specific subset of HD goals—by which the performance of development practice and policy became increasingly monitored. But professional and political conduct, in the sense alluded to above, has not been fully transformed, notwithstanding the power of the HD case. The main reasons for this lie in the field of political economy rather than of economic (or political) analysis. The effects of the implementation of HD policies are rarely zero-sum from the perspective of the short-run interests of the richer and more powerful groups. Somewhat surprisingly, and notwithstanding strong claims to the contrary, we find that even in the case of development aid for education, the direction and volume of support still tend to reflect the contemporary economic interests of DAC members (proxied by recipient country size and historical links to the metropolis) rather more than the pattern and intensity of HD needs.

Can we, then, provide an answer to the first question posed in this chapter: has HD become the dominant paradigm? The evidence is mixed. The enthronement of HD in the way suggested by the first column of Table 4.1 for 2000–10 seems justified on the basis of the stated balance of international advice and of stated policy intention. However, there is as yet limited evidence for significant changes in development practice (notwithstanding some important national exceptions, and given the continued unfolding consequences of debt-induced recession and financial crisis). This indicates that an affirmative answer to the question remains somewhat premature.

References

Alesina, A. and D. Dollar (2000). 'Who Gives Foreign Aid to Whom and Why?' *Journal of Economic* Growth, 5(1): 33–63.

Alkire, S. (2010). *'Human Development: Definitions, Critiques and Related Concepts'*. Human Development Research Paper 2010/01. New York: UNDP.

Balassa, B. (1982). *Development Strategies in Semi-Industrial Economies*. Baltimore: Johns Hopkins University Press (for the World Bank).

Bates, R. (1981). *Markets and States in Tropical Africa*. Berkeley, CA: University of California Press.

Broad, R. (2006). 'Research, Knowledge, and the Art of "Paradigm Maintenance": The World Bank's Development Economics Vice-Presidency (DEC)'. *The Review of International Political Economy*, 13(3): 387–419.

Chenery, H., M. Aluwhalia, C. Bell, J. Duloy, and R. Jolly (1974). *Redistribution with Growth*. New York and London: Oxford University Press for the World Bank and the Institute of Development Studies.

Colclough, C. (1991). 'Structuralism versus Neoliberalism: An Introduction'. In C. Colclough and J. Manor (eds), *States or Markets? Neoliberalism and the Development Policy Debate*. Oxford: Clarendon Press, 1–26.

Colclough, C. (2005). 'Rights, Goals and Targets: How Do Those for Education Add Up?' *Journal of International Development*, 17(1): 101–11.

Colclough, C. (2011). *Challenges for the Optimal Allocation of Education Aid: Should MDG Priorities Be More Prominent?*. RECOUP Working Paper 40. Available at: <http://recoup.educ.cam.ac.uk/publications/RECOUPAidallocationColcloughWP40.pdf>.

Colclough, C. and J. Manor (eds) (1991). *States or Markets? Neoliberalism and the Development Policy Debate*. Oxford: Clarendon Press.

Cornia, G. A., R. Jolly, and F. Stewart (eds) (1987). *Adjustment with a Human Face: Protecting the Vulnerable and Promoting Growth*, Vols 1 and 2. Oxford: Clarendon Press.

Deaton, A., A. Banerjee, N. Lustig, K. Rogoff, et al. (2007). *An Evaluation of World Bank Research 1998–2005*. Washington, DC: World Bank.

Kenny, C. and A. Sumner (2011). *More Money or More Development: What Have the MDGs Achieved?*. CGD Working Paper 278. Washington, DC: Center for Global Development.

Krueger, A. (1974). 'The Political Economy of the Rent-Seeking Society'. *American Economic Review*, 64(3): 291–303.

Kuhn, T. (1962). *The Structure of Scientific Revolutions*. Chicago: The University of Chicago Press.

Lal, D. (1983). *The Poverty of Development Economics*. Hobart Paperback 16. London: Institute of Economic Affairs.

Lewis, A. (1955). *The Theory of Economic Growth*. London: Unwin.

McGillivray, M. and E. Oczkowski (1992). 'A Two-Part Sample Selection Model of British Bilateral Foreign Aid Allocation'. *Applied Economics*, 24(12): 1311–19.

Meier, G. and D. Seers (eds) (1984). *Pioneers in Development*. New York: Oxford University Press for the World Bank.

Ravallion, M. (1997). 'Good and Bad Growth: The Human Development Reports'. *World Development*, 25(5): 631–8.

Raworth, K. and D. Stewart (2003). 'Critiques of the Human Development Index: A Review'. In S. Fukuda-Parr and A. Shiva Kumar (eds), *Readings in Human Development*. Oxford: Oxford University Press, 140–52.

Rodrick, D. (2006). 'Goodbye Washington Consensus, Hello Washington Confusion'. *Journal of Economic Literature*, 44: 1973–87.

Seers, D. (1969). 'The Meaning of Development'. *International Development Review*, 11(4): 3–4.

Seers, D. (1972) 'What Are We Trying To Measure?' *Journal of Development Studies*, 8(3): 21–36.

Seers, D. (1979). 'The Meaning of Development, and Postscript: The New Meaning of Development'. In D. Lehmann (ed.), *Development Theory: Four Critical Studies.* London: Frank Cass, 9–30.

Sen, A. (1980). 'Equality of What?'. In S. M. McMurring (ed.), *Tanner Lectures on Human Values,* Vol. 1. Cambridge: Cambridge University Press.

Sen, A. (1985). *Commodities and Capabilities.* Amsterdam: North Holland.

Sen, A. (1989). 'Development as Capability Expansion'. *Journal of Development Planning,* 19: 41–58.

Srinivasan, T. (1994). 'Human Development: A New Paradigm, or Reinvention of the Wheel?'. *American Economic Review, Papers and Proceedings,* 84(2): 238–43.

Sumner, A. and M. Tiwari (2011). 'Global Poverty Reduction to 2015 and Beyond'. *Global Policy,* 2(2): 138–51.

Thiele, R., P. Nunnenkamp, and A. Dreher (2007). 'Do Donors Target Aid in Line with the Millennium Development Goals? A Sector Perspective of Aid Allocation'. *Review of World Economics,* 143(4): 596–630.

ul Haq, M. (2003). 'The Human Development Paradigm'. In S. Fukuda-Parr and A. Shiva Kumar (eds), *Readings in Human Development.* Oxford: Oxford University Press, 17–34.

UNDP (1990–). *Human Development Report* (annual editions). New York: Oxford University Press for UNDP.

UNDP (2010). *Human Development Report 2010.* New York: Oxford University Press for UNDP.

UNESCO (2002–). *Education for All Global Monitoring Report* (annual editions). Oxford: Oxford University Press for UNESCO.

UNESCO (2003). *The Leap to Equality.* Education for All Global Monitoring Report 2003/4. Paris: UNESCO.

Wade, R. H. (1990). *Governing the Market.* Princeton, NJ: Princeton University Press.

Williamson, J. (1989). 'What Washington Means by Policy Reform'. In J. Williamson (ed.), *Latin American Readjustment: How Much Has Happened?* Washington, DC: Institute for International Economics, Chapter 2.

Williamson, J. (2004). 'A Short History of the Washington Consensus'. Paper presented the Fundación CIDOB conference 'From the Washington Consensus towards a New Global Governance', Barcelona, 24–25 September.

Wood, A. (2008). 'Looking Ahead Optimally in Allocating Aid'. *World Development,* 36(7): 1135–51.

World Bank (1979). *World Development Report 1979.* Washington, DC: World Bank.

World Bank (1980). *World Development Report 1980.* Washington, DC: World Bank.

World Bank (1981). *'Accelerated Development in Sub-Saharan Africa'.* Washington, DC: World Bank.

5

Social Protection
Consensus and Challenges*

Ravi Kanbur

5.1 Introduction

The global financial crisis of 2008 brought to the fore issues of financial-sector regulation. But its consequences for the poor of the world also fuelled an ongoing discussion and debate on social protection. Protection for the poor in the face of macroeconomic crises is just one aspect of social protection. Other macro crises such as natural disasters also have severe consequences for the poor. Moreover, alongside the macro shocks are the ordinary micro-level shocks, such as health and work accidents, that are important in the daily lives of the poor. Social protection in the face of a whole range of shocks is now firmly on the policy agenda.

This study presents a broad overview of the main areas of consensus and the challenges in the analytical and policy discourse on social protection. A simple framework for locating consensus and challenges is to begin by thinking of wellbeing outcomes (measured perhaps by income or consumption) as depending on (i) medium-term factors such as assets and access to opportunities, (ii) insurance mechanisms to cope with short-term shocks, and (iii) the magnitude of the consequences of the shocks even after insurance mechanisms have come into play. The reason for worrying about the consequences of shocks is twofold. First, there is the straightforward consequence on wellbeing in the short term. Second, however, is the fact that the short-term impacts can translate into medium-term negative impacts on assets, opportunities, and wellbeing.

---

* This study is a contribution to a Festschrift for Richard Jolly. It is based on my keynote address to the South–South Learning Forum, Addis Ababa, 30 May 2011.

In this framework, improving the wellbeing of the poorest thus depends on (i) increasing their assets and opportunities in the medium term, (ii) improving insurance mechanisms, and (iii) addressing the actual outcome of shocks when they hit. However, two sets of issues arise. First, the interventions in each category have consequences for the other categories. To give a few examples: public interventions in (ii) could diminish private arrangements, leaving (iii) unchanged; public intervention in (iii) is implicitly like intervention in (ii); intervention in (i) also helps with (iii). Second, given limited public resources, where is it best to use them—on (i), (ii), or (iii)? It is not good enough to duck the question and to say that we should do all three. Even if this were valid, it would pose the question 'in what combination?'.[1]

It will become clear that many of the challenges facing the social protection community arise from the issues introduced above, and this chapter will discuss a number of these challenges. However, the chapter begins by highlighting three areas where there appears to be consensus. Four areas of challenges are then discussed.

5.2 Consensus I: Importance of Risk and Volatility

The analysis of poverty and inequality has undergone a data revolution in the last twenty-five years. It is now difficult to picture the paucity of data with which analysts were faced two or three decades ago. The World Bank's Living Standards Measurement Survey (LSMS) website lists over sixty surveys from more than thirty countries—all of these are from after the mid-1980s. The Demographic and Health Survey programme has equally transformed the data landscape, providing a wealth of information on many dimensions of human development. Micro data for Africa have become available in ever greater quantities, to add to the data from countries such as India. Perhaps most important for the analysis of risk and volatility has been the development of panel datasets for a whole range of countries, including those in Africa.

This data revolution has made possible detailed and specific analysis of risk and volatility in wellbeing outcomes—quantification of its extent, and assessment of its causes and consequences. Further, there has been a coming together of qualitative and quantitative research, building on the strengths of each tradition to further sharpen the analysis.

Although there are many possible illustrations of the surge in research and policy analysis of risk and vulnerability, two will suffice for our purposes. First

---

[1] Of course, this brings up the bigger question of how much society should spend on social protection as a whole, but this takes us beyond the scope of this chapter.

is the symposium on shocks and vulnerability in the *Journal of Development Studies* (Volume 45, Issue 6, 2009). This collection of six papers ranges from the effects of rainfall uncertainty in Nepal (Menon 2009), through health risks in Pakistan (Heltburg and Lund 2009), and vulnerability in fishing communities in Congo (Bene 2009). The paper by Heltburg and Lund (2009) builds on earlier panel data analysis for Pakistan (for example, Alderman 1996), but uses a cross-section survey with a module that asks retrospectively about shocks. They find:

> ... high incidence and cost of shocks borne by households, with health and other idiosyncratic shocks dominating in frequency, costliness, and adversity. Sample households lack effective coping options and use mostly self-insurance and informal credit. Many shocks result in food insecurity, informal debts, child and bonded labour, and recovery is slow. Private and public social safety nets exist but offer little effective protection (Heltburg and Lund 2009: 889).

Second, more in the realm of policy reports and global syntheses, is the *Chronic Poverty Report* 2008–09 (CPRC 2009). However, even this report shows what it owes to the availability of panel data when it highlights the basic point that static poverty measures can mask significant poverty dynamics:

> Consider, for example, the significant reduction of 24 per cent in aggregate poverty apparent in rural Vietnam between 1993 and 1998. This tells us nothing about what happened to individual households. In fact, while about 30 per cent of households moved out of poverty, another 5 per cent fell into poverty (together considered as the transitorily poor), and about one-third of the population was poor in both periods (CPRC 2009: 5).

There is now no disagreement that the poor in developing countries do indeed face a significant range of shocks, that they have developed mechanisms and responses to address these shocks, that these mechanisms are inadequate and leave a significant amount of risk uncovered, that these uncovered shocks and responses to them have medium-term detrimental consequences, and that there is therefore a need for public intervention to provide protection against risk and volatility.

At the macro level, evidence and agreement have accumulated on increased growth volatility compared to the 'golden age' of growth from 1945 to 1979. Di Giovanni and Levchenko (2008) and Kose, Prasad, and Terrones (2006) are only two examples of papers in this genre. While higher growth is indeed associated with lower growth volatility, the first paper finds an association between trade openness and greater volatility, while the second paper finds that 'both trade and financial integration significantly weaken this negative relationship' (2006: 176). Formal statistical evidence has been strengthened by public and policymakers' perceptions of the consequences of the global financial crises of 1997 and 2008. Furthermore, evidence and agreement have also grown on the greater volatility in climate, and on the increasing ease of spread of infectious disease because of labour movements. These can both lead to macro-level shocks with consequences for economies as a whole and thus for the poor in those economies.

5.3 Consensus II: Systems, Not Programmes

Findings such as those by Heltberg and Lund (2009) on the ineffectiveness of public social protection programmes and interventions do not mean that these programmes do not exist. Quite the contrary. In fact, most countries have a bewildering range of interventions that fall under the label of social protection. Even focusing on just one institution and on the narrowly defined category of social safety nets, during 2000–10 the World Bank 'loaned $11.5 billion to support such programmes in 244 loans to 83 countries' (IEG 2011: xi). For any given country, a range of programmes, under different ministries and different budget headings, all contribute directly or indirectly to social protection.

Indeed, programmes that are not on the face of it designed to offer social protection against shocks can play a role in protecting the vulnerable against shocks. One example of this is the well-known *Progresa/Oportunidades* programme in Mexico, which is primarily designed to provide incentives to keep children in school. The essence of the programme is that in return for verified attendance at school over a given period, a cash transfer is made to the household. The programme has been evaluated and found to be highly successful in meeting its objectives (Levy 2006). However, consider now the implications of the fact that the programme is targeted at poor households. If there is a shock—at the micro or macro level—which results in the head of a household losing income, then this household is likely to fall into the target group and to begin to receive cash transfers as part of the programme. Of course, the transfer is conditional on keeping children in school, but it is nevertheless a transfer to a household that has suffered a shock. Indirectly, therefore, it is a form of social insurance.

There are many such examples in every country. The main conclusion is that a programme-by-programme assessment of social protection, important though that is, will be an incomplete analysis of social protection in the country as a whole. Elsewhere I have proposed the institution of a social protection assessment programme (SPAP) for each country, led by the government, but perhaps with the assistance of agencies such as the World Bank (Kanbur 2010a). Such an assessment would begin by an institutional description of the widest possible set of government programmes and interventions that can provide, directly or indirectly, protection against shocks at the micro and macro level. The second stage of the assessment would examine the overlaps and interactions between the programmes—for example, whether some programmes kick in simultaneously (perhaps in uncoordinated fashion) when a shock hits. Such an assessment would also identify portions of the population that are uncovered or under-covered by social protection.

I have argued (Kanbur 2010a) that a further piece of analysis could be conducted analogously to the World Bank and IMF's Financial Sector Assessment Programme (FSAP). An FSAP essentially 'imagines' macro shocks and traces through the consequences for the financial sector, identifying vulnerabilities. Such 'stress testing' is now commonplace in the macro/financial setting. But it could equally well be done in the social protection context—tracing through the consequences of potential macro-level shocks on incomes of the poor, and how existing programmes and interventions do or do not protect against a range of these shocks. Such analysis could then identify actions to close the gaps.

The more general point behind these specific points and proposals, a point on which there appears to be consensus, is that we need to see social protection in terms of systems, not individual programmes. Of course, implementation will ultimately be through programmes and interventions, and care will need to be taken to design and evaluate these in their own terms. But the overall frame needs to be one of the system as a whole, with all relevant institutions working together to provide social protection for the poorest.

5.4 Consensus III: Global Assistance for Crisis Response

The SPAP discussed in the previous section can lay the groundwork for a systemic view of social protection in the face of micro- and macro-level shocks. It can highlight gaps in the system and thus frame actions to rationalize and coordinate programmes as well as investment in new programmes to serve under-covered populations. However, even if such investment is undertaken in setting up systems, a key issue is whether resources will be available to finance higher levels of support when a crisis strikes.

The issue of resources arises both when the crisis strikes and when it recedes—will the political economy allow resources to be withdrawn when the crisis passes? Kanbur (2010a) contrasts generalized food (and fuel) subsidies and employment guarantee programmes in this regard. The political economy of generalized subsidies is relatively easy on the expansionary side because they benefit a wide range of the population; it is, of course, politically more difficult to withdraw the subsidies precisely for this reason. Public works programmes, on the other hand, are self-targeting. Since they offer employment at a given (relatively low) wage, there will only be demand at the time of crisis. As the crisis abates and wages and employment in the economy pick up, workers will leave the public works sites for better opportunities. The difficulty, rather, is in ensuring a sufficient budget for the wage bill at the time of crisis—and precisely because the programme is self-targeted to the poor, it will not have widespread support, unlike generalized food subsidies.

Mindful of these political difficulties with public works programmes, coalition partners in India's 'UPA-I' government in 2004 enacted an 'Employment Guarantee Act' so as to bind government to finding the budget at times of crisis. However, this is an issue that also faces the international community, which is called on to provide support at times of crisis. The experience of the food price crisis of the early 2000s, and then the financial crisis of the late 2000s, has been salutary, and has led to a consensus on the importance of rapid response and availability of resources when the crisis strikes. In fact, this was a key finding of Cornia et al. (1987) a quarter of a century ago.

In Kanbur (2010a) I argue that the key to such support is that it has to be *pre-qualified*. All the preparation work has to have been done before, and the amounts and triggers for tranche releases set out in advance, so that the whole process does not start only when the crisis hits. There are, in fact, some instruments which can be further enhanced to address this need. For example, the World Bank's deferred drawdown option (DDO) is one such instrument available to wealthier countries eligible for IBRD borrowing. For poorer countries, the World Bank's soft loan arm, IDA, has introduced a crisis response window (CRW) with an accelerated approval process. It is hoped that this window will be broadened, and the process moved closer to a pre-qualification of the type that is available for the DDO, where the agreement is made in 'normal times' and the drawdown can come whenever the crisis strikes.

5.5 Challenge I: Redistribution Versus Insurance

The various elements of consensus described above, especially the broad agreement on the extent of risk and vulnerability faced by the poor, and on the need for social protection, provide a good platform for global action. However, there remains a series of challenges and disagreement as we move to further analysis and especially to implementation. The next sections will review some of these issues and challenges.

The first of these issues can be posed in the form of a question: Is social protection primarily insurance or is it redistribution? In Kanbur (2010b)

I highlight the strong overlaps between social security and income redistribution schemes, and the difficulties of disentangling the two in practice.

Consider, first of all, a standard progressive tax system where payments rise disproportionately with income, starting with a subsidy at the lower end, financed by tax payments at the upper end. For simplicity, suppose that the system is self-financing. This system, the epitome of redistribution, in fact provides insurance in a world where incomes are risky. A negative shock leading to a shortfall of incomes leads to lower taxes, perhaps even to a subsidy if income after the shock is low enough. By the same token, a positive shock attracts a higher average tax rate. The variance of post-tax income is lowered, reducing risk. In effect, the tax system is providing insurance. In a previous section I have also highlighted how conditional cash transfer programmes can also, in effect, provide insurance against shocks to income, even though their stated objective is not at all to do so.

Now consider a relatively standard social security programme such as unemployment insurance. For this to be pure insurance, contribution should match benefits actuarially—over the long run, inflows and outflows have to be balanced in an appropriate sense. If they are not—for example, if benefits exceed contributions—the difference has to be made up from somewhere, presumably from general taxation. The overall system then involves, alongside insurance among workers in the scheme, redistribution to those in the scheme from the average taxpayer. If the excess is funded from, say, a tax on firms, then one would have to work out the incidence of this tax to assess the overall nature of the redistribution—but redistribution there will be.

The redistribution can be regressive, or progressive. Many so-called social security programmes for formal-sector workers in developing countries are not actuarially balanced. They require regular injections of resources from the fisc. Since in many cases (for example, schemes that cover highly paid government or state-owned enterprise employees) the beneficiaries are richer than average, these schemes are highly regressive redistributive programmes. On the other hand, other schemes, for example those that provide micro-insurance to small-scale informal-sector enterprises, are also not self-financing but require external financing from government resources. In this case the redistribution is progressive.

With this inherent overlap between insurance and redistribution in social protection, the challenge to the social protection (SP) community is thus:

(i)   analytical, to estimate the insurance and the redistribution components of each programme, or the system of programmes

(ii) political, to not hide behind the more palatable 'insurance' label but to be explicit about the redistributive dimension of social protection (positive or negative).

5.6 Challenge II: LICs Versus MICs

It seems to be generally accepted that government social protection programmes are more widespread in middle-income countries (MICs) than in low-income countries (LICs). This is not easy to establish quantitatively, not least because of the difficulties of defining what comes under the umbrella of social protection. However, one recent but indirect quantification comes from an evaluation of World-Bank-supported social safety net (SSN) programmes during the decade 2000–10 (IEG 2011: 12): 'The Bank lending, analytical, and capacity-building support for SSNs was significantly more concentrated in MICs than LICs throughout the decade'. Taking World Bank lending as a whole, 13 per cent of World Bank projects in MICs were devoted to SSNs, while the figure for LICs was 6 per cent.

In view of this stylized fact, an obvious set of questions arises. Is this the 'natural' order of things? Can social protection only be 'afforded' once the LIC/MIC threshold is crossed? Is the spread of social protection programmes greater in MICs because they are easier to implement in MICs than in LICs? There is a straightforward response to the 'affordability' question. It is that in fact protection against shocks is of particular importance to the poorest of the poor, because for these it is the protection against risk and vulnerability that stands between the next shock and destitution. So, if anything, the need for social protection is greater among the poorest, and in the poorest countries. In fact, anticipating the arguments in the next section, the likelihood of market failure in insurance is likely to be greater in the weak institutional environments of LICs, further underlining the need for state support in these areas.

Institutional development is, of course, key, linking back to the earlier argument about taking a systemic view of social protection. Two pieces of evidence throw interesting light on this issue. First, 57 per cent of the World Bank's SSN operations in MICs emphasized institution-building, while only 24 per cent in LICs did so. However, at the same time, the performance of SSN projects in MICs and LICs was similar. In fact, LICs did marginally better: using the well-established scale of the World Bank's Independent Evaluation Group, 88 per cent of projects score 'moderately satisfactory' or better in LICs, while the number was 85 per cent for MICs. This may well be because fewer of the projects in LICs were geared towards institution-building, which is more difficult and likely to result in less favourable project ratings. In any event, there does not seem to be a *prima facie* case for not engaging in building up social protection systems in LICs, where the need for them is equally great if not greater.

In light of the above, the challenge for the social protection community is to (i) argue that redistribution is required *as much if not more* in LICs than in MICs, (ii) show that there is indeed successful SP programme implementation in LICs (as evidenced by the recent review of SSNs by IEG (2011)), and (iii) to assess the characteristics of successful social protection programmes in LICs with a view to scaling up their implementation, which would, of course, reveal that the nature of success will vary from country to country and a 'one-size-fits-all' solution is not appropriate.

5.7 State Versus Private Insurance

Prior to any government social protection intervention, families, communities, and markets will have developed various ingenious insurance mechanisms. They are, of course, wholly inadequate, but they exist. Their presence raises three challenges for the social protection community: (i) to encourage expansion of these mechanisms, or introduce state mechanisms directly? (ii) if the former, how to encourage them? (iii) if the latter, what happens to the existing mechanisms?

There is a natural tendency in the social protection community—and this chapter has been no exception—to draw a line from market and community failure in the provision of adequate protection to the case for direct state intervention by setting up social protection programmes. The failures of the market in the provision of insurance are well known. Moral hazard means that insurance provision will not be complete. Adverse selection means that insurance markets may fail to exist altogether. Imposition of risk sharing, through requiring participation by state provision, is one solution to this. However, this perspective glides too easily over the issue of state failure. In particular, the political economy of elite capture is not as much discussed by advocates of social protection as it should perhaps be. I have already discussed how schemes that are ostensibly social insurance can turn out to be highly effective mechanisms for regressive redistribution—from the poor to the rich. While being alert to these issues, the social protection community needs also to weigh up the alternative of supporting and expanding community-level and civil-society-managed insurance and protection schemes.

How can the state support existing schemes, rather than supplant them with a full-blown government alternative? The experience of the Indian Self-Employed Women's Association (SEWA) is instructive. SEWA is a civil-society organization that works to support livelihoods and empowerment of women who work in the informal sector in India.[2] Insurance is a key dimension of this support, provided through Vimo SEWA.[3] Cover is provided for a range of contingencies including death, accident, widowhood,

---

[2] See <http://www.sewa.org>.   [3] See <http://www.sewainsurance.org>.

illness, and maternity. More than 60,000 women and their families are insured. SEWA's ground-level organization provides the infrastructure for servicing the needs, claims, validation, etc., for women. There is state support with subsidies to premiums through programmes of support to micro-insurance. However, in other dimensions state regulations are a hindrance to the operation of Vimo SEWA. The fundamental issue is that insurance regulations are written with large insurers in mind, and are not geared to small-scale micro-insurance programmes such as those of SEWA. Specifically, the capital requirements for insurers promulgated by the Insurance Regulation and Development Authority (IRDA) are too big for a micro-insurer such as SEWA. The result is that Vimo SEWA has to operate under cooperatives legislation and cannot expand to gain the benefits of scale. There is an ongoing dialogue in India, which has had to proceed in the difficult atmosphere of recent scandals associated with private-sector micro-insurance firms. Here is a case, then, where the state could support the development of a civil-society insurance mechanism through intelligent redesign of regulations.

The introduction of state mechanisms will affect existing non-state mechanisms. Subsidy for a non-state mechanism will affect the conditions for those non-state mechanisms that are not subsidized. In general, it may be assumed that non-subsidized non-state mechanisms will shrink in response. This is natural. Existing mechanisms were inadequate and needed to be supplemented. But the presence of alternatives will reduce the incentives for current mechanisms. The central point for the social protection community, however, is to guard against the tendency to overstate the benefits of a given state social protection programme by focusing on the gross benefits of the programme. Of course, these had better be positive—otherwise the programme will not pass the social cost–benefit test. However, the net social protection provided, after subtracting the shrinkage or disappearance of existing mechanisms, is bound to be less than the gross benefit. Yet the standard procedure in the social protection discourse is indeed to focus on the gross benefits of a programme and not on its net benefits, the calculation of which would require an analysis of the response of community and market mechanisms to state intervention.

5.8 Conditional Versus Unconditional Transfers

Conditional cash transfers (CCTs) are all the rage now. Although they have been part of the policymakers' toolkit for many years in Asia, well-documented successful experiences in Latin America from the mid-1990s onwards have put them onto a new global footing. Most Latin American countries now have them, and they have spread to other parts of the world—and have, indeed, been reintroduced to Asia (Fiszbein and Schady 2009). They have been evaluated using rigorous methods and found to deliver what they promise—for example, the impact of Mexico's *Progresa/Oportunidades* is, indeed, to reduce school dropouts, as per its main objective (Levy 2006; Fiszbein and Schady 2009). They are seen as an indispensable part of social protection.

The somewhat unconditional support for CCTs is disconcerting. There seems to be very little questioning of them in the policy discourse. One is reminded of a similar situation with microfinance fifteen years ago. A more sober assessment of the microfinance phenomenon and its impact on the poor is now coming into view. In particular, there are questions about whether the benefits flow to the poorest of the poor. So, here is a challenge for the social protection community on CCTs—at least on the first C, conditionality.

The basic structure of a CCT is as follows. First, identify target households. Second, define 'good behaviour' (for example, keeping children in school, attending antenatal health clinics, etc.) and monitor this behaviour. Third, let those who achieve a given behavioural standard receive a cash transfer. But what if the behavioural standard is more likely to be attained by wealthier households? Typically, for example, 'education' and 'health' are 'normal goods', i.e. households demand more of these as they get wealthier. Then, clearly, CCTs have an inbuilt regressivity. There is some evidence, for example, that the take-up rates in Mexico's *Progresa/Oportunidades* CCT are much lower for the poorest of the eligible households (Rodriguez 2011). It can also be shown theoretically (Rodriguez 2011) that with a fixed budget, unconditional cash transfers (UCTs) reduce the depth of income poverty more than CCTs. This result also holds for 'education poverty', when the objective is to reduce the shortfalls from a target level of years of schooling.

So the SP community must ask itself, 'What exactly is the gain of the first "C" in "CCT"?'

- Clearly, conditioning moves behaviour in the direction of the conditioning. There is a mountain of evidence on this, but this is perhaps not that surprising. The real question is what would UCTs, with the same budget, achieve in terms of average behavioural change and progressivity of this change. We do not have an extensive and systematic set of answers to this question.

- If, as seems possible from the analysis of Rodriguez (2011), CCTs are more likely to be regressive than UCTs, is the gain from conditioning political in nature, assuaging middle-class concerns about 'handouts' versus 'investment'? Of course, in reality a UCT may improve the schooling of the poorest even more than a CCT (with the same budget), but this may cut no ice in the political arena, where the notion of the poor being seen to do something in return for the cash they get may hold sway.[4]

Conclusion

The social protection literature and policy discourse is now vast, and it would be impossible to do a comprehensive review and to do justice to the myriad strands and perspectives one finds. Rather, my objective here has been to identify some areas of consensus and challenges in the social protection community—as I see them.

I have argued that there is now indeed a consensus among analysts and policymakers on the importance of risk and vulnerability in the lives of the poor, a development that has been helped by the greater availability of micro-level data on patterns of wellbeing. Further, there is consensus, at least at a certain level of generality, that the overall approach to social protection has to be systemic, even if implementation proceeds programme by programme. At the same time, I believe there is a consensus, especially after the global crises of the 1990s and the 2000s, that the international community needs to have mechanisms in place to provide resources rapidly to countries to protect their poor when a crisis hits.

However, there remain disagreements, and I have posed these as challenges to the social protection community. I have argued that there is a tendency in the community to hide behind the 'insurance' label when in fact social protection involves, and must involve, a large element of redistribution. There are also issues about whether resources are best spent on LICs or on MICs to strengthen social protection systems. How best to blend state and private, especially community-provided, insurance is another challenge. Finally, I have cautioned against the current fad for CCTs, and raised the challenge of whether UCTs might, in fact, be more progressive in their impact. These and other challenges provide a rich agenda for analysis and policy experimentation in social protection.

---

[4] Even where CCTs do better than UCTs on schooling, they do not necessarily do better on other dimensions such as teenage pregnancy (Baird et al. 2011). See also Schubert and Slater (2006).

References

Alderman, H. (1996). 'Saving and Economic Shocks in Rural Pakistan'. *Journal of Development Economics*, 51(2): 343–65.

Baird, S., C. Mcintosh, and B. Ozler (2011). 'Cash or Condition: Evidence from a Cash Transfer Experiment'. WB Policy Research Paper, 5259. Washington, DC: World Bank.

Bene, C. (2009). 'Assessing Economic Vulnerability in Small Scale Fishing Communities'. *Journal of Development Studies*, 45(6): 911–33.

Cornia, G. A., R. Jolly, and F. Stewart (1987). *Adjustment with a Human Face*. London: Clarendon Press.

CPRC (2009). *The Chronic Poverty Report, 2008–09*. [online] Available at: <http://www.chronicpoverty.org/publications/details/the-chronic-poverty-report-2008-09/ss> (accessed 11 August 2012).

Di Giovanni, J. and A. Levchenko (2008). *Trade Openness and Volatility*. IMF Working Paper, WP/08/146. Washington, DC: IMC. Available at: <http://www.imf.org/external/pubs/ft/wp/2008/wp08146.pdf> (accessed 11 August 2012).

Fiszbein, A. and N. Schady (2009). *Conditional Cash Transfers: Reducing Present and Future Poverty*. WB Policy Research Report. Available at: <http://www.siteresources.worldbank.org/INTCCT/Resources/5757608-1234228266004/PRR-CCT_web_noembargo.pdf> (accessed 15 August 2012).

Heltburg, R. and N. Lund (2009). 'Shocks, Coping and Outcomes for Pakistan's Poor: Health Risks Predominate'. *Journal of Development Studies*, 45(6): 864–88.

IEG (Independent Evaluation Group) (2011). *Social Safety Nets: An Evaluation of World Bank Support, 2000–2010*. Washington, DC: IEG, the World Bank Group. Available at: <http://ieg.worldbankgroup.org/Data/reports/ssn_full_evaluation.pdf> (accessed 11 August 2012).

Kanbur, R. (2010a). *Protecting the Poor against the Next Crisis*. Distinguished Lecture Series, Egyptian Centre for Economic Studies, Cairo, April. Available at: <http://www.kanbur.dyson.cornell.edu/papers/Protecting%20the%20Poor%20Against%20the%20Next%20Crisis.pdf> (accessed 11 August 2012).

Kanbur, R. (2010b). 'Conceptualising Social Security and Income Redistribution'. Keynote Address at the International Social Security Association, Luxembourg, September. Available in: *Bulletin Luxembourgeois des Questions Sociales*, 27: 31–41.

Kose, A., E. Prasad, and M. Terrones (2006). 'How Do Trade and Financial Integration Affect the Relationship between Growth and Volatility?'. *Journal of International Economics*, 69: 176–202.

Levy, S. (2006). *Progress against Poverty: Sustaining Mexico's Progresa-Oportunidades Programme*. Washington, DC: Brookings Institution Press.

Menon, N. (2009). 'Rainfall Uncertainty and Occupational Choice in Agricultural Households in Nepal'. *Journal of Development Studies*, 45(6): 889–910.

Rodriguez, C. (2011). *'Participation of the Poorest and Distributional Effects of Conditional Cash Transfers'*. Ithaca, NY: Cornell University. Mimeo.

Schubert, B. and R. Slater (2006). 'Social Cash Transfers in Low-Income African Countries: Conditional or Unconditional?'. *Development Policy Review*, 24(5): 571–8.

6

The Strange Neglect of Income Inequality in Economics and Public Policy*

Robert H. Wade[1]

> It is our job to glory in inequality and to see that talents and abilities are given vent and expression for the benefit of us all.
>
> MARGARET THATCHER
> *British Prime Minister*

> [O]f the tendencies that are harmful to sound economics, the most seductive and...poisonous is to focus on questions of distribution.
>
> ROBERT LUCAS (2004)
> *Professor of Economics at Harvard and Nobel Prize winner*

> [Those who oppose increases in incomes at the top are] spiteful egalitarians.
>
> MARTIN FELDSTEIN (1998)
> *Professor of Economics at Harvard, President of National Bureau of Economic Research (1978–2008), Chief Economic Advisor to Ronald Reagan*

> Poverty bothers me. Inequality does not. I just don't care.
>
> WILLEM BUITER (2007)
> *Professor of Economics, London School of Economics*

* Thanks to Gabriel Palma for useful comments.
[1] This essay draws on earlier essays, including Wade (2004, 2006, 2009, 2011a, 2011b).

Income inequality within countries has increased in most regions of the world since the 1980s. Yet rising inequality, especially income concentration at the top, has provoked little policy response. Conservatives claim that rising inequality is a natural and inevitable trend that could only be reversed by draconian growth-reducing state intervention. This chapter tackles the question of why such claims have prevailed and, more generally, why inequality has remained far down the list of public policy priorities even as it has soared. In contrast, 'poverty' has enjoyed periodic bouts of public policy attention, and a whole development industry is ostensibly directed at reducing it.

There is no question that, on the scale of the world over the past two centuries, the driver of continuous improvements in mass living conditions is the combination of technological change, accumulation of capital, and the demographic transition. The latter is the mechanism by which increases in production—going on for long before the Industrial Revolution—are converted into improvements in average living conditions rather than into more children. The fact that average income gaps between the poorest twenty countries and the United States are at historically high levels (of the order of 1:20) reflects the fact that many poor countries are still caught in the Malthusian trap, still to advance through the demographic transition. In any case, it is clear that for many developing countries, policies to redistribute downwards would be a less effective way to raise average incomes than policies to accelerate growth in national income.

The same conclusion does not hold in the already rich world, the focus of this chapter. Here the demographic transition is over, and technological innovation and capital accumulation are well institutionalized. At the same time the degree of income concentration at the top has reached the point where it generates high costs, of several kinds.

Here are some stylized facts about income concentration. In the 1920s the top 1 per cent in both developed and developing countries (those few more advanced developing countries for which data are available) received 15–20 per cent of national income before tax; and the share in the USA was more like 23 per cent (see Figure 6.1). The share of the top 1 per cent then fell substantially across all these countries during and after the Second World War, reaching 5–10 per cent by the late 1970s. Over the 1980s, coinciding with globalization, financialization, the erosion of trade unions, the decline of state funding for political parties, and the ascendancy of neoliberal doctrine in Anglo-American economies and many developing economies, the share of the top 1 per cent in these economies began to soar.

During 2002–6, the period of expansion during the Bush presidency, the richest 1 per cent of Americans accrued 73 per cent of the increase in national income (Palma 2011). This is not a misprint. Over the longer period of the three decades between 1978 and 2007 the share of the top 1 per cent

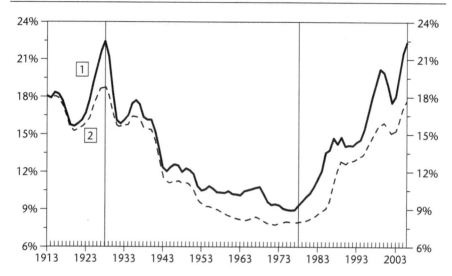

Figure 6.1 Share of top 1 per cent in US income, 1913–2006
Note: The solid line includes capital gains.
Source: Palma (2009).

before tax rose from 8 per cent to 18 per cent excluding realized capital gains, and 8.5 per cent to 23.5 per cent including capital gains. The top 1 per cent enjoyed real income growth of 4.4 per cent per year during these decades, compared with 0.6 per cent per year for the remaining 99 per cent (UNCTAD 2012: chapter 3), and accrued 57 per cent of the increase before tax and over 40 per cent of the increase after tax (Roemer 2011).

In terms of wealth, the richest 1 per cent of Americans owned about 35 per cent of reported household and corporate wealth in 2006–7 (the latest year for which statistics are available), a figure that is certainly too low because of all the wealth hidden in tax havens; but even taken at face value it is a far bigger share than in most other developed countries.

In the UK between 1979 and 2007 the share of the top 1 per cent rose from 6 per cent to 16 per cent, excluding capital gains. The average remuneration of FTSE100 chief executives rose by about 40 per cent in FY2010—a year of close to zero GDP growth—to reach £4.2 million, or 145 times the median wage.

In contrast, in continental Europe and Japan the share of the top 1 per cent remained fairly stable after the 1980s, at less than 10 per cent before tax. It is clearly possible for advanced capitalist economies to remain prosperous with much lower income concentration at the top than in the Anglo sphere.

The world total of high net worth individuals (HNWIs), with more than $1 million of liquid assets (excluding real estate), has surged since the great recession started in 2008. In 2010 the number exceeded the previous peak in 2007, even as governments of developed countries implemented austerity budgets. Though most are concentrated in the USA, Japan, and Germany (53 per cent of the world total live in these countries), the fastest increase in HNWI numbers is in Asia-Pacific countries, whose total exceeded Europe's for the first time ever in 2010 (Treanor 2011).

Hence the soaring demand for 'passion' purchases, from Ferraris to diamonds, art, and fine wines. Prices in the international art market are so sensational as to give Sotheby's and Christies their highest profits in years. Reviewing recent eight-figure sales in both the art market and homes, an *International Herald Tribune* article concludes, 'for the 0.001 per cent, life proceeds sweetly' (Goldfarb 2011: 21).

The Occupy Movement, which erupted in European and then North American countries in the summer of 2011, focused attention on inequality, framing the issue as the bottom 99 per cent against the top 1 per cent. One of its constructive effects was to couple the pre-existing mass resentment against 'welfare scroungers' with the new rage against the (undeserving) rich, so that the focus was no longer entirely on the former.

Pushed by budget pressures and public sympathy evoked by the Occupy Movement, some politicians began to talk of the desirability of higher taxes on the rich. President Obama endorsed the 'Buffett rule' that millionaires should not pay a lower rate of tax than their assistants. The British Conservative–Liberal Democrat coalition government floated the idea of a 'mansion tax' in the context of bringing the top income tax rate down. The French Socialist president proposed a 75 per cent tax rate on top incomes.

But these proposals everywhere run into fierce opposition, and the Occupy Movement had little follow-on once the occupations ended (the medium was its message). In the USA, hard-line conservative organizations advocate lower taxes (especially on the wealthy), less public spending (except for defence), free trade, and economic libertarianism. One such organization is the Club for Growth, which declared in early 2012, 'If we balance the budget tomorrow on spending cuts alone, it would be fantastic for the economy' (Krugman 2012b). Underlying the resistance is the proposition, widely accepted in policy circles and by the public at large, that public action to reduce top-level inequality is (i) infeasible and (ii) not legitimate.

The result is that politicians have done little to curb income concentration. They and commentators have tended to steer public debate along the track of 'Does individual X deserve his £1.4 million bonus?' and 'Why should people be rewarded for failure?', which leaves intact the premise that 'whatever-corporate-boards-will-bear' should be given for 'success'. Once on this track, the issues of the society-wide structure of income distribution and demand-generation are conveniently bypassed.[2]

The obvious answer to our question as to why inequality has been side-lined even as it surged is that the rich have a vested interest in boosting issues for public policy attention that do not question their relative position and ignoring those that do. Given that the rich have a vastly disproportionate influence in politics, civil service, and media, it is no surprise that the agenda of public policy does not draw attention to the need to change the structure of income distribution to make it less unequal—back to where it was in 1990, for example.

But 'the rich' and 'the top 1 per cent' are just statistical constructs. What interests and ideologies are in play?

6.1 The Change in Ruling Class Coalition

The class basis of 'the rich' changed after the 1980s. During the post-war decades politics in most Western countries rested on a class coalition or pact between the skilled working class, professional middle class, and capitalists who were either entrepreneurs running their own companies or investors for the long term (Bresser-Pereira 2012). The class coalition in turn rested on a 'pre-outsourcing' economic structure with a sizeable manufacturing base. Most companies' sales went to the domestic market, and employers' federations accepted that wages were both a cost of production and also a source of spending on domestic companies' products. Out of this came an 'establishment' governing elite, concerned to foster aggregate demand and the wellbeing of the whole society as a buttress to the elite's own position, which led it to support measures to limit income inequality, so that its members did not come to be seen as divorced from the rest of the society. Moreover, the elite had memories of the shared wartime sacrifices, and faced relatively strong

---

[2] The case of Leo Apotheker attracted condemnation. As newly appointed boss of Hewlett-Packard he received remuneration of almost US$10 million as a sign-on package, and just over US$13 million on his termination 11 months later, or US$23 million for 11 months of work. John Donohue, president of the American Law and Economics Association, commented, 'It's a shocking departure from capitalist incentives if you lavish riches on the losers.' He continued, 'Imagine if you were applying for a job, and you said, "I want to make it clear that if I do a terrible job, I want to walk away with a ton of money." Do you think you'd get hired? *Yet that's now standard practice in negotiating executive compensation*' (quoted in Stewart (2011), emphasis added). Another report says, 'A hallmark of the gilded era of just a few short years ago, the eye-popping severance package, continues to thrive in spite of the measures established after the financial crisis to crack down on excessive pay.' The report quotes a director of governance for a labour-affiliated investment fund saying, 'We repeatedly see companies' assets go out the door to reward failure. Investors are frustrated that boards haven't prevented such windfalls' (Dash 2011).

trade unions at home and an overarching 'us versus them' threat from the Soviet Union.

Since the 1980s the dominant class coalition has narrowed down to financiers, rentiers who draw their income from rents, interest, and dividends, and CEOs of companies selling products with a much higher import content than before, all operating on short time-horizons and a 'winner take all, devil take the hindmost' morality. The economic base changed from one in which most international trade involved whole products made by national companies at home and exported to foreign markets ('trade globalization') to one in which national companies shifted operations and employment to cheap-labour sites, China above all, and exported to the home market and elsewhere ('production globalization'). Manufacturing shrunk as a share of GDP in most Western economies, and with it mass trade unions, while the highly diverse and difficult-to-organize service sector grew. The labour market trifurcated into a class of super-rich ('top 1 per cent'), a middle class with tertiary education, and a large segment that lacks post-secondary training (currently some 85 million people older than 25 in the USA, giving the USA a rank of 14 in the world in terms of the proportion of 25 to 34 year olds with post-secondary education). The political marginalization of the bottom segment was signalled in the UK by Margaret Thatcher's evisceration of wages councils and John Major's axing of them in 1993, ending the era when governments saw low wages as their concern.

Out of these economic transformations came an 'oligarchic' elite, concerned to use the instruments of state power, including regulation (e.g. of banks), monetary policy, housing policy, taxation, and public spending, to redistribute upwards. The decline of state funding for political parties necessitated greater dependence on private donations, which came mainly from rentiers, financiers, and outsourced companies, whose donations carried the understanding that the parties, whether centre-right or centre-left, would refrain from policies the rich donors did not like, except at the margins. Meanwhile the new elite incumbents had no memory of Second World War shared sacrifices and faced no external threat from the Soviet Union, and no threat of internal communist or even trade subversion.

Turbocharging the economic transformation was an intense process of global corporate concentration, led by finance. A recent analysis identifies a super-cluster of 147 interlinked mega-firms accounting for a high share of the world's corporate revenues, which itself is dominated by finance: *all of the top fifty except one are financial firms* (Coghalan and MacKenzie 2011).

In 1997, shortly before the start of the East Asian/Latin American/Russian/Long Term Capital Management crises of the late 1990s, the value of financial transactions was about fifteen times the world's annual gross product. Today, even in the hard times following the crash of 2008, the ratio is almost seventy times. This jump from fifteen to seventy times in little more than a decade is testimony to the 'financialization' of the world economy and to the lock with which the financial sector of Anglo economies holds their governments. So too is the surging take-up of English as the compulsory second language in schools; for finance requires quick decisions, quick decisions need a single language, and English has become finance's lingua franca. (Car manufacturing does not require such quick decisions, allowing time for English communications to be translated into local languages.) Even Algeria, with its Francophone elite, switched to English as the compulsory second language in 1997, to the dismay of the former colonial master.

The sheer brazenness of the oligarchic elite in defending current institutional arrangements is caught in the justification given by Robert Rubin (long-time Goldman Sachs employee and board member, then US Treasury Secretary and champion of the repeal of the Glass-Steagall Act, then director and senior counsellor of Citigroup including through the period of Citigroup's bailout by the US Treasury, in which capacity he accrued $126 million in cash and stock) for not preventing financial firms reaching a size where they are 'too big [to be allowed] to fail'—and therefore have to be supported by taxpayers in the event of insolvency. Exclaimed Rubin, 'Too big to fail isn't a problem with the system. It is the system. You can't be a competitive financial institution serving global corporations of scale without having a certain scale yourself. The bigger the multinationals get, the bigger financial institutions will have to get' (quoted in Sharpe 2012: 141).

In the United States over the 2000s, high-income households have been paying their lowest share of federal taxes in decades, and corporations frequently avoid paying any tax. The 400 highest-income individual tax filers paid only 18 per cent of their income in federal income taxes in 2008, the most recent year available; in 2007, just 17 per cent; and they pay little by way of payroll taxes or state and local taxes, which are major burdens on middle-income families. They pay so little because most of their income is classed as capital gains, three-quarters of which go to the top 1 per cent. The tax rate on capital gains is the lowest since the days of President Hoover. President George W. Bush rammed the tax cut on capital gains and another on dividends through Congress in 2003 on the wave of euphoria over 'victory' in Iraq (Krugman 2012a). The Clinton administration, by contrast, was positively socialistic; during the first term the top 400 taxpayers paid close to 30 per cent of their income in federal taxes.

Yet during the Bush decade of frenzied tax-cutting for the rich the Republican Party also happened to lower some tax rates for the poor. (And earlier, the Reagan administration instituted the earned income tax credit, which became a remarkably effective anti-poverty programme by giving working families thousands of dollars a year in tax refunds.) Now Republican leaders want to correct such oversights and raise taxes on the poor and work-ing class in the interests of 'fairness' and eliminating welfare scroungers (*New York Times* 2011).

In Britain the Labour government over the 2000s deliberately refused to stand up to people who, through technically legal but morally reprehensible ruses, end up paying a minuscule amount of tax on their copious wealth. Labour Chancellor Alistair Darling boasted that he wanted London to be a welcoming home for Russians, Chinese, and Saudis, which meant low taxa-tion and 'light-touch regulation' (Kampfner 2011).

Similarly in Iceland. Over the 2000s the conservative, market-liberalizing, bank-privatizing Independence Party government shifted the tax burden onto the bottom half of the income distribution by almost eliminating the tax on capital gains and by lowering the threshold at which families had to start paying taxes. The ostensible aim was to boost incentives for entrepre-neurship. Instead it boosted the incentives for bankers to lend recklessly, eventually driving the economy over a cliff (Wade and Sigurgeirsdottir 2011).

6.2 Interests of the Middle Classes

It is hardly surprising that the already rich defend inequality and try to translate their riches into political power with which to limit redistribution downwards. But why have the middle classes mostly acquiesced? To under-stand middle-class acquiescence, consider trends in income distribution by income deciles.

Figure 6.2 shows the national income shares of population deciles in the USA from 1947 to 2006. Note, first, the sharp rise in the share of the top decile, D10, starting around 1980, the time of the Reagan/Thatcher neo-liberal reforms and the onset of the transformations described earlier, con-tinuing until the end of the series in 2006. Note, second, something more surprising: the share of the next 50 per cent of the population (D5–9) remained fairly constant at a bit more than 50 per cent through the whole period from 1947 to 2006, falling somewhat in the 1980s but then stabiliz-ing. (Not shown in the figure, the trends for both D7–9 and D5–6 are roughly constant.) Third, the share of the bottom 40 per cent (D1–4) fell steadily after 1980, proportionately more than the fall in the share of the middle 50 per cent. So as the share of the top 10 per cent rose after 1980, the bottom 40 per cent was squeezed proportionately more than the share of the mid-dle. All the concern with the 'hollowing out of the middle class' overlooks this point.

This pattern—the middle section of the income distribution (between the 40th and 90th percentiles) has managed to maintain a share of national

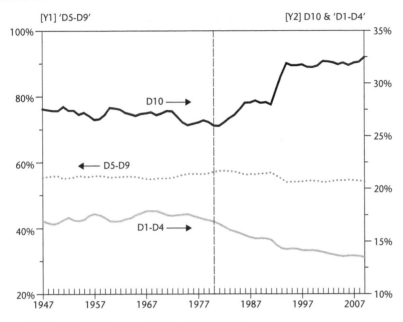

Figure 6.2 Share of US income deciles, 1947–2009
Source: Palma (2011).

Table 6.1 Decile shares (%) of national income, USA and average for 133 countries, 2009

	USA	133 countries
D10	33	32
D5–9	55	52
D1–4	13	17

Note: D10 is the top decile of the population by income, D5–9 the next 50%, D1–4 the bottom 40%.

Source: Palma (2011: Table 1).

income roughly in line with its share of population while the bottom 40 per cent has taken a disproportional cut in its share—is found in many other middle- and high-income countries (Table 6.1).

What are the political effects, in terms of support for or opposition to politicians who urge measures of downwards redistribution (e.g. higher taxes on the wealthy, a higher minimum wage, larger supply of public services that benefit poorer households disproportionately)? You might think that as the very rich soar ahead, leaving behind not just manual workers but also the middle-class masses (including doctors, academics, civil servants, and even

CEOs of small companies), the middle-class masses would mobilize politically to champion less concentration of wealth at the top. They don't. Why?

- As just noted, the middle classes have managed to sustain a share of national income roughly in line with their share of population. Just how is unclear, but part of the answer may be that many middle-class professions, especially in the public sector, have relatively strong unions or professional associations, as compared to the working class, and are better able to limit the supply of their numbers.

- Middle and upper-middle classes have been able to increase their consumption faster than their (slowly increasing) incomes by borrowing—from the financial resources available as wealth holders at the top seek to multiply their assets. Over the 2000s this rise in household debt to household income in the USA and other Anglo-American economies allowed aggregate demand to grow at the rate required to sustain the process of capital accumulation, despite stagnant wages; in effect, the capitalist elite operated a 'part-pay/part-lend' strategy rather than pay the required level of wages to utilize productive capacity.

- Some components of the economic conservative package are very appealing to the middle and upper-middle classes. In particular, the promise of lower taxes is a sure vote winner, even if the tax cuts benefit the rich most of all. When the British Labour Party's Gordon Brown became prime minister, he did so well in the opinion polls at first that he was tempted to call an early election. When the Conservative Party's Shadow Chancellor George Osborne promised to abolish inheritance taxes, the political balance changed so much that Brown called off the early election.

- The current generation of the middle classes has internalized the Reagan/Thatcher values of individualistic aspiration ('winners take all, let failures fail'). It expects to rely on its own efforts to get ahead—or at least, this is its self-image (Lakoff 2002).

- Fear of loss is a more powerful motivator than prospect of gain. Talk of 'reducing inequality' prompts middle-class anxiety that the government may try to pull up those *below* middle-class households, which worries them more than those above them rising even further away. Better to let the rich keep their income than allow tax-financed transfers to go to those below them—all the more so when, as now, many in the middle classes see themselves on the edge of the abyss, loaded up with debt and worried about unemployment and pensions. After all, their roughly constant share of national income means that they have been doing a lot better than the bottom 40 per cent, which is a measure of their *success*.

- The middle class holds a negative stereotype of the working class (bottom 40 per cent), which justifies resistance to downward redistribution. The stereotype rests on the second breakpoint in the income hierarchy (after the one at roughly the 99th percentile), between those with a college degree and those without. Over the past several decades the economic benefit of college education has steadily risen. In the USA, the average college graduate made 38 per cent more than the average high-school graduate in 1979, but makes 75 per cent more today. Moreover, college graduates are much better at passing their advantages on to their children, who are more likely to get married and stay married, less likely to have children out of marriage or to smoke or to be obese, and more likely to read to their children and have wider friendship networks. The bottom 40 to 50 per cent, in contrast, have more disorganized families and more disorganized social networks (Brooks 2011). With them as the reference group, the college-educated are not inclined to support calls for their taxes to go to 'welfare scroungers' lower down.

6.3 Conservative Ideology

Globalization, class interests, the concentration of corporate power, political-party funding, and the decline of trade unions cannot be the end of the story. Political ideologies and cognitive beliefs that justify the existing distribution of income are widely believed, including by people who accept that they have no prospect of becoming rich. Ideologies are not like holy water sprinkled onto interests; they do not simply justify whatever interests want. Rather, they have a causal role akin to 'switchmen' who determine the tracks along which human behaviours travel, to borrow a metaphor from Max Weber. Interests are then like the engines that pull or push the behaviours.

The ideational explanation for the neglect of inequality is that large parts of Western electorates—not just the rich and middle classes—have accepted a conservative ideology which pulls the switches in favour of *a vision of a moral society* where, in the name of 'freedom' and 'self-reliance', the role of government is to encourage largely free, private markets, and to accept the income distribution that results from the operation of those markets (provided the government does not rig the markets in favour of cronies). In this conservative worldview, government attempts to reduce income inequality only weaken the moral fibre of society by softening the link between law-abiding effort and reward. Such a society produces adults lacking in self-discipline and self-reliance—a welfare scrounger's haven (Lakoff 2002).

Philosophers have provided a raft of arguments to justify inequality and to reject John Rawls' partial defence of redistribution. For example, Robert Nozick, in *Anarchy, State and Utopia* (1974), argues that as long as exchanges between persons are voluntary, whatever distribution of rewards produced by those exchanges is legitimate. The book remains highly prized in conservative circles, though its supporters realize that in the real world many exchanges are not strictly voluntary.

The normal popular response to hard times is to demand more regulation and social insurance. Yet the hard times since 2008 have seen a surge in popular support for the conservative worldview. So Friedrich von Hayek's polemic *The Road to Serfdom*, published in 1944, rose to 240 on the Amazon Best Seller's List in 2010. Hayek argues that Beveridge's 1942 proposals for a welfare state in Britain (including a national health service) would curb economic freedoms and lead the government on a slippery slope to curb political freedoms too. The book's sales have been propelled upwards by conservative talk-show hosts prescribing it as a guide to the nefarious intentions of the Obama administration (Farrant and McPhail 2010). Ayn Rand's *Atlas Shrugged*, with its celebration of the captains of industry whom the government was always trying to tear down, has enjoyed a similar buzz, most of its enthusiasts failing to see that it is not only anti-government but also anti-democratic and anti-populist. The libertarian economist Ludwig von Mises, a leading figure in the post-war rise to dominance of the free-market policy paradigm, expressed the novel's message succinctly when he wrote to congratulate Rand on the book's publication in 1957:

> You have the courage to tell the masses what no politician told them: [that] you are inferior and all the improvements in your conditions which you simply take for granted you owe to the efforts of men who are better than you. (Frank 2011: 147)

It is no surprise that the same von Mises (1955) published *Ideas on Liberty* at about the same time, where he declares:

> ...inequality of wealth and incomes is the cause of the masses' well-being, not the cause of anybody's distress. [...] Where there is a lower degree of inequality, there is necessarily a lower standard of living of the masses.

The fuel for the current and historically unprecedented surge of popular support for the conservative, free-market ideology in hard times is the fear—even bug-eyed terror—of 'big government'. The Tea Party movement in the

USA had its genesis in 2009 in the battle over bank bailouts and went on to highlight the unholy alliance of big business and big government as the defining issue of public policy, holding up the 'free market' as the moral alternative. Get government intervention out of the way, it says, and every deserving person can climb the beanstalk, scramble through the hole in the sky, and arrive in the land of freedom, peace, and prosperity.

In an extreme case of 'false consciousness' Tea Party supporters overlook their movement's financing largely by millionaires and billionaires grown rich from big business, not by the entrepreneurs of small and medium-sized enterprises whom they celebrate. They, and anti-government conservatives more generally, also overlook the extent to which private firms in many sectors depend on government contracts.

But visceral anti-government sentiment in the United States now goes far beyond conservative circles. 'You can trust the government to do the right thing most of the time' now elicits an affirmative from only 10 per cent of respondents, down from three-quarters in the mid-1950s. In northern Europe, too, the near-consensus around 'austerity' as the way out of the current crisis ('Austerity is the only cure for the Eurozone,' declared German Finance Minister Wolfgang Schauble in September 2011) rests on an elite conviction that Europe can only compete in international markets by lowering costs, including taxes, and a popular conviction that 'the government is like a household writ large; just as a household has to tighten its belt in hard times, so must the government'. Both convictions reflect pre-Keynesian understandings of the economy, as though Keynes' conceptual breakthroughs about aggregate demand had never been made.

6.4 Economists' Intellectual Defence of Inequality

Generations of economists have provided intellectual justification for neglecting inequality and even opposing efforts to rein it in. If any profession could have raised the salience of inequality, economists could have. Instead, their modal stance on inequality is close to the one enunciated by Willem Buiter (2007): 'Poverty bothers me. Inequality does not. I just don't care.'

Economists have defended inequality with two instrumental (not moral) arguments. The first stems from the conception of the market as a *coordination* mechanism, allocating scarce resources to competing ends (Roemer 2011). Equilibrium prices in a competitive market (assuming no externalities or public goods) produce a Pareto-efficient allocation of resources. In particular, a competitive labour market produces the optimal functional income distribution, such that each factor of production earns the value of its marginal productivity. The relative remuneration of banker, bishop, and refuse collector must be fair, provided markets are competitive. This is comforting for the banker and the bishop.[3]

Extending this proposition from the model to the real world, mainstream economists tend to presume that any 'political' interference with the market-determined income distribution has efficiency costs, just like any other interference with the price system (managed exchange rates, tariffs, credit subsidies, industrial policy), and that the efficiency costs of political interference in market-determined income distribution are typically large. The premise is that 'markets may be imperfect, but governments are even more imperfect'. A senior advisor at the British Treasury remarked, critically, that when any policy proposal under discussion prompted the words 'price distortion' it was more or less dead in the water (personal communication, 2011).

To people not steeped in neoliberal economics this argument has some way to go before it can even be called simplistic; but it has commanded wide emotional agreement among economists, because it fits so well with mathematically tractable models of competitive markets as the core institution of a moral and prosperous society.

Economists' second instrumental justification for inequality is based on the conception of the market as a mechanism of *incentives* for the development of skills and innovation—or a mechanism for resource creation as distinct from resource allocation. Only by allowing individuals to keep most of the market value they (claim to) help to create will they be diligent and creative. The assumption is that individuals choose neither their occupations nor their balance between 'work' and 'leisure' on the basis of *intrinsic* satisfactions, but only on the basis of extrinsic material rewards. If they are allowed to retain a large fraction of the added value they help to produce, they will choose occupations that add more value to society and will choose more work and less leisure. Then their hard work and creativity will rebound to the benefit of the rest of the society, including the poor, through 'trickle-down'.

Underpinning these two arguments is the neoliberal conception of a capitalist economy as composed of a private and a public sector, the private sector and production for the market being the domain of the 'economic' (and 'natural') and the public sector and production of public goods being the domain of the 'non-economic' (and 'artificial'). This conception of the economy goes with the definition of economics as the study of choices under scarcity; as Lionel Robbins famously put it, 'Economics is a social science

---

[3] A fellow of the Institute of Development Studies at Sussex University sat next to the most senior civil servant at the Department for International Development at a dinner. The fellow told the permanent secretary that he [the fellow] could immediately double his salary by going to work for a specified firm for which he had been consulting. The secretary assured him, 'You must do it! You would double your contribution to society.'

which studies human behaviour as a relationship between ends and scarce means which have alternative uses.' The corresponding conception of society is a set of rationally self-maximizing individuals (or rats) competing with each other for scarce resources and learning, if at all, only by doing and not from each other. Altruism, community, cooperation, and solidarity feature only as means of obtaining scarce resources.

Economics education, especially in Anglo-American universities (among which are the world's top-ranked universities), inculcates individualism-based constructs. Teaching of the history of economic thought and comparative economic systems, which might expose students to other conceptions of economics, largely disappeared from university syllabuses as the Cold War wound down.[4] Strangely, the mainstream economics profession rarely talks of 'capitalism', referring instead to 'the market system', which makes it easier to avoid the literature on the inherent instabilities and unequalizing tendencies of capitalism. The upshot is that the (correct) proposition that some inequality of income and wealth is necessary and desirable tends to anaesthetize economists to the costs of inequality—economic, social, health, and political.

6.5 Right-Wing Think Tanks

Intellectual work to justify inequality and broadcast the rationale was going on long before the Reagan/Thatcher policy shifts. An active right-wing movement created well-endowed think tanks, such as the Hoover Foundation (1919), the American Enterprise Institute (1943), the Mont Pelerin Society (1947), and the Cato Institute, the Heritage Foundation, and the Manhattan Institute (all founded in the 1970s). The movement also financed advocates in other organizations, including political parties and university departments (Phillips-Fein 2009; Roemer 2011). As inequality began to rise in the late 1970s these organizations were ready to squash critics with arguments such as 'you are just practising the politics of envy', 'you are just being a spiteful egalitarian', and to advocate 'the market' as an efficient coordination and incentive mechanism.

---

[4] Asked what attainments contribute to success in the profession, only 3 per cent of 212 graduate students in American economics departments said that 'having a thorough knowledge of the economy' was 'very important', and 68 per cent said it was 'unimportant' (Colander and Klamer 1987). The argument of Frey and Eichenberger (1993) leads one to expect that continental European graduate students would rate knowledge of the economy more highly. However, the economics taught in the most prestigious European economics departments tends to be hard-line neoclassical/American economics. Girts Racko (2011) finds that Latvian students being educated at the Swedish Economics School in Riga, known for its hard-line neoclassical/American approach, acquired over two years much stronger beliefs in free markets and associated norms than a matched pool of students being educated at Latvian universities—including the belief that their beliefs had a strictly scientific non-ideological foundation.

Most of the thousands of groups that call themselves free-market or conservative think tanks refuse to disclose their sources of funding. But we know enough to know that they typically act as sophisticated corporate lobbying groups, cooperating to promote the views of the people who fund them. One expert has explained why such think tanks are more effective than other public-relations agencies:

> They are 'the source of many of the ideas and facts that appear in countless editorials, news articles, and syndicated columns'. They have 'considerable influence and close personal relationships with elected officials'. They 'support and encourage one another, echo and amplify their messages, and can pull together...coalitions on the most important public policy issues'. Crucially, they are 'virtually immune to retribution...the identify of donors to thinktanks is protected from involuntary disclosure'. (Jeff Judson, quoted in Monbiot 2011a)

The left has developed few equivalents to the well-endowed right-wing think tanks—seen in the fact that the mild-mannered centre-of-the-road Brookings Institution in Washington DC is regarded as the USA's most prominent 'centre-left' think tank.

Media ownership and media bias run overwhelmingly in favour of the conservative worldview. The British newspaper-reading public, for example, is exposed to a foghorn of right-wing opinion. Over the 2000s the right-wing national newspapers accounted for about 75 per cent of sales, the non-right-wing ones (including *The Financial Times*), 25 per cent.

The right-wing bias in the idea-generating and -promulgating organizations, coupled with the marginalization of mass trade unions, leaves the bulk of the population more exposed to anti-tax, anti-state, anti-solidarity ideology than in the post-war decades. With the track-switches in the hands of those providing intellectual justification for inequality, 'interests' of the rich pull public policies and institutions in the direction of income and wealth concentration at the top.

6.6 Centre-Left Political Tactics

Given the prevailing configuration of interests, organizations, and ideologies, centre-left parties made a tactical choice.[5] In the words of Roger Liddle (2007: 2), one of the principal ideologues of the British New Labour Party:

> In the mid-1990s, the leaders of New Labour made a fundamental policy choice. In government [they had been out of government since 1979] they would not explicitly prioritize a lessening of inequalities between top and bottom. Instead

---

[5] My thanks to Carlos Fortin for emphasizing this point.

their social justice priorities would be to tackle poverty, worklessness and economic and social exclusion.

Several reasons were clearly important in Labour making this choice. [...] [First, a sense] that intellectually Thatcherite neoliberalism was triumphant, and that the post-war welfare state consensus had irretrievably broken down and could only be rebuilt on a basis that incentivised (and did not penalize) hard work at all levels of society.

[Second], New Labour...seized on the discourse of globalization to provide a deeper intellectual rationale. [...] New Labour portrayed globalization as an inexorable force of nature beyond political control—making irrelevant old egalitarian and interventionist social democratic responses and requiring a thorough rethink of the means of achieving social justice, if not a redefinition of its goals.

But it was not just a matter of tactics. Leading centre-left figures really did believe in a vision of a moral society close to that of conservatives: one in which, to quote two British theorists of the 'Third Way', 'the key to justice as fairness can be seen in terms of the procedural securing of *opportunities* rather than a substantive commitment to patterned relative outcomes' (Buckler and Dolowitz 2000, emphasis added).

Another leading intellectual on the British centre-left, Will Hutton, likewise defines 'fairness' as rewarding individuals in proportion to the amount of discretionary effort they deploy to achieve socially useful results, provided they actually achieve them. The aim of a centre-left government should be to make access to riches dependent on 'talent, effort and virtue', as distinct from making outcomes more equal (Hutton 2010).

6.7 The Intellectual Case for Curbing Top-End Inequality

Academics on the centre-left can help to build a cross-class consensus for a more equal society by challenging more actively the intellectual arguments of the inequality defenders—so providing justification for pulling the switches in the other direction.

Moral criteria aside, we can ask questions such as 'Is the present degree of income inequality necessary for good economic performance?', 'Is it efficient?', and 'Are its negative societal spillovers small?'. These questions take the debate onto the same terrain as the inequality champions, engaging them on their own terms. We can bring a range of evidence to bear about the effects of different degrees of top-end inequality. The following points give no more than an indication of some of the evidence.

First, a standard argument of the inequality defenders is that sizeable top-level inequality (implicitly, close to the US level) is necessary to generate the innovation, corporate management, and productivity from which the whole population benefits. The figures given earlier on the divergence between the Anglo-American economies and the continental European and Japanese economies in the share of the top 1 per cent after 1980 challenge this proposition given that the performance of the Anglo-American economies was not noticeably better (Alvaredo et al. 2012).

Second, at the microeconomic level, it is simply implausible that top-end income recipients in the Anglo-American countries would be less productive at Scandinavian levels of post-tax remuneration relative to the median—implausible that at Scandinavian levels of remuneration they would retire and play golf. Can it be seriously argued that without a more than 40 per cent increase in remuneration in one year, FY2010, the CEOs of FTSE100 companies would have steered their companies less productively, or that—had they decamped to Switzerland or Hong Kong in protest—their replacements would have done so?

Third, Daniel Kahneman suggests that the apparent success of financial high-fliers is a cognitive illusion. In one study he followed twenty-five wealth advisors over eight years and found that the success of their advice 'resembled what you would expect from a dice-rolling contest, not a game of skill'. They can hardly be described as 'deserving rich'. Their riches are undeserved—that is, too big (Kahneman 2011; Monbiot 2011b).

Fourth, research on financial fragility shows a strong link with income inequality, suggesting that inequality above a certain level is *macroeconomically inefficient*, in that it raises the probability of financial crisis and economic slump (Lansley 2011). Above a certain level of inequality, economies tend to become 'debt-intensive', because the other side of income concentration at the top is stagnant or falling incomes lower down. In the face of stagnant incomes, a 'common interest' develops among firms, households, politicians, and financial regulators to allow private debt to fill the gaps between (i) the demand supported by incomes, (ii) the demand generated by aspirations to participate in the boom, and (iii) the demand needed to utilize productive capacity.

Fifth, the huge returns to financial operations distort business incentives, channelling investment away from productive uses into redistributive uses such as mergers and acquisitions, private equity funds, property and financial engineering, which focus more on transfers of ownership of existing assets rather than creation of new ones.

Sixth, high concentrations of income and wealth propel 'state capture', such that finance comes increasingly to dominate the state apparatus and the democratic process more generally, as discussed earlier.

Today, the power of Wall Street and the City of London remains largely intact despite the financial crash and economic slump. The initial effort at a great re-regulation of finance has for the most part turned into the 'great escape' (see the Dobbs–Frank Act and Volcker Rule in the USA, and the Vickers Report in the UK).[6] In the USA the dominance of monied interests has been accentuated by the recent Supreme Court decision (Citizens United) to grant the same 'freedom of speech' to corporations as to individuals, opening the floodgates to business purchase of politicians. This has come on top of the absence of limits to paid political campaign advertisements in the media, or of a requirement on every broadcast/cable/satellite provider to give equal time to major parties and candidates.

6.8 Conclusion

The sharp increase in income concentration at the top of national income distributions over the past two to three decades should have prompted a large body of social science research and public debate about the questions 'What are the costs of inequality?' and 'When are the rich too rich?'. Instead, the response has been muted, both in academia and in politics (except with reference to particular bosses seen to have failed at their job who nevertheless receive giant golden-handshakes). Inequality is kept in the background because of the wide acceptance of the idea that whatever distribution results from 'free markets' must be better than what results from 'government intervention' (beyond the limits of welfare transfers and tax exemptions for 'deserving poor').

How has the free-market ideology exercised such gravitational influence over policy? How have mega-corporations and dependent intellectuals been able to use the ideology as a conceit to hide the powerful influence of these

---

[6] A more extended account of the effects of vertical inequality should consider the evidence on health and social problems amassed by Wilkinson and Pickett (2009), drawn from twenty or so rich countries and across the fifty US states. They find that countries and states with higher income inequality tend to have lower life expectancy, higher infant mortality, more mental illness, more obesity, higher rates of teen births, more murder, less trust, and less upward mobility. More remarkably, they find (with less evidence) that countries and states with higher income inequality vary from those with lower inequality not only in terms of averages but also in terms of the frequency of the above 'problems' in the top income decile. In other words, higher levels of inequality act like a pollutant throughout the society. As for the magnitude of the effect, a study of mortality and inequality in 282 standard metropolitan areas of the USA found that 'Areas with high income inequality and low average income had excess mortality of 139.8 deaths per 100,000 compared with areas with low inequality and high income. The magnitude of this mortality difference is comparable to the combined loss of life from lung cancer, diabetes, motor vehicle crashes, human immunodeficiency virus (HIV) infection, suicide, and homicide in 1995' (Lynch et al. 1998). Among the rich countries, reducing inequality is the most powerful means for extending life expectancy (beyond the mysterious increase of two or three years for every decade that passes).

corporations in shaping public policy and rigging the 'free market' to their advantage?

In this chapter I have asked the more specific question of why electorates have acquiesced as the concentration of income and wealth at the top increased. Of the several factors discussed, I recap just three. First, economists, who constitute the most influential profession in shaping norms of public policy, are trained to presume that inequality is an *inevitable* outcome of the market as a coordinating mechanism, and a *necessary* outcome for the market to function as an incentive mechanism; and this presumption then marginalizes questions such as 'When are the rich too rich?'.

Second, middle and upper-middle classes have managed to protect their share of national income in many countries as the share of the top few percentiles rises, putting a disproportionate cut on the politically marginal bottom 40 per cent. This helps to diffuse middle-class anger at the rise of the super-rich, as does the fact that the middle class is rising relative to the bottom 40 per cent. Also, neoliberal fiscal policy packages normally include tax cuts from which they benefit. And they hear talk of 'redistribution' as meaning that they would have to pay higher taxes, which would fund benefits to the 'undeserving poor'. For these and other reasons the middle classes have not been responsive to centre-left parties trying to build a cross-class consensus for a more equal society in terms of both opportunities and outcomes. And so—the third factor—the centre-left parties differentiate themselves from conservatives by being more concerned about 'poverty', but not more concerned about 'inequality'.

Analysts on the centre-left can help to build a cross-class consensus for a more equal society by providing a sound intellectual basis for advocating more equal outcomes than exist in the Anglo-American economies. Part of this basis is the proposition that top-level income concentration at present levels is neither inevitable nor necessary for efficiency and creativity. Now, in the midst of a severe economic slump, minds may be more open to inequality-challenging arguments than in the past—for example, more open to understanding how the stagnation of income in most parts of the income distribution below the top contributed to a shortfall of aggregate demand, which was offset by rising consumption financed by easy credit, paving the way for the crisis (Wade 2011a).

The question remains of how to persuade political leaders and opinion-makers such as the World Bank to focus on inequality as a problem, separate from poverty. The short answer is that until radical changes are made in how political parties and candidates fund themselves, or until several more multi-country crashes have roiled the world economy, or until a mass revolt against oligarchic rule, or until the donors to political parties realize that they would better serve their own interest by not pressing for tax cuts and deregulation, inequality will remain on the margins of public policy even as corporate power and top-end income share remain at current or even higher levels of concentration. But at least we can strike a small blow for accurate description. When financiers and rentiers are able to privatize profits and to immunize themselves from losses (as in Robert Rubin's justification for banks that are 'too big to fail'), and when they and other wealthy entities are able to shape public policies to their liking through political-party financing and revolving-door appointments, our system is no longer 'democratic capitalism', but rather 'oligarchic impunity capitalism'.

References

Alvaredo, F., A. B. Atkinson, T. Piketty, and E. Saez (2012). *The World Top Incomes Database*. Available at: <http://www.g-mond.parisschoolofeconomics.eu/topincomes/>.

Bresser-Pereira, L. C. (2012). *Post-Crisis Developmentalist Pact?*. Personal communication, 11 September. Available at: <http://www.bresserpereira.org.br/Articles/2012/85.Pacto_desenvolvimentista_pos-crise-Trad.pdf>.

Brooks, D. (2011). 'The Wrong Inequality'. *International Herald Tribune*, 2 November.

Buckler, S. and D. Dolowitz (2000). 'Theorizing the Third Way'. *Journal of Political Ideologies*, 5(3): 309.

Buiter, W. (2007). 'Economists Forum'. *Financial Times*, 14 February.

Coghalan, A. and D. MacKenzie (2011). 'Revealed—the Capitalist Network that Runs the World. *New Scientist*, 19 October.

Colander, D. and A. Klamer (1987). 'The Making of an Economist'. *Journal of Economic Perspectives*, 1(Fall): 100.

Dash, E. (2011). 'Way out the Door Still Paved in Gold for Some US Executives'. *International Herald Tribune*, 1–2 October.

Farrant, A. and E. McPhail (2010). 'Does F. A. Hayek's *Road to Serfdom* Deserve to Make a Comeback?'. *Challenge*, July–August: 96–120.

Feldstein, M. (1998). 'Is Income Inequality Really a Problem?'. Paper presented to symposium sponsored by the Federal Reserve Bank of Kansas 'Income Inequality Issues and Policy Options', Jackson Hole, WY, 27–29 August.

Frank, T. (2011). *Pity the Billionaire*. London: Harvill Secker.

Frey, B. and R. Eichenberger (1993). 'American and European Economics and Economists'. *Journal of Economic Perspectives*, 7(4): 185–93.

Goldfarb, J. (2011). 'The Sweet Life of the 0.001 Per Cent'. *International Herald Tribune*, 15 November.

Hutton, W. (2010). *Them and Us: Changing Britain—Why We Need a Fair Society*. London: Little Brown.

Kahneman, D. (2011). *Thinking, Fast and Slow*. London: Allen Lane.

Kampfner, J. (2011). 'The Wealthy Should Pay More Tax. Why Has It Taken So Long?'. *The Independent*, 26 August.

Krugman, P. (2012a). 'Superlow Taxes at the Top'. *International Herald Tribune*, 21–22 January.

Krugman, P. (2012b). 'Moochers against Welfare'. *International Herald Tribune*, 18–19 February.

Lakoff, G. (2002). *Moral Politics: How Liberals and Conservatives Think* (2nd edition). Chicago: University of Chicago Press.

Lansley, S. (2011). 'Tinkering on the Brink'. *The Guardian*, 5 October.

Liddle, R. (2007). *Creating a Culture of Fairness. A Progressive Response to Income Inequality in Britain*. London: Policy Network.

Lucas, R. (2004). 'The Industrial Revolution: Past and Present'. 2003 Annual Report Essay. Minneapolis: The Federal Reserve Bank of Minneapolis.

Lynch, J., G. A. Kaplan, E. R. Pamuk, et al. (1998). 'Income Inequality and Mortality in Metropolitan Areas of the United States'. *American Journal of Public Health*, 88(7): 1074–80.

Monbiot, G. (2011a). 'Who Drives the So-Called Thinktanks Crushing Democracy for Corporations?'. *The Guardian*, 13 September.

Monbiot, G. (2011b). 'The 1% Are the Very Best Destroyers of Wealth the World Has Ever Seen'. *The Guardian*, 8 November.

New York Times (2011). 'The New Resentment of the Poor'. Editorial, *Times Digest*, 31 August.

Nozick, R. (1974). *Anarchy, State and Utopia*. New York: Basic Books.

Palma, J. G. (2009). 'The Revenge of the Market on the Rentiers'. *Cambridge Journal of Economics*, 33(4): 829–69.

Palma, J. G. (2011). 'Homogeneous Middles vs. Heterogeneous Tails, and the End of the 'Inverted-U'. *Development and Change*, 42(1): 87–153.

Phillips-Fein, K. (2009). *Invisible Hands: The Making of the Conservative Movement from the New Deal to Reagan*. New York: Norton.

Racko, G. (2011). 'On the Normative Consequences of Economic Rationality: A Case Study of a Swedish Economics School in Latvia'. *European Sociological Review*, 27(6): 772–89.

Rand, A. (1957). *Atlas Shrugged*. New York: Random House.

Roemer, J. (2011). 'Ideological and Political Roots of American Inequality'. *Challenge*, 54(5): 76–98.

Schauble, W. (2011). 'Austerity Is the Only Cure for the Eurozone'. *Financial Times*, 6 September.

Sharpe, M. (2012). 'The Corporation and the State against the Public'. *Challenge*, 56(1): 137–41.

Stewart, J. (2011). 'Failure in Business Should Be a Risk of Capitalism, not a Chance for Reward'. *International Herald Tribune*, 1–2 October.

Treanor, J. (2011). 'World's Wealthiest People Now Richer than Before the Credit Crunch: World Wealth Report Reveals Soaring Numbers of Rich Individuals in Asia Pacific Region—but Slower Growth in Britain'. *The Guardian*, 22 June.

UNCTAD (2012). *Trade and Development Report 2012*. Geneva: UNCTAD.

Von Mises, L. (1955). *Ideas on Liberty*. New York: Irvington.

Wade, R. H. (2004). 'On the Causes of Increasing World Poverty and Inequality, or Why the Matthew Effect Prevails'. *New Political Economy*, 9(2), 163–88.

Wade, R. H. (2006). 'Should We Worry about Income Inequality?'. In D. Held and A. Kaya (eds), *Global Inequality: Patterns and Explanations*. Cambridge: Polity Press, 104–31.

Wade, R. H. (2009). 'From Global Imbalances to Global Reorganizations'. *Cambridge Journal of Economics*, 33(4): 539–62.

Wade, R. H. (2011a). 'Global Trends in Income Inequality: What Is Happening and Should We Worry?'. *Challenge*, 54(5): 54–75.

Wade, R. H. (2011b). 'Globalization, Growth, Poverty, Inequality, Resentment and Imperialism'. In J. Ravenhill (ed.), *Global Political Economy* (3rd edition). Oxford: Oxford University Press, 372–415.

Wade, R. H., and S. Sigurgeirsdottir (2011). 'Iceland's Rise, Fall, Stabilization and Beyond'. *Cambridge Journal of Economics*, 36(1): 127–44.

Wilkinson, R. and K. Pickett (2009). *The Spirit Level*. London: Allen Lane.

7

Justice, Horizontal Inequality, and Policy in Multi-Ethnic Societies*

Frances Stewart

> Whichever way we look at it, we always return to the same con-
> clusion: namely that the social pact establishes equality among
> the citizens in that they all pledge themselves under the same
> conditions and all enjoy the same rights.
> Jean Jacques Rousseau (1762: 76)

Throughout his career, Richard Jolly's prime concern has been with poverty reduction and inequality. He regards inequality not only as presenting an important obstacle to the achievement of poverty reduction, but also as a source of injustice. Following this concern this chapter considers the issue of justice in heterogeneous societies, particularly in relation to horizontal (group) inequality.

While much attention has been given to inequality among individuals (vertical inequality) a critical issue in multi-ethnic societies is that of inequality across groups (horizontal inequality). The first part of this chapter contrasts the views of some philosophers and economists on the issue of vertical inequality and then attempts to draw some conclusions for horizontal inequality on the basis of their arguments. The conclusion of this part of the study is that, generally, multi-ethnic societies should aim to reduce inequalities across groups. The question then arises as to whether and when such redistribution is likely to gain support, particularly in the light of social psychologists' findings that people tend to see the 'scope of justice' as being mainly within their

* I am particularly grateful to Arnim Langer, who contributed greatly to the data collection in the second part of this chapter and gave very helpful comments on the chapter as a whole, to Patricia Espinoza for research assistance, and to Rolph van der Hoeven and Kristien Smedts for extremely helpful comments on a previous draft.

own identity group. The second part of the chapter reports on research on this issue using surveys in Kenya, Ghana, Nigeria, and Uganda.

7.1 Is Horizontal Equality Desirable?

There are many ways of approaching the complex question of why inequality is (or is not) undesirable both with respect to vertical inequality and to horizontal inequality. Different disciplines have taken different approaches. Philosophers start from basic principles and questions and explore the implications for equality arising from them. Conclusions differ according to the starting point. Economists are concerned to identify the distribution that maximizes accepted societal objectives, and their conclusions depend on how these objectives are defined, and how they are affected by different distributions.

Here, we explore three rather different philosophical approaches to the question of justice and distribution: first, those derived from a conception of what it means to be human (Kant 1785; Williams 1962); second, analysis of the implications of a posited social contract (Rousseau 1762; Rawls 1971); and third, the implications for distribution of giving primacy to libertarian principles (Locke 1689; Nozick 1974).[1]

The first approach, derived from the conception of common humanity, leads to an egalitarian conclusion in some respects, but people differ over the relevant domain that common humanity implies. For Kant, it consists in 'respect': 'equality of respect' is owed to everybody as rational moral agents ('treat humanity... in every case as an end, never as a means'). A difficult and controversial issue is how this should be interpreted in terms of the distribution of resources. It is arguable that the distribution of material resources has relevance to equality of respect; inequalities of wealth tend to be associated with inequality of respect, as wealthy people often treat others as of a lower order, and their wealth enables them to order poorer members of society around, including commanding their labour. Hence treating people as ends, never as means, does have egalitarian *material* content, although it clearly need not involve complete equality. How much inequality is consistent with equality of respect is likely to vary across cultures. Light could be shed on this by empirical investigations into the determinants of respect for others.

Williams also starts with a focus on people's common humanity. Although people are not equal in every respect, he argues that they are equal in capacity to feel and in their 'moral capacity'. But does this necessarily imply equality of resource distribution? He argues that it implies that any difference in

---

[1] Locke and Kant could also, of course, be placed in the contractarian category.

treatment must have justification and relevance: he distinguishes between goods demanded by need, exemplified by illness (the need) and medical treatment (the good), and goods distributed according to merit, exemplified by the capacity to benefit from university education (the merit) and university education (the good). For *needs* goods, there is a presumption of equality of treatment for all those with equal need; while for the merit goods, he argues that *equality of opportunity* is justified. Williams's principle of distribution according to need could be interpreted as supporting the universal provision of basic-needs goods and services, as advocated in the basic-needs approach to development (ILO 1976; Streeten et al. 1981; Stewart 1985), while the 'merit' part could be interpreted as broadly equivalent to Roemer's equality of opportunity (Roemer (1998), discussed below).

The fundamental principle behind human-rights approaches to development is the view that every person is morally equal and consequently entitled to certain basic rights. A human-rights approach implies equality in access to certain basic goods (adequate nutrition, housing, water, education, etc.); so long as these rights are realized, the human-rights approach is consistent with inequality in access to non-basic goods and services.

The second approach to be considered is the principle of distribution derived from a social contract. Rousseau argued that the social contract establishes 'equality among citizens' because 'they all pledge themselves under the same conditions and all enjoy the same rights', and his interpretation of this was that 'no citizen shall be rich enough to buy another and none so poor as to be forced to sell himself' (Rousseau 1762: 96). Rawls gives a more rigorous and detailed interpretation of distributional principles, derived from a social contract drawn up under a 'veil of ignorance'. The first Rawlsian principle is that everyone should have basic liberties, such as political liberty, freedom of speech, etc. The second is the 'difference principle':

> Social and economic inequalities are to satisfy two conditions: first, they are to be attached to offices and positions open to all under conditions of fair equality of opportunity (the principle of fair equality of opportunity); and second that they are to be to the greatest benefit of the least advantaged members of society (the difference principle). (Rawls 2001: 42–3)

Accordingly, equality of distribution is just, *unless it can be shown that the position of the poorest would be better in an unequal situation*, which would only occur if inequality raised growth to such an extent that the poor received more than in an equal situation. Whether inequality does indeed improve the position of the poorest, and how much inequality is optimal, is an empirical question that may differ across contexts. Rawls states that his principles are those that people would arrive at in a 'well ordered society': they apply within nations (our concern here) but not between them. In order to explore the implications for heterogeneous societies, we assume, perhaps controversially, that each such country qualifies as 'well ordered'.

The Locke/Nozick approach espouses the most inequality, since just outcomes for them are the outcomes that result from *just processes*, which may be consistent with high inequality. For Locke, property is a natural right, so long as it is acquired by a person's own labour.[2] Nozick drops the direct link with a person's labour, and argues that just outcomes are those that result from *legitimate* acquisition and transfer of goods and services. Since according to Nozick legitimate transfer includes bequests, any inequality, which may emerge even from an equal starting point, can lead to considerable and rising, yet just, inequality. Instrumental consequences of such inequality are not considered relevant. However, there is one major exception to this unconstrained situation. This is the principle of rectification that 'comes into play' if resources are not obtained legitimately. As Nozick accepts, 'Some people steal from others, or defraud them, or enslave them' (1974: 152). Where the resources were not acquired legitimately, including where inherited resources stem from illegitimate acquisition, 'rectification' (i.e. redistribution) is justified according to Nozick. How far this justifies redistribution depends on the interpretation of 'legitimate acquisition'. If one includes resources obtained by force, corrupt practices, and so on, the principle of rectification could apply extensively, thereby modifying the inegalitarian conclusions of this approach.

In sum, the assumption of common humanity, which can be interpreted as justifying a human-rights perspective, implies that everyone should have access to certain basic goods, which moderates inequality compared with laissez-faire outcomes; Rawls's social contract concludes that inequality is justified only if it improves the position of the poorest; and the process-focused approach of the libertarians tolerates any inequality that arises from *legitimate* processes, but not those that have their origins in illegitimate processes.

In general, economists consider inequality from both an intrinsic and an instrumental perspective. The intrinsic perspective is similar to and draws on philosophers' arguments about the justice of different distributions. The instrumental perspective (also implicit in some philosophers' conclusions, notably Rawls's) concerns how far inequality/equality affects other accepted objectives.

Utilitarianism, which forms the basis of much of economics, implies that the extent of inequality should depend on which distribution maximizes

---

[2] Locke (1689). Interpreting this principle becomes complicated if production involves machinery, employing people, and so on. Although it is normally interpreted as justifying property ownership and inequality, it could also be interpreted as a redistributory principle, involving a labour theory of value and ownership rights (Vaughan 1978).

utility, *irrespective of its distribution*. Pigou argues that this led to a highly egalitarian conclusion assuming that a person's marginal utility would diminish as they acquired more of it (Pigou 1920); but this assumption was famously disputed by Robbins, who argues that one cannot compare the utility gained by different individuals on the basis that 'in our hearts we do not regard different men's satisfactions from similar means as equally valuable' (Robbins 1938; 1945: 156–7). Robbins's argument was widely accepted, and economists since then have mainly shied away from making judgments about the desirable degree of inequality except from an instrumental perspective. This view was reinforced by those economists, such as Hayek, with libertarian views about the undesirability of restraints on individual actions.

Nonetheless, economists accept that there are instrumental considerations influencing the desirable distribution, with the optimal distribution being that which would maximize efficiency and output. A certain amount of vertical inequality may be needed, for example, to encourage people to work hard, use their talents, and direct their energies in a way that exploits their comparative advantage and maximizes societal output. But there is also an efficiency case *against* too much inequality—since it can reduce societal human capital, as poorer people are likely be more undernourished and undereducated, while highly unequal income distribution may reduce the size of domestic markets (leading to under-consumption and unemployment, though there are ways, of course, of compensating for this). Moreover, the converse point is often made: that inequality promotes savings. Thus there are efficiency arguments both for and against vertical inequality. This conclusion is supported by the findings of Cornia (2004), who has plotted inequality (as measured by the Gini coefficient of income) against growth of GDP per capita for 1960–98, which shows a concave relationship with growth rising as inequality increases from very low levels, and then declining with a further increase in inequality. One plausible conclusion from economists' instrumentalism is that the objective should not be *equality of outcomes* but *equality of opportunities* since, in principle, one would expect efficiency to be maximized if everyone faces the same opportunities (Roemer 1998).

There is an interesting similarity and contrast between the efficiency arguments of economists and those of philosophers (notably Rawls). Rawls starts with the presumption that equality is desirable but that *inequality* may be justified if it serves, instrumentally via efficiency effects, to improve the position of the *poorest* compared with an egalitarian situation. Economists, in contrast, argue that greater *equality* may be justified (compared with a market outcome) if it serves to improve the position of at least one person and not to worsen that of any other—or (allowing for compensation) if it raises national income, without regard to the consequences for the poorest.

Other instrumental reasons relate to societal effects, which may in turn affect output. For example, high vertical inequality tends to increase criminality, and this may lead to a reduction in investment and output. Moreover, inequality may be undesirable because it impedes the objective of reducing poverty. The implications of these instrumental reasons for redistribution depend on empirical relationships. For example, does inequality increase or reduce growth? Does it increase criminality? Does increased crime reduce growth? Is reducing inequality the most effective way of reducing poverty? (See, for example, Krahn et al. 1986; Alesina and Rodrik 1994; Persson and Tabellini 1994; Brush 2007; Bourguignon 2003; Eicher and Turnovsky 2003.)

Both the philosophers and economists cited above were mainly concerned with vertical rather than horizontal inequality. Here, we want to retrace the arguments, but consider them in relation to group or horizontal inequality. Our concern is with salient identity groups, including religious, racial, ethnic and gender groups. Despite the fluidity of group boundaries and their 'social-constructedness', these are groups that often form the basis of discrimination, and among which large inequalities are frequently observed. Here, we are not exploring what the various thinkers actually said about group equality, but rather are analysing whether one might come to different conclusions if we substitute groups for individuals in the arguments advanced by each approach.

There is not much to add to the first philosophical perspective—i.e. 'humans should be equal because they are human'—when taking a group perspective. The arguments of Kant and Williams essentially apply to individuals, and to groups only as consisting of a collection of individuals. However, in considering groups, one question that is much debated is whether group rights should be recognized as well as individual rights—for example, if there is a group right to the preservation of a culture/religion/language that goes beyond the rights of individuals to follow particular customs, practise a particular religion, or speak a particular language; and if there is, where there is a conflict between individual rights (e.g. not to speak a particular language) and group rights, which should have supremacy. We do not discuss these important issues here.

With respect to the social-contract approach of Rawls, applying a group perspective would imply maximin applied to groups (as well as individuals). It seems likely that this would lead to more egalitarian conclusions for groups than when applied to individuals, particularly where there are large numbers of individuals in both the poorest group and the rest of society. This is because where there are large numbers of people in both groups, an uneven distribution of talent or attitudes across groups is unlikely and consequently special incentives are unlikely to be needed for the privileged group(s) *as a whole* in order to increase total output so that the position of the poorest group improves. Consequently, maximin is unlikely to imply significant amounts of inequality across groups. This conclusion is reinforced when we recognize that the wellbeing of the poorest groups—or their freedoms—includes 'freedom to go about without shame', or self-esteem, and this freedom is likely to be debased rather than increased by a situation in which the privileged group(s) forge ahead leaving the poorest group behind. While for individuals in a society without marked differences in identities (a 'homogeneous' society) it is reasonable to assume a range of talents and of work propensities and tastes across individuals, so that special incentives may be needed to achieve maximum gains for the poorest individuals involving some vertical inequality, when we apply maximin to groups containing large numbers, a dispersion of talents and work propensities that would justify special incentives and inequalities *across* groups is less likely. Against this, it might be argued that some group cultures are disposed to a greater taste for leisure, for less ambition, less hard work, etc., and thus we might indeed observe such a dispersion across groups at a particular point in time. The question then is whether—if we do observe such differences—they are due to independent cultural differences, or rather to unequal treatment of group members over a long period. The latter is suggested by analysis of the origins of group inequalities (Stewart and Langer 2008). Nonetheless, if there is some genuine difference of cultural attitudes across groups—not due to a history of oppression and discrimination—maximin across groups may involve some group inequality, but this is still likely to be less than the inequality implied by the maximin principle when applied to individuals. However, Rawls's focus on the poorest individual must not be forgotten: if attaining group equality meant worsening the position of the poorest *person,* this would contradict the maximin principle. Consequently, any moves towards group equality must not worsen the position of the poorest person.

The third philosophical approach discussed is the most inegalitarian: i.e. Nozick's concern with property rights and exchange as a basis for just distribution. However, even this apparently highly inegalitarian approach may be interpreted in a much more egalitarian fashion when one takes a group as against an individual viewpoint. The reason is that much group inequality stems from unjust treatment at some prior (and often current) time: indigenous peoples generally had their lands taken from them; blacks in the USA were slaves; poorer groups in many African countries were discriminated against by the colonial authorities and then again by the independent governments; women as a group have been oppressed for millennia, often treated as near-slaves, forbidden property rights, etc. These injustices may no long exist (or exist only partially), but Nozick's principle of rectification still applies because many of those who are now privileged inherited some or all of their privilege from people in previous generations who did not acquire their initial resources legitimately. There is a general presumption, indeed, that this is the case with *all* inequalities between sizeable groups, because why otherwise would they be unequal?

Turning to economists' approaches, the egalitarian conclusion of Pigou was rejected by Robbins because he argues it is impossible to know whether one person gets more satisfaction from their resources than another. Maybe this is so, and some people have greater sensitivity so that they get more utility out of a given amount of income than some less sensitive person— although current happiness research does not support this view (Kahneman et al. 2006; Sacks et al. 2010).[3] But this is much more difficult to argue across groups that consist of large numbers of people: can we really assert that one identity group (blacks or women, for example) get less out of a certain income than others (whites or men), and on what basis? But if we reject such a clearly racist and sexist view, then we must reject Robbins's 'refutation' of Pigou, and consequently, from a utilitarian perspective, become egalitarians for group distribution.

The efficiency rationale for inequality might remain, but the same arguments that applied to the maximin approach apply here. When we are dealing with groups consisting of large numbers of individuals, there is no justification for assuming differences in talent and taste that would justify significant inequality. Moreover, the societal instrumental reasons for equality—for example, that they affect criminality and violence and thus impede economic growth—are also particularly strong for group inequality, given the consistent evidence that horizontal inequalities raise the risk of conflict (Østby 2008; Stewart 2008; Cederman et al. 2011).

This is much the same conclusion as Roemer (1998) and others come to in considering 'equality of opportunities' across individuals. If equality of opportunities is defined as equality of all factors over which the individual has no control, then virtually all group inequalities represent inequality of opportunities—since for most identity groups (race/gender/ethnicity) a person has little or no choice over the group to which they belong. Hence any inequality due to membership of that group represents inequality of opportunity. This might seem inconsistent with the conclusions of many econometric exercises identifying the contribution of identity to inequality in wages, for example, which usually show that only a portion of inequality is to be 'explained' by identity. But these exercises generally also include a number of variables, such as education or nutrition, to account

---

[3] Because of adaptive expectations and preferences, the results of happiness research should not necessarily be taken as a guide to distributional policy, since happiness reported depends (to some extent) on current circumstances.

for differences in outcomes, and attribute only the residual differences in returns to group membership. Yet cumulative disadvantage and advantage over generations means that these other variables—including education, health, etc.—are unequally distributed due to group membership (Stewart and Langer 2008). Adopting this perspective, differences in group outcomes can be used as an indicator of differences in opportunities. This, in fact, is broadly the approach adopted by Paes de Barros et al. (2009).

In summary, exploring the distributional conclusions of the philosophers and economists reviewed here suggests that it is difficult to find justification for much group inequality, and consequently societies should aim broadly for group equality, even if they tolerate some individual inequality as being justified from the perspective of efficiency (or by a libertarian approach). These egalitarian arguments apply where the groups in question include large numbers of individuals. As groups get smaller, they approximate more to individuals, and the justifications for some inequality from an efficiency perspective become relevant. We conclude that there are stronger arguments to support the view that justice requires equality across groups than across individuals. This does not imply complete equality, but implies a reduction in inequality in most societies where we observe large horizontal inequalities.[4] However, any move towards greater group equality should not be at the expense of worsening the position of the poorest, following a Rawlsian approach.

7.2 Do People Support the Reduction of Horizontal Inequalities?

Although, as argued in Section 7.1, the case for promoting horizontal equality is strong, in practice there exist large horizontal inequalities in many heterogeneous societies (Stewart 2002). This section of the chapter investigates whether this is due to lack of public support for redistribution across groups.

Social psychologists have recently[5] suggested that people's view of justice (fair rules and fair distribution) may be related to their identity in two ways. First, cultural norms of fairness can differ across groups. Second, the 'scope

---

[4] For reasons of space we have not discussed the dimensions in which such inequality is to be assessed. This is brilliantly analysed by Sen (1980), who argues that 'capabilities' provide the appropriate space. We would suggest that a subset of functionings (rather than capabilities, because of measurement problems) is the appropriate space. The most important functionings to assess are those that are essential for, or supportive of, other functionings, which we might term the dominant or primary capabilities.

[5] Wenzel noted in 2000, 'In four decades of social psychological research on distributive justice, the relationship between justice and identity has been more or less neglected' (quoted in Clayton and Opotow (2003)).

of justice' or the 'moral community'—i.e. who is regarded as being within a moral community and subject to accepted conceptions of fair rules and fair distribution and who is morally excluded (outside the scope of justice) may be determined by group identity. It is argued that people tend to support justice within their own group, but less so for those they regard as 'others' (Wenzel 2000; Opotow 2001; Clayton and Opotow 2003). 'What is viewed as fair and unfair differs for groups that are inside or outside one's scope of justice' (Clayton and Opotow 2003: 304). 'Moral exclusion can make it seem fair that one's own group is better off (has more resources) than other groups' (Clayton and Opotow 2003: 305).[6] This view of how people perceive justice implies that they would be more favourable to redistribution within their own group, and less favourable to redistribution across groups. There is some intuitive plausibility about this. It is widely accepted that people identify above all with their own families and are happy to redistribute within them, but much less outside the family; and this may extend to greater willingness to redistribute within a particular identity group than across groups. The finding that expenditure on public goods falls as ethnic/racial fractionalization rises may be due to this attitude, with people less willing to support public expenditures that would benefit other identity groups (Alesina and Glaeser 2004; Alesina and La Ferrara 2005). The greater acceptability of progressive taxation and relief of poverty within a nation than across nations may stem from similar reasons.

If this view of the scope of justice is correct, an unfortunate paradox emerges: that group inequality is difficult to justify, yet people are more likely to favour redistribution *within* their own group, and less likely to favour it across groups, since their 'scope of justice' is focused on their own group, and other groups are excluded from this moral universe.

In order to explore the validity of this conclusion, we report on surveys of perceptions from four countries in Sub-Saharan Africa. The aim is to investigate whether there is, indeed, little support for redistribution across groups, as suggested by the social psychology literature just cited. Of course, people might oppose redistribution in general, irrespective of group, and we do not have evidence on this. Hence disagreement with redistribution across groups is not necessarily related to the issue of the 'scope of justice' of those surveyed; however, approval for redistribution across groups does imply that the moral community extends across groups.

---

[6] Walzer (1983) takes a similar approach, arguing that principles of justice apply only among people with shared group membership; but he assumes that all citizens of a particular country form part of a single membership group, so that heterogeneous groups within a nation would qualify so long as they have citizenship.

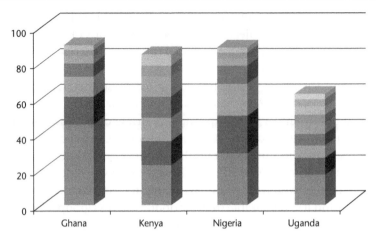

Figure 7.1 Ethnic composition of country: proportion of population in largest ethnic groups

Source: Derived from information contained in CIA World Factbook.

7.2.1 Attitudes Towards Redistribution in Four Heterogeneous Countries

This part of the study explores attitudes to redistributive policies in four African countries: Ghana, Kenya, Nigeria, and Uganda. Each is multi-ethnic and multi-religious, though the largest ethnic group in Ghana accounts for a much larger proportion of the population than in the other countries (Figure 7.1), while Nigeria is most evenly divided between Christians and Muslims, and Christians dominate in the other three countries (Figure 7.2). The issue of distribution across groups is relevant in each of these countries because of the presence of sharp horizontal inequalities (HIs). Tables 7.1–7.4 illustrate some prevailing socioeconomic HIs in the four countries by showing regional disparities with regard to a range of socioeconomic indicators, varying across the countries according to data availability.

NATURE OF SURVEYS AND VARIABLES EXPLORED

Surveys were carried out in major cities in each country in 2010–11 to investigate people's perceptions on a range of issues.[7] The surveys included a

---

[7] In Ghana, 324 people were randomly selected in Accra; in Nigeria, the survey was conducted among 412 randomly selected respondents in Lagos; and in Kenya (912 respondents) and Uganda (500), three sites were chosen in order to ensure representation of all major ethnic groups. The Kenyan survey covered Nairobi, Mombasa, and Nakuru, and the Ugandan one Kampala, Hoima (with 100), Mbarara, and Gulu (from the Central, Western, and Northern Regions). In all surveys, there was a 50–50 gender split and all respondents were 18 years or older. However, in each case, the surveys were in cities, so these results are not representative nationally, and particularly not of more isolated communities.

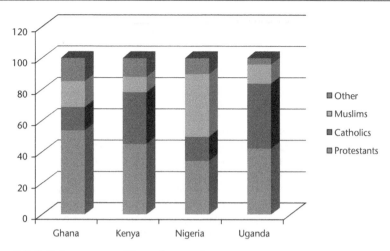

Figure 7.2 Religious composition of countries
Source: Derived from information contained in CIA World Factbook.

Table 7.1 Socioeconomic HIs in Kenya

Ratio to central province	Under-five mortality	Provincial health facilities	Secondary net enrolment rates		Spending on major roads, per person 1990–2000	Asset ownership, 2003[a]
			Boys	Girls		
Nyanza	3.81	0.74	0.96	0.63	0.4	0.54
Rift Valley	1.43	1.11	0.66	0.49	0.73	0.60
Western	2.67	0.44	0.75	0.63	0.33	0.52

Note: [a] The asset index is constructed as the sum of household ownership of five assets (television, car, motorbike, radio, refrigerator), with each asset weighted according to the proportion of the sample who do not own it.
Source: DHS (2003).

question on people's views of redistribution. Specifically, respondents were asked to what extent they agreed or disagreed with the following statement: 'The government should give extra economic assistance to the poorer ethnic groups'. The answering options were: strongly agree, agree, neither agree nor disagree, disagree, and strongly disagree. In the analysis below we include those who strongly agree with the view that the government should give economic assistance to poorer groups (REDCO). We excluded milder forms of agreement as many people might say they agree out of a sense of political correctness.

We identified a range of variables that appeared likely to be relevant to the question of the 'scope of justice'. These include gender, age, ethnic group, religion, poverty of the household, perception of being politically excluded, dissatisfaction with the position of the person's ethnic group, views of other

Table 7.2 Socioeconomic HIs in Ghana

Regions	Incidence of poverty 1				Infant mortality 2				Illiteracy 3	
	1998/99		2005/06		2003		2006		1998	
	%	Ratio (a)	%	Ratio (a)	%	Ratio (a)	%	Ratio (a)	%	Ratio (a)
Western	27.3	0.69	18.4	0.65	66	0.67	45	0.63	54	1.06
Central	48.4	1.23	19.9	0.70	142.1	1.44	69	0.97	55	1.08
Greater Accra	5.2	0.13	11.8	0.41	62	0.63	60	0.85	76	1.49
Volta	37.7	0.95	31.4	1.10	98	0.99	57	0.80	58	1.14
Eastern	43.7	1.11	15.1	0.53	89.1	0.90	61	0.86	66	1.29
Ashanti	27.7	0.70	20.3	0.71	78.2	0.79	72	1.01	64	1.25
Brong Ahafo	35.8	0.91	29.5	1.04	128.7	1.30	88	1.24	53	1.04
Northern	69.2	1.75	52.3	1.84	171.3	1.73	83	1.17	13	0.25
Upper East	88.2	2.23	70.4	2.47	155.6	1.57	68	0.96	20	0.39
Upper West	83.9	2.12	87.9	3.08	155.3	1.57	114	1.61	20	0.39
National	39.5	1.00	28.5	1.00	99	1.00	71	1.00	51	1.00

Note: ᵃ Ratio to the national average.
Sources: [1] Data derived from the Ghana Statistical Service, available at: <http://www.ghanainfo.org/> (accessed on 29 January 2008). [2] UNDP (2007: 35). Derived from DHS 1998.

Table 7.3 Socioeconomic HIs in Nigeria

	Infant mortality per 1000 live births	Under-five mortality per 1000 live births	Poverty rate, 2004, %
National	109	217	54.0
North-Central	103	165	67.0
North-East	125	260	72.2
North-West	114	269	71.2
South-East	66	103	26.7
South-South	120	103	35.1
South-East	69	113	43.0

Source: Derived from Higgins (2007).

groups, trust in people from other ethnic groups, loyalty to the nation and loyalty to a person's own ethnic group, inter-ethnic and inter-religious contacts, perceptions that ethnicity or religion is used in the public sphere (for example, in the allocation of government jobs), perceived treatment of a group by the government, and general dissatisfaction with government functioning. Details of the questions and how the answers were quantified are given in Appendix I.

Table 7.5 presents the average findings for the four countries. Some important observations from this are:

Table 7.4 Uganda: regional distribution of poverty, 1992–2003

	1992/93	1997	1999/00	2002/03	Change	
					1992/93–1999/00	1992/93–2002/03
Central	45.6	27.9	19.7	22.3	–25.9	–23.3
Eastern	58.8	54.3	35.0	46.0	–23.8	–12.8
Northern	72.2	60.9	63.6	63.3	–8.6	–8.9
Western	53.1	42.8	26.2	31.4	–26.9	–21.7

Source: Okidi et al. (2005: 5).

Table 7.5 Average findings from four surveys

	Ghana	Kenya	Nigeria	Uganda
REDECO	0.73	0.42	0.22	0.76
Male	0.51	0.50	0.50	0.43
Age	38.59	32.50	33.05	30.69
Yedu	10	12	12	11
Relig	0.19	0.15	0.42	0.15
Poverty	0.77	0.69	0.80	0.80
Dissat	0.33	0.21	0.16	0.37
polex1	0.29	0.30	0.22	0.49
polex2	0.02	0.04	0.02	0.05
polex3	0.18	0.20	0.19	0.36
Govfav	0.31	0.45	0.65	0.89
Inteth	0.60	0.63	0.64	0.64
Relpubd	0.40	0.32	0.28	0.32
Ethpubd	0.67	0.79	0.59	0.78
Nationident	0.14	0.26	0.11	0.09
Ethnicident	0.30	0.21	0.24	0.36
Ethcon	0.68	0.64	0.46	0.75
Relcon	0.51	0.61	0.47	0.80
Trust	0.54	0.42	0.55	0.61
Ethsatgov	0.50	Not asked	0.69	0.47
Disstate	0.52	Not asked	0.43	Not asked
Number of observations	324	907	412	500

- A high approval rate for economic redistribution towards other ethnic groups in Ghana and Uganda, with around three-quarters expressing strong approval, in contrast to a low rate in Nigeria of just 21.6 per cent, with Kenya in an intermediate position.
- In Uganda and Ghana, dissatisfaction with the position of a person's group was substantially above that in the other two countries, which

is interesting in view of the similarity of 'objective' inequalities (see Tables 7.1–7.4).

- Perceptions of political exclusion were markedly higher in Uganda than the other countries (almost half the sample saying they had less or much less influence than other groups). In the other countries, perhaps surprisingly in view of the differences in recent political histories, perceptions of political exclusion are rather similar.
- Coming to the questions relevant to the scope of justice:

  (a) First, perceptions of other ethnic groups are positive or very positive (INTETH) for over 60 per cent in each of the countries.

  (b) The proportion who trust in people from other ethnic groups (TRUST) is quite high, but below that for those with positive views of other groups, at 42 per cent for Kenya, 54 per cent and 55 per cent for Ghana and Nigeria respectively, and 61 per cent in Uganda. There is a surprisingly low correlation between these two variables.

  (c) Feeling *only* a national identity (NATION) is greatest in Kenya (but still only accounts for a quarter of the replies) and is just 9 per cent in Uganda; but feeling more national than ethnic (not shown in the table) applied to 36 per cent in Ghana, 58 per cent in Kenya, and just 25 per cent in Nigeria.

  (d) Those who feel more ethnic than national (including those who feel 'only' ethnic) (ETHNICID) accounted for over a fifth of the respondents in every country, and over a third in Uganda.

  (e) Perceptions of the importance of ethnicity in public life (ETHPUBD) are high. In Kenya and Uganda, nearly 80 per cent think ethnicity plays a role in the allocation of government jobs, contracts, and public housing, and in Ghana it is 67 per cent, both higher than the 59 per cent of Nigerian respondents, where ethnicity is, in fact, formally part of the process of allocation (Mustapha 2007). Religion is believed to play a smaller role in the governments' allocation of resources in all four countries.

  (f) High levels of intergroup contacts are shown, with most contacts in Uganda and fewest in Nigeria. The high level is not surprising, given the multi-ethnic nature of the sites surveyed.

- Satisfaction with the way a group is treated by the state (ETHSATGOV) was higher in Nigeria (nearly 70 per cent) than Ghana (50 per cent) and Uganda (47 per cent). The question was not asked in Kenya.

- Finally, perception of poor governance (DISSTATE) was over 50 per cent in Ghana and over 40 per cent Nigeria (not asked in Kenya or Uganda).

The differences across countries are interesting. While Ghana and Uganda had far higher approval rates of redistribution across groups, they were not any less 'ethnic' than the other countries in terms of people's identification as being ethnic rather than national, trust in people from other groups, views of other groups, the perceived importance of ethnicity in public life, or inter-ethnic contacts. It is clear that strong approval for redistribution is compatible with a strong ethnic identification, which suggests that the scope of justice is not simply determined by affiliation to an ethnicity or the perceived importance of ethnicity.

REGRESSION RESULTS: ATTITUDES TO ECONOMIC
REDISTRIBUTION

We conducted a logit-regression analysis to see whether we could find any systematic patterns across the multiple variables for each country. The dependent variable was strong approval for redistribution across groups. A summary of the significant findings is shown in Table 7.6. (Appendix Table A7.1 gives details). We did not find many significant relationships. Perhaps the most striking findings from the results are the major differences across the countries.

In Ghana, having positive views of other ethnic groups was positively related to approval for redistribution, while dissatisfaction with the

Table 7.6 Significant results of logit analysis

| | Approval for economic redistribution | | | |
	Ghana	Kenya	Nigeria	Uganda
Personal characteristics				
Male			Neg*	
Ethcon	Neg*			Pos*
Relcon				Neg**
Views of others				
Trust		Pos***		
Interethn	Pos*(*)			
Position of own group				
Polex	Pos [a] ***	Pos***	Pos***	Pos***
Dissat		Pos*	Pos**(*)	
Views of government				
Ethpub	Pos***			
Relpub				Neg**
Disstate	Neg**	Not asked	Neg**	Not asked

[a] Predicted perfectly so was dropped.
Notes: All variables shown are significant: $p < 0.01$***; $p < 0.05$**; $p < 0.1$*.
Source: Appendix Table A7.1.

functioning of the state was negatively related, as expected. Surprising results were that greater contacts across ethnicities were *negatively* related to approval for redistribution, and perceptions of an ethnicized state were *positively* associated with such approval. The strong political exclusion variable (POLEX 2) was perfectly related to approval for redistribution.

In Kenya, the variables significantly and positively associated with strong support for economic redistribution across groups were the extent to which people trusted members of other groups and perceptions of political exclusion (POLEX 1 and 3).

In Nigeria, males were less likely to support redistribution, dissatisfaction with the position of a person's group was associated with approval for redistribution, and one of the political exclusion variables is strongly positively associated with approval (POLEX 2). Perception of a poorly functioning state was negatively associated with approval for redistribution, as one would expect.

In Uganda, unlike Ghana, greater inter-ethnic contact was positively associated with approval for economic redistribution but greater inter-religious contact was negatively related. As with the other countries, perceptions of political exclusion led to greater approval for redistribution. Belief that religion influenced government allocations was negatively related to approval for redistribution.

The variables that appear significant across more than one country in relation to approval for redistribution are perceived political exclusion (all four countries), dissatisfaction with the group's position (Kenya and Nigeria), and dissatisfaction with state functioning (negatively in both Ghana and Nigeria—not asked elsewhere).

Grouping the variables into categories, as in Table 7.6, we see that having positive views of others was positively related to redistribution in two cases (Ghana and Kenya); the perceived relative position of the group to which a person belongs was important in three cases (Kenya, Nigeria, and Uganda); and views of the way the government functions influenced perceptions in three cases too (Ghana, Nigeria, and Uganda).

Perhaps of most interest are the relationships we did *not* find: neither of the variables relating to the way a person sees their own identity—notably feeling more national or feeling more ethnic—affected approval for redistribution.[8] Yet these were precisely the variables that would seem to indicate the 'scope of justice' hypothesis—i.e. one would have expected that those who felt more national identities would have shown more approval for redistribution across groups than those who felt more ethnic loyalties. Thus if

---

[8] One equation in Kenya showed 10 per cent significance for national identity, but in the opposite of the expected direction: more national identity led to less approval.

there is a 'scope of justice', it is more complex than simply a question of ethnicity (or religion) and its perceived importance.

Tentatively, we believe the differing results across countries are due to a country's political histories and policies from colonial times. These have varied markedly across these countries.[9] For example, Ghana's first President, Kwame Nkrumah, vigorously promoted national unity. Despite a turbulent political history subsequently, there has been a convention of shared power across regions and ethnicities and no serious inter-ethnic conflict has occurred (Langer 2009). In contrast, even before independence the various parts of Nigeria were administered separately, and since then power has been negotiated across groups; a major civil war and a number of serious but more minor conflicts have afflicted Nigeria, and have led to a constitution that is explicitly designed to share power across the groups, with distinctions among identities accentuated rather than suppressed (Mustapha 2005). Kenya represents an intermediate case, as the data suggest: there has been an implicit ethnic basis to policies and politics from colonial times, occasionally erupting into open conflict (Kimenyi and Ndung'u 2004; Stewart 2010). Uganda, like Nigeria, inherited a divided country on independence, and since then has also suffered extremely violent civil wars, with a regional and ethnic basis (Lindemann 2010; Tripp 2010). These differences extend to economic policies, with Ghana making most attempts to improve the position of the deprived areas (and groups), Nigeria focusing on political inclusion but not economic inclusion, and Kenyan economic policies mostly privileging the group in power (Stewart 2010; Kimenyi 2011). From this perspective, it is easy to understand why Ghanaians approve of redistribution more than Kenyans and far more than Nigerians. The very high approval rate of Ugandans is less easy to understand. However, it may be a response to the long civil war in the North, clearly associated with severe underdevelopment in the North (as both cause and consequence).

While in-depth study of the four countries is obviously needed to back up the historical explanation sketched above, the important conclusion from the empirical evidence presented here is that a high degree of pessimism about the possibility of gaining popular support for redistribution across groups in multi-ethnic societies is *not* warranted. As both the Ghanaian and Ugandan cases indicate, such approval can occur even in societies where ethnicity plays an important role in identity and politics.

---

[9] Size of country may also be relevant, with Nigeria having a much larger, more dispersed population than the other three.

7.3 Conclusions

The first part of this chapter argued that there were strong philosophical and economic arguments for greatly reducing horizontal inequality. Yet social psychologists have pointed to problems in heterogeneous societies because people's sense of fairness procedurally and in relation to resource distribution is thought to be limited to those within a particular moral community, which can plausibly be interpreted as those within particular ethnic or religious identity groups. This means redistribution across groups may not receive much support in heterogeneous societies.

Some empirical evidence from Ghana, Kenya, Nigeria, and Uganda, however, showed that support can be high even in societies with strong ethnic identification. In Ghana and Uganda, indeed, politicians may underestimate the extent of support for redistribution. But elsewhere, support is much lower, as is notable in the Nigerian data. Exploration of possible determinants of support for redistribution found that significant relationships vary across countries, but perception of being *politically excluded* is related to approval for redistribution across all four countries. The analysis finds no evidence to support the view that a person's expressed identity—ethnic or national—determines their support for redistribution, thus going against the 'scope of justice' hypothesis. The differences across countries may be due to political history and policies, but this needs further research.

In sum, what this suggests is that there is potential for redistributory policies in heterogeneous countries. Further investigation is needed on why redistributionary policies get support in some cases and not others, and how positive views can be promoted.

Appendix I

Variables likely to influence attitudes to government policies towards redistribution across groups:

1) **Gender**: We give a value of 1 to males and 0 to females (MALE).

2) **Age** of the respondent (AGE).

3) **Ethnic group**: Since different ethnic groups may have particular views, related to their norms, we included dummy variables for the main ethnic groups.

4) **Religion** (RELIGION): Likewise, we gave a dummy of 1 for non-Christians to see whether religion influenced people's views.

5) **Poverty** (POVERTY): It is plausible that poor people would favour economic redistribution more than rich people. Consequently, we included a dummy that took the value of 1 if a household has gone without enough food, enough clean water, enough fuel, cash, and/or medicines *at least once or twice* in the previous twelve months. Otherwise, the variable has the value of 0 (non-poor).

6) **Political exclusion** (POLEX): If a person believes they suffer from political exclusion it seems likely that they would favour redistribution of political appointments and plausibly economic assistance as well, since they may believe they are also economically excluded. Yet they might believe that economic redistribution would not go in their favour, given their political exclusion. To investigate the effects of perceived political exclusion, we developed three alternative measures:

   POLEX 1, which includes people who say they have less or much less influence in politics than other ethnic groups in the country;

   POLEX 2, which includes people who say they have much less influence than other groups and think that their ethnic group is seriously underrepresented in major political institutions;

   POLEX 3, which includes people who say they are much less *or* less represented and are seriously or somewhat underrepresented in political institutions.

7) **Dissatisfaction with the position of the respondent's ethnic group** (DISSAT): This variable includes all those who say the position of their ethnic group is worse or much worse than that of other groups in the country, who might be expected to favour redistribution.

8) **Inter-ethnic relations** (INTERETH): It seems likely that people who have a positive view of other groups might include them in their 'scope of justice' and consequently favour redistribution. This variable includes those who said their views of other ethnic groups were positive or very positive.

9) **Trust in others** [TRUST]: Similarly, it seems likely that those who trust people from other ethnic groups more would be more favourable to redistribution. A dummy of 1 was given to those who said they trusted people from other ethnic groups a lot.

10) **National loyalty** (NATIONIDENT): It seems plausible that those who think of themselves as primarily national rather than as members of an ethnic group would be more likely to approve of redistribution across groups. A dummy of 1 was given to those who said they 'felt only

Ghanaian' (or Kenyan or Nigerian) when asked to compare the relative importance of their ethnic identity and nationality.

11) **Ethnic identity** (ETHNICIDENT): People whose main loyalty is to their ethnic group may be more likely to oppose redistribution. A dummy of 1 was given to those who said they were more ethnic than national (including those who said they felt only ethnic).

12) **Inter-ethnic contacts** [ETHCON] might be likely to make people more favourable to redistribution. If a person had daily or almost daily contact with people from other ethnic groups in the neighbourhood, social, and work environments, the variable has a value of 1, and 0 otherwise.

13) **Inter-religious contacts** (RELCON) is calculated the same way for religious contacts as ETHCON.

14) Perceptions that **ethnicity is used in the public sphere** in the government's allocation of jobs, contracts etc. (ETHPUBD): Positive answers might imply a limited scope of justice, and distrust of the government to allocate additional assistance in the way desired. This was measured by adding up the 'yes' answers to the question of whether the government used ethnicity in the allocation of jobs, contracts, and public housing.

15) Perceptions of government using **religion in public sphere** (RELPUBD): This was measured as in point 14, but for answers to the question about religion.

16) **Treatment of a group by the government** (ETHSATGOV): If a person feels that his ethnic group is not well treated by the government, he may not favour redistribution. We gave a value of 1 to anyone who said that they were satisfied or very satisfied with the treatment of their ethnic group by the government.

17) **Poor opinion of the state** (DISSTATE): If people feel that the state does not function well, they may be more opposed to allocating the state a redistributive role. We gave a dummy of 1 to those who said they disagreed or strongly disagreed with the statement 'The state institutions in this country are highly effective and work really well'.

Table A7.1 Results of logit analysis (dependent variable: REDOCO (approval for economic redistribution to poorer groups))

Variables	Ghana			Kenya			Nigeria			Uganda		
	(1)	(2)	(3)	(1)	(2)	(3)	(1)	(2)	(3)	(1)	(2)	(3)
Male	0.341	0.337	0.333	-0.0137	-0.0160	-0.0114	-0.532*	-0.695**	-0.541*	0.0305	0.0419	-0.0335
	(0.286)	(0.287)	(0.286)	(0.144)	(0.143)	(0.144)	(0.278)	(0.288)	(0.278)	(0.234)	(0.232)	(0.235)
Age	-0.00372	-0.00271	-0.00345	0.00368	0.00499	0.00387	0.0117	0.0102	0.0119	-0.00834	-0.0107	-0.00873
	(0.00922)	(0.00918)	(0.00918)	(0.00749)	(0.00743)	(0.00747)	(0.00993)	(0.0101)	(0.00991)	(0.0100)	(0.00982)	(0.00996)
Yedu	0.0423	0.0486	0.0417	-0.00875	-0.0146	-0.0146	-0.000284	6.70e-05	0.00231	0.0106	0.0124	0.0122
	(0.0355)	(0.0358)	(0.0355)	(0.0194)	(0.0192)	(0.0192)	(0.0321)	(0.0320)	(0.0319)	(0.0255)	(0.0253)	(0.0254)
Religion	0.0724	0.154	0.0814	0.0581	0.189	0.123	0.187	0.196	0.160	-0.0111	0.0289	0.0481
	(0.374)	(0.377)	(0.375)	(0.215)	(0.214)	(0.213)	(0.296)	(0.295)	(0.293)	(0.313)	(0.309)	(0.313)
poverty1	0.118	0.0857	0.121	0.151	0.177	0.167	0.519	0.442	0.516	-0.0531	-0.0421	0.0192
	(0.326)	(0.326)	(0.325)	(0.164)	(0.162)	(0.163)	(0.347)	(0.347)	(0.347)	(0.283)	(0.280)	(0.284)
Disat	0.0628	0.0954	0.0533	0.165	0.299*	0.227	0.853**	0.713**	0.911***	0.112	0.248	0.0815
	(0.297)	(0.298)	(0.296)	(0.179)	(0.176)	(0.178)	(0.358)	(0.364)	(0.351)	(0.252)	(0.245)	(0.253)
polex1	0.459			0.606***			0.518			0.868***		
	(0.307)			(0.163)			(0.370)			(0.236)		
polex2		-na			0.0583			2.978***			0.581	
		-na			(0.362)			(1.133)			(0.645)	
polex3			0.326			0.368**			0.416			0.966***
			(0.369)			(0.183)			(0.382)			(0.274)
ethpubd	0.949***	0.972***	0.919***	-0.0717	-0.0795	-0.0996	-0.0623	-0.0231	-0.0599	0.206	0.272	0.205
	(0.326)	(0.325)	(0.324)	(0.181)	(0.179)	(0.180)	(0.296)	(0.298)	(0.296)	(0.283)	(0.276)	(0.281)
Ethloy	0.497	0.496	0.487	-0.380	-0.307	-0.355	0.0448	0.0145	0.0351	0.0665	0.0850	0.00476
	(0.611)	(0.608)	(0.609)	(0.262)	(0.263)	(0.262)	(0.355)	(0.364)	(0.355)	(0.305)	(0.302)	(0.306)
nationloy	-0.366	-0.297	-0.354	-0.298*	-0.236	-0.249	-0.490	-0.359	-0.466	-0.0555	-0.0978	-0.0870
	(0.398)	(0.399)	(0.397)	(0.167)	(0.164)	(0.165)	(0.507)	(0.510)	(0.506)	(0.376)	(0.375)	(0.379)
Inteth	0.537*	0.557**	0.536*	0.0269	0.0163	0.0264	0.00475	0.159	0.0153	0.334	0.341	0.349
	(0.282)	(0.284)	(0.281)	(0.150)	(0.148)	(0.149)	(0.281)	(0.291)	(0.281)	(0.231)	(0.228)	(0.231)

(*Continued*)

Table A7.1 (Continued)

Variables	Ghana			Kenya			Nigeria			Uganda		
	(1)	(2)	(3)	(1)	(2)	(3)	(1)	(2)	(3)	(1)	(2)	(3)
Ethcon	-0.715*	-0.670*	-0.665*	0.0801	0.103	0.127	-0.232	-0.158	-0.230	0.515*	0.533*	0.584*
	(0.392)	(0.390)	(0.389)	(0.300)	(0.297)	(0.298)	(0.361)	(0.363)	(0.361)	(0.303)	(0.300)	(0.302)
Relcon	0.143	0.102	0.104	0.0311	0.00839	0.000985	-0.224	-0.340	-0.254	-0.756**	-0.832**	-0.692*
	(0.350)	(0.349)	(0.348)	(0.290)	(0.288)	(0.289)	(0.358)	(0.354)	(0.356)	(0.367)	(0.367)	(0.366)
Trust	-0.0450	-0.0578	-0.0478	0.835***	0.802***	0.820***	-0.0953	-0.185	-0.105	-0.221	-0.226	-0.210
	(0.288)	(0.291)	(0.288)	(0.146)	(0.145)	(0.145)	(0.275)	(0.279)	(0.274)	(0.232)	(0.229)	(0.232)
Relpubd	-0.389	-0.385	-0.358	0.118	0.144	0.152	-0.0231	-0.0549	-0.0413	-0.516**	-0.566**	-0.556**
	(0.322)	(0.320)	(0.321)	(0.160)	(0.159)	(0.159)	(0.332)	(0.336)	(0.331)	(0.245)	(0.241)	(0.245)
ethsatgov	0.167	0.200	0.168	Not asked	Not asked	Not asked	-0.447	-0.627**	-0.479	0.0353	-0.0775	0.0486
	(0.277)	(0.278)	(0.278)				(0.333)	(0.306)	(0.336)	(0.231)	(0.225)	(0.230)
Distate	-0.576**	-0.591**	-0.613**	Not asked	Not asked	Not asked	-0.682**	-0.681**	-0.686**	Not asked	Not asked	Not asked
	(0.285)	(0.286)	(0.285)				(0.299)	(0.300)	(0.301)			
Constant	0.280	0.223	0.361	-1.004**	-0.859**	-0.871**	-1.348	-1.020	-1.303	1.059	1.470**	1.015
	(0.667)	(0.671)	(0.663)	(0.420)	(0.415)	(0.416)	(0.822)	(0.815)	(0.823)	(0.680)	(0.666)	(0.681)
Observations	322	316	322	902	902	902	412	412	412	495	495	495

Notes:
Robust standard errors are in parentheses; *** p < 0.01, ** p < 0.05, * p < 0.1.
-na Variable predicted success perfectly and was therefore dropped.

References

Alesina, A. and E. La Ferrara (2005). 'Ethnic Diversity and Economic Performance'. *Journal of Economic Literature*, 43(3): 762–800.

Alesina, A. and E. L. Glaeser (2004). *Fighting Poverty in the US and Europe: A World of Difference.* Oxford: Oxford University Press.

Alesina, A. and D. Rodrik (1994). 'Distributive Politics and Economic Growth'. *Quarterly Journal of Economics*, 109(2): 465–90.

Bourguignon, F. (2003). 'The Growth Elasticity of Poverty Reduction: Explaining Heterogeneity across Countries and Time Periods'. In T. S. Eicher and S. J. Turnovsky (eds), *Inequality and Growth: Theory and Policy Implications.* Cambridge, MA: MIT Press, 2–26.

Brush, J. (2007). 'Does Income Inequality Lead to More Crime? A Comparison of Cross-Sectional and Time-Series Analyses of United States Counties'. *Economic Letters*, 96: 264–8.

Cederman, L.-E., N. B. Weidmann, and K. Skrede (2011). 'Horizontal Inequalities and Ethno-Nationalist Civil War: A Global Comparison'. *American Political Science Review*, 105(3): 478–95.

CIA World Factbook. Available at: <http://www.cia.gov/library/publications/the-world-factbook> (accessed 10 September 2011).

Clayton, S. and S. Opotow (2003). 'Justice and Identity: Perspectives on What is Fair'. *Personality and Social Psychology Review*, 7(4): 298–310.

Cornia, G. A. (2004). *Inequality, Growth, and Poverty in an Era of Liberalization and Globalization.* Oxford: Oxford University Press.

Eicher, T. S., and S. J. Turnovsky (2003). *Inequality and Growth: Theory and Policy Implications.* Cambridge, MA: MIT Press.

ILO (1976). *Employment, Growth and Basic Needs: A One-World Problem.* Geneva: ILO.

Higgins, K. (2007). 'Regional Inequality and the Niger Delta'. Paper prepared for the *World Development Report*, Policy Brief No. 5. London: Overseas Development Institute, 1–10.

Kahneman, D., A. B. Kreuger, D. Schkade, N. Schwarz, and A. A. Stone (2006). 'Would You Be Happier If You Were Richer? A Focusing Illusion'. *Science*, 312(5782): 1908–10.

Kant, I. (1785). *Fundamental Principles of the Metaphysic of Morals.* Translated by T. K. Abbott, 1949. Indianapolis: Bobbs Merrill.

Kimenyi, M. S. (2011). *The Politics of Identity, Horizontal Inequalities and Conflict in Kenya.* Tokyo: JICA.

Kimenyi, M. S. and N. S. Ndung'u (2004). 'Sporadic Ethnic Violence: Why Has Kenya Not Experienced a Full-Blown War?' In P. Collier and N. Sambanis (eds), *Understanding Civil War: Evidence and Analysis.* Washington, DC: World Bank.

Krahn, H., T. F. Hartnagel, and J. W. Gartrell (1986). 'Income Inequality and Homicide Rates: Cross-National Data and Criminological Theories'. *Criminology*, 24(2): 269–94.

Langer, A. (2009). 'Living with Diversity: The Peaceful Management of Horizontal Inequalities in Ghana'. *Journal of International Development*, 21(4): 534–46.

Lindemann, S. (2010). *Exclusionary Elite Bargains and Civil War Onset: The Case of Uganda.* CSRC Working Paper 76. London: Crisis States Research Centre.

Locke, J. (1689). *Two Treatises of Government*. NewYork: Mentor (New American Library).

Mustapha, R. (2005). *Ethnic Structure, Inequality and Governance of the Public Sector in Nigeria*. CRISE Working Paper 18. Oxford: CRISE, Department of International Development, University of Oxford.

Mustapha, R. (2007). *Institutionalizing Ethnic Representation: How Effective Is the Federal Character Commission in Nigeria?*. CRISE Working Paper 43. Oxford: CRISE, Department of International Development, University of Oxford.

Nozick, R. (1974). *Anarchy, State, and Utopia*. Oxford: Blackwell.

Okidi, J. A., S. Ssewanyana, L. Bategeka, and F. Muhumza (2005). *'Distributional and Poverty Imapcts of Uganda's Growth: 1992 to 2003'*. Kampala: Economic Policy Research Centre (EPRC).

Opotow, S. (2001). 'Social Injustice'. In D. J. Christie, R. V. Wagner, and D. D. Winter (eds), *Peace, Conflict and Violence: Peace Psychology for the 21st Century*. New York: Prentis Hall, 102–9.

Østby, G. (2008). 'Polarization, Horizontal Inequalities and Violent Civil Conflict'. *Journal of Peace Research*, 45(2): 143–62.

Paes de Barros, R., F. H. G. Ferreira, J. R. M. Vega, and J. S. Chanduvi (2009). *Measuring Inequality of Opportunities in Latin America and the Caribbean*. Washington, DC: World Bank.

Persson, T. and G. Tabellini (1994). 'Is Inequality Harmful for Growth?'. *The American Economic Review*, 84(3): 600–21.

Pigou, A. C. (1920). *The Economics of Welfare*. London: Macmillan.

Rawls, J. (1971). *A Theory of Justice*. Cambridge, MA: Belknap Press of Harvard University Press.

Rawls, J. (2001). *Justice as Fairness: A Restatement*. Cambridge, MA and London: Harvard University Press.

Robbins, L. (1938). 'Interpersonal Comparisons of Utility: A Comment'. *Economic Journal*, 48: 635–41.

Robbins, L. (1945). *An Essay on the Nature and Significance of Economic Science* (2nd edition). London: Macmillan.

Roemer, J. E. (1998). *Equality of Opportunity*. Cambridge, MA and London: Harvard University Press.

Rousseau, J. J. (1762). *The Social Contract*. Translated by M. Cranston, 1968. London: Penguin.

Sacks, D. W., B. Stevenson, and J. Wolfers (2010). *Subjective Well-Being, Income, Economic Development and Growth*. NBER Working Paper 16441. Cambridge, MA: National Bureau of Economic Research.

Sen, A. (1980). 'Equality of What?' In S. McMurrin (ed.), *Tanner Lectures on Human Values*. Cambridge: Cambridge University Press, 196–220.

Stewart, F. (1985). *Planning to Meet Basic Needs*. London: Macmillan.

Stewart, F. (2002). *'Horizontal Inequality: A Neglected Dimension of Development'*. WIDER Annual Development Lecture 2001. Helsinki: UNU-WIDER.

Stewart, F. (ed.) (2008). *Horizontal Inequalities and Conflict: Understanding Group Violence in Multiethnic Societies*. London: Palgrave.

Stewart, F. (2010). 'Horizontal Inequalities in Kenya and the Political Disturbances of 2008: Some Implications for Aid Policy'. *Conflict, Security and Development*, 10(1): 133–59.

Stewart, F. and A. Langer (2008). 'Horizontal Inequalities: Explaining Persistence and Change'. In F. Stewart (ed.), *Horizontal Inequalities and Conflict: Understanding Group Violence in Multiethnic Societies*. London: Palgrave, 54–78.

Streeten, P. P., S. J. Burki, M. ul Haq, N. Hicks, and F. Stewart (1981). *First Things First, Meeting Basic Human Needs in Developing Countries*. New York: Oxford University Press.

Tripp, A. M. (2010). *Museveni's Uganda: Paradoxes of Power in a Hybrid Regime*. Boulder, CO: Lynne Rienner.

UNDP (2007). *Ghana Human Development Report, 2007: Towards a More Inclusive Society*. Accra: UNDP.

Vaughan, K. (1978). 'John Locke and the Labor Theory of Value'. *Journal of Libertarian Studies*, 2(4): 311–26.

Walzer, M. (1983). *Spheres of Justice*. London: Basic Books.

Wenzel, M. (2000). 'Justice and Identity: The Significance of Inclusion for Perceptions of Justice and the Justice Motive'. *Personality and Social Psychology Bulletin*, 26: 157–76.

Williams, B. (1962). 'The idea of Equality'. In P. Laslett and W. G. Runciman (eds), *Philosophy, Politics and Society* (2nd series). Oxford: Blackwell.

8

Employment, Poverty, and Development
Do We Have the Priorities Right?*

Rolph van der Hoeven

8.1 Introduction[1]

This chapter argues that it might be good to go back to Richard Jolly's concern during his early professional life: *employment* (Jolly et al. 1973). Now, just as then, we need a good mix of academic rigour, practical application, and political will to make employment an important, if not the number one, goal of development and of development aid.

An illustrative example is the 'Arab Spring' of 2011. In only a few months various Arab regimes were toppled by populations wanting not only more democracy but also, perhaps even more importantly, by the educated youth wanting good jobs and prospects of advancement in life. Yet this turmoil took place in countries that scored well on the progress in the millennium development goals (MDGs) much hailed by aid donors.

Tunisia and Egypt, as well as Jordan, are among the eight best performing countries with respect to progress in the MDGs. Yet, despite this progress on human development, youth unemployment was higher here than in other countries, such as Brazil and Vietnam, which had different levels of

* I would like to thank Tony Addison, Michael Lipton, Andy Sumner, and Frances Stewart, as well as the other participants at the UNU-WIDER conference on Development Aid in Helsinki (September 2011) and at the conference in honour of Sir Richard Jolly in Sussex (November 2011) for useful comments and suggestions.

[1] This is a condensed version of a longer working paper (van der Hoeven 2012).

development but similar achievement in MDG progress as these Mediterranean countries.

After the change in regimes in various Arab countries in the spring of 2011, the leaders of UNDP and other development agencies quickly recognized that something must be done about employment.[2]

It should be recalled that employment issues were notably absent from the MDGs when these were formulated in 2000. In a recent volume on employment, inequality, and globalization,[3] Mkandawire (2011) and Amsden (2011) argue that the lack of attention to employment issues resulted from too great a focus on poverty alleviation.

Amsden remarks:

> ...to slay the dragon of poverty, deliberate and determined investments in jobs above starvation wages must play a central role, whether for self-employment or paid-employment. The grassroots approach to solving poverty doesn't go far enough, because it aims only at improving the supply side of the labour market, making job seekers more capable, and not the demand side, making new jobs available for them. It acts as though new ways of earning a living emerge (at a positive wage) simply because the supply of job seekers is better clothed, housed, and fed, or enjoys more human rights—which is the same fallacious reasoning behind Say's Law.

Five years after the formulation of the MDGs, the World Summit 2005 Outcome contains reference (paragraph 47) to employment issues:

> We strongly support fair globalization and resolve to make the goals of full and productive employment and decent work for all, including for women and young people, a central objective of our relevant national and international policies as well as our national development strategies, including poverty reduction strategies, as part of our efforts to achieve the Millennium Development Goals. These measures should also encompass the elimination of the worst forms of child labour, as defined in International Labour Organization Convention No. 182, and forced labour. We also resolve to ensure full respect for the fundamental principles and rights at work.

This paragraph in the 2005 Summit Outcome led to the inclusion of a new sub-goal in 2007 (under MDG1): *Achieve full and productive employment and decent work for all, including women and young people,* with four indicators: (i) growth rate of GDP per person employed; (ii) employment-to-population ratio; (iii) proportion of employed people living below $1 (PPP) per day, and (iv) proportion of own-account and contributing family workers in total employment.

---

[2] See, for example, Helen Clark (2011), Administrator of the UNDP.
[3] Van der Hoeven (2011).

This addition has been welcomed by organizations such as the ILO, NGOs, trade unions, and various governments as it could give these organizations a handle to bring employment issues more forcefully into the discussion of development, development goals, and aid delivery. However, some criticize the inclusion of a goal for full employment, as it is not easy to measure and thus deviates from the intentions behind the original MDGs (Vandemoortele 2011).

Such criticism, however, reflects the somewhat ambivalent role the MDGs are playing in the current development discourse, namely that the MDGs were originally designed to set, measure, and monitor goals for certain important aspects of development without prescribing a concomitant development trajectory, so that all countries could agree with the goals without being obliged to adhere to the same policy prescriptions, something developing countries had become very wary of since the introduction of the structural adjustment policies in the 1980s and 1990s. Yet, despite the intention of not having an underlying prescribing development theory, the MDGs have paradoxically led to a situation where, as a result, the issues—such as employment—that were not explicitly mentioned in the MDGs received less attention from the development aid community.[4] So, in that respect, it is understandable and justifiable that full employment has been added as one of the (sub)goals of the MDGs.

But this leaves many questions open as to how to implement the goal. In recent discussions there has been a growing consensus that, although the goal of full employment has now been established, too little coordinated effort has been undertaken to achieve it. For example, a recent review of the MDGs (UNDG 2010), submitted five years after the inclusion of the employment (sub)goal, reports on the progress or regress in employment issues globally as well as in some countries by means of a number of employment indicators. It also gives examples of how particular development projects have contributed to more or better employment in individual countries, describing successful schemes for employment, training programmes for entrepreneurs or unemployed youth, improved collective bargaining, social security, etc.

However, looking at the different examples chosen in this review, it is not always clear how development aid in general has contributed to more and/or better employment. Most of the examples make no use of counterfactual analyses or even mention whether other schemes *mutatis mutandis* were also contributing to employment creation. Notably absent are macro analyses of the effects of total volumes of aid on growth and its possible impact on employment. It thus remains difficult to distil from the 2010 outcome review how successful development and development aid efforts have been with respect to creating more and better employment.

---

[4] A recent example is the way in which DFID has been analysing the 'effectiveness' of different UN organizations.

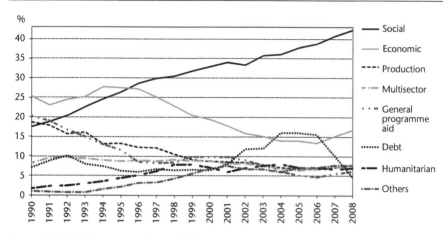

Figure 8.1 ODA by sector since 1990 as a percentage of total ODA, three-year average commitments
Source: OECD DAC Secretariat online database.

It remains equally difficult to distil from the DAC statistics how aid flows in general have contributed to employment creation. What statistics[5] have made clear is that the share of ODA commitments for the social sector (three-year moving averages) has greatly and steadily increased: from 16 per cent in 1990 to 34 per cent at the time of the introduction of the MDGs in the year 2000 to over 40 per cent in 2008, mainly driven by substantial increases in the share of ODA commitments to government and civil society and to a lesser extent to health, education, and population programmes (see Figure 8.1). Commitments to economic activities as well as to multi-sectoral activities all declined over the same period. In all major developing-country groupings, ODA commitments to social sectors were 42 per cent or higher in 2009 (see Figure 8.2).

These ODA statistics relate to the traditional ODA donors. New donors such as China and India almost certainly target a higher share of their aid on infrastructure, transport, mining, etc. These aid flows and projects may in the long run add to new capacity and to greater generation of jobs, although in the short run the employment effects might be quite limited or even offset domestic employment creation, as projects are often undertaken by contractors and temporary workers can even be imported from these donor countries. These flows are currently still considerably smaller than those from the traditional DAC countries, but are increasing faster than traditional ODA and therefore may in the future change the current trend of ODA, which is increasingly benefiting the social sectors.

---

[5] OECD DAC online (consulted 13 September 2011).

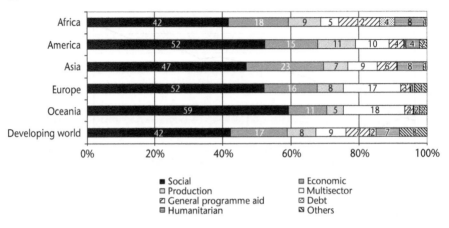

Figure 8.2 ODA by region and by sector, 2009, as a percentage of total ODA committed for each region
Source: OECD DAC Secretariat online database.

These changes in sectoral allocation cannot *prima facie* be taken as an indication of whether more or less attention is paid to employment in development aid. On the one hand, aid programmes to the social sectors, by increasing human capital and governance, could well contribute indirectly to increases in the quality of employment and to increased employment creation. But, on the other hand, by shifting resources away from investment in infrastructure and capital, these could lead to reduced growth of production and thus lower employment.

Hence we have to decompose the question of development aid efforts for employment into the following string of questions:

(i) Does aid contribute to growth (Arndt et al. 2010) and poverty alleviation?
(ii) Does growth contribute to employment creation?
(iii) Can aid interventions, while contributing to growth, be made to contribute more specifically to employment creation?

Furthermore, in the current context of integrated markets and globalization, it is not helpful to discuss the effectiveness of aid without consideration of the related issues of international governance and coherence in development and other policies.[6]

---

[6] For examples of the negative effects of cotton subsidies in the USA on cotton farmers and workers in Mali and of the de-industrializing effects in developing countries of the economic partnership programmes (EPA) proposed by the EU, see South Centre (2012).

This chapter, therefore, discusses first how globalization is leading to more precarious forms of work, through an overview of some major employment trends over the last twenty years.[7] This is followed by a discussion of which (national and international) employment policies seem to be warranted in the light of these trends of 'precarization'. The final section discusses how development aid can support these employment policies.

8.2 Employment Trends[8]

The ongoing process of globalization has in many countries resulted in a growing precarization of labour,[9] which we illustrate through the following six labour-market trends.

8.2.1 A Decline in the Employment-to-Population Rate for Most Regions in the World

For the world as a whole, the employment-to-population ratio seems to have remained rather constant, but there are important regional differences. All three Asian regions (at 73.8, 67.5, and 58.7 per cent) and Sub-Saharan Africa had the highest employment-to-population ratio at the beginning of the 1990s, but experienced declines of several percentage points between then and 2009.

In contrast, the employment-to-population ratio increased slightly from much lower levels in the Middle East, North Africa, and Latin America. The lower employment-to-population level in these regions at the beginning of the 1990s can be explained by (very) low female labour-force participation. At the global level, we notice two opposing trends, namely an increased ratio for female labour-force participation and a decline of male participation. The first trend can be ascribed to changes in customs and norms, and the second more to deterioration in employment opportunities as a consequence of globalization.

8.2.2 Changing Patterns in Production

For the world as a whole, the percentage of employment in the service industry has risen from 33.6 per cent in 1991 to 43.8 per cent in 2008. A high

---

[7] We will therefore not look at the effects of development aid on employment in developed or donor countries themselves, although this may be an important issue in the political discourse on development aid.

[8] This section draws on van der Hoeven (2010).

[9] See, for example, recent issues of the *World of Work Report* published annually by the ILO.

service-sector share in employment already prevailed in developed countries, Latin America, and the Middle East, with increases of around 9.5, 2.5, and 2 percentage points, respectively. However, a massive increase in this share took place in East Asia, where it almost doubled from 19.5 to 35.7 per cent, and in South Asia where it increased from 23.6 to 30.1 per cent.

Some analysts interpret the increase in service-industry employment as an indication of post-industrial society and as such an important indicator of progress in development. This fails to recognize that the service industry encompasses a wide range of activities, from hawking and peddling in the street to sophisticated financial services. Therefore a better indicator of development for developing countries is the size of the manufacturing sector. Here we notice differing trends over the last two decades. At the world level, the share of employment in industry has hardly changed between 1991 and 2008, remaining at 21.5 per cent. But there are again important regional differences. The most dramatic increase is in South East Asia and the Pacific, where the share increased from 12.7 per cent in 1991 to 19.4 per cent in 2000, and in South Asia where, over the same period, it increased from 15.4 to 22.4 per cent, thereby almost reaching the share in East Asia, where the share remained more or less constant over the period (around 23.5 per cent, with a dip of 3–4 percentage points around 1998 due to the Asian crisis). Notable are the very low and stagnant share in Sub-Saharan Africa (at around 8.5 per cent) and a declining share in North Africa.

It should be noted, however, that the share of employment in industry could underestimate the level of progress in industry. As Rada and Taylor (2006) point out, industry often has high productivity (or a low employment–value added elasticity). An important issue is, therefore, not only the size of employment in industry but also how the surplus generated in the industrial sector is used for reinvestment and how it is distributed in the rest of the economy.

8.2.3 The Increases in Non-Standard Forms of Employment

In developing countries, the important element of precariousness is most clearly manifested in the existence of a pervasive 'informal sector' in the economy or the 'informal economy'.[10] This phenomenon is not restricted to poor developing countries.

The existence of the informal economy is partly related to changes in the structure of employment: especially for the poorer regions, the increase in

---

[10] It has become common to talk about the 'informal economy' rather than the 'informal sector', as informal activities increasingly take place within established enterprises. It would thus be a misnomer to continue to talk about the informal sector.

employment in the service sector reflects an increase in the share of workers engaged in informal activities.

There are, however, contradictory explanations of the pervasiveness of the informal sector. Some (e.g. Maloney 2004) argue that the size of the informal sector is determined by the degree of labour-market inflexibility. According to them, the more inflexible the labour market, the greater the preference of employers to avoid employing workers formally and the stronger the inclination to act informally. Others (e.g. Kucera and Roncolato 2008) argue that the major cause of informal-sector activities is the lack of formal jobs. This interpretation has gained ground in the ILO, OECD, and other UN organizations.

There is evidence of a clear link between the increase in non-standard work and income inequality (Rani 2008), mainly due to widening wage differentials between standard and non-standard jobs. Some would explain this by the low education level of those engaged in the informal sector, as statistics show. But it is more likely the type of job rather than the educational attainment that drives inequality. An increase in education levels, in the absence of newly created formal jobs, will result in better-educated workers in the informal economy without a major decline in wage inequality.

8.2.4 A Declining Wage Share and the Growing Wage Inequality

The ILO (2008) reports that the wage share declined over 1995–2007 in two-thirds of the developing countries, including the major ones, as well as in the major developed countries. The only exception was the Latin American region, where some countries witnessed an increasing wage share. The ILO Report attributes the declining wage share to increasing trade and globalization and confirms earlier research findings (see Diwan 2001; Harrison 2002) that, contrary to the conventional wisdom that sees the labour share in GDP as relatively constant, the proportion of GDP that goes into wages and other labour income varies over time. Using a dataset from 1960 to 1997, Harrison (2002) splits her sample (of over 100 countries) into two even groups (based on 1985 GDP per capita). Her data show that in the group of poorer countries, labour's share in national income fell on average by 0.1 percentage point per year from 1960 to 1993. The decline in the labour share accelerated after 1993, to an average decline of 0.3 percentage points per year. In the richer subgroup, the labour share grew by 0.2 percentage points prior to 1993, but fell by 0.4 percentage points per year since then. Thus there was a post-1993 trend reversal for the richer countries, and an acceleration of an already downward trend for the poorer subgroup.

Harrison (2002) tests for factors that could explain changes in labour shares, combining detailed national accounts data from the United Nations with measures of trade openness, capital account restrictions, and capital flows. Overall, the results suggest that changes in factor shares are primarily linked to changes in capital/labour ratios. However, measures of globalization (such as capital controls or direct investment flows) also play a role. Harrison finds that frequent exchange rate crises lead to declining labour shares,[11] suggesting that labour pays a disproportionately high price (i.e. wages are more severely affected than GDP). Capital controls are associated with an increase in the labour share, an effect that Harrison attributes to the weaker bargaining position of capital vis-à-vis labour if the cost of relocating production increases with capital controls. Foreign investment inflows are also associated with a fall in the labour share. The weak bargaining position of labour in the context of open capital accounts is also a causal mechanism explored by Lee and Jayadev (2005). They find that financial openness exerts downward pressure on the labour share both in developed and developing countries for the period from 1973 to 1995. Harrison also finds that increasing trade is associated with a fall in the labour share. This result is robust across specifications. These results point to a systematic negative relationship between various measures of globalization and labour's share in GDP.

Diwan (2001), based on a large sample of countries, reports an average drop in the labour share of GDP in each crisis of 5.0 percentage points, and a modest catch-up thereafter. In the three years after the crisis, labour shares were still 2.6 percentage points below their pre-crisis average. Given the fact that most countries have undergone more than one crisis, the cumulative drop in the wage share over the last thirty years is estimated at 4.1 per cent of GDP, and is especially large for Latin America, where the share dropped 6.7 per cent between the 1970s and the 1990s. The overall decline in the labour share is partly explained by what some call the ratchet effect: after an economic shock or a financial crisis, the labour share in gross national income decreases and does not recover when national income recovers (van der Hoeven and Saget 2004).

However, not only has the inequality between wages and other components of gross domestic product increased, but the distribution among wage earners has also worsened. The ratio of the average wage of the top 10 per cent of wage earners in relation to the bottom 10 per cent is found to have increased in 70 per cent of the countries. Here also, one notices similar regional differences, an almost uniform pattern for most regions, but a mixed pattern for Latin America.

---

[11] Labour shares decreased with a real devaluation but failed to return to pre-devaluation levels during the recovery.

8.2.5 The Internationalization of the Production Process

Today there are some 82,000 transnational corporations (TNCs) in the world, with 810,000 affiliates. These companies play a major role in the world economy. For instance, exports from foreign affiliates of TNCs are estimated to have grown from about a quarter of total world exports of goods and services in 1982 to one-third in 2007. And the number of people employed by these corporations has increased fourfold since 1982, standing at about 77 million in 2008, and implying a much faster rate of growth than that of the labour force. These TNCs are dominated by a small number of large firms. The largest 100 TNCs account for 11 per cent of all employment in transnationals and for about 4 per cent of world GDP. Over the last 15 years, the largest TNCs have undergone a rapid process of internationalization. There has also been a progressive increase in the proportion of companies operating in the service sector and of TNCs based in developing countries (UNCTAD 2009: 17–18).

8.2.6 International Migration

Global figures of migration do not show a substantial change: in 1960 the stock of total migrants in the world population was 2.7 per cent and this percentage in 2005 had not changed.[12] This has led some commentators to argue that globalization is characterized by increased capital flows and increased trade and services flows but not increased labour flows. However, this characterization is misleading. If one looks at more disaggregated (by region) figures, one clearly sees a growing trend in some regions. In Europe, the stock of migrants as part of the population increased from 3.0 per cent in 1960 to 8.8 per cent in 2005. The same ratio increased from 6.7 to 13.6 per cent in North America, from 13.5 to 16.4 per cent in Oceania, and from 4.9 to 37.1 per cent in the Gulf States. By contrast, the ratio of the stock of migrants to the local population declined in Africa, Asia, and Latin America as a whole. The increase in the share of migrants in the local population in developed countries is quite substantial despite the severe restrictions most of these countries have put on inward migration.

This increased level of migration is leading to tension in the destination countries but is providing an increasing source of foreign exchange for the sending countries. Remittances for many developing countries represent a much larger flow than development assistance. For example, in East Asia and the Pacific in 2007, remittances stood at US$34 per capita compared with US$5 for ODA flow. Analogous figures for Latin America and the Caribbean are US$114 and US$10, and for South Asia US$33 and US$6. Only

---

[12] This figure excludes the former Soviet Union because Soviet citizens remaining after the independence of the former Soviet Republics are counted as migrants.

in Sub-Saharan Africa was the per-capita inflow of remittances (US$26) lower than that of ODA (US$39).

Using a broad definition, the World Bank estimates that remittances to developing countries amounted to US$166.9 billion in 2005, compared to US$85.6 billion in 2000 and US$31.2 billion in 1990 (World Bank 2005: 88). Remittances are not only a rapidly growing source of external finance, but they are generally steady across years and not prone to sudden reversals of direction (Sirkeci, Cohen, and Ratha 2012). They tend to be countercyclical to crises in developing countries (i.e. migrants send more money home to support their families) and hence help to smooth consumption volatility.

8.2.7 Summary

The trends described above all point to a growing precarization of labour. This is especially the case for the decline in labour participation rates in many regions, the declining wage share, and the growing wage inequality, as well as the continuing informalization of the labour force and the slow progress of structural change in many countries. Growing employment in multinational enterprises and their subsidiaries as well as growing migration in some areas of the world and growing workers' remittances have not been able to arrest the growing precarization.

8.3 Policies for Employment Creation

In the light of the trends just elucidated, particularly the 'precarization' of the labour market, we briefly review national policies, as well as the types of enabling international environment conducive to employment creation, in order to pave the way for a discussion on the nature of development aid interventions that might support such policies.

In discussing (national) policies for employment creation, it is important to distinguish between short-term (macroeconomic) policies and longer-term structural policies.[13] The first type basically should strive[14] for

---

[13] It should be noted that this distinction between the short-term and long-term policies for growth and employment creation was very much on the minds of the original architects of the Bretton Woods system in 1945, to the extent that the IMF and emergency funds of the UN were responsible for assisting and guiding shorter-term policies of the World Bank and UN specialized agencies over the long term. However, since the debt crisis of the 1980s and the ensuing structural adjustment policies (now frequently labelled 'poverty-reduction strategies'), the picture has become more complex. But for a clearer picture of employment policies, it is better to maintain the analytical distinction between the short term and long term in the first instance.

[14] It may not be possible to have full use of all productive forces given fixed factor proportions in the short run.

full capacity utilization, so that all productive forces, including labour, can be fully engaged in the production process, while the second should strive for an expansion of capacity and an increase in the employment content of growth, to the extent that increasing the employment content of growth does not jeopardize growth itself (or at least that it does not jeopardize growth to such an extent that the economy arrives at a declining growth and employment trajectory).

Although the question of the relation between development aid and employment was posed in terms of employment, it is important to qualify the term 'employment'.

In assessing outcomes of employment policy it is necessary to consider not only the quantity of employment but also the quality of employment, as in poorer countries most people cannot afford to be unemployed and have to be engaged in whatever survival mechanisms are possible. Statistics show that people in higher income-classes have higher unemployment rates than people in poorer income-classes (Ghose et al. 2008). Often quality of employment is measured by certain criteria: whether incomes among the self-employed or wages among employees exceed a certain level, or by the existence of a minimum level of secondary benefits such as social security and access to legally binding employment contracts. A combination of these three measures is also often applied. Terms used to describe those with adequate quality of work then are 'good jobs', 'decent work', or whether a worker or self-employed person belongs to the 'working poor' or not.

8.3.1 Shorter-Term Policies for Employment Creation: Some Illustrative Examples

In developed countries, policy debates on employment over the last thirty years have been dominated by the so-called NAIRU, the non-accelerating inflation rate of unemployment.[15] Given that many governments consider the control of inflation as the most important objective of short-term macro-economic policy, NAIRU becomes the target unemployment rate. The major problem with NAIRU, however, was—and still is—that it varies substantially, between 3 and 7 per cent in the USA, and that NAIRU is subjected to hysteresis: NAIRU, after a crisis period, is estimated to be higher than before the crisis (Ball 2009). This has led to macro-policy reactions that are too slow and too limited to solve the increasing unemployment in many developed countries. The influence of NAIRU, and the dominance of inflation corrections rather than employment creation as the principle aim of macroeconomic policy,

---

[15] See, for example, Ball (2009).

has also taken hold in policy prescriptions for many developing countries (Freeman 2007). We argue, through three examples, that such a policy stance is not appropriate and that greater concern for employment creation is good macroeconomic policy.

The first example of short-term policies for employment creation is in the realm of *macroeconomic policy*. Over the last five years the World Bank has become more concerned with growing inequality and has devoted various research publications to this topic. One example is the study on monetary and exchange rate reforms in Conway (2005: Chapter 2). It opens with a reference to the so-called 'policy trilemma' of international economic policies (see Mundell 1963; Cohen 1993; Obstfeld et al. 2004). This states that national economic policy space is circumscribed by the impossibility of pursuing the following three policies simultaneously: open capital account, fixed exchange rates, and independent monetary policy. The trilemma posits that only two out of these three policies can be combined. Under a system of an open capital account and fixed exchange rates, countries cannot pursue an independent monetary policy to stimulate employment growth, for example, since interest rates are determined by world interest levels. Conversely, if countries need to undertake an independent monetary policy, they either have to revert to flexible exchange rates or opt for a closed capital account.

The policy restrictions posed by this trilemma do hamper policies for full employment. But the policy trilemma, which has guided policymakers for several decades and is still guiding a majority of macroeconomists, can be relaxed by avoiding the rigid two-corner solutions referred to above by looking, for example, beyond the traditional opposing alternatives of fixed versus flexible exchange rates, or open versus closed capital accounts, to adopt intermediate options in these three policy domains—such as capital account management through the selective application of capital controls, or a managed real exchange rate (see Bradford 2004).[16]

Although capital controls—much like any other policy instrument—have not always been fully effective in reaching their stated objectives (see Ariyoshi et al. 2000), they have contributed to regaining greater policy autonomy in several cases, such as in Chile (Gallego et al. 1999; see also de Gregorio et al. 2000). The more controversial issue is controls on outflows. Edison and Reinhart (2001) argue that such controls enabled Malaysia to

---

[16] For example, in the case of China, research from the IMF argues that making the quasi-fixed exchange rate more flexible would allow the country to pursue a more independent monetary policy. The same paper also argues for a cautious approach to capital account liberalization, given the institutional weaknesses of China's financial system (see Prasad et al. 2005). The argument could be extended to many other developing countries. Rather than abandoning capital controls altogether, they should remain a policy tool to be used selectively.

stabilize exchange rates and interest rates during the East Asian crisis and to gain more policy autonomy. Kaplan and Rodrik (2001) conclude that the Malaysian approach has led to a faster economic recovery and to a smaller decline in real wages and employment than IMF policies would have done.

How could a system of a managed real exchange rate, the second element mentioned earlier, stimulate employment? Rodrik (2003) and Frenkel (2004) provide three channels. Active management of the real exchange rate would allow for higher capacity utilization in times of unemployment, if applied in combination with an appropriate mix of macroeconomic and fiscal policies. It would also stimulate output growth and hence employment if combined with appropriate industrial policies, as experience in various Asian countries has shown. It could furthermore shift the sectoral composition of exports towards more labour-intensive goods, and hence increase the employment elasticity of the economy as a whole.

Employing a policy mix with intermediate options such as a managed capital account or a managed real exchange rate requires more fine-tuning and coherence in policies than relying on rule-of-thumb policy interventions. To achieve this, therefore, requires national institutions that have explicit mandates for employment and decent work.

Another possible, supplementary, element to relax the policy trilemma is *to include one or two additional policy instruments to complement the fiscal and monetary tools* (see also Tinbergen 1970[1952]). Bradford (2004) suggests, for example, social pacts or coordinated wage bargaining to hold down inflation and so to 'free up' other policies aimed at growth and employment creation. It is thus very important to have employment creation and equitable distribution as explicit policy objectives for macroeconomic policies (van der Hoeven and Saget 2004).

A second example of employment conscious short-term policies is that of *considering central banks as agents of development*. Epstein (2007) argues that an employment-targeting approach to central bank policy may seem quite alien to those schooled in the orthodox tradition, but that this, in fact, has been quite common historically in both the currently developed and developing countries. Over the years, central banks have been agents of economic development, not just agents of economic stabilization. And while sometimes central banks have failed quite spectacularly in this mission, there have been other important success stories, including important periods in the USA, UK, France, Germany, Japan, South Korea, and India, to name just a few examples.

As for developing countries, Amsden (2001, 2007) describes the key role that investment banks in coordination with central banks played in the successful industrialization stories of countries such as South Korea, Taiwan,

Malaysia, Brazil, Argentina, and others, in mobilizing and directing savings to key industrial sectors, and in particular to those specializing in exports.

A third example of shorter-term policies stimulating employment and decent work is that of *setting minimum wages*. Several ILO studies (Saget 2001, 2008) have observed that as a consequence of structural adjustment and of a breaking-down of trade unions and labour-market institutions, the minimum wage in a sizeable number of countries is so low that it is does not contribute to reducing inequalities or poverty reduction and has become in effect meaningless. In a second set of countries, the minimum wage appears to fulfil its objective of reducing poverty without hampering employment creation.[17] But there is also third a set of countries where the minimum wage is too high to be considered a genuine minimum wage, with the risk of hampering economic growth and thus longer-term employment creation. In this so-called 'maxi minimum wage' situation (Saget 2008), minimum wage policies amount more to average wage fixation than to fixing minimum wages. Poorly developed collective bargaining is often a driving factor behind this. Thus both too low and too high minimum wages are an indication of malfunctioning labour-market policies.

Misconceived (short-term) macroeconomic policies can prevent economies from achieving sustained growth and employment. Taylor (2009) gives various examples of how stability in interest rates and foreign exchange can contribute to steady growth, but that with increasing financial openness, procyclical macroeconomic policies, especially for medium-sized and smaller economies, have become the rule rather than the exception affecting sustained growth.

8.3.2 Longer-Term Policies for Employment Creation

Having reviewed some of the short-term policies for employment creation, we now turn to the long-term policies for employment creation.

Although economic growth depends on many factors, one factor contributing to growth is structural change, a process where economic activity increasingly takes place in sectors with high value added, with diversification and sophistication of production. Although this process of structural change necessitates labour reallocation and can thus generate (frictional) unemployment, the higher value added created in the growth process results in higher incomes from wages and capital, which, together with increased demand from abroad, will lead to higher growth and employment. This

---

[17] It has been argued that the existence of minimum wages results in greater informal employment. ILO (1977) shows, however, that minimum wages up to two-thirds of the level of wages of unskilled workers will not produce substantial increases in informality.

virtuous picture, however, can be disturbed when structural change and expanded production and productivity increases in some sectors do not lead to higher national productivity. McMillan and Rodrik (2011), for example, argue that structural change in Asia has led to higher national productivity and growth, but that in Africa and Latin America, policies until recently were based on capturing comparative advantage in primary products, leading to lower labour productivity and lower growth, with negative consequences for employment and wages. Asian countries had, and have, an industrialization process in which industrial policies have been applied successfully, in contrast to Africa where industrial policies were mainly absent and in Latin America where, at least until recently, these policies, constrained by the legacy of the Washington Consensus, were not robust enough to be effective. The current debate is therefore not whether public policies for industrialization are useful or not, but which type of public policies will work best under which circumstances (Lin 2011).

It is thus important to consider appropriate policies for structural change and well-thought-out industrial policies in a meaningful debate on employment creation.

Melamed et al. (2011), based on the work of Khan (2007) and others, survey the literature on findings on the relation between growth, poverty, and sectoral employment. In twenty-four growth episodes detailed information on growth and employment was available, and out of these, poverty decreased in eighteen episodes, with rising employment in services and in manufacturing in most of them (see Table 8.1). The six cases where poverty increased or remained stable were mostly characterized by an absence of increases in employment in every sector. This analysis thus gives support for the link between growth and employment. However the link is far from robust and needs further research.

As argued above, policies for employment need to take into account both the quantity of employment and the quality of employment, or, as Khan (2006) puts it, 'policies for employment need to be concerned with the

Table 8.1 Growth, employment, and poverty: a summary of evidence

	No. of episodes	Rising agricultural employment	Rising industrial employment	Rising services employment
Growth episodes associated with falling poverty rates	18	6	10	15
Growth episodes associated with no fall in poverty rates	6	2	3	1

Source: Based on Melamed et al. (2011).

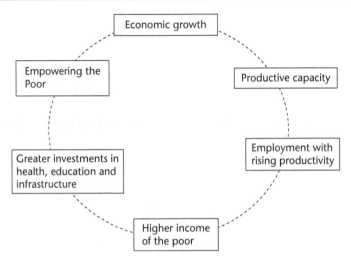

Figure 8.3 Virtuous circle of links among growth, employment, and poverty reduction
Source: Based on Ernst and Berg (2009).

quantity of employment, the factor productivity of employment, the factor remuneration of employment and the terms of employment'.

Ernst and Berg (2009) conceptualize these policy concerns in what they call the virtuous circle of links between growth, employment, and poverty reduction, namely economic growth, productive capacity, employment with rising productivity, higher incomes of the poor, greater investments in health, education, and infrastructure leading to an empowering of the poor, all contributing again to economic growth (see Figure 8.3). There are, however, many obstacles for such a virtuous circle to become effective in practice. Policy interventions are needed to overcome these obstacles and to stimulate employment creation.

Khan (2007) gives a useful overview of such policies. He distinguishes between five policy areas. The poor can escape working poverty when policies achieve a combination of the following:

- an increase in wage employment;
- an increase in the real wage;
- an increase in self-employment;
- an increase in productivity in self-employment;
- an increase in the terms of exchange of the output of self-employment.

But the poor face various constraints. One of the major constraints in the current context of globalization is a low output elasticity of demand for labour. Furthermore, economic growth, often in combination with exports to advanced markets, usually leads to growth in employment for which the poor do not possess the necessary skills. Also in the context of structural adjustment programmes, the employment impact of high growth is offset by a countervailing contraction of employment induced by economic reform. Another important factor is that growth might also fail to reduce poverty if the distribution of scarce productive resources is, and remains, highly concentrated.

In order to deal with these challenges, various longer-term employment policies are suggested: (i) rapid labour-absorbing growth that provides the poor with productive and reasonably well-remunerated employment; (ii) conversion of the poor in self-employment into productive entrepreneurs; (iii) an increase of productivity of poor workers both in wage and self-employment; (iv) labour-market policies that improve and adjust the skill composition of the poor; (v) macroeconomic policies that result in appropriate terms of exchange of the produce of the poor; (vi) in some countries an orderly dismantling of past systems of inefficient excess employment in the public or semi-public sector, with appropriate compensation rather than a disorderly and sudden dismantling; and (vii) a set of economic and social policies that incorporates special programmes designed for the households that cannot cover their basic needs from the proceeds of labour.

The effect of growth on employment is sometimes measured by the concept of employment elasticity of growth, that is, the percentage increase of employment that occurs with a one per cent increase in growth. Although various international reports use this concept, it is not without problems. First, since people in many developing countries cannot afford to be unemployed or to withdraw from the labour force, the employment elasticity of growth measures labour-force participation but does not give an indication of the quality of employment, as all activities performed by the poor are generally included in the measurement of employment. Second, high employment elasticity in itself does not convey success of an employment policy. For example, a country with a high employment elasticity (close to one), whose GDP grows slowly, say at 1 per cent a year, clearly does worse than a country with an employment elasticity of 0.5 but whose GDP grows at 7 per cent per annum. So when the concept of employment elasticity is used, it should be in conjunction with figures on growth and on the quality of the jobs created in different sectors and never as a single macroeconomic figure.

8.4 Aid and Employment

In combining the trends in employment and decent work, and the required national and international policies to promote good outcomes, the question is to what extent can development aid and development aid policies contribute to such policies?

Here, it may be useful to note that according to earlier observers, aid has often actually had a negative impact on employment of the poor. The analysis of the ground-breaking employment missions of the UN system in the 1970s pointed to a bias of aid against employment creation (e.g. the 1972 Mission Report to Kenya for the ILO; see also Jolly 1973). Major conclusions of these missions were that development aid often financed imports, which made capital cheaper vis-à-vis labour. Imported technologies were often also labour-replacing and big industries profited more than small industries from support and subsidies. The emphasis of aid was on urban areas, to the detriment of rural areas where most of the poor and underemployed lived. Some of these conclusions still hold true today, but in other cases aid donors have indeed shifted focus. But even this change in focus has not necessarily dealt with the root problems of employment creation, in particular, the need for investment to generate output and demand for employment and the distribution of profits emanating from productivity increases so that they can contribute to investment or increased wages to stimulate demand. Rather than deal with the structural changes necessary for increased productive employment, aid donors often supported social expenditure and programmes for small enterprises.

Thus a clearer conceptualization of the link between, on the one hand, the policies required to create employment and, on the other hand, the aid projects and policies to achieve this is clearly needed.

Table 8.2 summarizes potential policies directed towards the short-term objective of increased capacity utilization, and the longer-term objective of an increase in capacity, which might be supported by aid.

This table includes a number of policies that are favoured by current aid donors, but it also emphasizes policies for structural change and policies that affect the demand side of the economy. This follows our analysis above and is line with the recent observation by Taylor (2009) that orthodox economists

Table 8.2 Employment policies that might be supported by development aid

Capacity utilization	Capacity increase
Fiscal policies	Public investment
Monetary policies	Infrastructure
Exchange rate	Industry policy
Trade barriers	Education
Unemployment benefits	Vocational and management training
Cash transfers	Small enterprises
	HealthSocial security

Source: Author's compilation.

in short-term macro analysis place a great deal of emphasis on the supply side while ignoring the demand side, and that in relation to longer-term development, conventional economic analysis favours letting markets work rather than supporting the policies for structural change and industrial capacity-building.

As one can observe, the policies that influence employment creation and potentially interact with aid policies span a rather wide spectrum. As various analysts of structural patterns of development of successful countries have noted, a single general framework of development policy, such as the Washington Consensus, does not exist with respect to policies to promote structural change. Policies need to be time- and context-specific, and calls for 'best practice' are often a sign of intellectual laziness.

Therefore, in order to gain a better appreciation of the possible and desirable interaction between employment policies and development aid, a more detailed analysis of some of the aid-employment relationships seems to be necessary, taking into account context-specific situations (including the stage of development), as listed below:

- the effects of aid in increasing demand in situations of under-capacity and thus increasing employment;
- the effects of aid and Dutch disease in changing the balance between tradables and non-tradables and the consequences for employment;
- the effects of aid in increasing infrastructure and thus removing production bottlenecks in order to create more employment;
- the effects of aid in making capital more productive, with an ambivalent effect on quality and quantity of employment;
- the effects of aid in supporting structural change towards economic activity in sectors with high value added, with diversification and sophistication of production, which have a positive effect on employment and on the remuneration of unskilled and skilled workers in the long run;
- the role of aid in increasing education and hence human capital;
- the effect of aid on health issues so as to make work more productive; and
- the effects of aid on social security to make workers more productive and willing to adjust, etc.

8.5 Conclusions

This chapter has argued that in many countries the process of globalization has led to a 'precarization' of labour, which is especially manifest in the unstable working conditions of workers, in the growing inequality between the labour share and the capital share in national income in more than 75 per cent of the world's countries, as well as in the growing inequality in income and wages in many regions. Exceptions are some countries in Latin America where inequality declined from very high initial levels at the beginning of the century, and some countries in Sub-Saharan Africa and South East Asia. The lack of concern for employment and inequality in the formulation of the MDGs in 2000 and its consequences have been noted; moreover, the addition of a goal for full employment in a reformulation of the MDGs in 2005 did not lead to a change in focus in ODA. This chapter argues that if the growing concern for employment and inequality is taken seriously, a refocus of development efforts is necessary, combining a greater share of development aid for employment and productivity-enhancing activities with a change in national and international economic and financial policies, so as to make employment creation (together with poverty reduction) an overarching goal.

References

Amsden, A. (2001). *The Rise of the Rest: Challenges to the West from the Late-Industrializing Economies*. Oxford: Oxford University Press.

Amsden, A. (2007). *Escape from Empire: The Developing World's Journey through Heaven and Hell*. Cambridge, MA: MIT Press.

Amsden, A. (2011). 'Say's Law, Poverty Persistence, and Employment Neglect'. In R. van der Hoeven (ed.), *Employment, Inequality and Globalization: A Continuous Concern*. London: Routledge, 55–64.

Ariyoshi, A., K. F. Habermeier, B. Laurens, I. Oetker, J. C. Kriljenko, and A. Kirilenko (2000). '*Capital Controls: Country Experiences with Their Use and Liberalization*'. IMF Occasional Paper 190. Washington, DC: IMF.

Arndt, C., S. Jones, and F. Tarp (2010). '*Aid, Growth, and Development: Have We Come Full Circle?*'. WIDER WP, 2010/96. Helsinki: UNU-WIDER.

Ball, L. (2009). *Hysteresis in Unemployment, Old and New Evidence*. NBER Working Paper. Cambridge, MA: National Bureau of Economic Research.

Bradford, C. I. Jr (2004). 'Prioritizing Economic Growth: Enhancing Macroeconomic Policy Choice'. Paper presented at the XIXth G24 Technical Group Meeting, Washington, DC, 27–28 September.

CGD (Center for Global Development) (2011). *MDG Scorecards*. Washington, DC: CGD. Available at: <http://www.cgdev.org/section/topics/poverty/mdg_scorecards>.

Clark, H. (2011). 'Jobs, Equity and Voice: Why Both Economic and Political Inclusion Matter in the Arab World'. *Huffington Post*, 7 April.

Cohen, B. J. (1993). 'The Triad and the Unholy Trinity: Lessons for the Pacific Region'. In R. Higgott, R. Leaver, and J. Ravenhill (eds), *Pacific Economic Relations in the 1990s*. London: Allen and Unwin, 133–58.

Conway, P. (2005). 'Monetary and Exchange Rate Reforms'. In A. Coudouel and S. Paternostro (eds), *Analyzing the Distributional Impacts of Reform: A Practitioner's Guide*. Washington, DC: World Bank, 39–72.

de Gregorio, J., S. Edwards, and R. O. Valdés (2000). 'Controls on Capital Inflows: Do They Work?'. *Journal of Development Economics*, 63(1): 59–83.

Diwan, I. (2001). *'Debt as Sweat: Labour, Financial Crisis, and the Globalization of Capital'*. Washington, DC: World Bank. Mimeo.

Edison, H. and C. M. Reinhart (2001). 'Stopping Hot Money'. *Journal of Development Economics*, 66(2): 533–53.

Epstein, G. (2007). 'Central Banks as Agents of Employment Creation'. In J. A. Ocampo and K. S. Jomo (eds), *Towards Full and Decent Employment*. London: Zed Books, 99–122.

Ernst, C. and J. Berg (2009). 'The Role of Employment and Labour Markets in the Fight against Poverty'. In OECD, *Promoting Pro-Poor Growth: Employment*. Paris: OECD, 41–67.

Freeman, R. (2007). *Labor Market Institutions around the World*. NBER Working Paper 13242. Cambridge, MA: National Bureau of Economic Research.

Frenkel, R. (2004). 'Real Exchange Rate and Employment in Argentina, Brazil, Chile and Mexico'. Paper presented at the XIXth G24 Technical Group Meeting, Washington, DC, 27–28 September.

Gallego, F., L. Hernández, and K. Schmidt-Hebbel (1999). *Capital Controls in Chile: Effective? Efficient?*. CBC Working Paper 59. Santiago de Chile: Central Bank of Chile.

Ghose, A., N. Majid, and C. Ernst (2008). *The Global Employment Challenge*. Geneva: ILO.

Harrison, A. (2002). 'Has Globalization Eroded Labour's Share? Some Cross-Country Evidence'. Cambridge, MA: National Bureau of Economic Research. Mimeo.

ILO (1972). *Employment, Incomes and Equality: A Strategy for Increasing Productive Employment in Kenya*. Geneva: ILO.

ILO (1977). *Panorama Laboral 1997: América Latina y el Caribe*. Lima: ILO.

ILO (2008). *Global Wage Report, 2008/9: Minimum Wages and Collective Bargaining*. Geneva: ILO.

Jolly, R. et al. (eds) (1973). *Third World Employment, Problems and Strategies*. Harmondsworth: Penguin Education.

Kaplan, E. and D. Rodrik (2001). *Did the Malaysian Capital Controls Work?*. NBER Working Paper 8142. Cambridge, MA: National Bureau of Economic Research.

Khan, A. (2006). 'Employment Policies for Poverty Reduction'. In R. Islam (ed.), *Fighting Poverty: The Development–Employment Link*. London: Lynne Riemer, 63–103.

Khan, A. (2007). 'Growth, Employment and Poverty'. In J. A. Ocampo and K. S. Jomo (eds), *Towards Full and Decent Employment*. London: Zed Books, 123–57.

Kucera, D. and L. Roncolato (2008). 'Informal Employment: Two Contested Policy Issues'. *International Labour Review*, 147(4): 321–48.

Lee, K.-K. and A. Jayadev (2005). 'Capital Account Liberalization, Growth and the Labour Share of Income: Reviewing and Extending the Cross-Country Evidence'. In G. Epstein (ed.), *Capital Flight and Capital Controls in Developing Countries*. Cheltenham: Edward Elgar, 15–57.

Lin, J. Y. (2011). *'From Flying Geese to Leading Dragons: New Opportunities and Strategies for Structural Transformation in Developing Countries'.* WIDER Annual Lecture 15. Helsinki: UNU-WIDER.

McMillan, M. and D. Rodrik (2011). 'Globalization, Structural Change and Productivity Growth'. In M. Bacchetta and M. Jansen (eds), *Making Globalization Socially Sustainable.* Geneva: ILO and WTO, 49–84.

Maloney, W. (2004). 'Informality Revisited'. *World Development,* 32(7): 1159–78.

Melamed, C., R. Hartwig, and U. Grant (2011). *Jobs, Growth and Poverty: What Do We Know, What Don't We Know? What Should We Know?.* ODI Background Note. London: ODI. Available at: <http://www.odi.org.uk/resources/docs/7121.pdf>.

Mkandawire, T. (2011). 'How the New Poverty Agenda Neglected Social and Employment Policies in Africa'. In R. van der Hoeven, *Employment, Inequality and Globalization: A Continuous Concern.* London: Routledge, 35–54.

Mundell, R. A. (1963). 'Capital Mobility and Stabilization Policy under Fixed and Flexible Exchange Rates'. *Canadian Journal of Economics and Political Science,* 29(4): 475–85.

Obstfeld, M., J. C. Shambaugh, and A. M. Taylor (2004). *The Trilemma in History: Tradeoffs among Exchange Rates, Monetary Policies, and Capital Mobility.* NBER Working Paper 10396. Cambridge, MA: National Bureau of Economic Research.

OECD (2009). *Promoting Pro-Poor Growth: Employment.* Paris: OECD.

OECD-DAC (2011). *On-line database.* Paris: OECD-Development Assistance Committee.

Prasad, E., T. Rumbaugh, and Q. Wang (2005). *'Putting the Cart before the Horse? Capital Account Liberalization and Exchange Rate Flexibility in China'.* IMF Discussion Paper 05/1. Washington, DC: IMF.

Rada, C. and L. Taylor (2006). *Developing and Transition Economies in the Late 20th Century: Diverging Growth Rates, Economic Structures, and Sources of Demand.* DESA Working Paper 34. New York: UN-DESA.

Rani, U. (2008). *The Impact of Changing Work Patterns on Inequality.* IILS Working Paper 19308. Geneva: International Institute of Labour Studies.

Rodrik, D. (2003). *Growth Strategies.* NBER Working Paper 10050. Cambridge, MA: National Bureau of Economic Research.

Saget, C. (2001). 'Poverty Reduction and Decent Work in Developing Countries: Do Minimum Wages Help?'. *International Labour Review,* 140(3): 237–69.

Saget, C. (2008). 'Fixing Minimum Wage Levels in Developing Countries: Common Failures and Remedies'. *International Labour Review,* 147(1): 25–42.

Sirkeci, I., J. H. Cohen, and D. Ratha (2012). *Migration and Remittances during the Global Financial Crisis and Beyond.* Washington, DC: World Bank.

South Centre (2012). 'The EPAs and Risk for Africa, Local Production and Regional Trade'. *Analytical Note No. SC/TDP/AN/EPA/30.* Geneva: South Centre.

Taylor, L. (2009). *Growth, Development Policy, Job Creation and Poverty Reduction.* DESA Working Paper 34. New York: UN-DESA.

Tinbergen, J. (1970[1952]). *On the Theory of Economic Policy.* Amsterdam: North-Holland.

UNCTAD (2009). *World Investment Report.* Geneva: UNCTAD.

UNDG (2010). *'Thematic Paper on MDG 1: Eradicate Extreme Poverty and Hunger'.* New York: United Nations Development Group.

Vandemoortele, J. (2011) 'The MDG Story: Intention Denied'. *Development and Change*, 42(1): 1–21.

van der Hoeven, R. (2010). *Labour Markets Trends, Financial Globalization and the Current Crisis in Developing Countries*. DESA Working Paper 99. New York: UN-DESA.

van der Hoeven, R. (ed.) (2011). *Employment, Inequality and Globalization: A Continuous Concern*. London: Routledge.

van der Hoeven, R. (2012). *Development Aid and Employment*. WIDER Working Paper 2012/107. Helsinki: UNU-WIDER.

van der Hoeven, R. and C. Saget (2004). 'Labour Market Institutions and Income Inequality: What Are the New Insights after the Washington Consensus?'. In G. A. Cornia (ed.), *Inequality, Growth, and Poverty in an Era of Liberalization and Globalization*. Oxford: Oxford University Press for UNU-WIDER, 197–220.

World Bank (2005). *Global Economic Prospects 2006: Economic Implications of Remittances and Migration*. Washington, DC: World Bank.

Part III
Structural Adjustment, New Macroeconomic Approaches, and Remaining Challenges

9

The New Structuralist Macroeconomics and Income Inequality*

Giovanni Andrea Cornia

9.1 Introduction

During the last decade several developing countries adopted a new set of macroeconomic policies which, although sharing some similar elements, differs substantially from the liberal approach in several other respects. Important differences exist in relation to the *theoretical* Washington Consensus (WC) approach codified in the early 1990s by John Williamson and, in particular, to the *real-life* WC, which dominated policymaking in the 1980s and 1990s. In the developing countries that adopted it, the new approach appears to have improved growth and income inequality while helping to preserve a reasonable macro stability during the financial crisis of 2008–11. Unlike traditional macroeconomics (which broadly ignored social issues), the new approach constitutes an important tool to promote the achievement of social objectives too. This chapter aims to distil the common elements of this new approach—which, to follow Bresser-Pereira (2011), we name 'the new structuralist macroeconomics'—and to analyse its impact on income inequality.

The new approach was most frequently adopted in South America, although a few Sub-Saharan African (SSA) and South East Asian countries also introduced similar macroeconomic changes (Cornia and Martorano 2012). In contrast, most economies of Eastern Europe and the former Soviet

* The author would like to acknowledge the insightful comments of Carlos Fortin, Marco Dardi, Frances Stewart, Rolph van der Hoeven, and Nadia von Jacobi, as well as the excellent support of Bruno Martorano in compiling data and regression analysis. The usual caveats apply.

Union (EE-FSU) adopted in the 2000s liberal policies featuring fixed pegs, large current account deficits, and growing external indebtedness.

The past decade also witnessed a fall in income inequality in most Latin American countries as well as in some Sub-Saharan African and Asian economies. A question therefore spontaneously arises about the relation between macroeconomic policy changes and improvements in income inequality in developing countries.

9.2 Liberal Macroeconomics in Theory and Real Life

There is considerable ambiguity about the nature of the liberal macroeconomic policies adopted on a grand scale in the developing countries during the 1980s and 1990s, the transitional economies in the 1990s and 2000s, and most OECD countries during the last decade. Such an approach is normally referred to as the Washington Consensus, i.e. a set of ten policies on which a broad consensus had formed among Washington-based institutions (Williamson 1990). However, as Birdsall et al. (2010) observe, Williamson's ten policy points were quite different from the market-fundamentalist policies introduced during the last three decades. Paradoxically, as shown in Table 9.1, actual policy implementation was often much more extreme, particularly with respect to taxation, financial liberalization and exchange rate policy. Williamson (2002) himself noted later on that 'the Consensus [developed into]...an unjust set of neoliberal policies...imposed on hapless countries by the Washington-based international financial institutions'. Thus, popular references to the Washington Consensus relate to policies implemented in real life. As shown by Column 3 of Table 9.1, such policies were often at odds not only with the new structuralist macroeconomics but also with Williamson's original decalogue of 1990.

The scope of the liberal macroeconomic package was narrow and the number of its instruments limited (Blanchard et al. 2010). Macro policy had a main target—low inflation (2 per cent)—which had to be achieved through the policy rate set by an independent central bank focusing on inflation-targeting and the stabilization of inflationary expectations. The deep-seated belief was that as long as inflation was low and stable, the economy operated close to its output frontier while avoiding a rise in twin deficits and public debt. In such an approach fiscal policy played a secondary role due to lags in tax collection and expenditure cuts, the limited depth of domestic bond markets, and skepticism about the ability of governments to withstand the political pressures of interest groups.

The standard measures included in the real-life WC package included the following (Table 9.1, Column 3): a low budget deficit to be achieved quickly,

Table 9.1 Comparison of macroeconomic policy approaches

Policy area	Williamson's Washington Consensus 1993	Real-life Washington Consensus	New structuralist macroeconomics
1. Fiscal	• low deficit (2–3%) as precondition for growth • deficit not to be funded with inflation tax	• low deficits • procyclical cuts led to illusory fiscal adjustment • deficit to be closed by spending cuts, not by tax rises	• zero/small long-term deficit • countercyclical fiscal policy • stabilization funds/fiscal rules • gradual budget deficit cuts • targeted safety nets as automatic and discretionary stabilizers
2. Public expenditure	• public spending focus on areas with high returns (health, education, and infrastructure)	• deflationary adjustment policies led to large cuts in social spending and public investments	• increase in public social and infrastructural expenditure • sizeable increase in income-transfer programmes
3. Foreign indebtedness (public and private)	• not included	• large rise in public debt (from the 1970s) often leading to defaults	• reduce public debt/GDP • control rise of private debt • mobilize domestic savings
4. Taxation	• reduce efficiency cost of taxation • horizontal equity	• cut direct and trade taxes • expand scope of VAT • frequent drop in tax/GDP	• raise tax/GDP to potential level • greater use of progressive taxes • cuts in regressive excises
5. Monetary	• interest-rate liberalization	• large and persistent rises in interest rates	• low inflation not enough to minimize output gap • moderate and countercyclical stance
6. Exchange rate	• unified and competitive	• hard pegs or free floats	• SCRER in most cases • reserve accumulation • intervention in currency markets
7. Trade	• quantitative trade restrictions to be replaced by tariffs of around 10%	• similar	• free-trade policy with temporary controls in case of crises • diversification of exports/destinations • South–South trade
8. Current account	• not included	• a sustainable deficit financed by stable aid, FDI, and portfolio inflows	• long-term equilibrium or surplus
9. Openness to FDI	• barriers to FDI to be abolished • equal treatment of FDI	• same • FDI dominated by mergers and acquisitions	• similar approach, with some selectivity
10. Openness to portfolio flows	• not included	• encouraged, to finance development and for their disciplining role	• introduce temporary/permanent controls for inflows/outflows • steer their allocation to traded sector • sterilize growth in money supply
11. Financial and banking regulation	• financial de-repression	• financial de-repression • financial regulation not a macro policy tool	• prudential regulation is essential for macro stability • expand domestic credit during crises

Source: Author's compilation, in part drawing on Rodrik (2007).

including in periods of recession by cutting expenditure, as tax policy during this period was influenced by the belief that it was more appropriate to reduce the size of government than to increase the level of taxation significantly above historical levels; limited scope for discretionary countercyclical fiscal policy; a public debt/GDP ratio below 60 per cent; a monetary policy inspired by inflation-targeting; an exchange rate regime opting for a pure float or hard peg; acceptance of large current account deficits funded by stable aid, FDI, and liberalized portfolio inflows; neglect of financial and banking regulations (considered as outside the scope of macroeconomic policy), which, given the enthusiasm for financial deregulation, were seen as an intrusion in the functioning of credit markets.[1]

The success of this approach was to be assessed in terms of short-term changes in output gap, inflation, twin deficits, and public debt/GDP. Sound levels of these indicators were considered to be the preconditions for achieving private-sector-led growth, which depended on the availability of labour, physical and human capital, and technology, on which macroeconomics had no influence. In this sense, liberal macroeconomics was growth-neutral. This view contrasts with the development-oriented structuralist macroeconomics, which emphasizes public investments, competitive exchange rates, low dependence on foreign savings, and active credit policy as ways to stimulate long-term growth. During the 1990s macroeconomics set limits to private foreign indebtedness and introduced efficiency-enhancing measures such as privatization of state assets and liberalization of domestic markets, foreign trade, and the capital account (Table 9.2). This broader approach was expected to enhance allocative efficiency and therefore also needed to be assessed in terms of its growth impact. This broadening of evaluation criteria, however, did not extend to income distribution, as it was believed that the latter mainly depended on structural factors that had to be addressed through safety nets.

9.2.1 Results of the 'Real-Life' Washington Consensus

The real-life WC reforms succeeded in opening up the economy, promoting trade and financial integration, and reducing budget deficits, inflation, and, to a lesser extent, public debt and current account deficit (Table 9.2). Yet the deficit reduction was achieved by means of investment cuts that reduced medium-term growth and tax revenue, leading in this way to an illusory

---

[1] The IMF has gone through some rethinking (Blanchard et al. 2010). The extent of this rethinking, however, has been questioned by McKinley (2010), who notes that while these authors argue that policymakers should monitor multiple macro targets and use multiple instruments, low inflation in the end remained the IMF's top priority.

Table 9.2 Changes in policy stance on domestic and external liberalization

Regions	1982–90	1991–97	1998–2002	2002–10
*Average import tariff**				
South America	40.0	19.0	12.2	10.6
Central America and Mexico	46.6	18.1	8.8	7.2
Sub-Saharan Africa	26.7	24.9	14.5	13.2
MENA	29.7	21.9	17.3	16.2
South Asia	62.9	52.9	20.8	14.9
East and South East Asia	20.3	16.7	7.6	6.9
Asian economies in transition[1/]	44.5	38.9	15.5	12.6
EE-FSU	...	11.0	9.0	6.0
Advanced economies	8.5	7.1	3.3	4.2
*Trade/GDP ratio***				
South America	38.8	45.3	45.3	57.1
Central America and Mexico	63.0	79.4	84.5	89.3
Sub-Saharan Africa	66.9	68.3	73.9	79.3
MENA	64.1	68.1	62.9	78.7
South Asia	33.6	41.9	44.9	46.1
East and South East Asia	114.1	128.6	153.3	163.0
Asian economies in transition[1/]	29.5	58.1	75.2	106.0
EE-FSU	73.0	91.4	98.6	104.7
Advanced economies	60.6	62.3	74.1	77.5
*Kaopen index of capital account openness****				
South America	−0.78	−0.17	0.76	1.00
Central America and Mexico	−0.84	0.29	1.18	1.67
Sub-Saharan Africa	−0.91	−0.82	−0.59	−0.56
MENA	−0.64	−0.35	0.02	0.36
South Asia	−1.29	−0.74	−0.93	−0.90
East and South East Asia	0.85	0.96	0.50	0.57
Asian economies in transition[1/]	−1.73	−1.31	−1.07	−1.00
EE-FSU	−1.84	−0.53	0.01	0.65
Advanced economies	0.83	1.89	2.28	2.32
*Index of domestic financial liberalization**				
South America	5.1	6.8	6.9	7.7
Central America and Mexico	6.7	7.3	7.5	8.4
Sub-Saharan Africa	4.5	5.1	6.6	7.4
MENA	3.6	4.6	5.8	6.5
South Asia	4.7	5.6	6.4	7.4
East and South East Asia	5.9	6.9	6.6	8.2
Asian economies in transition[1/]	0.0	2.9	4.6	8.0
EE-FSU	0.5	3.2	7.4	8.7
Advanced economies	7.6	8.2	8.6	8.8

Notes: The Kaopen index ranges between 0 and 10 (complete liberalization). [1/] China and Vietnam.
Source: Author's compilation on the basis of * Gwartney et al. (2011), ** World Development Indicators (2011 version), *** Chinn and Ito (2008 and 2012 update).

adjustment, as the deficit widened in line with the adjustment-induced slowdown of GDP and tax collection.

After a steep rise in the 1980s and early 1990s (when Brazil, Russia, and other economies experienced hyperinflation), the rate of inflation fell to around 10 per cent in all regions except SSA and the transition economies (Table 9.3). This result was achieved by means of a restrictive monetary policy and fixed nominal pegs. However, where such an approach was sustained for years, the real exchange rate (RER) appreciated, affecting in this way the current account balance, growth, and inequality.

While the real-life Washington Consensus achieved important results in the field of stabilization, its growth, investment, and inequality performance was unsatisfactory. Growth slowed over 1980–2000 compared to 1960–80 (see Table 5 in Cornia 2012). The share of countries recording a negative growth of GDP/c rose from 6 and 12 per cent in the 1960s and 1970s to 31 and 32 per cent in the 1980s and 1990s. In contrast, growth accelerated and poverty declined (even though inequality rose) in China, India, and Vietnam, where macroeconomic policies differed from those of the real-life Washington Consensus. Unsurprisingly, with these exceptions, the investment rate stagnated or declined (Cornia 2012). While these disappointing outcomes might have been caused by endogenous changes in labour supply, prices, and technology, there is now agreement that they were mainly due to the implementation of real-life WC macro policies (Birdsall et al. 2010).

During the 1980s and 1990s domestic income inequality increased in 73 of the 105 countries with adequate statistical information (Table 9.4). The increase was almost universal in the OECD, Latin America, and EE-FSU. In China inequality rose slowly over 1978–90, but accelerated thereafter. A rise of inequality was observed also in the economies of East Asia, which had achieved a rapid and equitable export-led growth in the past, and in India. Inequality rose less markedly in SSA and Middle East and North Africa (MENA), where, however, data scarcity limits the scope of the analysis.

9.3 The New Structuralist Macroeconomics and Inequality

During the last decade many developing economies adopted defensive macroeconomic policies to protect themselves from the negative effects of rising global interdependence. The new structuralist macroeconomics is also a reaction to the deflationary bias of the real-life WC approach, i.e. the recurrent appreciation of the RER and the tendency of wages to grow below productivity. This bias, by depressing private consumption and exports, constitutes a major impediment to growth. The new approach has evolved also from

Table 9.3 Indexes of macroeconomic balance, 1982–2010

Regions	1982–90	1991–97	1998–2002	2002–10
*Budget balance/GDP (deficit < 0)**				
South America	−1.7	−2.0	−3.2	−2.5
Central America and Mexico	−2.4	−0.8	−2.8	−1.9
Sub-Saharan Africa	−5.1	−3.9	−3.5	−0.7
MENA	−1.8	−1.9	−1.8	0.1
South Asia	−6.9	−6.2	−6.0	−4.7
East and South East Asia	0.8	4.5	−0.7	−0.2
Asian economies in transition	−1.6	−1.7	−3.3	−2.5
EE-FSU	−10.1	−5.3	−3.2	−1.1
Advanced economies	−3.1	−4.1	−0.1	−1.5
*Average yearly rate of inflation**				
South America	386.3	111.7	11.7	7.6
Central America and Mexico	361.5	15.8	7.0	7.4
Sub-Saharan Africa	20.1	165.5	35.0	8.2
MENA	29.4	20.4	7.6	6.0
South Asia	10.3	9.3	5.9	8.3
East and South East Asia	6.5	5.7	5.9	3.9
Asian economies in transition	81.5	17.1	1.2	6.0
EE-FSU	15.0	528.2	16.6	6.7
Advanced economies	8.9	3.2	2.3	2.3
Average yearly variations in the real effective exchange rate index (2005 = 100) [a/, b/]				
South America	−8.5	3.6	−3.5	2.7
Central America and Mexico	−1294.7	2.5	1.4	0.1
Sub-Saharan Africa	−20.0	−2.1	−5.1	7.3
MENA	−7.4	−4.1	−0.1	0.5
South Asia	−8.5	−1.1	−1.6	0.8
East and South East Asia	−3.2	1.2	−4.0	1.2
Asian economies in transition	−20.2	−1.2	0.3	1.0
EE-FSU	−23.4	3.2	0.9	2.4
Advanced economies	0.3	−0.7	−0.5	0.6
*Public debt/GDP (per cent)**				
South America	56.8	47.7	52.5	44.4
Central America and Mexico	111.7	121.9	66.9	49.0
Sub-Saharan Africa	93.1	105.8	105.0	69.2
MENA	62.3	89.8	72.2	61.8
South Asia	92.1	80.4	76.9	76.9
East and South East Asia	46.6	39.8	52.6	46.4
Asian economies in transition	4.7	6.4	15.7	17.9
EE-FSU	32.1	72.7	45.1	31.9
Advanced economies	49.5	65.7	61.3	63.5
*Current account balance/GDP**				
South America	−2.8	−2.4	−1.7	2.0
Central America and Mexico	−4.9	−6.5	−5.9	−5.7
Sub-Saharan Africa	−6.9	−6.5	−6.7	−5.9

(*Continued*)

Table 9.3 (Continued)

Regions	1982–90	1991–97	1998–2002	2002–10
MENA	–3.5	–3.0	0.9	3.2
South Asia	–4.6	–3.2	0.0	–0.9
East and South East Asia	–2.1	–1.1	6.8	7.6
Asian Economies in transition	–2.0	–2.1	1.4	0.8
EE-FSU	–2.3	–6.0	–5.1	–4.6
Advanced economies	–1.3	0.2	0.3	–0.3
Foreign debt/Exports***				
South America	31	245	252	57
Central America and Mexico	39	405	161	89
Sub-Saharan Africa	42	616	497	79
MENA	25	228	191	78
South Asia	31	285	224	46
East and South East Asia	17	137	128	163
Asian economies in transition ᶜ/	67	113	86	39
EE-FSU	56	120	131	104
Advanced economies	…	…	…	77

Notes:
ᵃ/ Data cover 58% of 138 countries based on WDI 2011, BIS, and IDLA data.
ᵇ/ A minus sign signals REER depreciation.
ᶜ/ China and Vietnam only.
Source: Author's compilation based on * WEO (2011 version), ** ERS/USDA International Macro Database (2011 version), *** WDI (2011 version) and Reinhart and Rogoff (2010).

the critique of the 'growth with foreign savings' paradigm, as steady inflows attracted by high interest rates (considered necessary to target inflation) caused an appreciation of the RER, leading to persistent current account deficits that were financed by more inflows.

It is difficult to define a universal package of structuralist macroeconomic policies, as these depend on a long list of local conditions. Yet some broad principles apply fairly generally (Rodrik 2007). Indeed, the new macroeconomics pivots around policies aiming simultaneously at low inflation, budget deficit (or even surplus) and output gap, preventing external and internal crises, aiming at long-term growth of output and employment in the traded sector, lowering inequality, and neutralizing Dutch disease effects on industrialization and inequality by taxing commodity exports and creating offshore sovereign funds. The key elements of the structuralist macroeconomics include:

(i) *Reducing dependence on foreign savings, lowering foreign indebtedness, and mobilizing domestic savings.* Liberalization of the capital account has been presented as the golden opportunity to access a global pool of savings to speed up capital accumulation and job creation. These promises, however, have seldom materialized. Indeed, the evidence shows that open economies

182

Table 9.4 Trend in the Gini coefficient of the distribution of household income per capita, selected developed, developing, and transition countries, 1980–2000 and 2000–10[a]

A: 1980s and 1990s

	OECD	Transitional economies		Developing countries					World
		Europe	Asia	LatinAmerica	MENA	South East Asia	SouthAsia	SSA	
Specific period for each region[b]	1980–2001	1990–1998	1980–2000	1980–2002	1980–2000	1980–1995	1980–2000	1980–1995	
Rising inequality	14	24	2	14	2	5	3	9	73
No change	1	0	1	1	3	0	0	2	8
Falling inequality	6	0	0	3	3	2	2	8	24
Total	21	24	3	18	8	7	5	19	105

B: 2000–10 (or latest available year)

	OECD	Transitional economies		Developing countries					World
		Europe	Asia	LatinAmerica	MENA	South East Asia	SouthAsia	SSA	
Specific period for each region[b]	2000–2010	1998–2010	2000–2009	2002–2010	2000–2007	1995–2009	2000–2010	1995–2007	
Rising inequality	9	13	2	2	4	3	4	7	44
No change	4	5	1	1	0	0	1	1	13
Falling inequality	8	6	0	15	4	4	0	13	50
Total	21	24	3	18	8	7	5	21	107

Notes:
[a] The countries included in the table have at least ten well-spaced data over the thirty years considered. Each country was assigned to the rising, stable, or falling categories on the basis of a trend analysis.
[b] The periodization and turning points vary from one region to another. The 1980s have fewer data points.
Source: Cornia and Martorano (2012).

with sizeable domestic banking systems, savings, and investment rates have smaller portfolio inflows than countries with smaller banking systems and savings. Indeed, countries relying on external financing often end up in financial traps characterized by exposure to sudden stops, external shocks, unstable and costly risk premia, rises in domestic rates in line with those paid on foreign loans, and RER appreciation.

Reliance on foreign savings in the 2000s has become more selective, e.g. for loans to finance investments in the traded sector, while several countries reduced their public foreign debt.[2] As a result, the average ratio of foreign debt to exports fell markedly (Table 9.3). Spreads on international loans also fell as the perception of country risk improved, thanks to a rise in commodity prices that allowed some countries to improve their current account balance, accumulate reserves, and reduce foreign debt.

The experience of the EE-FSU stands in sharp contrast to this trend. Indeed, the region received a massive inflow of FDI and hard-currency loans at low interest rates (Aslund 2009). By 2008, Bulgaria, Estonia, Hungary, Latvia, and Slovenia had private foreign debts in excess of 100 per cent of GDP while their net foreign asset position deteriorated sharply (Figure 9.1), making them vulnerable to the sudden stop of inflows in 2009–10.

The new macro approach thus emphasizes that capital accumulation needs to be funded mainly through the strengthening of indigenous financial institutions and that macroeconomic credibility and effective banking/financial regulation are essential to increase domestic savings. The latter can be increased by harnessing the mandatory savings of pension funds, tightening consumption credit, and ensuring that there are incentives to invest. Finally, in countries with 'tax space' (i.e. in the sixty or so developing countries with tax/GDP ratios well below the potential level) public savings can be raised by increasing tax pressure.

(ii) *Controlling capital inflows and harnessing their sectoral allocation.* Greenfield FDI in labour-intensive manufacturing have often had an equalizing effect. In contrast, portfolio flows were often more problematic. Countries thus imposed 'price' (e.g. capital transactions taxes) and 'quantity' (e.g. minimum stay) requirements on capital inflows so as to avoid Dutch disease effects, bubbles, and RER instability. In addition, central banks limited the foreign exchange exposure of domestic banks, forbade them to borrow internationally to extend loans to the non-traded sector, and limited foreign ownership in sectors such as real estate, as was observed in Colombia, India, Malaysia,

---

[2] Brazil and Argentina prepaid their outstanding debt to the IMF, other countries restructured their foreign debt at a discount, and several low-income countries benefited from the HIPC programme. As a result, gross public foreign debt net of reserves fell in Latin America from 33 to 8 per cent of GDP.

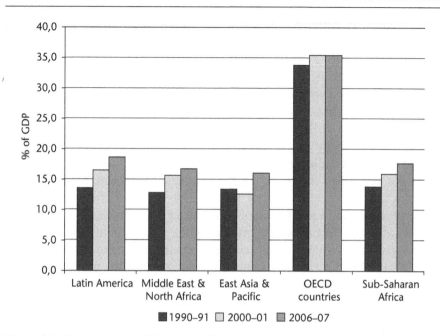

Figure 9.1 Average tax-to-GDP ratio in the main developing regions
Note: Latin America includes Argentina, Brazil, Chile, Colombia, Mexico, Peru, and Venezuela.
Source: Compiled by the author.

Singapore, Taiwan, India, South Korea, and Brazil in 2009–10. Central banks can also harness the inflows towards the labour-intensive traded sector by requiring commercial banks to allocate a share of their lending to agriculture and SMEs or by setting up loan guarantees in these sectors.

A key issue concerns the timing of the introduction, duration, and scope of capital controls. The IMF (2011) now fully supports temporary controls on inflows during crises, but the new approach suggests that they can be used as long as they are needed and can also be applied to outflows (Gallagher, Griffith-Jones, and Ocampo 2011). However, it is often argued that capital controls are not easily implemented, especially in countries with limited administrative capacity, that controls cannot replace sound macroeconomic policies, and that they can only slow down the flow of capitals but not eliminate it completely (Helleiner 1998). Yet, econometric evidence suggests that during the last fifteen years controls have been fairly effective (Gallagher, Griffith-Jones, and Ocampo 2011) and that they can, in conjunction with other measures, constitute a deterrent against massive shifts in capital movements.

(iii) *An exchange rate regime which reduces currency crises and promotes growth.* The crisis of the fixed-peg regimes epitomized by the collapse of the Argentinean currency board in 2002 encouraged a growing number of countries to opt for a stable and competitive real exchange rate (SCRER; see Frenkel and Rapetti 2008). Empirical research shows that a SCRER has been a key factor for kick-starting growth and improving long-term performance (Rodrik 2003; Gala 2008). This exchange rate regime tends to reduce the risk of currency crises, and at the same time provides adequate incentives for the expansion of the traded sector where many low-income workers are employed. This means rejecting the supposed superiority of the 'two-corner solutions' and recognizing that in small-to-medium open economies RER stability is a key policy objective. While a managed float, combining exchange rate flexibility with discretionary interventions in the currency market by the central bank, is now the tool of choice in a growing number of countries, much of the EE-FSU nations followed opposite policies. Only four opted for a managed float, while all others anchored their currency to the euro or dollar, or established a currency board (Aslund 2009). With fixed pegs, these countries could not devalue their currencies to respond to the balance-of-payments shock of 2008–10, and thus had to introduce a painful 'internal devaluation' consisting of raising interest rates, cutting nominal wages, and realizing large fiscal surpluses, i.e. measures which produced unequalizing effects (Purfield and Rosenberg 2010).

The management of a SCRER-type exchange rate regime requires the adoption of several supportive measures, starting with prudent fiscal and monetary policies that target inflation. Indeed, devaluation of the nominal exchange rate entails a slower decline of inflation than under other types of arrangements, as imported inflation rises in line with the nominal devaluations implicit in this approach. Inflationary pressures are aggravated by the SCRER's expansionary bias. In addition, the SCRER regime requires that the central bank accumulates large reserves (Table 9.5) to mitigate its appreciation during periods of financial/export bonanza or the collapse of the nominal exchange rate in the case of external shocks. Finally, the SCRER regime also requires the possibility of introducing capital controls. Several authors argue, however, that such an 'insurance policy' is inherently deflationary and can cost up to 3 per cent of GDP (Chandrasekhar and Ghosh 2009) as the reserves earn low interests on US bonds, while they could be used to import capital goods to speed up growth. Rodrik (2006), however, places such a figure at around 1 per cent of GDP, a tolerable amount when considering the favourable effects of holding large reserves on RER stability, the current account, and GDP growth.

(iv) *Long-term equilibrium or surplus of the current account balance.* As noted, the new structuralist macroeconomics is critical of the 'growth with foreign savings' paradigm and emphasizes the need for generating a current account surplus, so as to avoid problems of foreign indebtedness and inability to

Table 9.5 International reserves as a share of GDP

	1982–90	1991–97	1998–2002	2002–10
South America	7.4	10.7	11.1	15.4
Central America and Mexico	4.5	6.7	9.8	12.6
Sub-Saharan Africa	7.0	10.1	12.1	15.9
MENA	13.8	14.5	20.9	42.7
South Asia	3.8	7.8	8.6	12.0
East and South East Asia	17.0	24.8	34.1	40.6
Asian economies in transition	3.1	8.3	13.2	30.9
EE-FSU	2.7	9.2	14.5	21.5
Advanced economies	6.4	7.1	6.5	6.1

Source: Author's elaboration on the basis of UNCTADstat (2011 version).

control the exchange rate. As a result, during the 2000s all developing regions substantially improved their current account position and in three cases recorded surpluses (Table 9.2). The main exceptions were the non-oil economies of EE-FSU, where the current account deficit rose to 10 per cent of GDP. In Bulgaria, in 2007–8 the current account deficit exceeded 25 per cent of GDP.

(v) *Trade policy*. As was shown in Table 9.2, the free-trade policies adopted in the past have not been overturned during the 2000s, while there is evidence that their preservation did not generate additional unequalizing effects. In contrast, the structure of trade changed substantially as there was a decline in the share of trade with the advanced economies (again with the exception of EE-FSU countries, which increased their export dependence on Western Europe), a rise in intra-regional share trade, and a surge in the share of trade with the Asian economies. Thus, there has been a shift towards a trade regime that avoids a collapse of the import-competing sectors and actively seeks to diversify exports, while quickly removing any remaining anti-export-sector bias. However, rising trade with Asia often led to a 're-primarization' of exports in Latin America and Africa (Ocampo 2012).

(vi) *A countercyclical fiscal policy*. In the past, many economies lacked the ability to pursue countercyclical fiscal policies during crises owing to high levels of debt and future unfunded liabilities. In spite of this, the real-life Washington Consensus demanded a quick reduction of the deficit, with yearly cuts of up to 4–5 per cent of GDP. The new structuralist macroeconomics emphasizes instead the importance of being able to count on an adequate fiscal space, as shown by the growing number of countries recording a fall in deficits and public debt during the growth years of the 1990s and 2000s (Table 9.2). For instance, in 2008 seven of the ten South American countries analysed exhibited surpluses, thanks to the adoption in prior years of fiscal rules, fiscal responsibility laws, or discretional decisions aiming at correcting the pro-deficit bias of the past. At the same time, these countries allowed countercyclical increases in deficits during crises to support aggregate demand and limit the impact on output gap and inequality (Fanelli et al. 2011; see also Table 9.3).

A key issue in this regard concerns the pace of reduction of the deficit. The IMF argues that the deficit should be sustainable over the next five to ten years, but in determining this, it assumes the rate of growth, fiscal revenue, and interest rates as exogenous, while such variables and the deficit are, as argued above, jointly determined. Nor can the case for quick deficit reductions be argued on the basis that temporary deficits are costly, as there is no convincing evidence in this regard. In contrast, there is evidence—including for the European Union crisis of 2009–12 (Blanchard and Leigh 2013)—that large and rapid fiscal cuts reduce growth over the short and long term. Thus, while deficits certainly need to be reduced, this should be done gradually.[3] For instance, Adam and Bevan (2001) suggest that deficit reductions of up to 1.5 per cent of GDP per year help re-establish fiscal balance with a modest impact on output while larger reductions can hurt growth. There is also evidence that during the fiscal adjustment of 2009, many developing countries expanded public expenditure and the budget deficit. Though most of them reverted in 2010–11 to a more conservative stance, they still protected spending on infrastructure, health, and education (see Chapter 11).

(vii) *Greater role of automatic and discretionary stabilizers.* One area of the new consensus concerns the need to place greater reliance than in the past on both automatic and discretionary fiscal stabilizers. Even in the past, and increasingly so in recent times, commodity exporters set up stabilization funds aimed at offsetting the revenue effects of large fluctuations in the values of their exports. Such funds set aside resources during boom years (thus reducing the inflationary pressures arising from the non-traded sector) and released them automatically in crisis years to sustain public spending and aggregate demand. The orthodox view with respect to discretionary stabilizers was that they face design, timing, and organizational problems exactly when they are needed, with the result that their benefits generally arrive late. However, the last decade has witnessed the spread of equalizing social assistance transfers (currently reaching 860 million people worldwide), which can be expanded during crises.[4]

---

[3] During the recent crisis, deficits fell at a slower pace than in the past as the IMF came closer to playing the role of lender of last resort and as many developing countries had improved their financial resilience during the 2000s.

[4] See <http://papers.ssrn.com/sol3/papers.cfm?abstract_id=1672090>.

While these programmes were not considered as a component of macro policy, it now appears that they can play an important countercyclical role, making it possible to absorb shocks better and introduce policies that otherwise would generate hard-to-shoulder social and political costs.

(viii) *Tax policy*. More than before, the new approach emphasizes the macroeconomic and distributive advantages of an adequate level and progressiveness of taxation, and is less concerned with its presumed efficiency costs (Table 9.1). Indeed, the last decade witnessed a fairly universal rise in tax/GDP ratio (see Table 8 in Cornia 2012 as well as Figure 9.1). While the recent increase in commodity prices contributed to the surge in revenue in some countries, the rise in tax/GDP ratios (Figure 9.1) was mainly driven by tax reforms that placed greater emphasis on income, wealth, and financial transaction taxes, pragmatic presumptive taxation, and taxes on luxury items while reducing regressive excises. As a result, between the 1990s and 2000s the redistributive effect of taxation improved by between 0.6 and 3.8 Gini points in the ten Latin American countries with available data (Cornia et al. 2011). In contrast, in EE-FSU, tax reforms emphasized the introduction of VAT and a flat income tax that, with few exceptions, generated unequalizing effects on the post-tax income distribution (Cornia 2011).

(ix) *A countercyclical monetary policy*. According to the orthodox stance, inflation is costly and affects the poor the most. However, Stiglitz (1998) shows that driving inflation below 40 per cent produces no discernible benefits while rapid disinflation generally causes a contraction of GDP and—because of the endogeneity of tax revenue to GDP—a widening of the fiscal deficit. In addition, a policy of high interest rates increases the concentration of financial wealth in the hands of bondholders while, given the mark-up price formation mechanism prevailing in developing countries, a rise in interest rates raises production costs and prices.

In contrast, the new structuralist macroeconomics considers that, while the control of inflation is sacrosanct, its target value and speed of reduction must take into account other considerations, and be broadly driven by flexible inflation targeting. To start with, the inflation target should be raised (from 2 to 4–5 per cent in industrialized countries and in similar proportions in developing countries), so as to be able to cut interest rates during crises more markedly than in the past (Blanchard et al. 2010)—and be made more flexible. This policy should help to contain cost-push inflation and at the same time avoid a contraction in investment and growth that inevitably depresses employment. At the same time, monetary policy should aim at providing liquidity more broadly by allowing central banks to act as true lenders of last resort, sterilize unwanted changes in foreign exchange markets, and impose capital controls to preserve monetary autonomy. Finally, monetary policy should also focus on countercyclical regulation to prevent asset-price bubbles, excessive leverage, and current account positions that cause systemic risk (Chapter 13). For instance, capital-adequacy and liquidity ratios can be raised, loan-to-value ratios and risk-taking reduced, and margin requirements raised.

(x) *A stricter banking regulation and supervision.* The loosening of banking and financial regulation during the 1980s and 1990s allowed creating off-balance-sheet and shadow financial institutions not subjected to central bank regulations, which increased leverage and contributed to a long series of financial and banking crises. However, unlike in the OECD and European transition economies, the developing countries have recently experienced, even in 2009, few financial, sovereign debt, and banking crises. One reason for this crisis avoidance was the expanded role played by the IMF. Yet another reason was the banking reforms implemented in several countries. For instance, as Rojas Suarez (2010) argues, Latin American governments enhanced capitalization, funding, and supervision of their banking systems, encouraged the development of local capital markets, introduced a stricter prudential regulation of financial systems, enhanced risk-assessment mechanisms in large banks, developed appropriate legal, judicial, and accounting frameworks, and assigned a broader role to state banks in financing economic activity during crises.

9.4 The New Structuralist Macroeconomics and Inequality

Before econometrically testing the relation between macroeconomic policies and income inequality, we review from a theoretical perspective the pathways through which the former affects the latter.

- *The SCRER–unemployment reduction–inequality pathway.* A SCRER regime facilitates the shift of employment to the traded sector, which is generally more unskilled-labour-intensive than the non-traded sector (this might not be true in countries with a large urban informal sector). Second, as noted above, a competitive RER has been associated with periods of rapid growth and employment creation. Third, expansion of the traded sector relaxes the balance-of-payment constraint and generates positive externalities, including in terms of employment creation, in the non-traded sector too. Finally, a SCRER shifts the relative price ratio against the non-traded sector and so discourages the formation of unequalizing real estate bubbles.

- *The prevention of external crises–lower inequality pathway.* The new approach affects inequality also through the adoption of measures that minimize the frequency and impact of unequalizing foreign debt and currency crises. The new model, in fact, includes provisions to reduce foreign indebtedness, increase reserves, introduce capital controls, and adopt a SCRER regime that reduces the occurrence of current account crises.

- *The higher taxation–redistribution pathway.* Tax policy directly affects the distribution of disposable income as the increase in tax/GDP ratios obtained through progressive taxes improves the distribution of post-tax income in relation to the pre-tax distribution. A rise in tax revenue also permits a non-inflationary expansion of public expenditure on progressive social transfers, human capital formation, and infrastructure, thus improving the current distribution of disposable income as well as the future wage distribution, as the scarcity rents accruing to the educated rich decline in line with the increase in the supply of skilled workers. Third, even if the revenue increase is obtained through neutral or regressive instruments, taxation affects current inequality favourably by reducing the frequency of unequalizing budgetary crises, as an increase in revenue reduces the need to monetize the deficit or to borrow abroad.

- *The banking regulation–banking stability–inequality pathway.* Inequality is also affected favourably by a stricter regulation of domestic banking and the avoidance of banking crises, which, as Halac and Schmukler (2003) note in a study of five Latin American bank collapses, generate huge and lasting unequalizing effects. The continued decline of income inequality during 2008–10 in Latin America was certainly helped by a stricter regulation and supervision of the banking and financial sector.

- *The growth—inequality pathway.* The literature on endogenous growth suggests that the new structuralist macroeconomics affects GDP growth favourably. According to the Loyaza model, higher taxation increases the supply of public goods, which in turn raises the returns on private investments and human capital. Also, other policies of the new approach (e.g. the accumulation of reserves, capital controls, financial regulation, and so on) affect growth favourably. In turn, faster growth helps to create new employment and, in some cases, raises unskilled wages, thus equalizing the distribution of income. Such an effect is not automatic (indeed, some economies have experienced periods of jobless growth) but has been observed during growth spells in developing countries with flexible labour markets. Finally, the new approach helps to avoid rises in inequality by containing output and job losses during crises through the adoption of countercyclical fiscal and monetary policies.

We now test econometrically the above hypotheses on the basis of a panel of 124 countries with at least ten well-spaced Gini data points over the years 1980–2009. The dependent variable is the Gini coefficient of household disposable income drawn from SWIID (Solt 2009), the IDLA dataset (Martorano and Cornia 2011), Eurostat, and national sources. In some countries the definition of the income concept on which the Gini coefficients were computed is unknown. As argued above, the new structuralist macroeconomics affects inequality both directly (as, for instance, in the case of progressive taxation) and indirectly via the effect of these policies on growth. The regressors used in the analysis include the macroeconomic determinants of inequality discussed in the prior sections. (Appendix Table A9.1 presents the definitions and data sources of the variables included in the regression.) However, government deficit/GDP was dropped as redundant, as its effect is captured by the revenue/GDP and public debt/GDP ratios. As for the possible interdependence among other regressors, the very low values of the bilateral correlation coefficients (see Annex Table 2 in Cornia 2012) suggest the absence of multicollinearity. The panel nature of the data used for this test implies that the estimation procedure must take into account that each country is observed over several periods. Such a model takes the following form:

$$GINI_{it} = \alpha + \beta X_{it} + n_i + u_{it}$$

where $GINI_{it}$ is the Gini coefficient of the distribution of household disposable income per capita (or its closest approximation), X a vector of explanatory variables and two control variables (the average years of education of the workforce and its square), the subscripts i and t refer to the regions and years of the panel, u_{it} is a joint error term for regions and time periods, and n_i is the time-invariant regional fixed effect, while α and β are the parameters to be estimated. This estimation procedure generates for each region an intercept that captures specific fixed regional effects reflecting differences in geography, institutions, and unobservables.

The results of model 1 in Table 9.6 show that all variables are statistically significant and have the sign expected ex ante except for the Kaopen index of financial liberalization, which is non-significant, and the national saving/GDP ratio, which is significant but has a sign opposite to that expected. The subsequent four models present refinements of model 1 aiming at capturing regional or structural differences and at dealing with the two problems just mentioned. In particular, model 2 includes the interaction variable 'Kaopen index* dummy poor countries', which aims at capturing the effects of capital account liberalization in countries with a GDP per capita lower than the median of the countries panel, i.e. countries more likely to be affected by the instability of financial flows. In fact, model 2 confirms that while capital

Table 9.6 Fixed effects panel regression of the impact of macroeconomic variables on the Gini index of income inequality, 124 countries over 1980–2009

Regressors	Expected sign	Model 1	Model 2	Model 3	Model 4	Model 5
GDP growth rate	(−)	−0.0872**	−0.0867**	−0.0769**	−0.0855**	−0.0680*
Average yrs of education of workers	(+)	2.0383***	1.4137***	1.1819***	1.2618***	1.2429***
Average yrs of education of workers^2	(−)	−0.1232***	−0.0840***	−0.0712***	−0.0743***	−0.0737***
Gross national savings/GDP	(−)	0.1805***	0.1535***	0.3793***	0.2538***	0.2547***
Gross national savings/GDP* share VA in agriculture (s1)	(−)			−0.0035**		
Gross national savings/GDP* share VA in industry (s2)	(−)			−0.0046***		
Gross national savings/GDP* share VA in agriculture/share VA in industry (s3)	(−)				−0.1055***	−0.1065***
Capital controls (Kaopen index)	(+)	0.1060	−0.3088**	−0.4586***	−0.3745**	−0.3651**
Capital controls in poor countries (Kaopen index* dummy poor countries)	(+)		2.2923***	2.7001***	2.5600***	2.5805***
Reserves/GDP	(−)	−0.0348**	−0.0237	−0.0352*	−0.0290*	−0.0305*
Real exchange rate	(−)	−0.0001***	−0.0002***	−0.0002***	−0.0002***	−0.0002***
Government revenue/GDP	(−)	−0.2363***	−0.2325***	−0.2374***	−0.2280***	−0.2266***
Current account balance/GDP	(−)	−0.2188***	−0.1950***	−0.1755***	−0.1708***	−0.1680***
Bank deregulation (Frazer Institute Index)	(+)	0.9616***	0.8736***	0.7672***	0.7966***	0.8110***
Public debt/GDP	(+)	0.0080*	0.0027	−0.0035	−0.0023	−0.0028
% yearly change in public debt/GDP	(+)					0.0278**
Constant		39.66***	43.03***	44.90***	43.96***	43.86***
Regional dummies		Yes	Yes	Yes	Yes	Yes
Observations		1,274	1,274	1,219	1,219	1,219
R-squared		0.800	0.810	0.818	0.816	0.817

Note: ***, **, and * indicate that the parameters are significantly different from zero at the 99, 95, and 90 per cent probability levels respectively.
Source: Author's calculations.

account liberalization is equalizing on average (a result influenced by the presence of developed economies in the panel), it is unequalizing in poor countries.

In turn, model 3 adds to model 1 the interaction between the national savings rate and the share of value added in agriculture (s1) and industry (s2). Its results show that in economies where these two sectors are important, a higher gross national savings ratio is associated with lower inequality, possibly reflecting the fall in domestic savings in tertiarized societies with easy access to global finance. This effect is also captured in models 4 and 5 by the variable s3.

Overall, the results of models 1 to 5 confirm that accumulating reserves, adopting a SCRER, increasing government revenue/GDP, realizing a current account surplus, and experiencing rapid growth reduce inequality, while bank deregulation raises it. The public debt/GDP ratio is non-significant but its yearly variation is significant in countries where such a ratio exceeds 60 per cent (model 5). The parameters of models 1–5 are stable and—with the exceptions mentioned above—are highly significant, suggesting that they have been correctly estimated. While still subject to improvements (e.g. by verifying through a statistical test the possibility of endogeneity, which has been excluded here on theoretical grounds), the regression results are encouraging, as the control variables and the macroeconomics variables discussed in the prior sections have, in practically all models, the sign expected ex ante and are statistically significant. As noted, the Kaopen index of capital account liberalization, somewhat surprisingly, is equalizing on average but becomes unequalizing when interacted with the dummy 'low-income countries'.

In conclusion, the regression results tend to support to an unexpected extent the theoretical arguments, literature findings, and regional comparisons presented in Section 9.3. They also confirm that the adoption of real-life Washington-Consensus-type policies contributed to rising inequality in many developing countries during the 1980s and 1990s as well as in several countries of EE-FSU and South Asia during the 2000s. The case of China, which adopted some of the new macroeconomic policies while experiencing a rapid rise in income inequality, shows that other factors (such as growing regional disparity and weak labour-market policies) may override the gains due to the adoption of a sensible macroeconomics. Finally, further empirical and theoretical work is needed at the country or regional level to fully document what we argued to be the favourable inequality impact of the new structuralist macroeconomics that has gradually taken shape over the last ten-to-fifteen years in several developing countries.

Appendix

Table A9.1 Description of the variables used in the regression analysis

Variable	Description	Unit of measurement	Data source
Gini coefficient of disposable income per capita	Gini on income	Index (ranging btw 0 and 100)	Solt (2009); Martorano and Cornia (2011); EUROSTAT; World Development Indicators; African Development Bank database; ESCAP and national sources
GDP/c growth rate	Growth rate of GDP/c	Rate of growth	ERS/USDA International Macroeconomic Dataset (2011)
Human capital of workers	No. of yrs of education of adults (25+)	Absolute number	Barro and Lee (2010)
Gross national savings/GDP	Gross national savings	Percentage of GDP	World Economic Outlook (WEO) database 2011
Kaopen index of capital account openness	The Kaopen index is a positive function of openness.	Ranges btw –2.5 (close) and +2.5 (open)	Chinn and Ito (2008, and 2012 update)
Reserves/GDP	International reserves as a share of GDP	Percentage of GDP	UNCTADstat 2011
RER	Index of the real exchange rate	Index 2000=100	ERS/USDA International Macroeconomic Dataset (2011)
Revenue/GDP	Ratio of government revenue to GDP	Percentage of GDP	WEO database 2011
Current account balance/GDP	Current account balance	Percentage of GDP	WEO database 2011
Bank deregulation	Frazer Institute Index	Index varies between 0 (no deregulation) and 10 (complete deregulation)	Gwartney, Hall, and Lawson (2011)
Public Debt/GDP	Total public debt	Percentage of GDP	WEO database 2011, Reinhart and Rogoff (2010)

Source: Author's compilation.

References

Adam, C. and D. Bevan (2001). *Non-linear Effects of Fiscal Deficits on Growth in Developing Countries*. Working Paper. Oxford: Department of Economics, Oxford University. Available at: <http://www.economics.ox.ac.uk/Research/wp/pdf/paper120.pdf>.

Aslund, A. (2009). 'The East European Financial Crisis'. CASE Network Studies and Analysis 395/2009. Warsaw: Center for Social and Economic Research.

Barro, R. J. and J.-W. Lee (2010). *A New Dataset of Educational Attainment in the World, 1950–2010*. NBER Working Paper 15902. Cambridge, MA: National Bureau of Economic Research.

Birdsall, N., A. De La Torre, and F. Valencia Caicedo (2010). *The Washington Consensus: Assessing a Damaged Brand*. CGD Working Paper 312. Washington, DC: Center for Global Development.

Blanchard, O. and D. Leigh (2013). *Growth Forecast Errors and Fiscal Multipliers*. IMF Staff Working Paper (Research Department) WP/13/1. Washington, DC: IMF.

Blanchard, O., G. Dell'Ariccia, and P. Mauro (2010). 'Rethinking Macroeconomic Policy'. IMF Staff Position Notes, SPN/10/03. Washington, DC: IMF.

Bresser Pereira, L. C. (2011). 'An Account of New Developmentalism and Its Structuralist Macroeconomics'. *Brazilian Journal of Political Economy*, 31(3), 493–502

Chandrasekhar, C. P. and J. Ghosh (2009). 'Global Imbalances: Remarkable Reversal'. *The Monthly Review*, 5 December.

Chinn, M. D. and H. Ito (2008). 'A New Measure of Financial Openness'. *Journal of Comparative Policy Analysis*, 10 (3): 309–22. Updated version of 22 March 2012 available at: <http://www.web.pdx.edu/~ito/Chinn-Ito_website.htm> (accessed 8 January 2013).

Cornia, G. A. (2011). 'Economic Integration, Inequality and Growth: Latin America versus the European Economies in Transition'. *Review of Economics and Institutions*, 2(2): Article 2.

Cornia, G. A. (2012). *The New Structuralist Macroeconomics and Income Inequality*. DSE Working Paper, 24/2012. Florence: University of Florence. Available at: <http://www.dse.unifi.it/upload/sub/WP23_2012.pdf>.

Cornia, G. A. and B. Martorano (2012). 'Development Policies and Income Inequality: Main Trends in Selected Developing Regions, 1980–2010'. UNCTAD Discussion Paper 210. Geneva: UNCTAD.

Cornia, G. A., J. C. Gómez-Sabaini, and B. Martorano (2011). *A New Fiscal Pact, Tax Policy Changes and Income Inequality: Latin America during the Last Decade*. WIDER Working Paper 2011/70. Helsinki: UNU-WIDER.

Fanelli, J. M., J. P. Jiménez, and O. Kacef (2011). 'Volatilidad Macroeconómica y Respuestas de Políticas'. Santiago de Chile: CEPAL.

Frenkel, R. and M. Rapetti (2008). 'Five Years of Competitive and Stable Real Exchange Rate in Argentina, 2002–07'. *International Review of Applied Economics*, 22(2): 215–26.

Gala, P. (2008). 'Real Exchange Rate Levels and Economic Development: Theoretical Analysis and Econometric Evidence'. *Cambridge Journal of Economics*, 32(2): 273–88.

Gallagher, K. P, S. Griffith-Jones, and J. A. Ocampo (2011). 'Capital Account Regulations for Stability and Development: A New Approach'. *Issues in Brief 022*. Boston: The Frederick S. Pardee Center for the Study of the Longer-Range Future, University of Boston.

Gwartney, J., J. Hall, and R. Lawson (2011). Economic Freedom Dataset, published in *Economic Freedom of the World: 2010 Annual Report*. Vancouver, BC: Economic Freedom Network/The Fraser Institute. Available at: <http://www.freetheworld.com/datasets_efw.html>.

Halac, M. and S. Schmukler (2003). *Distributional Effects of Crises: The Role of Financial Transfers*. WB Policy Research Working Paper, 3173. Washington, DC: World Bank.

Helleiner, G. K. (ed.) (1998). *Capital Account Regimes and the Developing Countries*. London: Macmillan.

IMF (2011). 'Recent Experiences in Managing Capital Inflows: Cross-Cutting Themes and Possible Policy Framework'. Paper prepared by the Strategy, Policy, and Review Department of the IMF.

McKinley, T. (2010). *'Has the IMF Abandoned Neo-Liberalism?'*. Development Viewpoint, 51. London: Centre for Development Policy and Research, SOAS.

Martorano, B. and G. A. Cornia (2011). *The IDLA Dataset: A Tool to Analyze Recent Changes in Income inequality in Latin America*. Available at: <http://www.wider.unu.edu/research/current-programme/en_GB/Impact-of-Economic-Crisis/>.

Ocampo, J. A. (2012). *The Development Implications of External Integration in Latin America*. WIDER Working Paper 48/2012. Helsinki: UNU-WIDER.

Purfield, C. and C. Rosenberg (2010). *Adjustment under a Currency Peg: Estonia, Latvia and Lithuania during the Global Financial Crisis, 2008–9*. IMF Working Paper 2010/213. Washington, DC: IMF.

Reinhart, C. M. and K. S. Rogoff (2010). *From Financial Crash to Debt Crisis*. NBER Working Paper 15795. Cambridge, MA: National Bureau of Economic Research.

Rodrik, D. (2003). *Growth Strategies*. NBER Working Paper 10050. Cambridge, MA: National Bureau of Economic Research.

Rodrik, D. (2006). *The Social Cost of Foreign Exchange Reserves*. NBER Working Paper 11952. Cambridge, MA: National Bureau of Economic Research.

Rodrik, D. (2007). *One Economics, Many Recipes*. Berkeley, CA: Stanford University Press.

Rojas Suarez, L. (2010). *The International Financial Crisis: Eight Lessons for and from Latin America*. CGD Working Paper 202. Washington, DC: Center for Global Development.

Solt, F. (2009). 'Standardizing the World Income Inequality Database'. *Social Science Quarterly*, 90(2): 231–42.

Stiglitz, J. (1998). *'Broader Goals and More Instruments: Towards a Post-Washington Consensus'*. WIDER Annual Lecture 2. Helsinki: UNU-WIDER.

Williamson, J. (1990). 'What Washington Means by Policy Reform'. In J. Williamson (ed.), *Latin American Adjustment: How Much Has Happened?* Washington, DC: Institute for International Economics, Chapter 2.

Williamson, J. (2002). *Did the Washington Consensus Fail?*. Washington, DC: Peterson Institute for International Economics. Available at: <http://www.iie.com/publications/papers/paper.cfm?ResearchID=488>.

10

Trade, Exchange Rates, and Global Poverty
Policies for the Poorest*

Gerry Helleiner

10.1 Introduction

'Go ye into all the world and gather statistics'. This was a young, scripturally savvy, Richard Jolly assessing the likely instructions to recruits to the nascent Kuznets-inspired Economic Growth Center at Yale University in 1961. This trenchant commentary on what seemed to many of us (and the Ford Foundation) a golden opportunity and a significant international initiative has stayed with me over the past fifty years. It was entirely appropriate and devastatingly accurate; it was also funny.

Richard has always been one to go directly to the point. I remember equally well his telephone call from UNICEF headquarters in New York about twenty years later: 'Gerry, I want to take on the IMF.' That time he didn't exercise his sense of humour. But his often self-deprecating and ironic wit—even in the face of extreme challenges—has never left him. It is one of his most engaging traits.

Richard has been one of that rare breed—a highly talented economist of remarkable vision who has chosen to employ his skills in determined and highly practical pursuit of the most important of social objectives. I have valued his work and his friendship enormously.

In the Jolly spirit I shall seek to address some of the relatively neglected current concerns of some of the least advantaged members of the global community. There is much discussion in the academic and popular literature of the

* This study was prepared for the Richard Jolly festschrift conference, Institute of Development Studies, University of Sussex, 17–18 November 2011. For comments on an earlier draft I am very grateful to Giovanni Andrea Cornia, Roy Culpeper, John Loxley, Rohinton Medhora, Paul Shaffer, and Randy Spence, none of whom are to be held responsible in any way for its current contents.

changing international power structure—the rise of the BRICs—and emerging economic/financial imbalances. New concerns over financial crises, the volatility of financial flows, and concomitant exchange rate concerns have bred vigorous debate. Governmental interventions in the capital account have become almost commonplace in the 'emerging' economies and, remarkably, have even realized a degree of acceptance thereof on the part of the Washington financial institutions that used to decry them. In consequence there is ever-expanding anxious talk of 'beggar-thy-neighbour' currency practices and 'trade wars'. But this earnest discussion, to the extent that it addresses developing countries at all, tends to be confined to countries considered to be of systemic significance—Brazil, India, China, South Korea, and, to a lesser degree, the soon-to-be 'emerging countries' such as Chile, Thailand, Indonesia, Turkey, and South Africa. There has been precious little attention to what the poorer and/or smaller countries have been doing or should be doing. (An honourable and excellent recent exception is Berg et al. (2011).)

The discussions of capital flows and their interaction with trade and exchange rate policies have both short-term and long-term dimensions. Short-term concerns relate to stabilization objectives: the maintenance of external and internal macroeconomic balance in the face of exogenous and primarily temporary shocks. In the past the principal sources of such shocks were perceived as changes in the external terms of trade, weather, civil unrest or natural disaster. To these are now added flows of short-term private capital of unprecedented size. The macroeconomic management of short-term shocks is actually a topic requiring an entire paper of its own, addressing such matters as the appropriate management of foreign exchange reserves, the availability and use of offsetting international credit, including that of the IMF, and consequent debt management, appropriate short-term monetary, fiscal, trade, and exchange rate policies, and now macro-prudential policies relating to the domestic financial sector. The impact on poverty of shocks and short-term policy responses can obviously be significant. Indeed UNICEF, during the Jolly years, chose to engage vigorously and constructively in efforts to put a 'human face' upon 'adjustment' policies. In this chapter, however, my principal concern is with trade policies relating to longer-term development and poverty reduction, particularly, as already noted, in the poorest countries, and related capital account and exchange rate issues.

10.2 Trade, Development, and Poverty: Theory and Empirical Testing

Trade policy and the trade/development nexus have been featured, probably disproportionately so, in that part of the development literature written by economists. There has been controversy in this sphere, some of it continuing, but it is possible to discern an emerging professional consensus on many elements of the relevant theory and empirical record.

International trade may be an extremely useful instrument in the pursuit of economic and other objectives; but, some rhetoric notwithstanding, it is not and never has been an end in itself. Nor is it always and necessarily, as some would put it, an 'engine of growth'. As famously noted some time ago, it might better, and more typically, be described as its 'handmaiden'.

If trade is to be an instrument of such ultimate objectives as development in poor countries and reduction of their poverty, its effects in the particular circumstances in which it occurs should, ideally, be fully understood. Unfortunately, this is by no means an easy or straightforward matter.

It is easy to demonstrate, both in theoretical and empirical terms, that engagement in trade can provide benefits beyond those attainable in the total absence of trade: trade is better than autarchy. But how much trade and what kind of trade is best for a person or for a country at a particular time is a much trickier question to resolve. One generalization is possible: small countries self-evidently must rely upon trade more than large ones, and have much less room for manoeuvre in their trade (and industrial) policy. Beyond that it is difficult to go. There is always plenty of 'policy space' between total self-reliance in autarchy and totally free trade. Contrary to much of the more ideologically oriented literature of trade, it is a very long logical leap from the proposition that some trade is likely to be beneficial to the proposition that totally 'free' trade is always best.

Even the apparently self-evident gains from trade can be logically questioned. It has generally been assumed in the theoretical literature of economics that trade would not take place unless the parties to the trade both gained from the exchange. Such gains from trade may be immediate (static), attainable in the medium term (after some costly adjustment), or expected as 'dynamic' and longer-term in their effect. But even this convenient logical starting point may require qualification. Even in the simplest case, the economic argument appears to ignore totally the potential role of power—force, bullying, and threats—in bringing about the trade. It also ignores other non-trade relationships, including so-called 'side payments', e.g. provision of favourable treatment of foreign capital or intellectual property as a condition for a trade deal, that may be inseparable from the trading relationship per se.

When the parties to the trade in question are countries, rather than individuals, matters become even more complex. In particular, there may be individual 'losers' from international exchange as well as individual 'gainers'. There is plenty of empirical evidence linking expanded developing-country trade in recent decades to increased income inequality within these countries. How can one weigh such losses against the gains? And over what time horizon? For another example: what if the international 'trades' take place within the same firm, operating privately in two separate countries? The principal gains may then be realized by foreign firms rather than any domestic actors. Still another example: as in the case of trade among individuals, there are many dimensions to bilateral relationships. In many so-called 'trade' agreements among nations, there are non-trade provisions that cannot be ignored in any holistic assessment of the national gains or losses from them. They can include policy conditions relating to intellectual property, rights of establishment, the treatment of foreign investment and capital flows, development assistance, and various other issues, including non-economic ones relating to politics and foreign policy. Together, these may significantly offset (or indeed complement) the traditional gains from trade.

Complexity increases with consideration of the potential role of trade in increasing (or decreasing) poor countries' vulnerability to exogenous external shock. The impact of the global financial crisis of 2007–9 registered upon low-income countries primarily through its effects on their terms of trade and external demand for their exports (Berg et al. 2011). The degree of sectoral and product concentration of exports has also been relevant to the impact of exogenous shocks upon individual countries (Camanho da Costa Neto and Romeu 2011). Even if expanded trade was certain to bring increased income or income growth it might also bring increased instability, and policymakers could rationally trade off one against the other. These complexities are the bane of real-world policymakers—and the beginning of an understanding of the role of political and 'special interest' pressures upon policy processes.

It is extremely difficult to offer generalizations about the interactions between trade, trade policies, development, and poverty (or, for that matter, income distribution). The most that can be said on the basis of economic theory is that these relationships depend on a great variety of factors. Economic analysts have come some distance in identifying what they are likely to be. They include the factor-intensities and geographic location of alternative productive activities, linkages among productive sectors, consumption patterns of the poor, labour-market characteristics, the existence or nonexistence of governmental taxes and transfers, and the prior characteristics of income and asset distribution, not to speak of the very definition of poverty (and poverty profiles) in the country in question.[1] As trade policy changes and tradables (exports, imports, and import-competing activities) alter their roles in the economy, the prices of goods, services, and production

---

[1] See, for instance, Winters (2000).

factors can be expected to change. So can consumption and production patterns, employment, and income distribution.

Any attempt to provide a complete listing of the factors that matter to such relationships rapidly becomes excruciatingly boring to any but academic specialists. Policymakers do not usually have the time or inclination to plough through such long-winded and ultimately inconclusive theoretical analyses. They are likely to find frustrating the academic argument, however correct, to the effect that 'it all depends'. They seek simpler analyses and less ambiguous recommendations—and analysts, fortunately or not, have usually been happy to oblige. As they do so, they inevitably bring very strong 'priors', based upon the nature of their own training, ideology, experience, and, of course, the interests for whom they may be speaking. It should not, then, be surprising that analysts do not offer uniform advice.

Some have sought a simpler 'truth' in econometric investigations—with ever-improving datasets and increasingly sophisticated analytical tools. From the analyses of time-series, cross-sectional data, and combinations of the two, they seek to uncover statistical relationships and regularities that can shed overall light upon these complex relationships. The empirical tests typically pursue a two-stage logic. In the first, they have sought to uncover systematic relationships between measures of trade policy (usually described in terms of the degree of so-called 'openness') and economic growth. (Since 'development', as distinct from growth, is not unambiguously measured or even defined, it does not figure into the econometric literature.) In the second, they pursue the relationship between such growth and poverty reduction. (Some have attempted to relate trade policy directly to poverty reduction or income distribution but the underlying models for such relationships are not always clear.)

Although there remain wide and policy-relevant divergences in the *degree* to which growth is associated with poverty reduction, there is agreement on the typical second-stage relationship: growth is *usually*, though certainly not universally, associated with poverty reduction. (Relationships between growth and income distribution remain variable and controversial. When growth is heavily skewed towards the better-off, it is obviously quite possible for growth *not* to be poverty-reducing. In the best known study of this relationship, there was actually no poverty reduction in fully 45 out of 285 cases—16 per cent—of economic growth (Donaldson 2008: 2189; Dollar and Kraay 2002, 2004)). Efforts continue to try to elucidate the determinants (or at least correlates) of pro-poor growth, and alternative trade structures and trade policies are obviously only a few of the many possible pieces—not necessarily the most important—of this empirical puzzle (see, for instance, Ravallion 2005).

Agreement on the relationship between trade policy and growth has been more difficult. Econometricians are no better than other analysts. They too inevitably bring 'priors' and prejudgment to their work. The results are there-fore far from uniform across all such attempts. Different country samples, time periods, and measures of trade policy yield different results. Methodological controversies abound. Most liberalization-favouring researchers now con-cede that the econometric evidence for the link between trade policy and growth, which they have pursued for several decades, is inconclusive.[2] But even if this were not the case, what can 'average' statistical relationships, however complete with dummy variables for country characteristics, use-fully tell a policymaker working in his/her own particular place and time. How does he/she know that his/her particular case is not an 'outlier'?

10.3 Trade Policy Approaches to Global Poverty

In the face of all of these theoretical and empirical complexities and uncer-tainties, what are poor policymakers—at global or national levels—to do? For analysts and trade policymakers seeking to address global poverty there are two broad avenues of approach. There is obviously no reason why these two avenues of approach should be mutually exclusive. Ideally, one should both (i) direct special attention and more resources to the trade problems of the poorest countries *and*, at the same time, (ii) seek to improve the poverty impact of trade and trade policies within developing countries more gener-ally. The latter objective implies the preservation of a degree of policy space to permit its effective pursuit.

10.3.1 Focusing Supportive Trade Measures upon the Poorest Countries

By focusing trade gains upon the poorest countries (or other political or geographic units)—those with the greatest (average) incidence of poverty—there is a greater likelihood, on the balance of probabilities, that more and better trade will impact favourably upon poverty than with more 'neutral' level-playing-field approaches. That is the approach that draws preferential policy attention to the problems of such country categories as the (48) 'least

---

[2] For a comprehensive review and bibliography of the by-now quite extensive literature, see Singh (2010). An interesting more recent paper even finds, consistent with frequent earlier anxi-eties, that in low-income countries, openness is negatively associated with measures of develop-ment (Kim, Lin, and Suen 2011).

developed' or (40) 'low-income' or (44) 'IDA-only' countries. Preferential tariff treatment is the clearest example.

But such an approach, while providing a degree of international policy-making simplification, remains fairly crude and, by itself, is unreliable. It excludes the very significant numbers living in poverty in the BRICs and other middle-income developing countries. It neglects the many other major barriers to the possible poverty-reducing effects of expanded trade opportunities. In the absence of other requirements it may risk encouragement of traditional exports that generate few 'dynamic' effects, locking beneficiary countries into production patterns from which they seek longer-term escape. In any case, its effectiveness in actual practice has been compromised by overly complex rules of origin, non-tariff (technical or health-related) barriers, demands for complementary reciprocal commitments reducing the beneficiaries' potential 'policy space' and, as multilaterally agreed trade barriers fall and preferential trade agreements (PTAs) proliferate, declining preferential margins. The constraints upon poor countries' supply-side capacities to respond to preferential export opportunities have severely limited the impact of such preferential arrangements as exist. The latter limitations of such preference schemes have bred more recent attention to so-called 'aid for trade' for preferred poor countries, focusing upon their supply-side problems.[3]

Despite many declarations of intent, it has not been possible to get much beyond such preferences and 'aid for trade' within the multilateral trading system. The scope for consciously altering the terms of international trade in support of the poorest developing countries is typically limited more by political considerations in Northern countries than by objective trade policy possibilities. (Of course, other developments in global markets for goods and services—booms and recessions, technical changes, international investments, etc.—have usually, in any case, been of far greater significance to poor countries than conscious Northern policy changes.) Ostensibly mutually beneficial deals are somehow bargained in the tugging and pulling of international negotiation. But threats, bullying, specious analyses, and bribery have often been deployed against ministers from economically weaker countries, and outcomes have not always been clearly so beneficial to all. Despite the potential advantages of multilateral negotiations for weaker countries without much bargaining leverage, this has been as true of negotiations within the GATT and the WTO as with bilateral or regional negotiations. In any case, poverty and development effects have not normally been, by themselves, at issue in such negotiations. Those who negotiate within the World Trade Organization (WTO) on behalf of the major powers and the

---

[3] For a useful review see Njinkeu and Cameron (2008).

trade analysts upon whom they rely for advice are not mandated to pursue objectives other than 'national interest' (however defined) and have been singularly uncomfortable with the idea of introducing poverty reduction and development as primary objectives within the organization. Even the so-called Doha Development Agenda was so designated as little more than a public-relations sop to the developing countries rather than as a serious signal of trade policy intent. Although some have pressed for development/ poverty objectives to be primary in the EU's recent negotiations over economic partnership agreements (EPAs), its negotiators have not changed discernibly from their traditional approaches either.

Under the existing multilateral rules, very poor and small countries who are damaged by the trade practices of more powerful countries receive no compensation for their losses and, for obvious reasons (above all, heavy direct costs and fear of retribution), have difficulty mounting rules-based legal challenges to them. Still, as the West African cotton case has demonstrated, it may be possible—with careful preparation, good advice, and the support of the media and civil society—to make some headway with more aggressive rules-based approaches. As the WTO settles down to a system of rules administration and enforcement, rather than a succession of trade-liberalizing 'rounds', and as previous 'peace clauses' expire, such lawyer-intensive approaches, both on attack and defence, are likely to become more important. Analytical and legal assistance directed towards the legitimate grievances of the poorest and smallest developing countries may, therefore, become more productive. At the same time, these countries' domestic trade policies and practices (including exercise of their rights under international agreements) will have to be pursued within an increasingly intrusive and complex set of international rules and precedents, which must be fully understood by those developing their own policy approaches. Trade policymakers, therefore, need a firm grasp not only of the domestic economic (and political) implications of alternative policies, notably their likely consequences for development and poverty, but also the specific legalities of their translation into acceptable international practice.

Given the limited political and economic clout of the poorest countries, even if successfully exercised collectively (and that would be no mean achievement), significant Northern policy change in the direction of improved external conditions for poor countries' progress depends primarily upon the North's own more serious adoption of global anti-poverty objectives in holistic (including trade policy) practice rather than simply in rhetoric. Such further reform is possible but, on current evidence, it is not likely to appear soon or to make a huge difference, relative to other factors, if it comes. Nor can too much realistically be expected, in general, from increased legal challenges by the poorest countries. Hence the emphasis frequently placed by international development agencies and many poor and middle-income countries themselves upon their own trade policies and practices. Though international bodies have not always encouraged them and they have often proved difficult to implement effectively, these policies include preferential trade (and other economic) agreements among themselves, again subject enough for another paper.

10.3.2 Pro-Poor Trade Policies in the Poorest Countries

Perhaps more promising are efforts to understand better and improve the developmental and poverty-reducing impact of trade and trade policies in individual developing countries, both middle-income and the poorest. Improving the development effects and poverty-sensitivity of trade and trade measures in general can undoubtedly do more for continuing poverty reduction (within individual countries and regions) than preferential aid, trade, and other supportive arrangements for countries that are, on average, the poorest. Certainly, the provision of trade preferences or, more generally, better terms of trade will do little for poverty if the countries that receive them squander their possibilities with imperfect policies or are so constrained by supply-side and other constraints that they do not benefit much from them. As already implied, this approach may be considerably more difficult to implement successfully. Many are already engaged in the attempt—but it isn't clear that they have as yet been very successful.

In WTO circles, there has been considerable rhetoric and effort to 'mainstream trade' in development discourse in developing countries, not least in the poorest countries at which 'aid for trade' is directed. To many this terminology has seemed perverse. In the overwhelming majority of developing countries, and certainly in all of the smaller ones, there has never been any shortage of attention to trade or trade policy concerns. Indeed, their history of development has been, if anything, disproportionately concerned, from colonial times onwards, with the needs and possibilities of expanded external trade. The colonial powers and their firms had little interest in the overall development of their colonies, let alone poverty reduction, except insofar as it affected their own trading and investment activities. (No doubt some of their missionaries had a broader concern.) At the international level, it has been the developing countries who have long called for greater attention to the role of trade policies—everyone's trade policies—in their struggles for development and against poverty (even if their domestic policies in this regard left much to be desired). The early calls for 'trade, not aid' originated in the South, not the North. The UN Conference on Trade and Development (UNCTAD) was created under pressure from developing countries and continues to enjoy their support in the face of declining interest on the part of some Northern members.

What often seems to have been meant by those who have preached the 'mainstreaming' of trade is the adoption of trade policies of which they approve, above all greater trade liberalization. As already noted, any such broad policy recommendation on a one-size-fits-all basis is unlikely to be very helpful to policymakers in particular places at particular times. Rather, there would seem to be a much greater need to 'mainstream development' in trade policy discussion, not the other way around.

Certainly, sustained economic growth is necessary, though obviously not sufficient, for sustained poverty reduction. Equally certainly, sustained growth of export trade (strictly speaking, the domestic value added therein) can be one of the elements in sustained overall growth. In East Asia much of its growth has been, by most accounts, 'export-led'. Such export growth may arise from many sources. It may or may not be associated with conscious trade policy to that end; the favourable export and GDP growth experience in many African countries during the past decade, for instance, owed little or nothing to domestic trade policies. Sustained export growth has typically been associated with corresponding growth of imports and, where imports have previously been restrained by policy, export growth is frequently followed by some degree of import liberalization. There are few, if any, instances of sustained growth that can be associated with import liberalization alone.

Narrowly defined, trade policy refers to conscious policy influences (notably tariffs and trade barriers on imports, and taxes, other barriers, or subsidies on exports) upon the relative prices of goods and services within the tradables group (exportables and import-competing activities). Trade policy, that is, influences the domestic incentive structure.

But there are many other influences upon domestic incentive structures. As recent policy debate and practice in both rich countries and poor have demonstrated, exchange rates have a profound impact upon them. This is so important that it will be addressed in a separate section below.

But taking account of exchange rates is not the end of the policy/incentive story either. Other 'non-trade' governmental policies can also have a major impact upon incentive structures, and thus upon investment allocation, production structure, and trade—and thereby, of course, on development and poverty reduction. Governmentally directed and/or subsidized credit, government procurement policies, the terms of government deals with foreign investors (including local content and hiring requirements, location, domestic input prices, etc.), the provision of infrastructure, and the provision of specialized local human capital (skills) are all relevant to private-investor decisions. International 'standards' and 'technical barriers', over which poor and small countries have no control, but to which they must adapt, may also be highly relevant. Exclusive focus upon trade policy, narrowly defined, or even broadened to incorporate exchange rate policy, would clearly miss much of what matters to the determinants of export and import-competing production, trade, and development. Not least of the requisites for expanded production are the resources, whether domestically mobilized or foreign, for investment therein. It seems that it would be best either to interpret 'trade policy' very broadly (some would call it 'industrial policy'), or to consider it only within the much broader context of overall policies for development and poverty reduction, or both.

Economic development derives from an expanding production structure. In small and poor countries, production for export is a significant element in overall production, and it can be the most dynamic. The distribution of a poor country's income, the character of a country's infrastructure, and other development- and poverty-relevant factors can be greatly influenced by the composition of its expanding exports. (Concentration in primary product exports has actually been associated with declining overall productivity in recent years (McMillan and Rodrik 2011)). The longer-term global market prospects for particular exports are also relevant to development and they certainly vary. While it is possible, even likely, that different types of production, including those for export, exhibit different degrees of 'dynamism' in terms of potential for learning, innovation, positive externalities, and continuing productivity increases (manufacturing is frequently favoured over agriculture or tourism for such reasons), less is firmly known in this sphere. (Some argue that the latter such 'dynamics' are associated more with imports than with exports and, therefore, that as long as foreign exchange is earned so as to permit expanding imports, export composition is of secondary importance. Few, however, would question that the composition of output is likely to have considerable developmental significance.)

When petroleum or mining dominates the export bill, for instance, the bulk of the national gains are typically realized by the government, rather than by direct earners of export income. Infrastructure may be disproportionately concentrated around the relevant resource locations. The value of the currency, boosted by resource revenues, discourages other tradable activities (whether exporting or import-competing). It takes an unusually strong and foresighted government to preserve broader development and poverty-reduction objectives in the face of these elements of the 'resource curse'. Environmental side effects from these operations may also get in the way of overall development objectives.

An exporting economy in which smallholder farmers are the main exporters will, other things equal, show quite different characteristics. Infrastructure will be spread throughout the growing areas in the form of feeder roads and other supporting processing, storage, and marketing facilities. There are typically more opportunities for both forward and backward linkages, and for small-scale, bottom-up, income-earning activities than are usually found in a petroleum or mining (or, for that matter, plantation) enclave. Although the very poorest farmers are unlikely to be directly involved in export activity, income in smallholder exporting economies is therefore more widely distributed; the extent to which this is true, however, may be significantly affected by marketing arrangements.

When exports come from unskilled labour-intensive activities undertaken for foreign firms in an export processing zone (EPZ) or other urban area, the immediate distributional and developmental implications are different again. National gains take the form, almost exclusively, of formal employment (and wages) for nationals, often mainly for females. Outside the EPZ enclave or urban area there are typically very limited linkages or infrastructural or other developmental traces—at least until the wages earned in the EPZ are spent.

To some degree, policy can influence not only the volume but also the composition of expanding exports and thus overall development patterns and growth itself. New investments do not always 'just happen'—through impersonal market forces. They involve particular investments by particular firms in particular places. They require particular skills, particular infrastructure, and particular inputs. And they respond to specific incentives. Capably staffed governments, while not necessarily seeking themselves to 'pick winners' (to use the usually abusive terminology of those inclined to disapprove of any governmental activity), can assist in shaping outcomes in a development-oriented and poverty-reducing direction.[4]

In the African context, where so many of the poorest countries are found, poverty is typically at its most severe in the rural areas, and particularly in 'lower potential' areas. More than 70 per cent of Africa's poor are believed to work in agriculture, most of them primarily producing food for local consumption. It would seem to follow that if short-term poverty reduction is a major objective, special efforts should be made to develop new agricultural and related production, and agriculture-linked economic activities (inputs, processing, marketing, etc.), with special attention to smallholder farmers and poorer areas. In many poor African countries, facing rising and volatile prices for imported foods, there may be scope for increased smallholder food production for domestic consumption; but limited domestic markets for food products are likely to set bounds upon the prospect for profitable expansion of production for them. Development and/or expansion of

---

[4] For a recent useful discussion of possibilities and problems in this sphere, see Lin et al. (2011).

non-traditional agricultural (and other) exports, including the domestic processing of some materials previously exported in raw form, seems an obvious further route to explore, particularly when unskilled labour or smallholders are involved. Overt urban unemployment suggests that expanded unskilled labour-intensive activities in urban areas, some of which could find export markets, with or without the assistance of foreign investors, also deserve major attention. But such general, and already well-rehearsed, suggestions are not much help to hard-pressed policymakers. They need greater specificity—with reference to their particular national circumstances; and for this they need relevant local analysis.

The challenge for those trade analysts concerned, above all, with development and anti-poverty objectives is to insert their analytical perspectives into ongoing trade policy discussions and negotiations so that they are a normal and expected part of the policy discourse. There is no 'general theory' of the relationships between trade, trade policies, and development or poverty. Nor will there ever be one. Indeed, much of the struggle such analysts constantly face is that they must contend against the one-size-fits-all mentality, which is buttressed by the enormous strength of simple theory based upon simplified assumptions generating strong and apparently universal solutions, and is backed by powerful interests favouring unimpeded and untaxed economic activities for international and trading firms. Some elements of effective poverty-oriented trade policy are nonetheless probably universal: unskilled labour-intensive activities are to be encouraged; extreme complexity is likely to be costly and inefficient; market-based instruments (direct subsidies and tariffs) are usually more efficient than quotas and controls; exceptional arrangements should always be time-limited. But each country and each time period has its own unique attributes and constraints; and, in order to address any set of objectives effectively, they need to be adequately understood. And, as has already been said, the objectives must also be clear. If poverty reduction is the primary objective, either immediate or prospective, then that should be the yardstick that is applied to all manner of economic policies. The age-old policy question is still the right one: *'cui bono'*, for whom is this good? But, as should by now be evident, there is little reason to think that trade policies are the most important in a poverty-focused policy arsenal.

10.4 Exchange Rates, Capital Flows, and Reserves: Emerging Concerns

Arguably, exchange rates typically matter much more than trade policies to trade volume in individual countries—at least in the short to medium

Table 10.1 Real effective exchange rate (REER) changes and weighted mean tariff rates, selected African countries, 2000–8

	REER change		
	2000–08%	2005–08%	Weighted mean tariff, 2008%
Cameroon	+19	+10	13 (2007)
Côte d'Ivoire	+23	+6	10
Ghana	+9	−6	10
Malawi	−49	+11	8
Nigeria	+45	+9	9
Uganda	−7	+2	11
Zambia	+46	+23	5

Source: World Bank, World Development Indicators.

term. Real (inflation-adjusted) exchange rates often move far more, and with greater abandon, than taxes, subsidies, and trade barriers. Indeed, short- to medium-term movements in the real exchange rate often exceed the height of tariffs and trade barriers (assumed, for the present purpose, to be unchanging). Table 10.1 illustrates, in a sample of African countries (for which there happen to be readily available data) the great relative importance of recent changes in the real exchange rate over short- and medium-term periods (2005–8 and 2000–8 respectively).

By increasing the relative price of tradables vis-à-vis non-tradables, real currency devaluation (appreciation) encourages (discourages) domestic production of all tradables and discourages (encourages) their domestic consumption. (Trade taxes and barriers apart, all domestic tradables prices are the product of their world prices, as expressed in foreign currency, and the local exchange rate. In what economic theorists describe as 'small' countries, world prices are exogenously set, and can safely be taken as given.) In small countries the 'equilibrium' real exchange rate (or, if one prefers, the rate towards which it tends to gravitate in the absence of governmental intervention in the foreign exchange market) is influenced by a number of exogenous variables—the external terms of trade, export volume, private capital flow, and official development assistance (Williamson 1994). The real exchange rate is also, in part, and particularly in the short to medium run, the product of governmental policies, those of the finance ministry and/or the central bank. Since the incentive effects of changing real exchange rates can easily swamp those of more sluggishly changing trade policies, sensible overall development- or poverty-oriented incentive policies must involve central banks and treasuries no less than trade ministries. Since governmental 'management' of the exchange rate through intervention in the market for foreign exchange has domestic monetary implications, there must be care to develop appropriately complementary fiscal, monetary, and financial policies. Chinese and East Asian experience demonstrates the feasibility of consciously sustained real 'undervaluation' in governmental pursuit of export expansion and an overall growth strategy. One can make a strong developmental and poverty-fighting case for such active governmental support for the domestic production of tradables, both import-competing and exportable, through the exchange rate instrument (e.g. Rodrik 2008). The production of tradables is typically characterized by higher potential for overall productivity improvements than that of non-tradables, and is much more likely to be favourably affected by continuing global dynamic influences. (In some of the poorest countries, however, where production structures are relatively rigid and prospects for relatively easy reallocation of production towards tradables are severely constrained, the urban poor could be hurt by real currency undervaluation's positive impact upon the price of such tradables as food and fuel, important in their consumption.)

Such governmental involvement implies the possibility of 'currency wars'. But where countries are economically small, while one could worry about the fallacy of composition (what is true for one may not be true of the collectivity) the prospect of retaliation and negative global externalities from such policies is probably quite limited. The rules of the WTO impose no constraints upon this element of policy space. Nor has the IMF so far discouraged real currency undervaluation in systemically insignificant countries; their concern has typically focused upon the negative macroeconomic consequences of currency overvaluation.

There is now, however, a serious 'fly' in this otherwise potentially productive small-country 'ointment'. External shocks can wreak havoc with exchange rate policy intentions in poor countries. To the long-standing problems of instability and unpredictability in export revenues and flows of official development assistance there is now added a further source of shocks. In an increasingly globalized financial system private capital flows have become both larger and more volatile than heretofore—even in very poor countries. The size of such flows to small and medium-sized economies is negligible in the global scheme of things; but their size may be great enough to cause serious disruption in individual small countries. The size and volatility of exports and flows of official development assistance have long been understood to complicate macroeconomic management and the creation of appropriate incentive structures in poor countries. It is now much more evident than it previously was that even if these could be stabilized, the problem of international private capital flow, even in the poorest countries, remains.

Surges of private capital can drive the (real) exchange rate in counterproductive directions and create undesirable and costly exchange rate instability.

No less costly may be their impact upon fragile domestic financial institutions, generating both 'overheating' in inadequately monitored or managed financial booms and/or costly financial 'busts'. Such surges can be driven by completely exogenous forces, notably interest-rate changes in source countries and/or contagion from financial crises elsewhere in the global economy. In poor and small countries it does not take an absolutely large flow of foreign capital to swamp other influences on the economy and overwhelm macroeconomic managers and supervisory authorities. (These characteristics and other differences from typical Northern financial sectors would seem to call for significant modification of standardized regulatory regimes devised by and for developed countries (Rojas-Suarez 2008).)

A common popular misconception concerning the problems of financial surges and the use of capital controls has been that they have to do with the prospect of undesirable capital *outflows*. In fact, as recent events in emerging markets have demonstrated, macroeconomic managers in developing countries must be equally concerned with the domestic impact of (frequently volatile) capital inflows. In order to minimize undesirable macroeconomic effects it may be productive not only to deploy offsetting monetary and fiscal policies but also to resort to taxes or controls on capital inflows, as many developing countries now do. In times of financial crisis, in order to protect domestic financial institutions against 'flight' to stronger resident branches of foreign-owned ones, it may also be necessary for financial policies explicitly to favour the former (that is, to abandon the WTO principle of 'national treatment'). It is therefore essential that developing countries, poor and small as well as emerging markets, proceed prudently and cautiously with any international undertakings relating to the management (or not) of the capital account. In the 1990s the IMF, WTO, and OECD all actively pushed capital account liberalization upon developing countries; happily these countries were able to resist the introduction of new capital account liberalization rules. There is now, at least in the IMF, much greater recognition of the inappropriateness of such overly simplified and inappropriate rules for the capital account (IMF 2011; Ostry et al. 2011). But Northern financial interests continue to press for them in bilateral, plurilateral, and regional 'trade' agreements, including the EU's economic partnership agreements.

Developing-country negotiators need to be particularly wary of international agreements that appear to relate primarily to the foreign direct investment that virtually all seek. The definition of 'foreign investment' in such agreements can readily be written or interpreted so broadly as to encompass portfolio and other short-term flows. More fundamentally, much academic writing to the contrary, foreign direct investment can be as volatile and unpredictable as any other foreign capital flows. For instance, by borrowing from domestic financial institutions on the security of their domestic fixed capital, foreign owners can quickly 'liquefy' their local direct investment in order to achieve rapid capital outflow in times of crisis or perceived trouble. Nor is it generally recognized that high proportions of so-called foreign direct investment flows are in the form of loans to already controlled local firms rather than fresh equity investment. Foreign direct investment flows should be subject to general rules no less stringent than those applicable to portfolio flows.

In the new circumstances of globalized and turbulent financial markets, developing countries therefore need to be extremely cautious about premature across-the-board liberalization of international financial flows. Any new rules to which they subscribe should leave their policymakers with full autonomy to manage their capital accounts and their domestic financial systems in the interest of their own macroeconomic stability and development and, in particular, to permit measures to discourage short-term inflows and outflows of private capital and, in carefully defined circumstances, to favour domestic financial institutions over foreign-owned ones in the resolution of financial crises.

Needless to say, there are further issues in the management of external shocks in low-income countries. The most obvious need at the global level is further access for these countries to fast-disbursing low-conditionality international credit when required. Failing such reform, if they seek to protect themselves against such shocks they have no option but to hold increased (costly) foreign exchange reserves, either alone or in concert with others. As might be expected, there is solid evidence that those low-income countries holding greater reserves were not impacted as severely by the latest global recession (Berg et al. 2011). But this is, of course, a longer story.

It should by now be clear that the trade components of holistic international economic cooperation agreements, which typically receive the bulk of attention (at least in the popular press), may not be the only, or even the most developmentally important, ones. Surges in international capital flows and related exchange rate changes and other effects can easily dwarf trade impacts upon growth and development. Getting rules and policies wrong in this sphere can have catastrophic consequences. Policy space must be preserved in this arena no less than in the trade one. Other domestic policies and practices can, in any case, dwarf both trade and exchange rates in their impact upon development, income distribution, and poverty.

10.5 Capacity-Building for Pro-Poor Trade and Exchange Rate Policies

Ultimately, to achieve the objective of global poverty reduction through international trade and capital flow, there must be the relevant analytical capacity and political will, both in richer countries and in poor. Probably the weakest points today are political will in the rich (and middle-income) countries, and analytical and institutional capacity in the poorest. There are unfortunately early limits to what may be expected from change in the former, even in the longer run. It may, however, be quite productive to make greater conscious effort to improve the latter. (And any paper honouring Richard Jolly needs little excuse to discuss capacity-building in Africa; that was, after all, the topic of his Yale PhD thesis.)

Capacity-building is not simply a matter of improving national individuals' knowledge, experience, and skill, as important as that obviously must be. For a country, as distinct from an individual, to experience increased capacity for good policy formation there must be strong and credible institutions and processes through which its skilled individuals can have an impact upon economic policies and practices. Through appropriate governmental organization, available relevant knowledge and experience, wherever it exists, must be mobilized and connected to political and policy processes. Government interchange and dialogue both with business and with civil society can assist in the development of consensus as to policy approaches. Forums and relevant networks can both inform a wider public as to possible policy directions and, through the generation of further learning and political institutions, help to influence decisions. Strong local research, education, and training institutions can support such meetings, networks, and political processes so as to increase the probability that relevant analysis, knowledge, and skills will be made available to decision-makers, both in the public and private sectors.

Strong institutions can also help to mitigate the ubiquitous turnover problem. Individual turnover of skilled personnel within major government and other institutions is often distressingly high. Governmental and institutional effectiveness can obviously be negatively affected by the loss of key individuals with accumulated knowledge and experience in specialized fields. If strong enough, institutions and established processes, with continuing lives of their own, can limit some of the resulting damage. For sustained capacity to be built, maintained, and productively employed, then, careful thought must be given to the best institutional means, in the particular country context, for doing so. This is likely to involve appropriate remuneration for key professionals, means for maintaining professional morale, and other institutional reforms.

Ultimately, in each specialized sphere of international economic policy, one must return to the need for relevant knowledge, experience, and skills. The shortfalls in this respect are at their greatest in the poorest countries. What are the most significant gaps in the analytical and experiential skill sets available at present in these countries, particularly in Africa? What kind of people now populate the relevant ministries, and how have they been trained? Do they possess the kinds of knowledge, skills, and experience that they require to do their jobs well?

Well-trained economic policy analysts can be found in the poorest countries but are typically still quite scarce. The best can usually be found in finance ministries, development and planning ministries, central banks, presidential offices, and policy research institutions or universities. The number of such analysts who specialize in international economic policies (trade, balance of payments, exchange rates, capital flow), is, however, very small; and the number of those who purportedly have specialized in these areas and are at the same time familiar with the legal issues and niceties of WTO, IMF, or EPA negotiations is minuscule. The vast majority of those who are responsible for international economic files in African countries have little formal training in either international economics or international law. Nor is there usually much help available through local research institutions, universities, or consultants. The result has frequently been a high, and inherently undesirable, degree of reliance upon external 'technical cooperation' and external advice.

The need for capacity-building in international economic analysis and relevant negotiation skills in these cases is obvious. The case for assigning especially high priority to trade-related skills is particularly compelling at a time of negotiation and implementation of new trade and trade-related agreements in the WTO, with the EU, the USA, and China, and at regional levels. No less important is the need to build capacity for such analysis that, unlike much of what can be found in academic institutions or multilateral institutions' courses, is both interdisciplinary (especially economics, law, and politics) and clearly focused upon development and poverty objectives. Needless to say, an important further required element in capacity-building of the type most needed, again sometimes missing in academia, is practical usefulness.

What are required, then, are programmes that combine much of the usual theoretical and methodological rigour offered in traditional international (and other) economics and politics courses—with the practical, international institutional, and legal knowledge proffered in law faculties and international business schools—all within the overall context of a clear focus upon development and poverty objectives.

Small and poor countries doing the relevant cost-benefit calculations may reasonably conclude that the likely impact of their participation in many multilateral decision-making activities is so small that the specialized expertise required for their effective participation is not worth too much of their scarce investment. Their very scarce human talent may more profitably be used at home for other purposes. In such instances, as has already been seen in the Caribbean (with its regional negotiating machinery) and in the various African regional groupings, much can be gained through improved cooperative endeavours with others with related interests. This obviously applies no less to training and capacity-building endeavours, as undertaken by the African Economic Research Consortium (AERC), African Capacity-building Foundation (ACBF), and others. In these instances it may be particularly helpful for much of the training and capacity-building efforts to be less specialized, with improved collective arrangements for drawing upon foreign specialized knowledge only where it is especially necessary.

In the construction of the kind of longer-term capacity-building programmes for improved public policy now needed and wanted, it is often easier to specify what has *not* worked well and is *not* wanted rather than what exactly one is after. Among the principal problems often experienced in previous and existing programmes, both postgraduate and undergraduate, are the following:

i) too much abstract and/or irrelevant theory, drawn from the developed country 'shelf' relative to exposure to models more accurately reflecting developing-country characteristics;

ii) too much time spent on sophisticated econometric methodology relative to more practical statistical knowledge and analysis, including the capacity to assess data quality;

iii) too narrow, and even ideological, an approach to the role of public policy at the expense of a broader and more relevant approach to historical experience and political understanding;

iv) particularly in programmes in foreign countries, the provision of too narrow a range of institutional and legal knowledge and too much attention directed at irrelevant (foreign) national specifics;

v) too little attention devoted to the particular characteristics of poor countries and the specifics of their various trading, legal, and development experiences; and

vi) too little attention directed at the particular objectives of development and poverty reduction.

A further major problem with existing programmes, which must be addressed, is the subsequent relative isolation and potential demoralization and/or obsolescence of specialized graduates who return to work in their own countries.

A list of the problems associated with short courses and seminars intended to build economic policy capacities might not look too dissimilar. In addition, motivation for attendees at short courses and conferences is sometimes dubious, and the learning acquired there, while no doubt valuable in itself, is often of questionable relevance to their working responsibilities.

At a minimum, it ought to be possible to construct a network or networks of like-minded institutions and individuals who are working to increase and improve multidisciplinary capacity-building that aims at improving economic and other policies directed at development and poverty reduction in the poorest developing countries. Its members could include specialists in trade law, international business, international economics, or international political economy, as well as 'generalists' in public policy or other related fields with an interest in international economics (both trade and finance), poverty, and development issues. It would surely be helpful to be able, on a regular basis, to exchange information, course materials, and ideas—and perhaps, at some point, even students and faculty. All could be welcomed: those who offer short courses (whether academic institutions, NGOs, or international institutions), those who offer undergraduate courses, those with relevant postgraduate programmes, and individuals in relevant law firms.

10.6 Conclusions

It seems that the interaction between trade *cum* exchange rate policies and global poverty problems is often complex; but it undoubtedly deserves greater research attention than it has received. Much of what passes for conventional wisdom in this sphere is oversimplified and unreliable as a guide to policymakers in specific places and times.

Attempting to address global poverty by providing preferential trade arrangements for the poorest countries has proved neither very effective nor politically promising. On the other hand, attempting to do so via 'improvement' of developing countries' own trade and exchange rate policies, not least those of the poorest, requires both resources to deploy and a sophisticated understanding of such policies' potential role in stimulating growth and addressing poverty. It also requires a degree of political support that may be no less difficult to obtain. Unfortunately, there remains considerable professional uncertainty as to the likely impact of trade and trade policy upon growth—both in theory and in the empirical record—thereby making appropriate policy formation in particular circumstances even more difficult. In any case, a great many governmental policies other than those on trade influence the structure of overall incentives, and thereby trade, growth, and poverty reduction. In particular, and especially in the short to medium term, exchange rates play at least as great a role as trade policies in this regard. The real (inflation-adjusted) exchange rate that establishes the overall relative price of tradables (both exportables and import substitutes) can be a major determinant of the structures of production and demand, and thus of economic development and poverty reduction; its appropriate management usually deserves greater care than trade policy. In the poorest countries the specific factor-intensity and other development-relevant characteristics of the production in which they choose (or have been forced) to specialize also deserve more careful policy consideration.

In the recent (and current) widespread analyses of the causes and consequences of the global financial crisis and recession of 2007–9, and the role of international private capital flows therein, the poorest developing countries—since they are of little systemic importance—have been largely ignored. It is important to recognize, however, that newly resurgent and volatile private capital flows to these countries, as well as developing countries more generally, while small in the aggregate, create significant new problems for their policymakers. It has become far more difficult for all developing countries to achieve and maintain a development-sensitive real exchange rate, indeed more generally to macro-manage their economies, in this new environment. It is far from evident that complete international capital account liberalization, such as is often promoted in these countries by powerful negotiators from developed countries, would be in their development interest.

Again, these policy issues are complex. There are no simple formulae that can be applied to all situations. One size does not fit all. There is ultimately, therefore, no escape from the need for each poor country that aspires, within its inescapable constraints, to develop its economy and reduce poverty, to build the capacity to develop its own uniquely appropriate trade and exchange rate (and other) policies. This is a matter not only of individual skills but also of strong and relevant institutions and processes, not least political ones. Unfortunately, appropriate educational programmes for the creation of the required skills scarcely exist in (or for) the poorest countries, where the shortfalls are greatest, and their relevant institutions are typically weak. There is an obvious logic, particularly for the poorest countries, in the pursuit of scale economies via cooperation with others in such endeavours. The most useful contribution that outsiders can probably make in this sphere is to assist the poorest developing countries, in whatever ways they can, to build their own capacities to make sensible development and poverty-reducing policy decisions of their own. It seems to me that this is pretty much what Richard Jolly was saying fifty years ago—and has spent a lifetime trying to do.

References

Berg, A., C. Papageorgiou, C. Pattillo, M. Schindler, N. Spatafora, and H. Weisfeld (2011). *Global Shocks and Their Impact on Low-Income Countries: Lessons from the Global Financial Crisis*. IMF Working Paper 11/27. Washington, DC: IMF.

Camanho da Costa Neto, N. and R. Romeu (2011). *Did Export Diversification Soften the Impact of the Global Financial Crisis?*. IMF Working Paper 11/99. Washington, DC: IMF.

Dollar, D. and A. Kraay (2002). 'Growth Is Good for the Poor'. *Journal of Economic Growth*, 7(3): 195–225.

Dollar, D. and A. Kraay (2004). 'Trade, Growth, and Poverty'. *Economic Journal*, 114(493): F22–F49.

Donaldson, J. (2008). 'Growth Is Good for Whom, When, How? Economic Growth and Poverty Reduction in Exceptional Cases'. *World Development*, 36(11): 2127–43.

IMF (International Monetary Fund) (2011). *Recent Experiences in Managing Capital Flows—Cross-Cutting Themes and Possible Policy Framework*. Washington, DC: IMF. Available at: <http://www.imf.org/external/np/pp/eng/2011/021411a.pdf>.

Kim, D-H., S-C. Lin, and Y-B. Suen (2011). 'Nonlinearity between Trade Openness and Economic Development'. *Review of Development Economics*, 15(2): 279–92.

Lin, J., C. Monga, D. W. te Velde, S. D. Tendulkar, A. Amsden, K. Y. Amoako, H. Pack, and W. Lim (2011). 'Growth Identification and Facilitation: The Role of the State in the Dynamics of Structural Change'. *Development Policy Review*, 29(3): 259–310.

McMillan, M. and D. Rodrik (2011). 'Globalization, Structural Change and Productivity Growth'. In M. Bacchetta and M. Janson (eds), *Making Globalization Socially Sustainable*. Geneva: ILO–WTO, 49–84.

Njinkeu, D. and H. Cameron (eds) (2008). *Aid for Trade and Development*. New York: Cambridge University Press.

Ostry, J. D., A. R. Ghosh, K. Habermeier, L. Laeven, M. Chamon, M. S. Qureshi, and A. Kokenyune (2011). *'Managing Capital Inflows: What Tools to Use'*. IMF Discussion Note SDN/11/06. Washington, DC: IMF.

Ravallion, M. (2005). *'Inequality Is Bad for the Poor'*. WB Policy Research Working Paper 3677. Washington, DC: World Bank.

Rodrik, D. (2008). *The Real Exchange Rate and Economic Growth. Brookings Papers on Economic Activity*, Fall. Available at: <http://www.brookings.edu/~/media/projects/bpea/fall%202008/2008b_bpea_rodrik.pdf>.

Rojas-Suarez, L. (2008). 'Volatility: Prudential Regulation, Standards and Codes'. In Jose Marie Fanelli (ed.), *Macroeconomic Volatility, Institutions and Financial Architectures*. New York: Palgrave Macmillan, 73–100.

Singh, T. (2010). 'Does International Trade Cause Economic Growth? A Survey'. *The World Economy*, 33(11): 1517–64.

Williamson, J. (ed.) (1994). *Estimating Equilibrium Exchange Rates*. Washington, DC: Institute for International Economics.

Winters, L. A. (2000). 'Trade and Poverty, Is There a Connection?'. In D. Ben-David, H. Nordstrom, and L. A. Winters, *Trade, Income Disparity and Poverty*. Geneva: WTO, 43–69.

11

Human Development and Fiscal Policy
Comparing the Crises of 1982–5 and 2008–11

Bruno Martorano, Giovanni Andrea Cornia, and Frances Stewart

11.1 Introduction

The financial crisis of the late 2000s assumed a global dimension, affecting many countries around the world, in contrast to the debt crisis of the early 1980s, which mainly affected developing countries, leading to the famous 'lost decade'. In comparing these two crises, it is relevant to examine not only the extent and characteristics of the macroeconomic shocks, but also the differing government responses. While deflation and monetarism prevailed in the early 1980s, a Keynesian approach dominated the policies implemented by different governments during the first phase of the late 2000s crisis. Indeed, policymakers felt the need to react promptly to limit the negative economic and social consequences of the macroeconomic shocks. However, fiscal austerity measures were introduced during the second phase of the late 2000s crisis due to growing levels of public deficits and indebtedness, pressure from financial markets, high public debt problems of the EU countries, and a resurgence of orthodox influence over policy.

This chapter has dual objectives: on the one hand, we attempt to contrast the management of public social expenditure during the crises of the 1980s and 2008–11; on the other, we investigate whether the factors contributing to changes in social expenditure differed between the two crises and whether the debate on human development, which increasingly dominated the policy scene from 1990, affected fiscal policy during the crisis.

11.2 The Macroeconomic Shocks and Their Origins

The recent crisis and that of the early 1980s have different origins, characteristics, and effects. The origin of the 1980s crisis was related to the large indebtedness of developing countries following heavy borrowing in the 1970s, changes in the monetary policy in the USA and the UK in the late 1970s, and the subsequent recession in advanced economies. The crisis spread from advanced to poor economies because of the large rise in interest rates, a drop in commodity prices and export volumes resulting from the slowdown in global demand, and the sudden contraction in capital flows to developing countries. The fall in exports and increase in interest rates and the consequent inability to cope with servicing the debt generated the so-called debt crisis. The worst affected regions were Sub-Saharan Africa (SSA) and Latin America and the Caribbean (LAC), where the level of debt had increased, respectively, by more than 50 and 70 percentage points of GDP from the late 1970s to the mid-1980s. Asia was relatively unaffected as the countries of this region generally had not accumulated significant amounts of debt in the 1970s.

In contrast, the financial crisis in the late 2000s had its origin in the housing and banking sectors of developed countries. Attempts to save their financial systems led to a dramatic rise in public debt that pushed some rich countries into a sovereign debt crisis, especially in the Eurozone, where countries were unable to devalue their currency. In contrast to previous crises, developing countries were less affected. The African countries had reduced their large stock of debt, thanks to the Heavily Indebted Poor Countries Initiative of the early 2000s, while the LAC countries had done likewise through a series of renegotiations, defaults, debt cancellations, and fiscal policy changes aimed at achieving a low level of public external indebtedness and a high level of reserves.

Nonetheless, the crisis in rich economies affected developing countries via real channels, that is, via declines in export receipts, foreign investments, and migrant remittances. A dramatic worsening in the value of primary commodity exports was mainly driven by a large drop in international prices following a major fall in demand. In 2009, negative changes in the terms of trade were recorded by the countries belonging to the Commonwealth of Independent States (CIS), LAC, Middle East and North Africa (MENA), and SSA (Table 11.1).

Due to the fall in world output as well as rising tariffs and quantitative restrictions, the volume of world trade as a percentage of GDP decreased by 10 percentage points between 2008 and 2009. All the regions reduced their

Table 11.1 Percentage changes in the international terms of trade of goods and services

	2005	2006	2007	2008	2009	2010	2011
Advanced economies	−1.5	−1.1	0.3	−2.0	2.3	−1.0	−1.7
Central and Eastern Europe (CEE)	−0.8	−1.3	2.0	−2.3	3.8	−1.5	0.4
Commonwealth of Independent States (CIS)	13.8	7.7	2.3	18.5	−19.4	12.7	12.0
Developing Asia	−0.9	−0.8	−0.2	−3.1	5.6	−5.5	−1.7
Latin America and the Caribbean (LAC)	3.7	7.0	2.5	3.3	−6.1	8.3	5.5
Middle East and North Africa (MENA)	17.6	5.9	1.2	11.1	−16.7	6.1	11.4
Sub-Saharan Africa (SSA)	9.3	3.0	1.8	4.4	−13.6	20.0	3.6

Source: WEO database.

imports of goods and services, with the largest variation recorded by CIS (26 percentage points). Similarly, in 2009 the volume of exports of goods and services fell in all regions with the exception of SSA, where it remained stable. There was also a reduction in private financial flows from advanced economies to developing countries (Figure 11.1), especially in the case of portfolio investment. In 2008, capital inflows dropped by more than half of their 2007 real value, with the largest declines recorded by CEE and some CIS countries in terms of access to bank lending (UNDESA 2011). Also, the foreign direct investments (FDI) declined from 2.5–3 per cent of GDP in 2007 to 1–2 per cent in 2010. Only in SSA did FDI increase by more than 1 per cent of GDP between 2007 and 2008, although they decreased in the following two years.

Furthermore, remittances dropped in the emerging and developing countries, losing their traditional countercyclical role in difficult times. In particular, they fell by 1 per cent of GDP in LAC, and by more than 1.5 per cent in MENA and CEE–CIS. However, remittances remained stable in SSA, while they increased slowly in South Asia (Cornia and Martorano 2012).

These were the main shocks responsible for the worsening conditions in the developing countries in the late 2000s. There are noticeable differences from the 1980s crisis and across regions. In the early 1980s, LAC and SSA were the most affected regions (Table 11.2). Conversely, CEE–CIS, LAC, and the rich countries were the most affected in the recent crisis, while Asian, MENA, and SSA countries showed a positive performance (Table 11.2). Above all, a remarkable difference is noted in the trend of world GDP over the two periods. Although world GDP growth recorded a deceleration during the early 1980s, it remained on average positive, whereas in 2009 the average world GDP growth rate turned negative (Table 11.2).

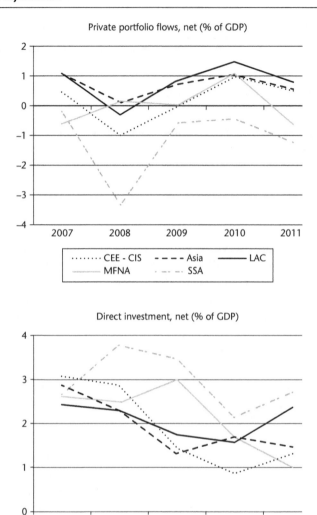

Figure 11.1 Private capital flows to developing regions, 2007–11
Source: WEO database.

11.3 Public Policy Response

11.3.1 The Initial Stimulus

The early 1980s crisis affected poor economies more severely and many of them sought support from the IMF. However, the standard fiscal and

Table 11.2 Annual percentage change in GDP in constant prices, 1980–4 versus 2007–11

	1980	1981	1982	1983	1984	2007	2008	2009	2010	2011
World	1.8	2.2	0.7	2.8	4.9	5.4	2.8	–0.6	5.3	3.9
Advanced economies	0.9	2.0	0.2	3.1	4.9	2.8	0.0	–3.6	3.2	1.6
Emerging and developing economies	3.8	2.8	1.8	2.0	4.9	8.7	6.0	2.8	7.5	6.2
– CEE	–1.1	–1.0	1.1	4.5	3.8	5.4	3.2	–3.6	4.5	5.3
– CIS	–	–	–	–	–	9.0	5.4	–6.4	4.8	4.9
– Developing Asia	5.9	5.8	5.6	7.0	7.9	11.4	7.8	7.1	9.7	7.8
– LAC	6.5	1.1	–0.5	–2.8	3.9	5.8	4.2	–1.6	6.2	4.5
– MENA	–1.9	2.5	1.3	2.7	3.5	5.6	4.7	2.7	4.9	3.5
– SSA	4.5	6.8	0.5	–0.8	2.8	7.1	5.6	2.8	5.3	5.1

Source: WEO database.

monetary policies recommended by the IMF amplified the size of the macroeconomic shock and increased its duration as adjustment policies focused mainly on the spending side. As a result, 'real government expenditure per capita fell in over half the countries of the developing world, with a greater proportion declining among countries with the adjustment policies than among those without' (Andersen et al. 1987: 73).

The scenario was completely different at the beginning of the recent crisis due to a broad consensus about the need to adopt countercyclical fiscal policies. Beyond expansionary monetary policies, 'during the first phase, most countries—in both the developing and developed world—moved swiftly to introduce fiscal stimulus packages and boost spending' (Ortiz et al. 2012: 174). According to EC-ILO (2011), this fiscal stimulus was on average close to 4 per cent of GDP with some packages exceeding 15 per cent of GDP, as in the cases of Georgia and Thailand. Considering twenty-two countries, Khatiwada (2009) shows that stimulus packages mainly encompassed public expenditure measures, while tax cuts were represented in less than one-quarter of the packages. Furthermore, there are interesting differences between developed and developing countries. While the latter concentrated mainly on infrastructure spending, fiscal packages in developed countries involved more of other types of additional spending and a greater proportion of tax cuts (Table 11.3).

According to Ortiz et al. (2012), more than eight out of ten countries increased public expenditures in the face of the crisis, with the result that fiscal balances deteriorated everywhere (Figure 11.2). The largest increase in public spending and worsening of fiscal balance was recorded in MENA countries, followed by the advanced economies.

Table 11.3 Composition of fiscal packages (% of total stimulus)

	All countries	Developed countries	Developing countries
Infrastructure spending	27.8	14.9	46.5
Employment measures[a]	1.8	2.9	0.2
Direct transfers to low-income households[b]	9.2	10.8	6.8
Other spending	39.8	37.2	43.5
Tax cuts	21.5	34.1	3.0

Notes:
[a] As reported by Khatiwada (2009: 18), 'employment measures include increasing the number of training centres and services like job search and placement'.
[b] This refers to direct cash transfers, conditional cash transfers, and unemployment benefits (Khatiwada 2009).
Source: Khatiwada (2009).

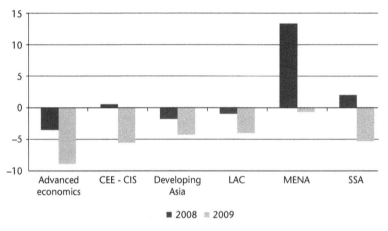

■ 2008 ▩ 2009

Figure 11.2 Fiscal balance (% of GDP) in 2008 and 2009
Source: WEO database.

Because of the poor economic conditions prevailing in many countries, the IMF regained some of its role as economic advisor and emergency lender, establishing new and much enlarged loan facilities with easier access. Moreover, its response to the crisis differed from its previous stance, with more flexibility in conditionality and more tolerance for unorthodox policies (Broome 2010). Indeed, the IMF considered a fiscal stimulus useful and, to some degree, necessary in the first phase of the crisis (Spilimbergo et al. 2008).

However, the persistence of the economic downturn led to a drop in government revenues, especially in CEE–CIS and SSA (by 2.4 and 5.4 per cent of GDP respectively between 2008 and 2009). As a consequence of this and of the fiscal stimulus, almost all regions experienced large and widening fiscal deficits (Figure 11.2).

11.3.2 From Fiscal Stimulus to Consolidation

The initial Keynesian approach in developed countries was swept away by the rapid accumulation of sovereign debt and the return to a neoliberal policy stance. As Aizenman and Jinjarak (2010: 7) explain, 'the sense of urgency and the will to move policies in tandem during the peak of the crisis has been replaced with extensive debates among countries regarding the future course of macro policies, and growing "fiscal fatigue"'.

Also, the IMF soon reverted to its traditional position, emphasizing a new need for fiscal austerity and especially the necessity to cut public spending (IMF 2010b). In particular, 'the consolidation strategy, particularly in advanced countries, should aim to stabilize age-related spending in relation to GDP, reduce non-age-related expenditure ratios, and increase revenues in an efficient manner' (IMF 2010b: 4). Nonetheless, there continued to be some differences compared with the past. For instance, the IMF (2010a: 11) suggested that 'an abrupt, front-loaded tightening is risky and should be avoided, except when market conditions make it inevitable'.

Although the negative effects of fiscal tightening on GDP growth and employment were clear, it was believed that fiscal adjustment was inevitable to gain credibility with international markets and to reduce the negative impacts of high debt on economic performance. This was especially marked in the Eurozone, where countries were unable to adjust their exchange rates and the accumulating debt threatened the stability of the Eurozone as a whole.

Consequently, many countries implemented austerity packages from 2010 onwards. In the developed countries, the aim was not only to reduce the high levels of public indebtedness but also to rebuild the fiscal space that had been eroded in 2008 and 2009. Although their level of indebtedness was much lower, fiscal consolidation was recommended also in the developing countries in order to avoid an escalation of debt and the risk of rising inflation.

Based on a review of 158 IMF country reports, Ortiz et al. (2012) show that in more than seven out of ten countries, wage cuts and salary caps had occurred or were planned. For example, the government of Ireland introduced wage cuts in the public sector and some African countries adopted caps on the hiring of civil servants and a freeze on public-sector salaries. Moreover, several countries planned to reduce the value of subsidies on energy and food (Ortiz et al. 2012).

With respect to tax changes, the most common measures concerned indirect taxation. Among the most common responses was an increase in VAT rates or the introduction of new excise taxes. In addition, as reported by Ortiz et al. (2012), several countries were considering the possibility of taxing more products, such as basic foods (e.g. Ethiopia and Moldova) or fuel and energy (e.g. Mexico and others). It is a known fact that these taxes have a regressive incidence. In contrast, some countries—such as Ghana—tried to increase taxation in a more equitable way, raising taxes on luxury goods, while other countries aimed to compensate for the increase in the fiscal burden by introducing exemptions or reducing taxes on goods with a high incidence in the budgets of the poor (e.g. on fuel and food staples in Kenya). Generally, the programmes of fiscal consolidation implemented in 2010 differed among developed and developing countries. While advanced economies and CEE countries preferred to introduce cuts on expenditure, emerging economies relied mainly on revenue recovery.

Finally, several countries tried to strengthen their fiscal institutions by changing fiscal rules. Compared with the past, the second-generation fiscal rules are more sophisticated and assure more flexibility and autonomy for policymakers in tackling cyclical changes by disciplining local governments and coordinating policy among the different levels of government during fiscal consolidation, as occurred in Latin America in the early 2000s.

Overall, public expenditure decreased in most countries: on average about one out of two developing countries and about three-quarters of the countries in CEE–CIS and MENA implemented cuts (Ortiz et al. 2012). In particular, public expenditure decreased by 3 per cent of GDP in CEE–CIS and MENA and 2 per cent in advanced economies (Figure 11.3). Conversely, public expenditure remained stable in the Asian developing countries and increased slightly in LAC and SSA (Figure 11.3).

However, the contraction during the austerity period was not enough to offset the expansion in public spending recorded during the first phase. Consequently, so far, public expenditure showed a positive change in each region during the overall crisis of the late 2000s in contrast to what happened during the crisis of the early 1980s.

11.3.3 Is It Old Hat? A Comparison of the Management of Public Social Expenditure in the Crisis of the 1980s and that of the 2008–10/11 Period

In this section we compare the changes in the level and composition of public expenditure during the two crises. In particular, we classify public

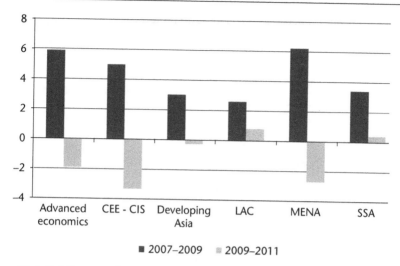

Figure 11.3 Public expenditure changes (GDP points) over the period 2007–9 and the period 2009–11

Source: Authors' compilation.

expenditure by function over the period 1981–5 and over the periods 2007–9 and 2009–10 so as to capture the different impact of the fiscal stimulus efforts and of the fiscal consolidation during the latter crisis.

SOCIAL PROTECTION EXPENDITURE[1]

Social protection includes expenditures on transfers to people, such as pensions, unemployment benefits, and other transfers, which in principle should increase during economic difficulties. Yet many studies suggest social protection expenditure has historically been less protected than other expenditures during fiscal adjustment. Indeed, Table 11.4 shows that social protection expenditure dropped in all regions in the early 1980s, decreasing on average in almost half of the countries included in our analysis. This percentage increased to more than 50 per cent in developing Asian, MENA, and SSA countries, while in Latin America about one out of two countries introduced cuts.

The scenario was completely different during the recent crisis. Indeed, Zhang et al. (2010) show that additional social protection measures constituted about one-quarter of the total cost of the stimulus packages and close to 50 per cent in some countries (e.g. South Africa, Singapore, and

---

[1] According to the IMF's (2001: 76) functional classification of expenditure, social protection includes spending on sickness/disability, old age, survivors, unemployment, family/children, housing, R&D social protection, social exclusion n.e.c., and social protection n.e.c.

Table 11.4 Changes in public spending for social protection (% of GDP) by period

	Change in social spending/GDP (*Variation in percentage points*)			Percentage of countries where public social spending increased (decreased)		
	1981–85	2007–09	2009–10	var 1981–85	var 2007–09	var 2009–10
Advanced economies	−0.2 (−1.6)	2.6 (18.7)	−0.2 (−1.2)	27 (14)	100 (0)	17 (4)
CEE—CIS		2.6 (26.0)	0.0 (0.2)		86 (0)	16 (26)
Developing Asia	−0.2 (−13.5)	0.2 (21.4)	−0.1 (−9.6)	33 (50)	85 (14)	13 (38)
LAC	0.0 (−0.7)	0.7 (13.4)	−0.1 (−3.8)	27 (45)	80 (20)	27 (45)
MENA	−0.1 (−2.6)	−0.1 (−1.0)	−1.0 (−10.9)	29 (57)	60 (20)	33 (66)
SSA	−0.1 (−6.6)	0.3 (12.4)	0.1 (3.4)	33 (56)	71 (14)	60 (40)

Notes: The number of countries included in each region varies across the different periods. Countries that experienced variations between −5% and +5% are considered stable.
Source: Authors' elaboration based on GFS–IMF data and Martorano and Cornia (2012) database.

Taiwan). Table 11.5 shows that almost seven out of ten countries, especially in SSA, developing Asia, and LAC increased resources devoted to social protection rather than cutting them as they had done in the 1980s. In advanced countries and CEE–CIS, the percentage of countries increasing their expenditures on social protection rose to more than 90 per cent.

The majority of the increases in social protection expenditures were concentrated in the first phase (2007–9). In 2010, social protection spending decreased slightly in all regions except CEE–CIS, where it remained stable, and SSA, where it continued to increase (Table 11.4). However, the decline in public expenditure on social protection during the years of fiscal austerity (2009–10) did not fully offset its previous expansion during 2007–9.

When looking at the composition of social benefits during the recent crisis, it is important to underline the differences among countries. The largest increases in advanced and CEE–CIS economies were on contributory social security benefits. In contrast, in LAC and East Asia the biggest increase was in expenditures for non-contributory social assistance benefits. Indeed, in the developing countries, governments introduced new cash transfer programmes or extended existing ones. In China, a new rural pension scheme was introduced to cover 24 per cent of eligible rural residents by the end of 2010 (Lei et al. 2011). New welfare programmes were also introduced in Pakistan and the Philippines in 2008.

In LAC, governments expanded or increased the benefits from existing cash transfer programmes; for instance, the Argentinian and the Brazilian governments respectively expanded the coverage of the *Asignación Universal por Hijo* and *Bolsa Família*. In SSA too, existing programmes were extended or new programmes were implemented to protect people from the effects of the crisis. For example, 'Ethiopia introduced wheat subsidies to ease the impact of inflation on the urban poor and vulnerable rural populations. Senegal created a cash transfer programme for mothers and young children, and Namibia and South Africa enhanced support grants for the elderly and children, while increasing spending on health and low-income housing' (UNDESA 2011: 87).

EDUCATION AND HEALTH EXPENDITURES
In *Adjustment with a Human Face*, Andersen et al. (1987) show that governments cut health and education expenditures in reaction to the crisis of the early 1980s. Indeed, education spending decreased in three-quarters of the Latin American countries, while health spending remained stable or decreased in the vast majority of SSA countries (Tables 11.5 and 11.6).

These cuts led to difficulties in the education and health sectors in both regions. For example, Andersen et al. (1987) report that in Ghana there were problems with immunization against yellow fever while in Mozambique there were deficiencies in primary healthcare services. Similarly in the education sector, the introduction of fees in African countries reduced enrolment rates in primary schools and the quality of educational services deteriorated (World Bank 1995).

In the 2000s crisis, the situation was completely different. As part of the fiscal stimulus packages, governments increased their expenditures on health. UNDESA (2011: 86) reports that several countries 'announced direct or indirect health funding, such as increased spending on public health (China, Honduras, Indonesia, Japan, Kenya, Peru, South Africa, Thailand, United States), compensation for contributions to statutory health insurance schemes (Germany), and health insurance assistance (Switzerland, United States)'. Consequently, public expenditure on health increased in every region over the period 2007–9 (Table 11.5).

Nonetheless, governments did implement some spending cuts during the fiscal consolidation period (2009–10). For example, 'Ireland has reduced both pay and non-pay outlays in the health sector (including through voluntary redundancy schemes and reduced fees), and Greece and Portugal have advanced reforms of their healthcare systems with a view to containing spending' (IMF 2012: 24). With the exception of SSA, health expenditures decreased in every region, although the size of the changes was not large enough to offset the previous increase (Table 11.5).

Table 11.5 Changes in public spending on health during the two crises

	Change in public health spending/GDP (variation in percentage points)			Percentage of countries where public health spending increased (decreased)		
	1981–85	2007–09	2009–10	var 1981–85	var 2007–09	var 2009–10
Advanced economies	0.4 *(12.6)*	0.8 *(12.3)*	−0.1 *(−1.1)*	36 (23)	92 (0)	4 (13)
CEE–CIS		0.5 *(13.4)*	−0.1 *(−2.4)*		76 (10)	18 (32)
Developing Asia	0.2 *(16.6)*	0.2 *(16.6)*	−0.1 *(−5.5)*	63 (25)	70 (30)	40 (30)
LAC	−0.1 *(−4.5)*	0.6 *(20.2)*	−0.2 *(−6.7)*	27 (27)	83 (11)	13 (33)
MENA	0.2 *(9.9)*	0.2 *(7.7)*	−0.3 *(−13.4)*	43 (29)	50 (17)	0 (50)
SSA	−0.2 *(−11.7)*	0.2 *(9.6)*	0.2 *(7.7)*	11 (33)	50 (31)	60 (20)

Note: See Table 11.4.
Source: Authors' elaboration based on GFS–IMF data and Martorano and Cornia (2012) database.

Table 11.6 Changes in public spending on education during the two crises

	Change in public spending on education/GDP (variation in percentage points)			Percentage of countries where public spending on education increased (decreased)		
	1981–85	2007–09	2009–10	var 1981–85	var 2007–09	var 2009–10
Advanced economies	−0.2 *(−5.5)*	0.5 *(9.6)*	0.0 *(0.6)*	14 (41)	87 (0)	13 (9)
CEE–CIS		0.5 *(10.8)*	−0.2 *(−3.9)*		80 (10)	5 (42)
Developing Asia	0.3 *(13.6)*	0.2 *(7.8)*	0.1 *(2.3)*	75 (0)	50 (40)	29 (43)
LAC	−0.3 *(−11.6)*	0.7 *(16.2)*	−0.1 *(−2.2)*	8 (75)	76 (12)	9 (18)
MENA	0.3 *(5.9)*	−0.5 *(−9.1)*	−0.3 *(−5.7)*	57 (29)	0 (50)	0 (50)
SSA	−0.1 *(−2.1)*	0.0 *(−0.3)*	0.2 *(4.9)*	33 (33)	36 (27)	33 (0)

Note: See Table 11.4.
Source: Authors' elaboration based on GFS–IMF data and Martorano and Cornia (2012) database.

Stimulus packages also included measures directed towards the education sector. Indeed, several poor countries concentrated their efforts on primary education for poor households, while other countries, such as China, tried to expand the supply of educational services (Khatiwada 2009). As a result, education expenditure increased in all regions except MENA (Table 11.6). In education, as in government expenditure as a whole, it is possible to distinguish two trends: one covering the phase of fiscal stimulus (2007–9) and the other characterizing austerity (2009–10). In the first period, education spending increased by more than 15 per cent in Latin America and by about 10 per cent in advanced economies, CEE–CIS, and Asian developing countries. In the second period, this type of expenditure dropped slightly in MENA, CEE–CIS, and Latin America, but remained stable in rich countries and rose in SSA and developing Asia.

Comparing government responses during the two crises, it is evident that countries targeted more attention on the health and education sectors in the second crisis. In general, although the second phase of the 2000s crisis was similar to the early 1980s, the changes implemented then were not sufficient to completely offset the increases introduced during the fiscal stimulus phase. Of course, as this austerity phase is not over at the time of writing, continued cutbacks may mean a net worsening in expenditure over subsequent years.

OTHER EXPENDITURES

With respect to the remaining public expenditures, there were no significant changes in terms of defence, public order and safety, environment protection, housing, or communities and recreation expenditures in either crisis (Table 11.7).

More evident were the changes in expenditures on economic affairs and general public services. Over the period 1981–5, public expenditure on economic affairs fell in all the regions considered with the exception of the SSA countries, where it remained stable; the largest cuts were implemented in the LAC and Asian countries. During the first phase of the recent crisis, economic expenditures increased slightly almost everywhere, as spending on infrastructure was one of the most important components of the stimulus packages implemented by developing countries. In the fiscal consolidation phase, expenditures on economic affairs continued to increase in MENA and SSA. Although the governments of the other regions reduced this expenditure, these reductions did not offset the previous increases (Table 11.7).

Table 11.7 Changes in public spending on general services and economic affairs (% of GDP)

	General public services			Economic affairs		
	1981–85	2007–09	2009–10	var 1981–85	var 2007–09	var 2009–10
Advanced economies	−0.2	0.4	−0.2	−0.1	0.7	−0.1
CEE–CIS		0.6	−0.4		0.4	−0.3
Developing Asia	0.5	0.7	0.4	−1.3	0.5	−0.5
LAC	0.0	0.4	0.1	−1.6	−0.1	−0.1
MENA	0.5	−1.6	0.9	−0.3	0.2	0.7
SSA	−1.1	1.3	−0.4	0.0	1.2	0.7

Note: The number of the countries included in the different periods analysed is not the same.
Source: Authors' elaboration based on GFS–IMF data and Martorano and Cornia (2012) database.

Government responses were far more heterogeneous in the case of expenditures on general public services. In the early 1980s, the most evident change was among SSA countries (Table 11.8). In contrast, the same expenditure rose by 1.3 percentage points of GDP in the late 2000s. Expenditures on general and public services also increased during the fiscal stimulus period in other regions with the exception of MENA, where they decreased. Moreover, during the fiscal consolidation period these expenditures remained stable, again with the exception of MENA.

CHANGES IN PUBLIC EXPENDITURE COMPOSITION
The changes in public expenditure composition give an indication of government priorities during crises. A component of public expenditure can be defined as either 'protected' or 'vulnerable' depending on whether its share in total expenditure increases or decreases.

Using this approach, Table 11.8 shows that expenditure on economic affairs was particularly vulnerable in the early 1980s as its share in total expenditure decreased the most. Although economic affairs expenditure was on average protected in the SSA, a disaggregated analysis shows that it was protected in less than 50 per cent of the countries and that cuts were significant in more than 30 per cent of them. Expenditure on social protection was vulnerable in high-income countries, while the health sector maintained its share in total public expenditure. Finally, expenditures on general public services and on education were protected in the Asian and MENA countries (Table 11.8).

A completely different pattern can be observed during the recent crisis. During its first phase, with the exception of MENA countries, the most protected expenditure was that on social protection. During the second phase of the recent crisis, the share of social protection expenditure continued to increase in CEE–CIS and remained stable in the other regions. With regards to the health sector, the situation was similar to that of the early 1980s. A noticeable difference is observed for education spending in the LAC countries, which, in contrast to the previous crisis, was more protected than other sectors. As for the expenditure on economic affairs, in most cases governments had reactions similar to the early 1980s, introducing cuts especially in the second phase of the recent crisis. Thus, between 2009 and 2010, there were no major changes in public expenditure composition.

11.4 Which Factors Contributed to the Change in Social Expenditure During the Two Crises?

We now investigate the factors that contributed to the differences in social public expenditure during the crises of the early 1980s and late 2000s. As

Table 11.8 Changes in public expenditure composition

		Advanced economies	CEE–CIS	Developing Asia	LAC	MENA	SSA
General public services	1981–85	=		↑	=	↑	↓
	2007–09	=	=	↓	=	↓	=
	2009–10	=	=	↑	=	=	↓
Economic affairs	1981–85	=		↓	↓	↓	↑
	2007–09	=	=	=	↓	=	↑
	2009–10	=	=	=	↓	↓	=
Health	1981–85	=		=	=	=	=
	2007–09	=	=	=	=	↑	=
	2009–10	=	=	=	=	=	=
Education	1981–85	=		↑	↓	↑	=
	2007–09	=	=	↑	↑	↓	=
	2009–10	=	=	=	=	=	=
Social protection	1981–85	↓		=	=	=	=
	2007–09	=	↑	↑	↑	↓	=
	2009–10	=	↑	=	=	↓	=

Note: The number of countries included in each region varies across the different periods. = means a variation of between –1% and +1%.
Source: Authors' elaboration based on GFS–IMF data and Martorano and Cornia (2012) database.

noted, the two crises are different and the factors affecting the changes in social spending could also have been different.

One of the most important factors is, of course, the economic environment. According to the accepted view, social expenditure should be countercyclical so as to protect people during bad times. In high-income countries, social protection instruments—such as unemployment insurance, food stamps, social security, and so on—work as a cushion during worsening economic conditions. While developing countries have traditionally had underdeveloped tools of social protection, many of them recorded important improvements in this area over recent decades.

To increase social expenditures a policymaker needs adequate fiscal space. Both in the early 1980s and in the second phase of the 2000s crisis, high public deficits and rising debt ratios constrained policy options for a variety of reasons. In the 1980s, the possibility of taking countervailing action against the critical economic and social conditions was restricted in the developing countries by the conditionality involved with loans from international agencies, which imposed a strict discipline on total expenditures. Indeed, several scholars have criticized the influence of international agencies on the decisions taken by developing countries during crises.[2] The IMF (1995) guidelines

---

[2] There is, however, no general consensus. Using data for 140 countries over the period 1985–2009, Clements et al. (2011) show that education and health grew more in countries

for adjustment emphasized the necessity of expenditure rationalization to achieve stabilization, including limits on expenditure on social benefits and the introduction of targeting. In addition, countries had to reduce the size of subsidies or replace them with vouchers and had to liberalize food markets. In terms of public services, it was suggested that countries should rely more on fees, especially for education and health, while profitable activities could be privatized.

The adverse consequences of the 1980s crisis on poor people fuelled an important debate on 'human development'. 'The UN was left to take on the role of constructive dissent. In 1985, the United Nations Children's Fund (UNICEF) began promoting the need for "adjustment with a human face" and issued its two-volume study in 1987. By 1990, UNDP had prepared the first of its annual human development reports, setting out a more fundamental alternative to Bretton Woods orthodoxy' (Jolly 2005: 55). All in all, there was a growing consensus about the necessity to move from 'structural adjustment' to a 'recovery with a human face'.

The changing environment pushed international agencies to include poverty issues directly in their programmes. Thus, 'the introduction of the Poverty Reduction and Growth Facility in November 1999 was an important step in the history of the International Monetary Fund' (Oberdabernig 2010: 22). As a result, international agencies in the first phase of the recent crisis were more tolerant of budget deficits and less restrictive on policy choices 'allowing more accommodative policy responses' (IMF 2009: 44). For example, some countries under IMF-supported programmes (such as Costa Rica and Pakistan) expanded their social protection systems (IMF 2009).

Also, the adverse social outcomes associated with the structural adjustment programmes in the 1980s generated a growing call for equity that acquired strength following the gradual consolidation of democracy in many developing countries. Indeed, authoritarian regimes in the 1980s often disregarded the wellbeing of low-income groups, who were not protected from social cuts. In contrast, the increase in people's political participation and party competition clearly affected the decisions of policymakers. As shown by several works, democratic regimes are more cautious during recessions about cutting social spending (Kaufman and Segura-Ubiergo 2001), independently of their ideology, because, it is suggested, of *the politics of blame avoidance* (Weaver 1986).

Moreover, it is necessary to emphasize that, compared to the past, developing countries benefited from greater autonomy from the recommendations of

under IMF-supported programmes. In contrast, Basu and Stewart (1995) report that social spending declined more in countries that embarked on an SAP, and Andersen, Jaramillo, and Stewart (1987) show that the adjustment programmes introduced under the aegis of the IMF included important cuts on social protection expenditures.

international agencies because of their low debts and accumulation of reserves (Stewart 2012). The example of Latin America, a region known in the past as the laboratory for the Washington Consensus, is illustrative. During the 1980s and 1990s, austerity produced a continuous deterioration in economic and social outcomes. Indeed, cuts in public expenditures hampered economic growth and consequently reduced tax revenue, resulting in increased fiscal deficits and producing what has been described as an 'illusory adjustment' (Easterly 1999). From the early 2000s, Latin American countries implemented a new policy model based on a combination of growth, redistribution, and macroeconomic stability, and similarly to other regions were able to implement countercyclical policies in the recent crisis, including expanding their social protection system (Cornia et al. 2012).

Finally, in contrast to the early 1980s, a Keynesian wind dominated the first phase of the recent crisis, affecting the economic policy implemented by different countries. Since market fundamentalism was believed to be the source of the crisis, the implementation of Keynesian policies was considered essential to reverse the weak economic situation. In this context, social expenditures played a central role in supporting demand. Nonetheless, Keynesianism had a short life, partly due to the special problems of the Eurozone, and the nightmare of default began to loom in the minds of policymakers, first in advanced economies and then, to a lesser extent, in developing countries. The growing level of debt, the threat of speculation from financial markets, and a resurgence of the influence of orthodox economists convinced many policymakers of the necessity to reduce deficits and limit indebtedness. At the same time, the international financial agencies reverted to their original stance, advising that cuts in public spending were essential. Although this view was widely challenged, it dominated policy partly because it fed into the anti-state views of conservatives and dominated the Eurozone, where German influence was paramount.

We now test whether the factors discussed above contributed to changes in social expenditures (i.e. public expenditure on social protection, health, and education) during the two crises. For this purpose, a database was built that included annual data for forty-five and eighty-seven countries respectively over the periods 1980–5 and 2007–10. Given the macro-panel nature of the data, we use a fixed-effects estimation procedure which takes the following form:

$$\Delta(Social_{EXP_{it}}) = \alpha + \beta X_{it} + \eta_i + u_{it} \qquad\qquad i = 1, 2, \ldots N; \, t = 1, 2, \ldots, T \quad (1)$$

where i and t denote the country and the time period respectively, η_i is the time-invariant country's fixed effect and u_{it} a joint error term for countries and time periods. The dependent variable is the social expenditure variation

Table 11.9 Definition, description, and data sources of the variables used in regression analysis

Variable	Description	Unit of measure	Source
Variation of social expenditures	Variation of public social expenditure (social protection, education, and health)	Percentage points variation of social expenditure on GDP	ADB database; Easterly (2001); EUROSTAT; Government Finance Statistics (GFS); IDLA database; National sources; OECD stat; World Development Indicators (WDI); World tax database
GDP growth rate	Growth rate of GDP per capita	Rate of growth	ERS/USDA international macroeconomic dataset (2011)
Public debt	Level of public debt	Public debt/GDP	WEO database 2011; Reinhart & Rogoff (2010)
Poor countries	Developing countries	1 (developing countries) 0 (advanced economies)	Authors' compilation
IMF	Countries under an IMF-supported programme	1 (IMF-supported programme) 0 (otherwise)	Clements, Gupta, and Nozaki (2011) IMF's country information online database
Democracy	Index of democracy	Index ranges between 0 and 100	Vanhanen (2011)
Right	Dummy denoting a country run by a right-wing party	1 (right-wing party), 0 (all other cases)	Keefer (2010)
Keynesian	Dominance of Keynesian policies	Dummy equals 1 for the period 2007–09	Authors' compilation

Source: Authors' compilation.

in percentage points as share of GDP, which we expect to be countercyclical, especially in the recent crisis when the need for protective action was more widely accepted. In turn, X is a vector of explanatory variables (Table 11.9), which are grouped as follows: (i) macroeconomic conditions; (ii) external pressures; and (iii) other factors.

(i) Macroeconomic conditions. We consider two variables: the growth rate of GDP, which proxies the size of the macroeconomic shocks,[3] and the level of debt as a share of GDP, which proxies the country's initial

[3] The growth rate of GDP is only a proxy of the macroeconomic shocks, which are equal to the sum of the drop in export receipts/GDP, capital inflows/GDP, and remittances/GDP. GDP growth rate is closely related to these variables but is also influenced by the policy responses adopted, amount of external financing available, and other factors.

fiscal conditions and its inherent vulnerability to shocks. As discussed above, we would expect social expenditure to move in the opposite direction to the level of debt.

(ii) External pressures. As reported above, the international agencies had an important role during the crises analysed in this chapter. Thus, we test what happened to social spending under IMF-supported programmes for the early 1980s and the late 2000s, extending the data compiled by Clements et al. (2011) for the early 1980s. The IMF dummy variable equals 1 if a country has an IMF-supported programme and 0 otherwise. We expect that the presence of an IMF agreement in the 1980s crisis would be associated with a reduction of social expenditures, while the expected sign is less clear for the 2007–9 crisis due to the greater autonomy of the developing countries as compared to the past and the influence of the human development debate.

(iii) Other factors. We introduce the Vanhanen democracy index among the regressors to test the impact of the spread of democracy on social expenditure. This index measures both the extent of political pluralism and citizen participation in political life. Moreover, we introduce a dummy to denote whether a country is run by a right-wing government dominated by 'parties that are defined as conservative, Christian democratic, or right-wing' (Keefer 2010: 7). As argued above, in a democratic context (irrespective of a government's political ideology), it is, in fact, more difficult to cut social expenditures than other components of public expenditure. Finally, we try to investigate whether an effective Keynesian wind dominated the first phase of the recent crisis and thus affected the economic policy implemented by different countries. To proxy for this, we introduce a Keynesian dummy variable that controls for the first phase of the recent crisis (2008–9).

11.4.1 Regression Results

As can be seen in Table 11.10, the factors that contributed to the variation in social public expenditure during the crises of the early 1980s and the late 2000s are completely different. In the early 1980s, the variation in social expenditure was affected by a country's level of indebtedness, especially in the developing countries. While the level of debt/GDP becomes non-significant when other variables are included, the interaction between the level of debt/GDP and the dummy for non-rich countries is negative and significant, meaning that a high level of indebtedness pushed the developing countries to introduce social protection cuts. The macroeconomic shocks

Table 11.10 Regression results (dependent variable: percentage points variation of social expenditure/GDP)

	Early 1980					Late 2000				
	1	2	3	4	5	1	2	3	4	5
GDP growth rate	-0.0064**	-0.0034	-0.0032	-0.0038	-0.004	-0.0126***	-0.0138***	-0.0140***	-0.0148***	-0.0124***
Debt		-0.0023***	-0.0011	-0.0013	0.001		-0.0021**	-0.0017	-0.0008	0.0012
Debt*poor					-0.0025*					
IMF			-0.1156**	-0.1194**	-0.1174**			-0.0364	-0.0475**	-0.0422*
Democracy				0.003	0.0032				0.0028	0.0054*
Right				-0.0182	-0.0212				-0.0164	-0.0142
Keynesian										0.0637***
Constant	0.0342***	0.1569***	0.1188***	0.0861*	0.0564	0.0768***	0.1800***	0.1695***	0.0675	-0.1425
Obs	171	117	117	117	117	298	295	295	286	286
R-squared	0.034	0.077	0.151	0.16	0.166	0.243	0.26	0.267	0.333	0.378
N countries	41	29	29	29	29	83	82	82	80	80

Notes: * significant at 10%; ** at 5%; *** at 1%.
Source: Authors' compilation.

(proxied by the GDP growth rate) had no significant impact, indicating that social expenditures were not countercyclical. Also, the democracy index is not significant, probably due to the fact that the majority of developing countries were run by authoritarian regimes. The regression results confirm the view that the situation in the late 2000s was different. Table 11.10 shows that the most important determinant of social expenditure variations, then, was the severity of the economic shock experienced. In particular, a worsening of economic conditions favoured a countercyclical expansion of social protection spending. At the same time, the spread of democracy increased governments' contribution to social protection independently of their political orientation. Although the IMF imposed conditions less stringent than in the past, the results were not different in the late 2000s compared with the previous crisis due to the promotion of fiscal austerity during the last years of the recent crisis. In addition, the Keynesian dummy is positive and significant, meaning that such an approach led to a more robust countercyclical fiscal policy, which was completely different from that adopted in the early 1980s and in 2010.

11.5 Conclusions

The size of the recent macroeconomic shock was greater than that of the early 1980s. While world growth decelerated in the early 1980s, it turned negative in 2009. It appears that the governments' reactions during the recent crisis were different compared to those implemented in the early 1980s. In the vast majority of countries, policymakers tackled the initial phase of the crisis through the implementation of fiscal stimulus packages in which an increase in social spending represented one of the main components.

The factors that contribute to explaining this difference in approach include greater country autonomy as compared with the past and the spread of democracy. Moreover, the negative consequences of the structural adjustment policies in the 1980s pushed policymakers to pay greater attention to human development. Lastly, it was evident that a Keynesian approach dominated the early phase of the recent crisis. Nonetheless, fear of debt default in 2010 and continuous pressures from international financial markets pushed many policymakers to introduce austerity packages, offsetting in part their previous actions. Since the crisis is not over at the time of writing, their net effect over the crisis and adjustment period may well eventually prove to have been negative in many countries.

Another major difference between the crises is that the advanced countries were most directly affected in the 2000s, and the poorest countries relatively unscathed, a complete reversal of the 1980s situation. This means that the poorest people are likely to have suffered less in the 2000s than they did in the 1980s. This was helped by social protection that was extended extensively due to the growing acceptance of the need for 'human development'—itself largely a response to the adverse conditions accompanying and following the crisis of the 1980s—and to the spread of democracy.

Unfortunately, no data are yet available after 2010. However, according to available fiscal projections, it appears that a growing number of countries will undergo new cuts in public expenditure and will turn more to indirect taxation. As noted by Ortiz et al. (2012: 177), 'overall, an additional thirty-two countries are forecasted to undergo public expenditure cuts between 2011 and 2012, with the largest changes occurring in the poorest region: Sub-Saharan Africa'. Moreover, about one out of three countries are trying to cut their social protection expenditure (Ortiz, Chai, and Cummins 2012). These policies have been implemented or are in discussion especially in high-income countries.

So, while the path followed by most countries during the first phase of the recent crisis limited the consequences of the economic downturn, a return to an austerity stance increases again the risk of a vicious circle dominated by an illusory fiscal adjustment and a worsening of social conditions. Cuts in social spending are detrimental to the reduction of poverty and inequality; reducing expenditures on education and health will have negative effects on the future shape of income distribution; and cutting investments in physical and human capital could be counterproductive both in terms of macroeconomic stabilization and long-term growth.

To conclude, 'pushed to extremes, austerity is bad economics, bad arithmetic, and ignores the lessons of history' (Jolly et al. 2012: 1). Policymakers have a fundamental responsibility to avoid irrational cuts in social spending and at the same time to promote economic development and human capital formation to ensure better living conditions for their populations.

References

Aizenman, J. and Y. Jinjarak (2010). 'The Role of Fiscal Policy in Response to the Financial Crisis'. Background paper for the *World Economic Situation and Prospects 2011*. Available at: <http://www.un.org/esa/policy/index.html>.

Andersen, P., M. Jaramillo, and F. Stewart (1987). 'The Impact on Government Expenditure'. In G. A. Cornia, R. Jolly, and F. Stewart (eds), *Adjustment with a Human Face*, Vol. 1. Oxford: Clarendon Press, 73–89.

Basu, A. and F. Stewart (1995). 'Structural Adjustment Policies and the Poor in Africa: An Analysis of the 1980s'. In F. Stewart (ed.), *Adjustment and Poverty: Options and Choices*. London: Routledge, 138–70.

Broome, A. (2010). 'The International Monetary Fund, Crisis Management and the Credit Crunch'. *Australian Journal of International Affairs*, 64(1): 37–54.

Clements, B., S. Gupta, and M. Nozaki (2011). *'What Happens to Social Spending in IMF-Supported Programmes?'*. IMF Staff Discussion Note, SDN/11/15. Washington, DC: IMF.

Cornia, G. A. and B. Martorano (2012). *'Development Policies and Income Inequality in Selected Developing Regions, 1980–2010'*. UNCTAD Discussion Paper 210. Geneva: UNCTAD.

Cornia, G. A., J. C. Gómez-Sabaini, and B. Martorano (2012). *A New Fiscal Pact, Tax Policy Changes and Income Inequality*. Working Papers Series wp2012_03. Florence: Department of Economics, University of Florence.

Easterly, W. (1999). 'When Is Fiscal Adjustment an Illusion?'. *Economic Policy*, 28: 57–86.

Easterly, W. (2001). *Global Development Network Growth Database*. Available at: <http://econ.worldbank.org/WBSITE/EXTERNAL/EXTDEC/EXTRESEARCH/0,,contentMDK:20701055~pagePK:64214825~piPK:64214943~theSitePK:469382,00.html>.

EC-ILO (2011). *'A Review of Global Fiscal Stimulus'*. EC-IILS Joint Discussion Paper Series 5. Geneva: ILO-IILS.

IMF (1995). *'Guidelines for Fiscal Adjustment'*. Pamphlet Series, No. 49. Washington, DC: IMF.

IMF (2001). *Government Finance Statistics Manual 2001* (GFSM 2001). Available at: <http://www.imf.org/external/pubs/cat/longres.cfm?sk=15203.0>.

IMF (2009). *'Review of Recent Crisis Programmes'*. Staff Paper SM/09/246. Washington, DC: IMF.

IMF (2010a). *Fiscal Monitor. Fiscal Exit from Strategy to Implementation*, November. Washington, DC: IMF.

IMF (2010b). *From Stimulus to Consolidation: Revenue and Expenditure Policies in Advanced and Emerging Economies*. Washington, DC: IMF.

IMF (2012). *Fiscal Monitor: Balancing Fiscal Policy Risks*, April. Washington, DC: IMF.

Jolly, R. (2005). 'UN and Development Thinking and Practice'. Forum for Development Studies, No 1-2005.

Jolly, R., G. A. Cornia, D. Elson, C. Fortin, S. Griffith-Jones, G. Helleiner, R. van der Hoeven, R. Kaplinsky, R. Morgan, I. Ortiz, R. Pearson, and F. Stewart (2012). *Be Outraged: There are Alternatives*. Available at: <http://policydialogue.org/files/events/Be_Outraged-finalhi_rez_1.pdf>.

Kaufman, R. R. and A. Segura-Ubiergo (2001). 'Globalization, Domestic Politics, and Social Spending in Latin America: A Time-Series Cross-Section Analysis, 1973–97'. *World Politics*, 53(4): 553.

Keefer, P. (2010). *Database of Political Institutions: Changes and Variable Definitions, DPI2010*. Washington, DC: Development Research Group, World Bank.

Khatiwada, S. (2009). *'Stimulus Packages to Counter Global Economic Crisis: A Review'*. *ILO Discussion Paper, DP/196/2009*. Geneva: ILO.

Lei, X., C. Zhang, and Y. Zhao (2011). *'Incentive Problems in China's New Rural Pension Programme'*. Beijing: China Center for Economic Research, Peking University. Mimeo.

Martorano, B. and G. A. Cornia (2012). *'Development Policy and Income Inequality Database'*. Florence: University of Florence. Mimeo.

Oberdabernig, D. A. (2010). *'The Effects of Structural Adjustment Programmes on Poverty and Income Distribution'*. Paper presented at the wiiw Seminar in International Economics, Vienna, 4 March.

Ortiz, I., J. Chai, and M. Cummins (2012). 'Austerity Measures and the Risks to Children and Poor Households'. In I. Ortiz and M. Cummins (eds), *A Recovery for All: Rethinking Socio-Economic Policies for Children and Poor Households*. New York: Division of Policy and Practice, UNICEF, 172–230.

Reinhart, C. M. and K. S. Rogoff (2010). *From Financial Crash to Debt Crisis*. NBER Working Paper 15795. Cambridge, MA: National Bureau of Economic Research.

Spilimbergo, A., S. Symansky, O. Blanchard, and C. Cottarelli (2008). *'Fiscal Policies for the Crisis'*. IMF Staff Position Note, SPN/08/01. Washington, DC: IMF.

Stewart, F. (2012). 'The Impact of Global Economic Crises on the Poor: Comparing the 1980s and 2000s'. *Journal of Human Development and Capabilities*, 13(1): 83–105.

UNDESA (2011). *The Global Social Crisis, Report on the World Social Situation 2011*. New York: UN-Department of Economic and Social Affairs.

Vanhanen, T. (2011). Measures of Democracy 1810-2010 [computer file], FSD1289, version 5.0 (2011-07-07). Tampere: Finnish Social Science Data Archive [distributor].

Weaver, K. (1986). 'The Politics of Blame Avoidance'. *Journal of Public Policy*, 6(4): 371–98.

WEO (World Economic Outlook) (n.d.). *World Economic Outlook* (WEO) database 2011. Available at: <http://www.imf.org/external/pubs/ft/weo/2011/02/weodata/index.aspx>.

World Bank (1995). 'Social Impact of Adjustment Operations'. Report No. 14776. Washington, DC: World Bank, Operations Evaluation Department.

Zhang, Y., N. Thelen, and A. Rao (2010). *Social Protection in Fiscal Stimulus Packages: Some Evidence*. UNDP/ODS Working Paper. New York: UNDP/Office of Development Studies.

12

Innovation for Pro-Poor Growth
From Redistribution with Growth to Redistribution through Growth*

Raphael Kaplinsky

12.1 Introduction

It is perhaps unusual to begin a chapter with a table. But the data in Table 12.1 tell a compelling story.

The first decade of the twenty-first century witnessed an acceleration of growth in many low- and middle-income countries. These rates were high in comparison to the last decade of the twentieth century (and even more so in comparison to the lost development decades of the 1980s), and by comparison with global average growth rates in the same periods. Rapid and accelerating growth was most pronounced in China and India, but was also evidenced in middle-income countries as a whole, as well as in SSA. At the same time, the numbers living globally below the MDG1 US$1.25pd benchmark (hereafter referred to as MDG1) fell by 339 million between 1988–90 and 2007–8. This is often taken to indicate progress in global poverty reduction. Yet the decline in the poverty number in China (516 million) exceeded the global total (339 million), which means that outside of China, the number of people living globally below MDG1 increased by 177 million. In SSA, a more than a doubling of the annual average growth rate resulted in a 59 per cent increase in absolute poverty numbers. In India, the recent growth miracle has been associated with a further 42 million people living below

* I am grateful to Giovanni Andrea Cornia for his insightful and constructive comments on an earlier draft. Some of the material in this study draws on a report prepared for the PRMED Division of the World Bank, 'Bottom of the Pyramid Innovation and Pro-Poor Growth' (2011).

Table 12.1 GDP growth rates and numbers living below MDG1, 1990–2008

	GDP growth p.a. (%)		Millions of people living below US$1.25 per day (MDG1) (US$2005PPP)	
	1990–2000	2000–08	1988–90	2007–08
World	2.9	3.1	1,668	1,329
China	9.9	10.4	724	208
India	5.5	7.0	414	456
SSA	2.2	4.9	224	355

Source: Poverty numbers from Chen and Ravallion (2008) and Sumner (2010). Growth rates from WDI (accessed October 2011).

MDG1. Strikingly, despite rapid economic growth, there was more than a doubling of the number of the absolutely poor in middle-income countries and currently more than 70 per cent of those living below MDG1 live in this rapidly growing group of economies. These trends with regard to absolute poverty occurred despite the fact that the first decade after the millennium saw a reduction in relative poverty (that is, inequality) in many economies (Cornia and Martorano 2012).

What these numbers point to is the structural character of the dominant growth model, in which a significant proportion of the population in many countries is being excluded from the fruits of growth. This impoverished population is made up of two groups. The first are those living in Lewis's traditional sector, eking out a living in subsistence agriculture or in low-paid formal-sector employment. The second are the truly marginalized, those living without access to land or formal-sector employment. This bifurcated structure between the haves and the have-nots shows superficial similarities with Lewis's two-sector model. However, his 'traditional sector' had the means of subsistence (Lewis 1954). To this we now need to add a rapidly growing 'third sector'—that of the wholly excluded.

There are three primary and related reasons that explain this structural character of the current dominant global growth trajectory. The first is that it arises as a direct result of deepening globalization (Kaplinsky 2005). Globalization allows high-income earners who possess various forms of rent (such as natural resources, skills, entrepreneurship, and patents) to valorize these rents over a larger market. At the same time it exposes those with low incomes and without rents to intensified competition. For example, in the case of unskilled labour, the global labour pool has doubled in the past two decades, following the entry of China, India, and the former Soviet Union into the global economy.[1]

---

[1] China's success in reducing absolute poverty in the context of its rapid outward-oriented growth and deepening participation in the global economy is often used to argue that the

The second factor explaining the distributional character of this global growth trajectory is the financialization of the global economy (Lazonick 2010). This has placed a growing emphasis on high-income-yielding arbitrage rather than production, with this arbitrage being a function confined largely to the high-income economies and to the capital cities of a select few middle-income countries. It has led to a change in the terms of trade between financial services and the producers of goods and non-financial services, shifting distributional patterns in favour of the financial sector. It has also led, and is likely to continue to lead, to growing volatility of incomes throughout the global economy.

The third factor that explains why enhanced growth coexists with, and indeed in some cases causes, absolute poverty arises from the dominant trajectory of innovation. Its capital-intensive nature, its scale intensity, its dependence on high-quality networked infrastructure, its reliance on skilled labour, and its product portfolio (producing products that meet the needs of the rich) all have the effect of disadvantaging the poor, both as consumers and producers, and of excluding in many countries large segments of the population from productive employment.[2] Moreover, much contemporary technology is also destructive of the environment, not least in relation to its energy intensity, and this has disproportionately negative impacts on the global poor. While innovation is only a partial contributor to the persistence of global poverty, it is an important one, and one that is largely neglected in the theorization of innovation (Cozzens and Kaplinsky 2009).

12.2 In What Way Has Innovation Contributed to Exclusionary Growth?

Schumpeter defines entrepreneurship as the act of innovation, that is, the application of a new idea to meet the needs of consumers. His primary focus was on the search by entrepreneurs for new combinations that would enable

---

dominant growth model is indeed poverty-reducing. However, this focus on the success of China ignores the impact of its growth on other economies. Chinese competitiveness in third-country markets places pricing pressures on the exports of other economies (Kaplinsky and Santos-Paulino 2006; Fu et al. 2012; Wood and Mayer 2011) and displaces low-income-economy exports from these markets (Kaplinsky et al. 2010). Its exports also undermine domestically-oriented manufacturing in other low-income economies. Generalizing from China's experience thus suffers from the familiar fallacy of composition argument.

[2] The seeming exception to these trends is the employment of unskilled and semiskilled labour in export processing zones in some developing economies that have managed to insert themselves into global value chains. This does not negate the capital-intensive trajectory of innovation, but reflects the slicing up of value chains and the geographical relocation of the unskilled and semiskilled workers who continued to be employed in production.

them to escape, at least temporarily, from competition and thereby to earn higher profits ('entrepreneurial rents').

With a view to developing pro-poor innovation policies, three lessons can be drawn from this Schumpeterian perspective. First, while a profit-driven agenda explains the bulk of innovation in the global economy, there is no intrinsic reason why innovation should always occur as a commercial activity. Social innovation—by national health services, for example—is an important realm of technological change. Second, the Schumpeterian perspective highlights the role of social actors in the innovation cycle. Amongst other things, this helps us to understand that technologies are predominantly shaped by their social context rather than a result of unfolding 'natural laws'. Third, as a consequence of the social context of innovation, it highlights the limits to interventions that are confined to physical technologies without addressing the social, institutional, and economic context of innovation. As we shall see below, these three insights have important implications for the trajectory of innovation and for pro-poor innovation policies.

Value chain theory augments our understanding of innovation by adding two further forms of integration to the product and process innovation that has long preoccupied innovation theory (Humphrey and Schmitz 2000). Functional innovation reflects repositioning within the chain (for example, moving from production to design), and chain integration reflects movement to a different chain of activity.

Working with these two theoretical frameworks, we can observe the dominant trajectory of global innovation over the past century. As a general rule the consumers whose needs have historically been targeted by the global innovation system (product innovation) have been those of the higher-income consumers located in the relatively rapidly growing Northern economies. The physical 'embodied' technologies that have been developed (process innovation) have, in general, been increasingly large-scale and have depended on reliable, high-quality, and network-driven infrastructure (such as electricity grids, fixed telecoms, integrated water and sanitation systems). They have also generally been labour-saving (and within this have been increasingly reliant on skilled labour) and capital-using. And the widespread availability of relatively cheap energy sources has meant that they have been energy-intensive, and often also heavily polluting in nature. The organization of value chains, which have become increasingly fragmented and global (functional innovation), has led to the clustering of producers in low-income economies in highly competitive niches of the value chains, often confined to simple labour-intensive assembly and subject to intense wage competition. Moreover, meeting the needs of high-income consumers in high-income Northern economies has also led to a situation in which value chains are increasingly standards-intensive (Kaplinsky 2011), thereby placing barriers to entry to small-scale informal and often illiterate producers. Finally, moving to new lines of activity (chain upgrading) in an increasingly knowledge-driven economy has required a range of complex capabilities that are beyond the reach of poor producers and low-income economies.

The theory of induced innovation provides a framework for understanding how this exclusionary technological trajectory has evolved. It identifies three factors that determine the nature and trajectory of technological progress (Ruttan 2001). The first is the nature of demand, with innovators responding to the effective demand of consumers with disposable cash incomes. The large and growing markets in the post-war era were of high-income consumers in developed economies rather than low-income consumers in developing economies. The second is factor prices and the quality, nature, and price of infrastructure. Innovation occurring in high-income economies reflects these operating conditions and has been capital-intensive, large in scale, and dependent on reliable, widely diffused, and centralized infrastructure. The third factor identified by Ruttan, based on insights from institutional economics (Dosi 1982), reflects the path-dependencies of innovating firms. Their bounded rationality means that Northern-based firms innovated in areas closely related to their past success, were reinforcing a trajectory of innovation that was largely focused on meeting the needs of high-income consumers, and were reflecting the operating conditions in high-income economies. We can add to Ruttan's threefold induced innovation framework the role of regulatory systems. An increasingly tight and enduring system of global intellectual property rights has created major barriers to the entry of new innovators. The underpricing of the real cost of energy and environmental externalities (a reflection of inadequate regulatory systems) has led to the development of energy-intensive and polluting innovation streams.

Until very recently, the overwhelming proportion of resources that go into innovation have been located in the high-income economies. The Sussex Manifesto of 1970 (Singer et al. 1970) estimated that around 98 per cent of global R&D expenditure occurred in high-income economies, and much of the 2 per cent that took place in the developing world was focused on the needs of high-income consumers and the formal sector. But R&D is only one source of technological change and, although unrecorded, a very large proportion of the incremental change in production was similarly located in high-income economies. Where incremental innovation has occurred in low-income economies, much of this has been in transnational corporations (TNCs) originating in the high-income economies and has been geared to meeting the routines of their global operations.

12.3 A Response to Marginalization: The Rise (and Fall) of the Appropriate Technology Movement

It is not surprising, therefore, that the dominant global innovation path has, until recently, contributed in important ways to the persistence of global poverty and to a widespread increase in global inequality in many economies, particularly before the turn of the millennium, with destructive consequences for the environment. One response to this Northern-focused innovation trajectory—which produced products for high-income consumers and technologies that saved on labour, were large in scale, and depended on reliable and centralized infrastructural networks—was the development of the appropriate technology (AT) movement. This comprised a growing spread of NGOs, often with a global reach, such as the Intermediate Technology Development Group in the UK (ITDG, now Practical Action). In spirit, many of these AT NGOs drew their inspiration from the values of Gandhi's Swadeshi Movement in India and were promoted globally by Schumacher (1973). They promoted the development of new ATs, often comprising a blending of traditional and new technologies (Bhalla 1984) and the diffusion of existing ATs both within and across national boundaries.

In principle, the development of AT offers the prospect of providing the underpinnings of a more inclusive and less environmentally damaging growth path. But four problems have beset the AT movement. First, empirical enquiry showed that most ATs were 'economically inefficient' (that is, making greater use of both capital and labour per unit of output), a critique widely recognized in the literature (Eckaus 1955, 1987; Stewart 1979; Bhalla 1975; Emmanuel 1982). Second, 'appropriateness' is inherently contextual, and involves trade-offs between objectives (Kaplinsky 1990). Many labour-intensive and small-scale technologies are relatively energy-intensive. The AT movement often failed to recognize these trade-offs and was guilty of 'over-promise', undermining the credibility of the technologies it was promoting. Third, the social context of innovation was not conducive to their diffusion. The dominant innovators in the global economy were located in Northern economies, operating in large-scale ventures, and had little or no interest in meeting the needs of the incomeless global poor, or of incorporating the poor in global value chains. And fourth, much of the output produced by ATs failed to meet the growing demand for standards in high-income country export markets.

Given these constraints, the diffusion of ATs has generally been undertaken by not-for-profit NGOs. They have been widely scorned in many low-income countries, particularly by the urban elites who have modelled their consumption patterns and life trajectories on their peers in high-income countries. The AT movement may have grown rapidly in the 1970s and early

1980s, but it was a truncated growth and it was consigned to the margins of the economy.

12.4 The World Is Changing: Forces of Disruption

We are now witnessing the emergence of a series of developments that threaten to disrupt the dominance of a global innovation system that targets the needs of high-income consumers by utilizing capital-, scale-, and standards-intensive technologies that are sensitive to the quality, reliability, and ubiquity of networked infrastructure. They offer the potential to provide ATs that are efficient and that provide opportunities for profit-seeking innovation. We consider four of these emerging disruptive factors: the dynamism of low-income markets, the availability of new radical technologies, the global diffusion of innovative capabilities, and the emergence of new innovation actors.

12.4.1 The Character and Dynamism of Low-Income Markets

Despite the revival of economic growth in the USA and other Northern economies after the financial crisis of 2008, most of the high-income markets continue to experience two structural deficits. The first is with regard to debt, where, despite a narrowing of deficits in the private sector, sovereign debt remains high and continues to grow. The second, less widely recognized but equally germane to our discussion, is the level and persistence of balance of payments. The structural rebalancing required to meet both of these deficits will necessarily lead to a decline in demand in high-income markets, whether resulting from an orderly or disorderly process of adjustment (Kaplinsky and Farooki 2011). By contrast, growth in China, India, Brazil, and other emerging economies is likely to remain high and robust, at least by comparison with the Northern economies. The Africa–Asia–Central Europe head of Unilever estimated in 2010, for example, that by 2020 nearly 80 per cent of incremental consumption growth will come from emerging economies.

These growing low-income-economy markets are distinctive. On the one hand, they reflect a rapid growth in demand by an urban middle class that is not very different from most consumer markets in the North, searching for globally branded, differentiated and high-quality positional goods. For example, in 2010 the most rapidly growing market for Mercedes-Benz and Rolls-Royce cars was in China. But, on the other hand, there is a rapidly expanding and very large market of low-income consumers. In both China and India, there is a clustering of households with total household incomes

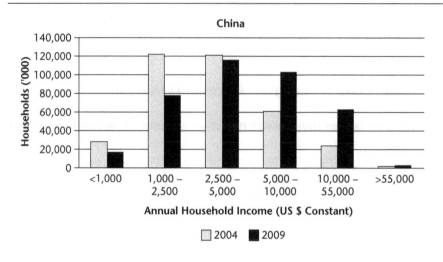

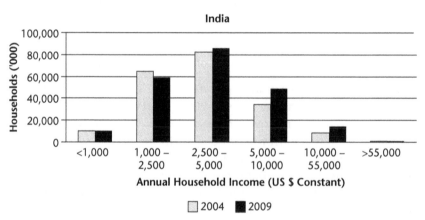

Figure 12.1 Number of households, by disposable income, China and India, 2004 and 2009

Source: Compiled from <http://www.portal.euromonitor.com> (accessed July 2010).

of less than US$5,000 in 2009, comprising 56 per cent of all households in China, and 71 per cent in India (Figure 12.1).

In all probability, or at least by hypothesis (drawing on Ruttan's induced innovation framework), the driving of consumption by low-income households will induce a different set of products from those induced by high-income earners in Northern economies. These product innovations are likely to be differentiated to meet the environments in which they are developed. As McKinsey advises its clients, these innovations will be distinctively different from those produced for high-income global consumers, somewhere between the positional goods of high-income consumers and the basic-function and low-acquisition-cost goods of the very-low-income con-sumers defined by Prahalad (2005) as those at the 'bottom of the pyramid'. It is this 'bottom-of-the-pyramid' market that has begun to draw the attention of many of the world's largest TNCs, particularly those selling final consumer goods such as Unilever, Procter and Gamble, and Nestlé. Low-income con-sumers may prefer 'high-quality' branded goods, but they lack the incomes required to both acquire and then consume these more expensive goods. In these circumstances they will make do with what they can afford, rather than what they would prefer to consume.

A further important reflection of the changing geography of global con-sumption has been the shift of final market in many sectors from high-income to low-income countries. This has had important implications for the role of standards in global value chains. Products destined for high-income consum-ers and countries have tended to involve the extensive use of both product and process standards. There is considerable evidence that these standards have acted to exclude low-income producers from global value chains. By comparison, products destined for low-income markets have been relatively devoid of standards (Kaplinsky et al. 2011), removing some of the barriers to entry for small-scale producers.

Beyond low-income households as sources of consumption is their role as providers of wage labour. The incomes that they earn reflect wage rates that are far lower than those in high-income economies. Despite rapid rises in wages in China, for example, even in the coastal regions where wage rates have risen dramatically, most factory workers earn less than US$2 per hour. Beyond China are regional Asian labour forces where wages are even lower. These low wage rates reduce the incentive for entrepreneurs to develop and commercialize capital-intensive technologies.

12.4.2 The Emergence of New 'Radical' Technologies

In the current era, we can witness the emergence of four new technologi-cal families, each of which has widespread potential significance for pro-ducing products for poor consumers and/or for including poor producers in efficient production processes. The first of these is the rapid growth and diffusion of information and communication technologies. Perhaps the out-come most relevant to pro-poor innovation has been the benefits provided by mobile telecommunications. While most attention has been placed on their contribution to consumer welfare, it may well be that the capacity that mobile telephony provides as a capital good is of greater historical sig-nificance. Farmers and distributed producers in other sectors have greater access to market information and increasingly also to knowledge-intensive extension and business services. The second relevant emerging technology is the new forms of energy production, renewables such as solar power, wind power, and biomass. As in the case of mobile telephony, these new technologies both enhance consumer welfare and producer incomes, providing the potential for low-cost and distributed energy supply. The distributed character of both mobile telephony and renewable energy is particularly relevant for poor consumers who were previously prevented from benefiting from these services, because with previous technologies, access followed from large and capital-intensive investments in network-intensive infrastructure. The final two sets of emerging pro-poor relevant technologies are nanotechnology and biotechnology. Both of these provide the scope for radically new technologies that have important potential applications in meeting the needs of poor people and small-scale applications through, for example, new diagnostic kits and new water purification systems.

Each of these technologies provides the potential for shaping technological progress in particular directions. For example, the feed-in tariffs incentivizing the adoption of solar PV and other renewable forms of energy in many Northern economies have led to a system in which the energy generated is fed into the national energy grid. However, these new sources of energy production can be consumed directly at-source by producers, allowing for distributed production and use.

12.4.3 The Global Diffusion of Innovative Capabilities

The very rapid increase in the share of global manufacturing value added in low- and middle-income economies in general, and China in particular, has been associated with a pervasive increase in capabilities in these economies. These capabilities have been built on a number of strands of activity. The first has been the widespread increase in levels of education across the globe. The second has been relatively passive processes of learning by doing, and the more active processes of 'learning by adaptation' and 'learning by capacity expansion' (Katz 1987; Bell 2007). These firm- and farm-level activities, generally associated with efforts to make maximum use of purchased, and often imported technologies, arise out of incremental changes undertaken in the operation of equipment. They are often also acquired through participation in global value chains (Kaplinsky and Morris 2001; Gereffi et al. 2005). Formally constituted R&D is another important component of innovation (although often overestimated in importance). By 2000, more than one-fifth of global R&D was located in the developing world (Hollanders and Soete 2010), an increase of major significance given the estimated share in 1970 of only 2 per cent (Singer et al. 1970). An increasing share of this dispersed R&D occurs as a result of outsourcing by global TNCs, particularly to China and India (Bruche 2009). This global diffusion of capabilities to countries with large populations of low-income consumers provides the scope for a new source of innovation, potentially disruptive to the historic dominance of Northern sourced technological change.

12.4.4 Disruptive Entrepreneurs

The existence of capabilities, the availability of radically new technologies, and the growth of effective demand from poor people do not in themselves result in innovation. Instead, as Schumpeter highlighted, innovations arise as a consequence of purposive action by entrepreneurs developing and utilizing inventions in product, process, and organization in the search for supernormal profit.

We can distinguish a number of different categories of entrepreneurs who might play a role in the innovation of pro-poor products and services and process technologies. One key set of actors is the established global TNCs seeking to capture the 'fortune at the bottom of the pyramid', particularly in the FMCG (fast-moving-consumer-goods) sector. Prahalad was one of the first to spot the potential of the growth that these low-income markets offered for profitable production and drew attention to the market potential of this new class of consumers (Prahalad and Hammond 2002). He observes that there were four billion people living at per-capita incomes below US$2,000 per annum. Crucially, and perhaps not surprisingly given that he worked in Northern business schools, Prahalad believes that this provided a profitable market opportunity for TNCs rather than for the small-scale and locally owned firms long identified in the appropriate-technology and informal-sector literature as being key providers for low-income consumers. He argues:

> By stimulating commerce and development at the bottom of the economic pyramid, [Northern-based] MNCs could radically improve the lives of billions of people...Achieving this goal does not require multinationals to spearhead global social development initiatives for charitable purposes. They need only act in their own self interest, for there are enormous business benefits to be gained by entering developing markets. (Prahalad and Hammond 2002: 4)

But this belief that Northern TNCs would be able to grasp this market is an untested assertion. As Christenson's widely cited work points out, large firms that dominate industries are often extremely good at hearing the demands of their existing customers, but very poor at hearing those of new customers. His argument is essentially that this weakness arises directly as a consequence of their core strength, which is that they have invested considerable resources in acutely understanding the needs of their core customers. Thus when a new technology arrives that fails to address these known needs effectively, the major innovating firms are dismissive. They fail precisely because they listen to their customers so well: 'the logical, competent decisions of management that are critical to the success of their companies are also why they lose their positions of leadership' (Christenson 1997: xiii).

If the leading Northern-origin TNCs are unable to exploit this emerging low-income market effectively, there are a variety of domestic firms in low-income economies that recognize the potential for profitability in targeting the needs of low-income consumers, and addressing these needs through innovations of basic, labour-intensive technologies. A widely cited example (which is not without its teething problems) is the Tata Nano in India, a basic car priced at less than US$2,500 and aimed at low-income consumers moving up from two-wheeled scooters. One conception of this car is also to produce it in kit form so that consumers can tailor the body to meet their needs (by adding a trailer, for example) so that the car becomes a capital good. In China, Haier (which is now the world's second-largest producer of white goods) discovered that some rural consumers used their washing machines both for clothes and to wash potatoes. So they redesigned their machines to make them more robust and to serve both consumer needs effectively.

Less visible, and below the radar, are a plethora of small- and medium-scale entrepreneurs in the South who are introducing small-scale innovations without inputs of formal R&D, and with little attention being paid to intellectual property rights or product and process standards. For example, DMT Mobile Toilets is a commercial enterprise that produces, rents, and maintains safe, sanitary, portable toilets in West Africa. Lifeline Energy conducts extensive end-user research and then develops and distributes appropriate, clean energy products, including radios, a range of lights, solar panels, and MP3-enabled Lifeplayers that allow pre-loaded educational content as well as Internet access.

Another relatively new carrier of innovation is the public–private partnerships (PPPs) constructed by international organizations such as the Bill and Melinda Gates Foundation, the Global Alliance for Vaccines and Immunization (GAVI), and the International AIDS Vaccine Initiative (IAVI) to deal with global health problems. These involve building innovation consortia combining Northern and Southern research institutions, universities, and firms. Unlike private-sector entrepreneurs who seek to tap into growing bottom-of-the-pyramid cash markets of private consumption, this PPP entrepreneurship tends to focus on innovation in sectors where poor consumers either do not have the incomes to allow the private entrepreneurs to capture the fortune at the bottom of the pyramid, or where the public-good nature of the product and service does not allow private entrepreneurs to appropriate their innovations.

12.4.5 The Combined Impact of Disruptive Forces on the Innovation Trajectory

The single most important conclusion that emerges from the above analysis is that there has been a sea change in the determinants of pro-poor innovation. In the past these were often inefficient in nature, were promoted by civil-society organizations, and were generally scorned by both consumers and formal-sector producers (although in some countries, such as India, there was a greater degree of acceptance of AT products). By contrast, as a result of the disruptive factors discussed above, ATs have moved from the margin of economic accumulation. Critically, their diffusion is driven by a profit-seeking Schumpeterian rather than a normatively driven Schumacherian motor. There is widespread evidence that market-driven diffusion is occurring and that this has resulted in pro-poor outcomes. For example, in Cameroon (Khan and Baye 2011) Chinese motorcycles are less durable than Japanese motorcycles and require more repairs. However they only cost one-third as much as the higher-quality products and this has provided the opportunity for low-income school-leavers to enter the market as taxi drivers and logistics providers. Similarly, Chinese-produced batteries have half the operating life of Northern-branded products, but cost only one-third as much. In both cases, the Chinese products both lower the entry costs for purchases and reduce the unit costs of consumption. Efficient and profitable ATs are also being generated within Africa:

> South African companies are paying much more attention to the rest of the continent, which some once made a habit of ignoring. MTN controls half of the Nigerian telecoms market, which is doubling in size every year. Shoprite is Africa's largest food retailer, operating in 18 African countries. South African companies are also discovering the 'bottom of the pyramid' in their own country. Several companies have pioneered the art of using cell phones to map the distribution of informal shops (spaza) and truck stops. Blue Label Telecoms, which sells pre-paid tokens, has blazed a trail in forming relationships with tribal chiefs and popular gospel singers to help sell its products. Knowledge of the bottom of the pyramid is now being used to expand in emerging markets. SABMiller produces beer for Uganda using cheap local ingredients rather than expensive imported malt. MTN provides solar-powered phones to fishermen. (*The Economist*, 10 September 2011)

12.5 Pro-Poor Innovation, Redistribution, and Growth

How, then, do these developments in the trajectory of innovation relate to the debate on redistribution and growth in which Richard Jolly was a core participant during the 1970s and 1980s?[3] In considering these issues, we need to preface the discussion by recognizing a series of framing issues. The first concerns the blurring of both the categories and the interrelationship of categories used in this debate. On the one hand, we have 'redistribution', and on the other, 'growth'. Then we have the prepositions—'and', 'from', 'before', and 'with'. There is the further complication of whether the linking words begin with 'growth' ('growth-preposition-redistribution') or with 'redistribution' ('redistribution-preposition-growth'); the ordering is suggestive of causal explanations and the ranking of normative objectives. A second framing issue is that insofar as we are concerned with global poverty, we need to keep in mind that (as Peter Townsend (1979) observed some decades ago), poverty has two dimensions—an absolute one (the MDG1 target) and a relative one (equity). It might seem that these are unrelated concerns, but there is now growing recognition that equity has a bearing on the absolute incidence of poverty (Wilkinson and Pickett 2009).[4]

There are two overlapping perspectives on the link between growth and distribution, notwithstanding the above-mentioned confusion of nomenclature and the blurring of categories. The first is a set of explanations that see poverty reduction (in both its absolute and relative sense) as arising as an outcome of an ex-post redistribution of the gains arising from growth. This fits under the 'redistribution and/with growth' heading. The second is an analysis in which redistribution—or, perhaps, a more equitable pattern of distribution—arises endogenously as a core component of the growth path itself. This fits under the 'redistribution with/through growth' heading. The developments that I have addressed in the foregoing discussion are very much centred on the second of these perspectives, that is, that we are witnessing the emergence of disruptive forces that will contribute to a growth trajectory in low-income economies that is characterized by less unequalizing patterns of growth.

With these caveats in mind we can now consider the overlaps between the putative new trajectory of innovation discussed in previous sections and the 'redistribution/growth and/from/with growth/distribution' debate. Here it is possible to identify three issues common to both: redistribution as a positive or normative phenomenon;[5] the character of technology; and the role played by South–South trade in technology.

---

[3] In addressing this debate I draw on the references cited in Jolly's recent note for UNESCO (Jolly 2011), namely the ILO Kenya Report (ILO 1972), the various contributions in Chenery et al. (1974), the contributions in Cairncross and Puri (1976), the *IDS Bulletin* (IDS 1975), and the 2006 *World Development Report* (World Bank 2006).

[4] Wilkinson and Pickett's analysis is based on data from the higher-income group of countries. It is impossible that the conclusions do not apply in the low-income group of economies.

[5] Here, and in the discussion below, I draw on economic theory to distinguish 'what ought to be' normative statements from 'what is and why' positive explanations.

12.5.1 Normative and Positive Determinants of Distribution

The central thrust of the ILO Kenya Report (ILO 1972) was to identify a set of policies that would provide for a win-win outcome in which all incomes would expand as a consequence of economic growth, but with those at the bottom of the pile growing more rapidly. The report was explicitly normative in nature. That is, it sought to persuade the rich that it was in their interest to raise the living standards of the poor and that this could be achieved through the introduction of a package of policies to be implemented by the state, but with the acquiescence of the private sector.

Colin Leys is widely recognized as the prime critic of the Kenya Report (Leys 1975a, 1975b). Leys, who unlike most of the participants in the Kenya Report was a political scientist rather than an economist, argues that this normative policy drive lacked analytical content, and in particular that it failed to recognize the political significance of class. In so doing, it failed to identify a politically coherent category of actors who had meaningful common objectives other than those of improving their living standards: 'The condition of the masses in the third world is not purely a matter of material want, but also of subordination, oppression, exploitation, and disregard' (Leys 1975a: 8). This analytical failure, he argues, meant that policy prescriptions would have little traction in the real world. With the benefit of hindsight, there can be little doubt that Leys's critique was spot-on. The four decades since the ILO Report was published have seen a systematic deepening of inequality and a growth in absolute poverty in Kenya. The political structures that have emerged show conclusively that whatever the rhetoric—and Kenya's politics are replete with commitments to poverty reduction—there has been a systematic and steady increase in inequality, both within high- and low-growth periods. (As Jolly (2011) shows, the apparent fall in the Gini coefficient between 1990 and 1995 was almost certainly a statistical aberration.) According to the World Development Indicators, the incidence of sub-MDG1 poverty in Kenya was 19 per cent in both 1988 and 2005, suggesting an increase in the absolute numbers living below US$1pd from 5.7 million to 7.02 million.

By contrast, the developments that I have sketched out in the previous sections are of a 'positive' rather than a 'normative' nature. It is my belief that while the diffusion of efficient ATs can be speeded up through policy (see below), their diffusion will occur even without this policy support. Most of the new breed of efficient ATs will be driven by the market. Unlike the era in which the Kenya Report and *Redistribution with Growth* were written, their adoption will be fuelled by the capitalist motor.

12.5.2 Embodied Technology, and Products for the Poor

Issues of technology and the choice of technique were central to the ILO Report. This was in part because unemployment was increasingly recognized as a major developmental challenge in the 1970s and in part because of the make-up of the ILO Team (which included Ajit Bhalla, Charles Cooper, and Hans Singer). This focus on technology spilled over into the *Redistribution with Growth* report. The particular focus adopted towards technology was heavily influenced by Sen's seminal book, *Choice of Techniques*, which had been published a few years before the Kenya Mission (Sen 1968), and was preceded (and subsequently complemented in the ILO World Employment Programme) by a series of empirical studies on the choice of techniques. In all of this material, technology was almost exclusively seen as a set of physical embodied artefacts, and was largely confined to process technology. There were exceptions—for example, Lancaster (1966), Langdon (1981), and Stewart (1976 and 1979) all focused on products as an important category of technological change—but 'engineering man' dominated the discourse. As we saw in the earlier discussion, this emphasis on process rather than product technology is echoed in much of the contemporary literature on innovation and technical change (Ruttan 2001).

Yet, the distinctive feature of much of the recent pro-poor innovation is that it centres on business models as much as embodied technologies, and on product innovation as much as process innovation. For example, Prahalad's treatise identifying the 'fortune at the bottom of the pyramid' is replete with examples of new forms of organization, including eye-care and the marketing of soap and shampoo in India, and banking in Mexico (Prahalad 2005). Perhaps an even better-known example of pro-poor innovation that reflects changes in business models is the explosion in microfinance. The product, 'money', is constant, but the business model involved in delivering the product is very different. In other cases, particularly when TNCs are involved, the core feature of pro-poor innovation lies in the product offering. Examples of this include the stripping-out of costly functions that make the original product attractive to rich consumers (but unaffordable to the poor), or dual-purpose products such as Haier's washing machines (washing clothes and potatoes), or the low-cost medical-imaging technology developed by GE in India (Immelt, Govindarajan, and Trimble 2009). Increasingly, there is also a combination of new and business models in pro-poor innovation as in the diffusion of Mpesa telecoms in Kenya, which allow for money transfers via mobile phones. In all these cases, there appears to be a distinctive difference in the character of technical change compared to that envisaged in the redistribution from/and/with/ through growth schools.

12.5.3 South–South Trade in Technology

As we have seen in the earlier discussion, perhaps the single most important disruptive feature of the new technological trajectory is its Southern origin. I have argued that by virtue of four factors intrinsic to Southern economies—low-income consumers, factor prices and infrastructure, the build-up of technological capabilities, and new and distinctive entrepreneurship—the character of emerging Southern technology will differ from that originating in Northern economies. This is, of course, not true for all Southern-origin technology, since there are many cases of Chinese firms (Huawei), Indian firms (Tata Consulting), Brazilian firms (Embraer), and South African firms (Sasol) competing at the global frontier and in Northern markets. But it is true for much of Southern technology, particularly that emerging 'below the radar' from small and medium-sized firms, often with their origins in the rural sector (such as Chinese township and village enterprises, TVEs) or in provincial towns.

This is a relatively new phenomenon, but it is not something that was unanticipated in the earlier literature. For example, Stewart concluded in 1976, 'To get technological change responsive to the conditions in the LDCs the change must originate in the LDCs' (Stewart 1976: 133). It was also central to some of the discussion in *Redistribution with Growth*. Thus, Ahluwalia concludes (1974: 89):

> ...closely related to the problem of technical choice is the problem of capital-goods production... It is unlikely that the capital-goods producing sectors of developed countries will respond to demand for such goods in underdeveloped countries. Capital-goods producing industries in the more advanced of the underdeveloped countries will have to take a lead in producing the appropriate capital goods and indeed exporting them to other underdeveloped economies.

The difference between then and now is that in 1974 this was a normative objective; today it is a positive fact.

12.6 Conclusion

In the preceding discussion I have presented a story that suggests that, unlike in earlier decades when AT was diffused through non-profit organizations, in the current era AT is likely to be diffused by the market. While this will not in itself eliminate global poverty, I believe that it has the potential to make a significant impact in poverty alleviation by contributing to a new growth path. The more this redirection of technological utilization in low-income economies is allied to changes in the macro-context of growth, the greater the prospects for the emergence of a more equal global economy, and a reduction in the numbers living in absolute poverty.

So far, my argument has been a 'positive' one, seeking to show how the Schumpeterian motor of entrepreneurial rent-seeking will be associated with the generation and adoption of technologies more appropriate to the operating conditions of low-income economies, and producing products of greater relevance to the needs of the global poor. I can visualize Richard's response to this: 'That's all very interesting, *but surely* [his emphasis] you don't really mean that there is nothing we can do to influence these developments?' So I have to respond to this, and here are some suggestions for a normative response to these 'positive' developments.

12.6.1 Removing Market Imperfections

The task is to identify those market imperfections that are intrinsic to pro-poor innovation. Perhaps the most widely cited imperfection in the literature on AT is that which relates to factor prices, where it is widely considered that the wages of the organized sector's working class in low-income countries are higher than their opportunity cost, that the cost of capital is lower than its opportunity cost, and that environmental and social externalities are either not represented in the price system or the prices at which they are represented do not reflect their true environmental cost. Clearly, factor pricing is an important issue with regard to the diffusion of ATs, but the policy conclusions are not always as clear-cut as they seem. For one thing, in many low-income economies, high formal-sector wages support a large number of people and are consumed as extended family household incomes rather than as personal incomes. Moreover, wages are also a source of demand for the output of ATs. And, further, investment in ATs will undoubtedly be furthered by low-cost capital; the trick is to direct this low-cost capital to investors in ATs, and this may involve innovations in the delivery of investment (as in the case of micro-credit), which is in itself a form of appropriate technology. The point is not that different factor prices will not make a difference, but rather that they will only make a limited difference.

Second, since poor producers and consumers are often illiterate and/or lack access to the Internet and print media, they are particularly prone to knowledge imperfections. For example, users of innovations will characteristically lack knowledge of the nature and extent of relevant innovations. Mirroring this are producers of innovations who lack knowledge of final markets, particularly those that are not geographically proximate. These knowledge imperfections are especially problematic in the case of pro-poor innovations since, by their nature, many are produced by SMEs in rural areas, unconnected to high-quality infrastructure, and are 'below the radar'.

A mechanism needs to be established to fill these knowledge gaps within countries and in trade between countries. Unlike the existing policy trajectory, which seeks to connect poor producers to rich consumers, the task is now to connect poor producers to poor consumers, particularly those outside their region.

Third, a systematic sweep is required of the regulatory structure to determine the extent to which these may adversely affect poor producers and poor consumers. This is not to suggest that regulations be abolished. Many regulations exist to protect the public interest. But it is important to determine whether the regulations that affect the development and diffusion of innovations are unevenly weighted against poor producers and consumers. For example, a regulation that specifies the minim weight of a loaf of bread may either be determined by the weight of an average loaf (allowing for variable loaf-size with manual, labour-intensive manufacturing) or the minimum weight of an individual loaf (favouring mechanized mixing and dividing).

12.6.2 Reorienting National, Regional, and Sectoral Innovation Systems

Optimizing the flow of pro-poor technologies requires an alignment of the relevant actors in the innovation system. This recommendation slips off the tongue easily, but is a more daunting task than is often recognized. Connecting private-sector firms in the innovation value chain is relatively easy and is generally supported as an outcome of market forces. But getting the supportive institutions aligned to meet the needs of poor producers and to develop products and services for poor consumers is more difficult, since the price system plays only a marginal role. Often 'quality' standards and criteria—let alone the direction of research—reflect connections in the system of innovation with the global community of peers rather than with the needs and capabilities of the marginalized domestic populations. This misalignment is evident in the CGIAR system, where the selection of problems for investigation often ignores the needs of poor and marginalized producers.[6] For example, drawing on the successful development of Green Revolution seeds, for more than twenty years ILRAD sought to find a 'high-science' vaccine for trypanosomiasis. This failed, but in the interim a low-tech approach to vector control was largely ignored, and veterinary services were wound down, with severe consequences for poor livestock farmers (Clark and Smith 2010).

---

[6] I am grateful to Norman Clark for alerting me to this issue.

12.6.3 Strengthening the Role of Non-Market Actors

In the case of public goods, the market is unlikely to be able to serve the needs of poor consumers and poor producers. This is classically the case in the provision of health services, which are particularly important in meeting the needs of the poor. Related to this are network problems where capital costs are high and where unit costs decline sharply with large-scale provision. This tends to occur in the case of infrastructure. It not only limits the development of networks, but creates particular difficulties when users are dispersed and have low incomes. In these cases, there will be pervasive market failure and pro-poor innovations are unlikely to emerge without the active participation of non-market actors.

This does not necessarily mean that market actors will be excluded from participating in the development of these pro-poor innovations. As we saw above, there are a number of cases of new innovation actors entering the innovation cycle in collaboration with private-sector firms. They have played a particularly important role in the provision of innovative public goods in the health sector, targeting neglected diseases or diseases that disproportionately affect the poor. But there has been a less active presence of non-market actors in the development and diffusion of pro-poor innovations with regard to infrastructure. The beneficial impact of infrastructure on poor producers is often underestimated.

12.6.4 Redistributing Income

As we have seen, the character of the market is a major factor inducing and biasing the trajectory of innovation. Historically, the needs being met by the global innovation system have been those of high-income consumers. However, in recent years we have seen a critically important change in this inducing factor, one in which the growing market power of low-income consumers has led to the development of a growing number of products and services designed to make profit out of poor consumers, and production technologies aimed at poor producers. It stands to reason, therefore, that the faster this market of poor consumers grows, and the larger this market is, the greater will be the inducement for pro-poor innovation. We can therefore anticipate a self-reinforcing virtuous circle in which pro-poor growth stimulates pro-poor innovation, which, in turn, reinforces pro-poor growth.[7]

---

[7] The outcomes of redistribution may not always be as obvious as they seem. For example, in the 1970s a PhD student at IDS (Roger Berry) explored the employment consequences of income distribution in India and estimated that there would be no net positive impact, since at the margin the rich consumed (labour-intensive) services and the poor consumed durable manufactured goods involving capital-intensive production processes.

It is probable that this is the single most important factor underlying the development of a pro-poor growth path. This is not just because of the links between income levels and the direction of technological change, but the political environment in which income redistribution occurs is likely to favour a number of complementary developments that reinforce other elements of the pro-poor growth agenda. It is thus abundantly clear that while pro-poor innovation provides the scope for more equalizing patterns of growth, it is merely one factor, albeit an important and largely neglected one, leading to a development strategy that rapidly erodes absolute (and perhaps also relative) poverty in the global economy.

References

Ahluwalia, M. S. (1974). 'The Scope for Policy Intervention'. In H. Chenery, M. S. Ahluwalia, C. L. G. Bell, J. H. Duloy, and R. Jolly (eds), *Redistribution with Growth*. Washington, DC: World Bank, 73–90.

Bell, R. M. (2007). 'Technological Learning and the Development of Productive and Innovative Capacities in the Industry and Infrastructure Sectors of the Least Developed Countries: What Roles for ODA?'. Paper prepared for UNCTAD Division for Africa, Least Developed Countries Specialized Programme. Brighton: Science Policy Research.

Bhalla, A. S. (ed.) (1975). *Technology and Employment in Industry*. Geneva: ILO.

Bhalla, A. S. (ed.) (1984). *Blending of New and Traditional Technologies: Case Studies*. Dublin: Tycooly Publishing.

Bruche, G. (2009). '*A New Geography of Innovation: China and India Rising*'. Columbia FDI Perspectives, 4. New York: Columbia University.

Cairncross, A. and M. Puri (eds) (1976). *Employment, Income Distribution and Development Strategy: Problems of the Developing Countries, Essays in Honour of H. W. Singer*. London: Macmillan.

Chen, S. and M. Ravallion (2008). *The Developing World Is Poorer than We Thought, but No Less Successful in the Fight against Poverty*. WB Policy Research Working Paper 4703. Washington, DC: The World Bank Development Research Group.

Chenery, H., M. S. Ahluwalia, C. L. G. Bell, J. H. Duloy, and R. Jolly (1974). *Redistribution with Growth*. Washington, DC: World Bank.

Christenson, C. (1997). *The Innovator's Dilemma*. Cambridge, MA: Harvard Business School Press.

Clark, N. and J. Smith (2010). '*The CG System as a Innovative Programme: Implications for Climate Change Policy for Developing Countries*'. Cambridge: Climate Change Secretariat.

Cornia, G. A. (2012). *Inequality Trends and their Determinants: Latin America over 1990–2010*. WIDER Working Papers 2012/09. Helsinki: UNU-WIDER.

Cornia, G. A. and B. Martorano (2012). '*Development Policies and Income Inequality: Main Trends in Selected Developing Regions, 1980–2010*'. UNCTAD Discussion Paper 210. Geneva: UNCTAD.

Cozzens, S. E. and R. Kaplinsky (2009). 'Innovation, Poverty and Inequality: Cause, Coincidence, or Co-evolution?'. In B.-A. Lundvall, J. K. Joseph, C. Chaminade, and J. Vang (eds), *Handbook of Innovation Systems and Developing Countries: Building Domestic Capabilities in a Global Context*. Cheltenham: Edward Elgar, 57–82.

Dosi, G. (1982). 'Technological Paradigms and Technological Trajectories'. *Research Policy*, 11(3): 147–62.

Eckaus, R. S. (1955). 'The Factor Proportions Problem in Underdeveloped Areas'. *American Economic Review*, 45(4): 539–65.

Eckaus, R. S. (1987). 'Appropriate Technology: The Movement Has Only a Few Clothes On'. *Issues in Science and Technology*, 11(2): 62–71.

Emmanuel, A. (1982). *Appropriate Technology and Underdevelopment*. Chichester: J. Wiley.

Fu, X., R. Kaplinsky, and J. Zhang (2012). 'The Impact of China on Low and Middle Income Countries' Export Prices in Industrial-Country Markets'. *World Development*, 40(8): 1483–96.

Gereffi, G., T. Sturgeon, and J. Humphrey (2005). 'The Governance of Global Value Chains'. *Review of International Political Economy*, 12(1): 78–104.

Hollanders, H. and L. Soete (2010). 'The Growing Role of Knowledge in the Global Economy'. *A World of Science*, 8(4): 2–10.

Humphrey, J. and H. Schmitz (2000). *Global Governance and Upgrading: Linking Industrial Cluster and Global Value Chain Research*. IDS Working Paper 120. Brighton: Institute of Development Studies.

IDS (1975). 'Redistribution with Growth'. *IDS Bulletin*, 7(2), 4–8.

ILO (1972). *Employment, Incomes and Equality: A Strategy for Increasing Productive Employment in Kenya*. Geneva: ILO.

Immelt, J., V. Govindarajan, and C. Trimble (2009). 'How GE is Disrupting Itself'. *Harvard Business Review*, 87(10): 56–65.

Jolly, R. (1975). 'Redistribution with Growth: A Reply'. *IDS Bulletin*, 7(2), 9–17.

Jolly, R. (2011). *Kenya, Actions towards Equity: The Reduction of Inequality in Kenya. Note prepared for UNICEF*. Brighton: Institute of Development Studies. Mimeo.

Kaplinsky, R. (1990). *The Economies of Small: Appropriate Technology in a Changing World*. London: Intermediate Technology Press.

Kaplinsky, R. (2005). *Globalization, Poverty and Inequality: Between a Rock and a Hard Place*. London: Polity.

Kaplinsky, R. (2010). *The Role of Standards in Global Value Chains and their Impact on Economic and Social Upgrading*. WB Policy Research Working Paper 5396. Washington, DC: World Bank.

Kaplinsky, R. (2011). 'Bottom of the Pyramid Innovation and Pro-Poor Growth'. Paper prepared for the World Bank's PRMED division. Milton Keynes: The Open University.

Kaplinsky, R. and M. Z. Farooki (2011). 'What are the Implications for Global Value Chains when the Market Shifts from the North to the South?'. *International. Journal of Technological Learning, Innovation and Development*, 4(1/2/3): 13–38.

Kaplinsky, R., D. McCormick, and M. Morris (2010). 'Impacts and Challenges of a Growing Relationship between China and Sub-Saharan Africa'. In V. Padayachee (ed.), *The Political Economy of Africa*. Abingdon: Routledge, 389–409.

Kaplinsky, R. and M. Morris (2001). *A Handbook for Value Chain Research*. Prepared for IDRC. Available at: <http://www.prism.uct.ac.za/Papers/VchNov01.pdf>.

Kaplinsky, R. and A. Santos-Paulino (2006). 'A Disaggregated Analysis of EU Imports: Implications for the Study of Patterns of Trade and Technology'. *Cambridge Journal of Economics*, 30(4): 587–612.

Kaplinsky, R., A. Terheggen, and J. P. Tijaja (2011). 'China as a Final Market: The Gabon Timber and Thai Cassava Value Chains'. *World Development*, 39(7): 1177–90.

Katz, J. M. (1980) 'Domestic Technology Generation in LDCs: A Review of Research Findings'. ECLA/IDB/IDRC/UNDP Research Programme. Buenos Aires: ECLA.

Khan, S. A. and R. M. Baye (2011). 'China–Africa Economic Relations: The Case of Cameroon'. Report submitted to the African Economic Research Consortium, Dept. of Economics and Management, University of Yaoundé II.

Lancaster, K. J. (1966). 'Change and Innovation in the Technology of Consumption'. *American Economic Review*, 56(1/2): 14–23.

Langdon, S. (1981). *Multinational Corporations in the Political Economy of Kenya*. London: Macmillan.

Lazonick, W. (2010). *The Fragility of the US Economy: The Financialized Corporation and the Disappearing Middle Class*. Available at: <http://www.theairnet.org/files/research/lazonick/Lazonick%20FUSE%2020101003.pdf>.

Lewis, W. A. (1954). 'Economic Development with Unlimited Supplies of Labour'. *The Manchester School*, 22(2): 139–91.

Leys, C. (1975a). 'The Politics of Redistribution with Growth'. *IDS Bulletin*, 7(2), 9–17.

Leys, C. (1975b). *Underdevelopment in Kenya: The Political Economy of Neo-Colonialism*. London: Heinemann.

Prahalad, C. K. (2005). *The Fortune at the Bottom of the Pyramid: Eradicating Poverty through Profits*. Upper Saddle River, NJ: Pearson Education/Wharton School Publishing.

Prahalad, C. K. and A. Hammond (2002). 'Serving the World's Poor, Profitably'. *Harvard Business Review*, 80(9): 48–57.

Ruttan, V. W. (2001). *Technology, Growth and Development: An Induced Innovation Perspective*. New York: Oxford University Press.

Schumacher, F. (1973). *Small Is Beautiful*. London: Blond and Briggs.

Sen, A. K. (1968). *The Choice of Techniques* (3rd edition). Oxford: Blackwell.

Singer, H., C. Cooper, R. C. Desai, C. Freeman, O. Gish, S. Hall, and G. Oldham (1970). *The Sussex Manifesto: Science and Technology for Developing Countries during the Second Development Decade*. IDS Reprints No. 101. Brighton: Institute of Development Studies.

Stewart, F. (1976). 'Capital Goods for Developing Countries'. In A. Cairncross and M. Puri (eds), *Employment, Income Distribution and Development Strategy: Problems of the Developing Countries, Essays in Honour of H. W. Singer*. London: Macmillan, 120–39.

Stewart, F. (1979). *Technology and Underdevelopment* (2nd edition). London: Macmillan.

Sumner, A. (2010). *'Global Poverty and the New Bottom Billion: What if Three-Quarters of the World's Poor Live in Middle-Income Countries?'*. Brighton: Institute of Development Studies. Mimeo.

Townsend, P. (1979). *Poverty in the United Kingdom: A Survey of Household Resources and Standards of Living*. Harmondsworth: Penguin Books.

UN-Habitat (2010). *State of the World's Cities 2008/2009*. New York: UN-Habitat.

Wilkinson, R. and K. Pickett (2009). *The Spirit Level: Why More Equal Societies Almost Always Do Better*. London: Allen Lane.

Wood, A. and J. Mayer (2011). 'Has China De-industrialised Other Developing Countries?'. *Review of World Economics*, 147(2): 325–50.

World Bank (2006). *Equity and Development: World Development Report, 2006*. Washington, DC: World Bank.

13

Helping Control Boom–Bust in Finance through Countercyclical Regulation*

Stephany Griffith-Jones and José Antonio Ocampo

13.1 The Case for, and Early Proposals of, Countercyclical Prudential Regulation

The long history of financial cycles, of which the North Atlantic crisis that started in 2007/08 and is still ongoing at the time of writing in early 2013 is a major example, shows that procyclical behaviour is inherent to the functioning of financial markets, and is indeed perhaps the major market failure in finance! Procyclicality is characterized by excessive risk-taking and financial activity in good times, followed by insufficient risk-taking and financial activity in bad times. During times of boom, risk premia decline, credit expands, and strong balance sheets and increasing competition bring an expansion of lending and loosening of credit standards, partly in an effort to compensate for the fall in profitability derived from lower interest-rate margins. In a self-fulfilling cycle, credit expansion is largely backed by collateral whose value increases with the expansion of lending. On the other hand, during a recession, and even more if a financial crisis happens, when non-performing loans rise and banks face higher provisions and tighter capital buffers, financial intermediaries turn very conservative and tighten credit standards well beyond what fundamental conditions would warrant. This leads to major costs to growth, employment, investment, and development.

There are ample theoretical explanations and empirical evidence of this pattern. That instability is inherent to the functioning of financial markets was, of course, one of Keynes's (1936) insights, which was emphasized by his

* The authors would like to thank Ariane Ortiz for her excellent research assistance.

follower, Minsky (1982). The basic reason is that finance deals with future outcomes that cannot be forecast with certainty. Therefore, opinions and expectations about the future rather than factual information dominate financial market decisions. This is compounded by asymmetries of information that characterize financial markets (Stiglitz 2001). Financial agents thus rely to a large extent on the actions of other market agents, leading to interdependence in their behaviour, which is particularly manifested in the twin phenomena of contagion and herding. Contagion of opinions and expectations, both positive and negative, is a central feature of the alternating phases of euphoria and panic (Ocampo 2008).

Moreover, herding and volatility are accentuated by the increasing use of similar market-sensitive risk-management statistical techniques (Persaud 2003) and the dominance of investment managers aiming for very-short-term profits, evaluated and paid at very-short-term intervals (Griffith-Jones 1998).

The procyclical nature of finance calls for regulation that leans against the wind. After the East Asian crisis in 1998, some analysts began proposing that countercyclical prudential regulation should be put in place, as part of broader countercyclical macroeconomic policy frameworks. However, prior to the North Atlantic crisis, support for countercyclical regulation was very limited and restricted mainly to a few academics and some international organizations, particularly the United Nations Economic Commission for Latin America and the Caribbean (ECLAC) and the Bank for International Settlements (BIS). Spain pioneered implementing countercyclical regulation, indicating that it is both feasible and effective.

In 1999, the United Nations pointed out in its report *Towards a New International Financial Architecture* that the unpredictability of key macroeconomic variables needed to be taken into account in designing prudential regulation and supervision (ECLAC 1999). It suggested in particular that capital-adequacy requirements should be raised during periods of financial euphoria to take account of the increasing financial risks intermediaries incur. ECLAC (2000: ch. 8) emphasized soon after that, depending on the type of operation, higher capital or complementary liquidity buffers should be required in a countercyclical way, and limits should be set on the proportion of the value of financial or fixed assets that can be used as loan collateral when asset prices are rising.

In the same line, at the BIS et al. (2001: 1–57) argued that procyclicality stems from inappropriate responses by financial system participants to changes in risk over time, and proposed the use of regulation and supervisory instruments in an explicitly countercyclical fashion to limit the development and consequences of serious financial imbalances. The instrument proposed should encourage the building up of a protective cushion in good times that can be drawn down in bad times.

Furthermore, the concern that risk assessment and traditional regulatory tools, including Basel II standards, had a procyclical bias in the way they operated, adding to the procyclical nature of the credit cycle, began to be raised (Goodhart 2002). Indeed, in a system in which loan-loss provisions are tied to loan delinquency, precautionary regulatory signals are ineffective during booms, and thus do not hamper credit growth.

On the other hand, the sharp increase in loan delinquency during crises reduces financial institutions' capital and, hence, their lending capacity (Ocampo 2003). This, in conjunction with the greater perceived risk, triggers the credit squeeze that characterizes such periods, thereby reinforcing the economic downswing.

In 2003, Ocampo (2003; see also Ocampo and Chiappe 2003) argued for comprehensive countercyclical prudential regulation to manage the effects of boom–bust cycles. Such comprehensive regulation should include: (i) specific provisions for latent risks of new lending (the system that Spain had already introduced); (ii) strict regulation of currency and maturity mismatches, particularly in the first case for non-tradable sectors in developing countries; (iii) liquidity requirements to manage imbalances in the maturities of assets and liabilities on banks' balance sheets; and (iv) limits on loan-to-collateral value ratios and rules to adjust the values of collateral to reflect long-term market trends in asset values rather than cyclical variations.

Proposals to include countercyclical elements in the Basel II Capital Accord, to mitigate the inherent procyclicality of the internal-ratings-based approach (IRB), were put forward as early as 2002 (Griffith-Jones et al. 2002; Griffith-Jones and Ocampo 2003; Ocampo 2003). They included suggestions for introducing countercyclical instruments, such as Spanish-style provisions or countercyclical capital charges, simultaneously with Basel II, to compensate for the procyclical nature of the Basel Accord (see also Banco de España 2005). As discussed below, it is very valuable that countercyclical provisions were finally included in the Basel III Capital Accord in 2010.

13.2 Basel III, Especially in Relation to Countercyclical Regulation

In September 2010, the twenty-seven countries of the Basel Committee on Bank Supervision agreed in principle rather major changes to bank capital-adequacy regulations, the so-called Basel III proposals (BCBS 2010). Their stated aim is to strengthen banks so that 'never again' can a crisis like that which started in 2007–8 happen.

These Basel III proposals have a number of positive elements, such as increasing risk-weighted capital requirements, plus introducing a leverage ratio for solvency, an additional capital buffer, a countercyclical buffer (through dynamic provisioning based on expected losses), and liquidity provisions. As regards increasing risk-weighted capital-adequacy requirements, the minimum for common equity, considered as the highest form of loss-absorbing capital, will be raised from 2 per cent to 4.5 per cent after the application of stricter adjustments. The Tier-1 capital requirement, which includes common equity and other qualifying financial instruments, will increase from 4 to 6 per cent over the same period, while the minimum total capital ratio remains unchanged at 8 per cent.

Major questions have been asked about the appropriateness and sufficiency of the above measures. First, are the increases of capital requirements enough, and will they be implemented soon enough, given that the implementation schedule is very slow? Most observers, even fairly conservative ones, think the answer to these questions is 'no', especially for banks with very risky assets. Several authors, including senior figures in the Bank of England, argue that the established changes are too small to increase resilience of the system enough. Instead they suggest, for example, that core capital should be much higher as a proportion of risk-weighted assets (Admati et al. 2010; Miles et al. 2011). A more radical critique asks whether focusing on risk-weighted assets is the best approach, and if this will lead to new forms of arbitrage. Would a greater emphasis on leverage (total assets divided by capital) be better, for example?

Returning to the main topic of our chapter, it is positive that Basel III introduced a countercyclical buffer, within a range of 0 per cent and 2.5 per cent of common equity up and above general core-capital requirements. The focus is on excessive aggregate credit growth on a national level. The advantage of a countercyclical buffer is that it adjusts the expected loss from credit to the average of a business cycle, thereby fighting excessively optimistic predictions and building up buffers beyond core-capital charges as protection against unexpected losses. Banks that do not meet the buffer will be subject to restrictions on capital distributions (dividends, share repurchases, and discretionary bonus payments to staff) until they do, which is also a positive measure.

Basel III advises the use of the credit-to-GDP gap as the leading indicator for the calculation of the countercyclical capital buffer. Repullo and Saurina (2011) argue that this measure lacks a clear relationship to business cycle indicators, and is thus not inherently anticyclical. Therefore national banking regulators need to assess the relationship between the business cycle indicators and the credit-to-GDP ratios, as well as considering the use of other indicators that relate credit growth to the business cycle. Repullo and Saurina (2011) suggest, for example, the deviation of credit growth from the trend and other measures. A debate is ongoing on how best to implement countercyclical regulation, including in emerging and developing economies, given the different structures of their economies and financial sectors, as well as issues related to data availability.

Countercyclical measures proved their worth during the crisis in the case of Spain, and is also already used to a certain extent in some Latin American countries. As the current Eurozone crisis unfolds in Spain, where it was partly caused by excessive mortgage growth, it seems that the countercyclical changes for Spanish banks may have been too limited. Though Spanish statistical (countercyclical) provisions have helped strengthen the large Spanish banks, particularly problematic in Spain was that specific limits or regulations were not imposed on the very rapid expansion of lending for mortgages. This, however, does not disprove the idea of countercyclical requirements, but on the contrary means that regulators should react more strongly to sectoral credit growth that moves sharply out of line. As Spanish regulators themselves argue, the rapid increase of the value of collateral linked to the property boom probably prevailed over the higher lending costs derived from dynamic provisioning (see also what we will refer to as the *Geneva Report*, Brunnermeier et al. 2009). One way to deal with these issues, as we discuss below, is to introduce limits on loan-to-collateral value ratios and rules to adjust the values of collateral to reflect long-term market trends in asset values rather than cyclical variations.

13.3 The Emerging New Consensus on Countercyclicality

As the global financial crisis grew more acute, the depth of discussion on countercyclical regulation, as a way to avoid the build-up of systemic risk in the future and to dampen economic cycles, became clearer and widespread. All major reports on regulatory policy responses to the crisis (such as Brunnermeier et al. 2009; Turner Review 2009; Stiglitz 2009; Warwick Commission 2010) highlighted the importance of countercyclical, as well as macro-prudential, regulation. Also, national reports (such as those of the US and UK Treasuries) increasingly supported not just the principle of countercyclicality, but started entering the specifics of how to implement it. In fact, some countries, such as Switzerland, moved quickly to implement a simple version of countercyclical regulation, distinguishing between imposing minimum capital-adequacy requirements for bad times and doubling them for good times.

Furthermore, since their first November 2008 meeting the G20 leaders have endorsed the need for countercyclical regulation. So have international regulatory bodies, such as the now expanded Financial Stability Forum (Board) and the Basel Committee on Banking Supervision. The BIS, in its

2009 *Annual Report*, provided an in-depth analysis of how countercyclicality could be implemented (BIS 2009). The consensus indicates that it is not enough simply to reduce procyclicality of existing regulations, but it is also necessary to design new, proactive countercyclical regulations—to offset the impact of unavoidable procyclicality elsewhere, as the Turner Review puts it. In the terms of the UN Stiglitz Commission (Stiglitz 2009), the basic aim is to improve the stability of the macroeconomy and particularly to reduce the procyclicality of finance and its effects on the real economy. It is all this analysis and support that led to the introduction of countercyclical changes in Basle III, as discussed above.

Most of the aims of macro-prudential regulation are widely shared. Thus, the US Treasury Statement of 3 September 2009 gives the following objectives for countercyclical regulation: (i) to reduce the extent to which capital and accounting framework permits risk to accumulate in boom, exacerbating credit cycles; (ii) to incorporate features that encourage or force banks to build large capital cushions in good times; (iii) to raise capital requirements for bank and non-bank financial firms that pose a threat to financial stability due to their combination of size, leverage, interconnectedness, and liquidity risk, and for systemically risky exposures; and (iv) to improve the ability of banks to withstand specific and system-wide liquidity shocks.

In spite of the decision of Basle III, there continues to be a debate on what instruments are best to introduce countercyclicality, i.e. whether limits on leverage should relate to capital or provisions (reserves in US/UK terminology).

In the case of solvency, with current accounting practices, which do not allow or severely limit statistical or forward-looking provisions, countercyclical capital-adequacy requirements should be the preferred instrument. However, the current dialogue between international regulators and accounting associations may facilitate the active use of provisions. If Spanish-style statistical provisions are allowed, they may be preferable, as they follow the international principle that provisions should cover *expected* losses, while capital should be able to cover *unexpected* losses (Stiglitz 2009; Ocampo 2003). By restricting total assets to capital, maximum overall leverage ratios could also be an important regulatory tool. Complementary liquidity requirements are also desirable, as the Basle Committee has recognized (see below).

The case for provisions or similar mechanisms comes also in different forms in other reports. Thus, as the UK Treasury and the Turner Review have pointed out, countercyclical buffers, both of capital and provisions, should be held in the form of non-distributable reserves, which therefore cannot be distributed either as excessive dividends, share buy-backs, remunerations, or bonuses. This is the essence of the Spanish system. It is encouraging that in their Pittsburgh meeting the G20 leaders endorsed this principle and Basle III incorporated it.

Some reports and official statements tend to opt for a combination of policy instruments. This may reflect a 'belt-and-braces' philosophy, given the seriousness of the problem and the limitations of different instruments. Interestingly, the US Treasury also sees this as a way to avoid regulatory arbitrage: although it may be relatively easy for banks to arbitrage any free-standing risk-based capital requirement and relatively easy for firms to arbitrage any free-standing simple leverage constraint, it is much more difficult to arbitrage both frameworks at the same time.

Some reports (for example, the Turner Review and the UN Stiglitz Commission) argue for complementary instruments to be included, such as making rules on loans to value more restrictive, or even varying them with the cycle, especially in good times. Though this may add to complexity, it will tackle directly one of the key problematic links during booms: rising credit increases asset prices (especially real estate), but then higher credit feeds into asset-price bubbles. Furthermore, the UN Stiglitz Commission, as well as our previous studies, argues that limiting or discouraging currency mismatches, especially for banks, is essential to limit financial risks for emerging and developing economies, which are subject to strong procyclical capital flows. We return to these issues below.

To a certain extent, different proposals reflect the features of different countries' financial systems and the problems they have encountered. Thus, when the September 2009 US Treasury Report argues from a macro-prudential perspective for higher risk-based capital charges for certain systemically risky exposures, due to their high correlation with the economic cycle, they refer in particular to exposures like the structured finance credit protection purchased by banks from the American International Group (AIG) and other thinly capitalized special purpose derivatives companies. For a developing or emerging economy, higher risk-based capital charges would refer to far simpler instruments (e.g. mortgages), which are also highly correlated—but in a more traditional way—with the business cycle.

The emphasis that the US Treasury and other reports place on higher capital requirements for systemically important institutions draws on the research at the BIS and elsewhere, which shows that large banks, and those more exposed to system-wide shocks, contribute more than proportionally to systemic risks. Both the size of individual banks, and of the total banking—or even financial—system are important, as in situations of crisis they may need to be bailed out. To an important extent, therefore, the total amount of acceptable systemic risk is determined by how much the public sector can afford to spend without creating major future damage to the economy. Thus, as Buiter (2009) argues, a solution may be to limit the size of the banking sector, by making capital requirements of individual banks a function not only of their own size, but of the size of the total banking balance sheet relative to the government's capacity to raise taxes and cut spending. The emphasis in the BIS analysis, however, is not particularly on size of institutions, though this is important, but on the degree of correlation among institutions' balance sheets. However, as correlations tend to change so much during crisis periods, it seems difficult—though potentially worthwhile—to try to determine ex ante which institutions are more systemically risky, so their capital and other requirements will not just reflect the likelihood of their own failure, but also their potential contribution to systemic risk. Furthermore, if stricter regulation (e.g. tighter capital requirements) is imposed on systemically important institutions, the list of such institutions must be carefully revised as the financial system evolves.

13.4 Outstanding Issues and Complementary Policies

13.4.1 Rule-Based versus Discretionary Interventions

One important choice that has emerged is whether countercyclical buffers (capital or provisions) should be designed as a discretionary instrument or, rather, as a formula-driven rule. As the Turner Review points out:

- With a discretionary system, bank regulators would need to judge appropriate level of required capital ratios in the light of analysis of the macroeconomic cycle and of macro-prudential concerns. The discretionary system would have the advantage of allowing a nuanced analysis of macroeconomic and macro-prudential conditions to guide decisions, but it would depend crucially on the quality and independence of the judgments made.

- Under a formula-driven system, the required level of capital would vary according to some predetermined metric such as the growth of the balance sheet. It would provide a pre-set discipline not dependent of judgment and, particularly important, not subject to the influence of lobbying and to cycles of optimism and pessimism, which also affect regulators. Indeed, the Spanish system, based on a pre-set formula that determines statistical provisions, is a practical proof that rules defined ex ante can work, and thus provides a template on which the international community can draw, even though the Spanish system was insufficient to stop excessive credit growth, as shown ex post by the problems of the banking system during the Eurozone crisis.

The Turner and other (e.g. Geneva) reports believe that there is merit in making the regime, at least to a significant extent, formula-driven. This could be combined with regulatory discretion to add additional requirements on top of the formula-driven element if macro-prudential analysis suggested that this was appropriate. This is also the approach suggested by Ocampo (2003), who recommends mixing the Spanish provisioning rules with discretionary rules that would be put in place if overall credit growth were considered excessive by the authorities, if there is a bias in lending towards sectors subject to strong cyclical swings (e.g. real estate), in which case such lending would be subject to additional provisions, and if credit growth by individual banks expands relative to a benchmark. Interestingly, during the last boom, some countries did establish additional provisions for credit in specific sectors that were experiencing rapid growth (India in relation to real estate, for example).

The third approach is probably the most appropriate. It is important, indeed, to put in place fairly simple countercyclical rules that cannot be weakened in good times, when 'this time is different' arguments try to undermine regulatory criteria. The rule or formula could be tightened by imposing additional requirements if there is a very large and long boom that poses threats to financial and macroeconomic stability, or if loans to certain sectors grow very rapidly.

Furthermore, financial innovations, some of which may have been designed precisely to arbitrage regulations, may also require further tightening of countercyclical rules if they are deemed by regulators to pose increased systemic risk (D'Arista and Griffith-Jones 2009b; UK Treasury 2009). More broadly, it is essential that regulations should be similar for similar types of financial transactions, whether they are undertaken by the banking system or in capital markets. Thus, as argued in Section 13.6 below, security issuance in capital markets, which is equivalent to bank lending, and derivatives should also be subject to countercyclical regulations (e.g. on collateral and margin requirements).

Furthermore, financial innovations increase during booms, when new and untested instruments that are difficult to value become widespread. This exacerbates procyclicality, as such new and often opaque, as well as complex, instruments hide and underprice risk. Regulators should either limit or ban the use of such instruments, or at least tighten countercyclical rules for financial institutions that extensively use them.

A more direct approach was suggested as an option by Joseph Stiglitz in his October 2008 Testimony to the House Financial Services Committee. This direct approach would imply designing 'speed limits restricting the rate at which banks can expand their portfolio of loans'. This is an interesting alternative to implementing indirect incentives to achieve the same objective.

Indeed, in the past, countries such as the UK and developing countries, and even the USA, pursued such an approach rather effectively, when they fixed limits for growth of total lending by individual banks and for the banking system. Should indirect approaches for countercyclical regulation prove to be insufficient, there seems to be a strong case for the use of a more direct approach, which could perhaps also be done through limiting the expansion of leverage. This could be easier in developing countries, especially those which do not have excessively large and complex financial sectors.

Assuming countercyclical indirect policy instruments are used, a key issue is what indicators are best to determine when capital charges or provisions would need to be built up or could be drawn down as bad times come. The BIS 2009 *Annual Report* provides an analysis of the impact of three possible variables suggested in the literature: credit spreads (the variable suggested by Gordy 2009), change in real credit (by Goodhart and Persaud 2008), and a composite indicator that combines credit/GDP ratio and real asset prices (by Borio and Drehmann 2009). The conclusion that it draws is that it seems possible to identify macroeconomic indicators that signal correctly when buffers should be built up, but deciding their release is more difficult, especially for the latter variable. For this reason, they recommend more discretion, combined with a rule that creates predictability and helps avoid regulatory capture during the boom.

13.4.2 The Regulation of Liquidity

There was increasing support in different reports and statements on the need for regulating liquidity, including introducing a countercyclical element into this regulation. This is because the recent crisis showed that the risk profile of banks and financial institutions in general critically depends on the way that they fund their assets. As the US Treasury September 2009 Report argues, excessive funding of longer-term assets with short-term debt by a bank can contribute as much or more to its failure as insufficient capital. Furthermore, the report states that 'liquidity is always and everywhere a highly procyclical phenomenon'. Indeed, because capital, even though high, may be insufficient to deal with liquidity problems in a crisis, sufficient independent liquidity requirements are also very important.

In fact, it was a major and absurd omission of the pre-crisis framework that there was practically no regulation of liquidity. This has not always been the case. Thus, in 1951, US banks held reserve balances with the Federal Reserve at a level of over 11 per cent of bank deposits, giving them a very comfortable cushion. By the early 2000s, this cushion had practically been wiped out with banks' reserve balances shrinking to 0.2 per cent of their deposits (D'Arista and Griffith-Jones 2009b). There is now growing consensus on the need for a strong regulatory framework that focuses not just on safeguarding the liquidity positions of banks in the face of firm-specific stress events, but also helps preserve the funding liquidity of banks if system-wide liquidity contractions occur.

There was initially relatively less specific international discussion on the best method to ensure sufficient liquidity, and possibly to do it counter-cyclically, than on the issue of solvency relating to capital and provisioning requirements. One approach can be to estimate liquidity requirements on the basis of the residual maturity of financial institutions' liabilities, thus generating a direct incentive for the financial system to maintain an appropriate liability structure. The quality of the assets with which liquidity requirements are met is also crucial (Ocampo and Chiappe 2003). An alternative, which draws from the system of reserve requirements typical of past practices, would be to establish a regime that facilitates central banks to increase and reduce liquidity to financial institutions through accounts held on the liability side of institutions' balance sheets (D'Arista and Griffith-Jones 2009a).

Regulation of liquidity needs to be complementary with regulation of solvency. Though arguing that the liquidity regime should be independent from the regulatory capital regime, the September 2009 US Treasury Report correctly says that it is equally important to recognize that they are highly complementary. Indeed, this report considers the merits of making regulatory capital requirements a function of the liquidity risk of banking firms. Though clearly higher capital cannot be totally relied on to prevent a run by creditors, it may be consistent with macro-prudential goals to require banks with larger structural funding mismatches, or that rely on volatile short-term funding sources, to hold more capital. This would force the banks to internalize the cost its higher liquidity risk imposes on the financial system, thus encouraging them to seek longer-term funding.

The Geneva and Warwick Reports went further by recommending that regulators increase the existing capital requirements by two multiples, one linked to the growth of credit, and the other to maturity mismatches. The first multiple for capital-adequacy requirements would be a function of the growth of lending. A second multiple on capital requirements would relate to the mismatch in the maturity of bank assets and liabilities. One significant lesson of the crisis is that the risk of an asset can be determined largely by the maturity of its funding. Northern Rock as well as other banks might well have survived with the same assets if the average maturity of its funding had been longer.

A liquidity multiple to capital-adequacy requirements would be added to discourage banks from a reliance on inappropriately risky sources of funding. Assets that cannot be posted at the central bank for liquidity are assumed to have minimum maturity of two years or more. If a pool of these assets were funded by a pool of two-year term deposits, there would be no liquidity risk and no liquidity charge. But if the pool of funding had a maturity of one month and so had to be rolled over every month, the liquidity multiple on the base capital charge would be near its maximum. Liquidity multiples would give banks an incentive to find longer-term funding, and where they cannot do so, to hold a liquidity buffer or liquidity reserve that could be drawn down in times of stress.

One of the biggest innovations in Basel III is the regulation of liquidity. However, they have not introduced the approach recommended by the Warwick Commission.

The liquidity coverage ratio and the net stable funding ratio introduced by Basle III are responses to the problems of funding liquidity experienced during the crisis. Banks will have to prove that they can fund themselves for one month (liquidity coverage ratio) and for one year (net stable funding ratio):

> The liquidity coverage ratio identifies the amount of unencumbered, high quality liquid assets an institution holds that can be used to offset the net cash outflows it would encounter under an acute short-term stress scenario specified by supervisors…The net stable funding (NSF) ratio measures the amount of longer-term, stable sources of funding employed by an institution relative to the liquidity profiles of the assets funded and the potential for contingent calls on funding liquidity arising from off-balance sheet commitments and obligations. The standard requires a minimum amount of funding expected to be stable over a one year time horizon based on liquidity risk factors assigned to assets and off-balance sheet liquidity exposures. The NSF ratio is intended to promote longer-term structural funding. (BCBS 2010)

The liquidity coverage ratio is intended to make sure that no re-occurrence of the failure of banks is possible due to liquidity guarantees of banks granted to the shadow banking sector or other reasons. It aims at preventing banks from taking on liquidity risks they cannot shoulder, whereas the net stable funding ratio is aiming to decrease the likelihood of another bank run in the wholesale financial markets. One of the important innovations is to include off-balance sheet obligations of the banks. However, the extent to which these measures will increase the resilience of the financial system cannot yet be gauged, because they will only come into force in 2018 and in the meantime will be tested via impact studies and, if necessary, adjusted so as not to disturb the markets too much. Thus, one might fear a potential softening of these rules during the phase of implementation. A more radical question is why off-balance sheet obligations are allowed to persist, and whether it would not be better to put all these transactions on the balance sheet.

13.4.3 Accounting Rules

It is important that the building of countercyclical buffers as required by financial stability be matched by the integrity and transparency of financial statements. An important issue is the design of accounting rules that would allow provisions for latent loan losses to be built up during periods of credit growth, indeed possibly shifting to a system in which provisions are made when credit is *disbursed*, as the Spanish system implies. There are reasons to believe that accounting standards setters will modify standards to include macro-prudential regulation. The Financial Stability Forum (FSF), along with the G20 leaders in the London Summit in April 2009, urged cooperation between accounting standards setters and regulators to improve standards of valuation and provisioning, and this collaboration has moved forward.

The Turner Review had suggested an approach that would imply that existing accounting rules would be used to determine profits and losses, reflecting fair-value mark-to-market approaches for the trading book and known information on actual loan servicing and incurred loss on the lending book. This would be complemented by the creation of a non-distributable 'economic cycle reserve' that would set aside profits in good years to anticipate losses likely in the future. This economic-cycle reserve would also appear on the profit and loss account, allowing profits and earnings per share to be estimated before and after the reserve. Thus, two measures of profitability could be reported: the traditional accounting one and another calculated after countercyclical reserves.

13.4.4 Complementary Regulations

Given the role that foreign-currency-denominated loans have played in emerging- and developing-country financial crises, as indicated again in several Central and Eastern European countries and Iceland during the initial phases of the North Atlantic crisis, preventing currency mismatches in portfolios should be an important regulatory objective in these countries. One simple approach, which some countries follow, is actually to forbid currency mismatches in the portfolios of financial institutions and to prohibit or discourage lending in foreign currencies to agents who have no revenues in those currencies. Thus, for example, Uruguay increases capital requirements by 25 per cent (from 8 to 10 per cent) if there are such currency mismatches.

Besides regulating currency and maturity mismatches, it is also important—mainly for emerging and developing economies, but also for other economies—to limit loan-to-value ratios, especially for loans to real estate. Rules to adjust the values collateral for cyclical price variations can also be used. A complementary mechanism that seems to work well is minimum limits on down-payments by borrowers for mortgages, which can be fixed (e.g. Canada) or vary with the cycle (e.g. China). Such methods can also be applied to other very cyclical instruments, such as credit cards. Thailand has used variable minimum payments of credit cards as a countercyclical tool.

13.5 The Trade-Offs between Tighter Regulation and the Supply of Credit

There is a trade-off that needs to be struck in increasing strictness of regulation of both solvency and liquidity when determining optimal levels of overall bank capital and liquidity adequacy (an important issue that needs to be decided together with the degree of countercyclicality). This relates, first, to the issue of optimal level of capital. The trade-off has first to consider the economic benefits of higher bank capital, which both decreases the probability of bank defaults (and major crisis) and the reduced danger that, in bad times, insufficient capital will lead to a credit squeeze with negative efforts on the real economy. However, it also has to consider that the requirement of higher overall capital may increase the cost of intermediation in good times, and thus can have some negative effect on borrowers, particularly less creditworthy ones. This could be most serious for small and medium-sized enterprises with limited access to other sources of funding.

After the major financial crisis that started in 2007, the optimal level of capital is recognized to be significantly higher than what regulators considered appropriate in the past. This re-evaluation is based on the massive scale of economic and financial losses suffered across the world due to the crisis. Increasing capital requirements may increase costs of financial intermediation. However, the benefits of reduced probability of bank failure and economic harm are seen as extremely high, and this tips the balance in favour of setting higher capital requirements. This argument is similar to that used by economists who favour controls on excessive capital inflow to developing countries in boom times. Whilst recognizing that there are certain microeconomic costs, they feel the benefit of diminished risk of future crises outweighs those benefits.

Similarly, limiting maturity transformation by banks, as discussed above, to safeguard their liquidity in periods of stress, may have some negative effects on their borrowers in that it allows less long-term lending. This cost will, however, be accompanied by a reduction of the major systemic risk caused by large maturity transformation by banks, which has required massive central-bank liquidity assistance during the current crisis to avoid the collapse of banks and to help restore lending.

Should in future more tightly regulated banks provide more expensive and shorter maturity credit, there may be a need to design new instruments to provide, for example, more long-term credit, as well as provide access to cheaper and more abundant credit to key sectors. It may be necessary to use public development banks, or other public interventions, to achieve such purposes.

13.6 How Comprehensive Should Countercyclical Regulation Be?

13.6.1 At a National Level

The case for tighter and countercyclical regulation of banks is increasingly accepted. However, stronger and more countercyclical regulation of banks alone would encourage migration of transactions and risk from banks to non-banks. Banks would be tempted to hide their own lending in associated off-balance sheet vehicles such as conduits and special investment vehicles (SIVs). This would pose new threats to financial stability (US Treasury 2009a, 2009b, as well as other reports).

There is therefore a very clear case for more countercyclical and stronger equivalent regulation to be applied to all markets (including over-the-counter derivatives (OTC) trading), to all banking and non-banking financial institutions, such as hedge funds and investment banks, and to all instruments, such as derivatives. Furthermore, equivalent regulations need to be applied to banks and capital markets (BIS 2009; Stiglitz 2009; D'Arista and Griffith-Jones 2009a).

The principle of comprehensive countercyclical regulation seems the clearest and most transparent one. As the BIS 2009 *Annual Report* puts it, no part of the financial system should be allowed to escape appropriate regulation. This will reduce the likelihood of future crises.

This would imply that all off-balance sheet transactions of banks would have to be placed on their balance sheets. Securities issued in capital markets should also be subject to equivalent regulation. The Financial Stability Forum 2009 Report on Addressing Procyclicality of the Financial System also recommends enforcing minimum initial margins for over-the-counter derivatives and securities to reduce leverage while requiring margins or haircuts to be relatively stable over the cycle. This is very welcome, as it would reduce the tendency for margining and collateral practices to fall in boom times and create adverse effects in times of market stress. Making collateral and margin requirements cycle-neutral, so they do not decline in booms, as the FSF suggests, would be positive. An issue to explore is whether such collateral and margin requirements (which are conceptually equivalent to capital require-ments) should not go beyond this, and also have countercyclical elements. This would seem desirable, as when security issuance and derivatives were growing excessively (e.g. well beyond historical average) collateral and capi-tal requirements could be increased.

Similarly, all financial institutions (including hedge funds and other pri-vate pools of capital) should have equivalent regulation, both of solvency (especially their leverage) and of liquidity, to avoid the migration of risky activities to less regulated institutions. There seems to be growing rhetorical international consensus for this, but it is essential that such broad consensus is reflected in sufficiently comprehensive and countercyclical regulation in practice. This has inevitably been opposed by those who would be regulated, driven more by their wish to maximize short-term profits rather than by the aim of financial stability. The importance of a clear commitment by policy-makers and legislators to financial stability is essential in this regard.

13.6.2 At an International Level

Clearly, financial risks and crises are transmitted from one country to the other through contagion. However, given that cycles do have some national features, there is growing consensus (e.g. in the Geneva, UN Stiglitz Commission, and Warwick Reports) that regulation, in general, and coun-tercyclical policies, in particular, should be implemented mainly nationally and by the host country, thereby shifting some of the emphasis in regula-tion from the home to the host country. This would imply that branches of foreign-owned banks would be required to become separately capitalized subsidiaries. This is also linked to the fact that most bailouts are done by host national authorities, so that the country that is the lender of last resort would also need to be the regulator. Indeed, the economic authority design-ing the countercyclical rules in the host country should probably be the central bank, as it focuses on macro and financial stability broadly defined.

Even though countercyclical measures should be implemented nationally, it would be best if the criteria for implementing them were to be coordinated internationally, to avoid regulatory arbitrage. Certainly, at the level of the European Union, countries should coordinate countercyclical measures on a wider regional basis. In fact, the European Union has the precise instrument, the Capital Adequacy Directive (CAD) that implements Basel regulation within the EU, which has been modified for such a purpose. The creation of EU-level (and/or Eurozone-level) regulatory bodies is further facilitating European coordination of national countercyclical regulation.

There are strong reasons for going further, and having international coor-dination of countercyclical regulation. (The fact that Basle III includes criteria for countercyclical regulation facilitates this task.) The need for such coordination is related, first of all, to the fact that international economic and, especially, financial linkages have been steadily growing as markets become increasingly globalized. As White (2009) points out, this greater integration implies that purely domestic indicators of procyclical behaviour will underestimate the threat to financial stability, to the extent that other countries are subject to similar pressure. Therefore, account needs to be taken of relevant pressures in related countries or globally. Second, a crisis in another important country (especially if it is a creditor or debtor, or a major trading partner) can have a significant effect on the financial stability or output of countries linked to it through strong financial or trade links, even though they themselves did not build up any national systemic risk. Therefore, from a policy perspective, greater integration implies that all countries have a legitimate concern to avoid procyclical excesses occurring in other countries, especially in large ones. Third, for short-term competitive reasons, countries, and especially their financial institutions, may be more willing to implement countercyclical regulations if they know that other countries are also doing so. One basic reason is, of course, that if some countries were to implement countercyclical regulation, while others did not, this would inevitably lead to regulatory arbitrage. It could, however, be argued that in the long term, better regulated (including via countercyclical rules) financial centres will be more financially stable, and therefore should become more competitive.

For all these reasons, it seems desirable that the criteria for designing countercyclical regulation be agreed internationally. As has been pointed out, the fact that Basle III includes criteria for countercyclical regulation facilitates this task and is very positive. An important issue that may require further research is the extent to which in implementing national countercyclical regulation purely domestic variables should be examined, or whether some account should be taken of international trends, such as global credit or asset-price growth.

This regulation would then be implemented nationally by host countries. In doing so, countries need to adapt it somewhat to the specific features of their financial systems and their economies. However, increasingly strengthened international regulatory bodies should strongly encourage all countries, especially larger ones and ones with more internationalized financial systems, to implement countercyclical regulation.

13.7 Conclusions

In a modern market economy, regulation is very important, as it significantly influences the level of credit at particular moments, and its evolution through time. As Greenwald and Stiglitz (2003) have shown, the level of credit is the critical variable in the determination of output and employment. Indeed, the important role of credit had been underestimated by academics and policymakers, who tend to place more emphasis on monetary policy. To the extent that credit is an important macroeconomic variable, good and effective regulation becomes an important policy tool.

The need for regulation to be countercyclical was initially recognized by only a small and fairly isolated group of academics and some international institutions. However, after the global crisis became acute, international commitment by policymakers to countercyclical regulation became widespread. Countercyclical regulation is increasingly accepted to be an important part of economic strategies aimed at stabilizing the economy by reducing the procyclicality of finance and its effects on the real economy. It does so by explicitly incorporating the impact of macroeconomic risks, and by changing crucial regulatory variables in a countercyclical way to discourage lending booms and prevent credit crunches. As agreement on implementing countercyclical regulation is very broad amongst policymakers, there is also ever-growing consensus that it is not enough to reduce procyclicality of existing regulations (as Basel II did), but it is also essential to design strictly countercyclical regulations, to offset the natural tendency of banking and financial markets towards boom–bust patterns (as Basle III has done to some extent). The key questions are now practical: how should countercyclical regulation best be implemented?

Initially, there was a debate about what instruments would best be used to achieve regulatory countercyclicality, especially in solvency requirements, but also for liquidity. There is now increasing agreement that several instruments need to be used in parallel. In the case of solvency, those instruments include countercyclical capital requirements and loan provisioning, as well as countercyclical leverage ratios and loan-to-value ratios. An alternative for the latter are rules to adjust the values of collateral for cyclical price variations, especially for real estate prices.

The only problem with using such a large array of instruments may be their excessive complexity, which partly reflects the complexity of problems posed by the financial system. An alternative, more direct approach would be for regulators to limit the growth of bank credit. This could become relevant if the more indirect countercyclical regulation instruments discussed above were not sufficiently effective.

Countercyclical provisions have the virtue that they have already been implemented by the Spanish authorities for a long period, though they were not sufficient to curb credit growth, especially for real estate. One problem has been tensions between implementing countercyclical provisions and accounting rules. However the dialogue between international regulatory bodies and accounting associations after the global crisis is helping to ease this problem.

The choice between implementing countercyclicality through rules or in a discretionary way is an important one. There seems to be an overall preference for predetermined rules, which will reduce the risk of regulatory capture, either by narrow interests or by the overenthusiasm that characterizes booms. Rules could be tightened in special circumstances, but never loosened during booms. Appropriate indicators (such as growth of credit and/or asset prices) need to be chosen to ensure countercyclical capital buffers vary more effectively with the cycle.

Though solvency, assuring enough capital and provisioning, is key for financial stability, so is liquidity. As solvency and liquidity are complementary, there may be a case for implementing requirements jointly, which would imply requiring more capital in a countercyclical way for institutions with large maturity mismatches. However, as capital will never be enough to deal with serious liquidity problems, there is a clear case for having a separate liquidity requirement, as Basle III does, even though it will only be implemented in 2018.

As regards accounting disclosure rules, these should satisfy both the needs of investors and those of financial stability. An optimal approach may be to rely on a dual disclosure approach, where both current profits and losses are reported, and profits after deducting a non-distributable economic-cycle reserve that sets aside profits in good years for likely losses in the future.

There are some important trade-offs between stronger and more counter-cyclical regulation and access to credit. Such stronger regulation will result in higher spreads in domestic financial intermediation. They may result in a suboptimal supply of financing, especially in the supply of long-term credit for small and medium-sized firms (SMEs). Therefore, additional instruments may be necessary to provide sufficient, and sufficiently long-term, credit, particularly to SMEs. Higher spreads may also generate incentives for corporations with direct access to international capital markets to borrow abroad, thus increasing the likelihood of currency mismatches in the portfolios of these agents. Hence the need for international coordination of regulatory policies, as well as specific policies to deal with currency mismatches in financial portfolios. It may also be necessary to find other institutions, such as development banks, to grant loans to sectors such as SMEs.

To avoid regulatory arbitrage, the comprehensiveness of countercyclical regulation is an important issue, both nationally and internationally. The best approach seems to be equivalent comprehensive countercyclical regulation for all institutions, instruments, and markets. This would include also all non-banking financial institutions, such as hedge funds (the so-called shadow banking system), as well as all instruments within banks, by consolidating all activities onto the balance sheet; it should also include countercyclical margin and collateral requirements on all securities and derivatives instruments.

Countercyclical regulation needs to be implemented nationally, as cycles vary by countries; and it should be implemented by host countries. However, the broad criteria need to be defined nationally or regionally (e.g. within the European Union) but coordinated internationally, as markets are subject to contagion. Thus, a crisis in another important country (especially if an important creditor, debtor, or trade partner) can seriously harm financial stability or output in countries, even though they have not accumulated systemic risk. Therefore, in the context of intense globalization, all countries have a legitimate concern to avoid procyclical excesses in other countries. The case for international coordination for defining broad criteria for countercyclical regulation is therefore strong.

References

Admati, A. R., P. M. DeMarzo, M. F. Hellwig, and P. Pfleiderer (2010). *Fallacies, Irrelevant Facts and Myths in the Discussion of Capital Regulation: Why Bank Equity is not Expensive*. The Rock Center for Corporate Governance at Stanford University, Working Paper Series No. 86; Stanford GSB Research Paper No. 2063. Stanford. Available at: <http://www.coll.mpg.de/pdf_dat/2010_42online.pdf>.

Banco de España (2005). *'Financial Stability Report'*. May. Madrid: Banco de España.

BCBS (Basle Committee for Bank Supervision) (2010). *A Global Regulatory Framework for More Resilient Banks and Banking Systems*. December. Basel: BIS. Available at: <http://www.bis.org/publ/bcbs189_dec2010.htm>.

BIS (Bank for International Settlements) (2009). *Annual Report*. Basel: BIS.

Borio, C. and M. Drehmann (2009). 'Assessing the Risk of Banking Crises: Revisited'. *BIS Quarterly Review*, March: 29–46.

Borio, C., C. Furfine, and P. Lowe (2001). *'Procyclicality of the Financial System and Financial Stability: Issues and Policy Options'*. Background paper for the meeting *'Marrying the Macro- and Micro-Prudential Dimensions of Financial Stability'*. BIS Paper No. 1. Basel: BIS.

Brunnermeier, M., A. Crockett, C. Goodhart, A. D. Persaud, and H. Shin (2009). *Fundamental Principles to Financial Regulation [Geneva Report]*. London: Centre for Economic Policy Research.

Buiter, W. (2009). 'Forget Tobin Tax: There Is a Better Way to Curb Finance'. *Financial Times*, 1 September.

D'Arista, J. and S. Griffith-Jones (2009a). 'Agenda and Criteria for Financial Regulatory Reform'. In S. Griffith-Jones, J. A. Ocampo, and J. Stiglitz (eds), *Time for a Visible Hand: Lessons from the 2008 World Financial Crisis*. New York: Oxford University Press.

D'Arista, J. and S. Griffith-Jones (2009b). *Agenda and Criteria for Financial Regulatory Reform*. G-24 Working Paper, August. Available at: <http://www.g24.org/TGM/sgjda0909.pdf>.

ECLAC (United Nations, Executive Committee on Economic and Social Affairs) (1999). *Towards a New International Financial Architecture*. March. Santiago: ECLAC.

ECLAC (2000). 'A More Stable Macroeconomy'. In *Equity, Development and Citizenship*. Santiago: ECLAC, 65–9.

Financial Stability Forum Report (2009). *Addressing Procyclicality in the Financial System*. April. Available at: <http://www.financialstabilityboard.org/publications/r_0904a.pdf>.

Goodhart, C. (2002). 'Basel and Procyclicality'. In A. Hilton (ed.), *Bumps on the Road to Basel*. London: Centre for the Study of Financial Innovation [CSFI], 26–8.

Goodhart, C. and A. Persaud (2008). 'A Party Pooper's Guide to Financial Stability'. *Financial Times*, 4 June.

Gordy, M. B. (2009). 'First, Do No Harm; a Hippocratic Approach to Procyclicality in Basel II'. Paper presented at the conference 'Procyclicality in the Financial System', jointly organized by the Netherlands Bank and the Bretton Woods Committee, February.

Griffith-Jones, S. (1998). *Global Capital Flows: Should They be Regulated?* Basingstoke and New York: Macmillan/St. Martin's Press.

Griffith-Jones, S. and J. A. Ocampo (2003). *What Progress on International Financial Reform? Why So Limited?* Stockholm: Almqvist & Wiksell International for EGDI.

Griffith-Jones, S., S. Spratt, and M. Segoviano (2002). 'The Onward March of Basel II: Can the Interests of Developing Countries be Protected?'. Paper presented at the 'Enhancing Private Capital Flows to Developing Countries' conference organized by the Commonwealth Secretariat and the World Bank. London.

Keynes, J. M. (1936). *The General Theory of Employment, Interest and Money*. London: Macmillan.

Miles, D., J. Yang, and G. Marcheggiano (2011). 'Optimal Bank Capital'. Bank of England Discussion Paper 31. London: External MPC Unit.

Minsky, H. P. (1982). *Can It Happen Again? Essays on Instability and Finance*. Armonk, NY: M. E. Sharpe.

Ocampo, J. A. (2003). 'Capital Account and Countercyclical Prudential Regulation in Developing Countries'. In R. French-Davis and S. Griffith-Jones (eds), *From Capital Surges to Drought: Seeking Stability for Emerging Markets*. London: Palgrave Macmillan, 217–44.

Ocampo, J. A. (2008). 'A Broad View of Macroeconomic Stability'. In N. Serra and J. E. Stiglitz (eds), *The Washington Consensus Reconsidered: Towards a New Global Governance*. New York: Oxford University Press, 63–94.

Ocampo, J. A. and M. L. Chiappe (2003). *Capital Account Regulations in Developing Countries*. Stockholm: Almqvist & Wiksell International for EGDI.

Persaud, A. (2003). 'Market Liquidity and Risk Management'. In A. Persaud (ed.), *Liquidity Black Holes: Understanding, Quantifying and Managing Financial Liquidity Risk*. London: Risk Books, 177–94.

Repullo, R. and J. Saurina (2011). *The Countercyclical Capital Buffer of Basel III: A Critical Assessment*. CEMFI Working Paper 1102. Madrid: Center for Monetary and Financial Studies.

Stiglitz, J. (2001). 'Principles of Financial Regulation: A Dynamic Approach'. *The World Bank Observer*, 16(1): 1–18.

Stiglitz, J. (2008). *'Testimony on the Future of Financial Services Regulation'*. Washington, DC: United States House Financial Services Committee.

Stiglitz, J. (2009). *Report of the Commission of Experts of the UN General Assembly on Reforms of the International Monetary and Financial System* [UN Stiglitz Commission]. New York: UN. Available at: <http://www.un.org/ga/econcrisissummit/docs/FinalReport_CoE.pdf>.

Turner Review (2009). *The Turner Review: A Regulatory Response to the Global Banking Crisis*. March. London: Financial Services Authority.

UK Treasury Committee (2009). *Banking Crisis: Regulation and Supervision. Fourteenth Report of Session 2008–09*, July. London: House of Commons Treasury Committee.

US Treasury Department (2009a). *Financial Regulatory Reform. A New Foundation: Rebuilding Financial Supervision and Regulation [The White Paper]*. Washington, DC: US Treasury Department.

US Treasury Department (2009b). *Principles for Reforming the U.S. and International Regulatory Capital Framework for Banking Firms*. September. Washington, DC: US Treasury Department.

Warwick Commission (2010). *Warwick Commission Report on International Financial Reform*. Coventry: University of Warwick.

White, W. R. (2009). *Should Monetary Policy "Lean or Clean"?*. Working Paper 34. Dallas: Federal Reserve Bank of Dallas, Globalization and Monetary Policy Institute. Available at: <http://www.dallasfed.org/assets/documents/institute/wpapers/2009/0034.pdf>.

Name Index

Index